New Approaches to International Law

José María Beneyto · David Kennedy
Editors

Justo Corti Varela · John Haskell
Assistant Editors

# New Approaches to International Law

## The European and the American Experiences

T·M·C·Asser Press    Springer

*Editors*
José María Beneyto
Instituto de Estudios Europeos
Universidad CEU San Pablo
Madrid
Spain

David Kennedy
Institute for Global Law and Policy
Harvard Law School
Cambridge, MA
USA

*Assistant Editors*
Justo Corti Varela
Instituto de Estudios Europeos
Universidad CEU San Pablo
Madrid
Spain

John Haskell
Mississippi College School of Law
Jackson, MS
USA

ISBN 978-90-6704-878-1 ISBN 978-90-6704-879-8 (eBook)
DOI 10.1007/978-90-6704-879-8

Library of Congress Control Number: 2012942922



Published by T.M.C. ASSER PRESS, The Hague, The Netherlands www.asserpress.nl
Produced and distributed for T.M.C. ASSER PRESS by Springer-Verlag Berlin Heidelberg



Printed on acid-free paper

Springer is part of Springer Science+Business Media (www.springer.com)

# Preface

Everywhere we can see the impact of things foreign and far away. People everywhere feel vulnerable to global economic and political forces. But how do these things threaten us and what levers are available to respond? So much about global society remains obscure. What holds it together? How much is chaos, how much system? How are we governed at the global level? Urgent issues implicating people and places across the globe seem to call out for a coordinated global response. How might we aspire to govern?

The local—and diverse—impact of faraway things makes a global response to them difficult, even when it seems most necessary. Although the economic crisis is "global," it is felt differently by each person and each nation. Just as the costs and opportunities of climate change will fall unevenly across the planet. This disconnect between local and global and the diverse distribution of gains and losses ensures that many significant issues will be solved neither by one city or nation or corporation alone, nor by the United Nations and the routines of global summitry. We might conclude that improved "global governance" is the answer: a diffuse global public policy capacity to aggregate interests, resolve conflicts, manage risks, address common problems, and promote prosperity. International law might well be the material from which such a capacity might be wrought. Intellectuals and policy professionals have ploughed these fields for more than a century, imagining and promoting international law as a tool for global governance.

In their work, we can follow the emergence of global governance as an idea, a promise, and a reform proposal. Indeed, to trace the contours of global governance is to follow the hand of knowledge in arrangements of power, if only because global governance is so often an assertion, an argument, a program of action, or a call to resistance. Indeed, when it comes to global governance, saying it is so can make it so. Indeed, saying it is so is often all there is to it. Global public authority always comes into being and functions as an assertion. In other contexts, we forget the power of claims to right. Other than in moments of revolutionary turmoil, we forget that the sovereign is just a person who says he is King. Institutionalization makes public power and sovereign authority seem "real," just as it makes distinctions between things like "public" and "private" or "national politics" and the "global economy" seem natural.

In global governance, the saying and performing are right on the surface. Global governance must be claimed through an assertion that this or that military deployment or human rights denunciation is the act of a global public hand, the "international community" in action. Moreover, the world to be governed must also be identified and thereby made. Forty years ago it was common to say that the most significant product of the space race was a distant photo of planet earth and there was something profound in the observation. Such things constitute our world before we begin to identify actors or structures, assert rulership or solve problems. Of course, such ideas arise from somewhere. Without a space program, perhaps without a Cold War, without Life magazine, we might not have had those photos at that moment in that way, and the idea may have arisen differently, at a different moment, or have seemed less compelling. For the globe, the constitution of a world is ongoing. It is technical and institutional work, as well as a communicative and performative accomplishment of the imagination.

The assertive and performative dimensions of global power are equally significant for those who would resist global governance. Identifying the global hand in local unpleasantness is also an assertion and an allegation of responsibility. Where jobs are lost at our local factory, we might finger Wall Street or the transnational corporate elite, just as we might blame our national government, or the currency—even the butterflies—in China. Whether one aspires to bring global governance into being or fears its power, one must name it, assert it, and identify it, before it becomes something to build or destroy.

We might say that what we mean by "global governance" is simply the sum of what those who wish to manage and to resist globally have jointly drawn to our attention as governance. We can read the ideas that compose the world and aspire to rulership both in the centrality of law to the effort—the proliferation of legal institutions, rules and modes of argument across what remains a dispersed, and ad hoc terrain for the exercise of public authority—and in the role played by expertise in global order—the striking transnational effects of shared expert vernaculars for thinking about everything from economic life to war. Policy makers, pundits, and politicians are all hard at work asserting a world, identifying the players and their powers, attributing responsibility, distinguishing cause and effect.

Scholars of global law and governance have periodically paused to ask how this work of world making is going. We are passing through such a moment of self-reflection now. I routinely ask my students how they see the world now. Is it like 1648 or 1919 when it seemed everything needed to be rethought? Or is it like 1945, when the international order seemed to need reforming but not remaking. Tweak the League Covenant and you have the UN. Replace European empire with self-determination under American hegemony and continue. Or is this like 1989, when the demand was not reform but implementation: finally, with communism defeated we could implement the solutions put forward a generation before. Many opt for the middle position: reform, add Brazil to the Security Council, sort out the democracy deficit and currency travails in Europe with another round of treaty drafting, and keep going. But an ever increasing number come to the study of international law feeling this is or should be another 1648 or 1919. The essays collected in this volume reflect in various ways on scholarly work, including some of my own, written over the last few decades in this spirit. What if we thought it was 1648 and we could start again? What if we saw existing institutional arrangements and proposals for reform as hopelessly inadequate to the tasks at hand? Could we understand where our predecessors went wrong? Might we begin anew? That, it seems to me, is the aspiration behind the search for "new approaches" to international law.

It is immensely flattering that the authors collected here have found my own writings useful. I am grateful for the sustained engagement, commentary, and criticism. These essays differ a great deal in emphasis and direction. That is surely partly a matter of geography, of generations, and of each author's own preoccupations and projects. Nevertheless, to my mind, those who seek "new approaches" to international law today do share a common impulse. An impulse to step back from contemporary common sense about the nature of global order and the available paths for reform, as well as a recognition that despite decades of careful study, we still lack a good picture of how we are, in fact, governed at the global level. Simply mapping the channels and levers of influence and public capacity remains an enormous challenge.

Nor do we have a persuasive program of action. The International Criminal Court could triple its budget and jurisdiction, the United Nations could redouble its peacekeeping efforts, the international human rights community could perfect its machinery of reporting and shaming—and it would not prevent the outbreak of genocide, the collapse or abuse of state authority. Every American and European corporation could adopt standards of corporate responsibility, every first world consumer could be on the outlook for products which are fairly traded and sustainably produced, and it would not stop the human and environmental ravages of an unsustainable global economic order. America could sign the Kyoto Protocol, could agree with China and the Europeans on various measures left on the table at Copenhagen, and it would not be enough to prevent global warming. The United Nations' Millennium Development Goals could be implemented and it would not heal the rupture between leading and lagging sectors, cultures, classes. The Security Council could be reformed to reflect the great powers of the twenty-first, rather than the twentieth century, but it would be scarcely more effective as a guarantor of international peace and security. Global administrative action could be everywhere transparent and accountable without rendering it politically responsible.

Each of these efforts might be salutary. Some may be terribly important. Yet the intuition that this would all somehow not be enough has become widespread. We know that these well-meant projects may do more to render problems sustainable for the regime than to resolve them. Just as we know the most well-intentioned efforts to strengthen global governance and reinforce international law may, in fact, be as much part of the problem as of the solution. As a result, restating these proposals is not a recipe for reform or revival. It is a recipe for disenchantment and for a withdrawal of confidence, affiliation, and interest from the machinery we know as international law or "global governance." At such a moment, it is not surprising that many are rethinking our capacity for global governance and reassessing the role of international law. Striking off in new directions today requires more than stepping back from the classical international law tradition. By now, we know that international law is more complex than simply adding up national law and international law, public law and private law. For a century, international lawyers have known that the Westphalian vision of states interacting with one another in a horizontal public legal order has been demoted. For years it has been said that the state has been opened up, broken apart, replaced by the shifting internal dynamics of national bureaucracies and local powers. Already in 1949, the ICJ redefined sovereignty as "an institution, an international social function of a psychological character, which has to be exercised in accordance with the new international law."

The twentieth century was an enormously rich one for disciplinary renewal. The structure of international law was radically rethought, shifting focus from assessments of normative validity to depictions of an interactive dynamic of persuasion and legitimacy. New international legislative, administrative, and judicial institutions were built only to have their activities be reimaged as functions and dispersed, exercised wherever two were gathered in their name. The language of law was marked off from political discourse, articulated in hundreds of codifications, only to be re-integrated with political life as the mark, measure and language of legitimacy. Across the last century, international lawyers, policy makers, intellectuals, and statesmen built new modes of world public order by reinterpreting dispersed institutions in legal terms, as a transnational policy process, a transnational judicial network, a global civil society. The big ideas of the mid-twentieth century, such as transnational law, policy science, and functionalism broke disciplinary boundaries and framed a more sociological inquiry into the operations of law in the world. They taught us that if it worked like law, we could learn a lot by treating it as law, and they remind us that things may not, in fact, all add up. Legal and institutional pluralism is our fate. Twentieth century scholars spawned new fields like "international economic law" or "international environmental law" or "global administrative law" to foreground new institutions, new problems, new ideas about how governance works across great distances. All these ideas were born as responses and challenges to the Westphalian regime. These are the reinventions which have faltered. Today, approaching the world anew demands more.

If we step back for a moment, we could say that international law promises to play a series of quite distinct functions in international society. Many look to international law for the expression of universal values, most commonly in the human rights canon. But we now know that people disagree about the most fundamental things, that values are not universal, and that even human rights can often be part of the problem as of the solution. Even virtues have dark sides. I am not the first to notice that human rights was a late twentieth century project and that is now, in some sense, over. At the same time, international law also promises to identify the legitimate actors and their powers, most formally by enumerating the "rights and duties of states." This is partly sociological, simply registering the powerful and their capacities. And of course it is also normative, offering a measure of the legitimate uses and misuses of power which may be useful in resolving disputes about who can do what. But international law no longer catalogs the sites of power, nor delimits their authority, for all the functional reinventions of the last century. Too much remains off screen, even there. We are neither describing the world as it is nor imagining a world that could be.

Perhaps most importantly, international law promises a catalog of policy tools and institutional arrangements with which to confront global problems. We have long said that like the European Union, only more so, the international order governs in the key of law rather than that of budgets or a monopoly of force. Yet the tools for addressing the most severe global challenges facing us are not to be found in international law, even after the dispersion and functional re-imagination of global governance as a matter of networks sharing common vernaculars of legitimacy. It would be more accurate to identify the cramped channels of public order entrenched by our legal system as among the root causes of the difficulties we face.

A new approach to international law and global governance would begin where these efforts have left off. A first step would be realizing that global governance is not only about management and problem solving. It concerns the making of the world. And in this it may indeed be up to our problems, for they are not technical or political challenges. They are structural. Their roots run deep. To develop a new approach, we must grasp the depth of the injustice of the world today and the urgency of change. We must realize that the most egregious problems are not those that "cross borders" or threaten the sustainability of the current order. They are precisely those occluded and reproduced by that order—and, often, by our best efforts to set things right

Imaginary boundaries have become fault lines built into the world: public and private, national and international, family and market. A conceptual separation between economics and politics has become a startling mismatch between a global economy and a political order lashed to local and territorial government structures. The result is a rupture between a national politics on the one hand, and a global economy and society on the other. At the top and the bottom of the economy, we have deracinated ourselves, moving ever more often across ever greater distances. In relative terms, the middle classes are the ones who have become locked to their territory. Increasingly, the relative mobility of economics and territorial rigidity of politics have rendered each unstable as political and economic leadership have drifted apart.

Government everywhere is buffeted by economic forces, captured by economic interests, engaged in economic pursuits. Everywhere governments operate in the shadow of disenfranchised and disillusioned publics who have lost faith in the public hand, in its commitment to the "public interest," in its sovereignty, its relevance, its capacity to grasp the levers that affect the conditions of social justice or economic possibility. In the face of integrated supply chains, global markets, financial uncertainty, workers, corporations, banks—all turn to the nation state for redress, bailout, support—only to find there is often little their sovereign can or will do.

Just as the global economy has no "commanding heights," so the political system has no sovereign center. The institutional structure for each has been broken up. Political life has drifted into neighborhood and transnational networks, been caught up by the media, transformed into spectacle. Politics is diffused into the capillaries of economic and social life and condensed in the laser beam of media fashions. The institutional roots of the economy are informal networks, embedded in local and private rules, rather than the regulatory schematics of any nation, let alone the institutions of the "trading system" or the WTO. Think of the network of obligations which tied our global financial system in knots: collaterized debt obligations, credit default swaps and securitization so complex, and markets so rapid no regulatory authority can unravel them. Corporate governance so fluid and inscrutable one rarely knows who calls the shots. We have only begun to understand private law or corporate governance as global governance. But credit default swaps stand in a long line of private arrangements, including slavery, made in one place that restrict public policy alternatives elsewhere.

The result: the old worlds of diplomacy, foreign policy, and national economic management have become obsolete and left to play catch up with forces for which they were not designed. In such a world, we can dream about global governance, but we cannot have it. Not until the political economy of the world has been rebuilt. The relationship between the institutional frameworks for economic life and the channels for politics will need to be remade, a project demanding institutional innovation and experimentation.

Effective governance is no longer a matter of eliminating the corruption or capture of public authorities—difficult as that is. Nor is it a matter of sound corporate governance, corporate social responsibility and effective regulatory supervision—difficult as those are. Effective governance requires that public and private actors become adept at something none are now well organized—or well disposed—to attempt: managing the distribution of growth, linking the leading and lagging, managing the political economy of dualism. And they must do this not only in their backyard, in their territory, in their sector—but in a new world of shifting relations and linkages. Where small things have large effects, where local rules govern global transactions, and where very little is transparent or predictable.

If that is our world, how might scholars of international law contribute? How might we articulate the values, map the world, proffer the necessary policy tools? How might we speed politics, rewire economic life, encourage institutional innovation and experimentation? New approaches for this century might begin by clearing the ground. The debris of the traditional Westphalian narrative—and of its twentieth century modernizations—will need to be hauled away. Indeed, perhaps that is all we can offer now—vigilance against the repetition of renewal, vigilance cultivated in the gnarled vines of critique that have grown up alongside a century of optimistic renewals.

We can at least offer these—mistakes to avoid, bridges to nowhere built once too often. We will want to remember that the fragmentation of economic and political power has not de-legalized them. The governance challenge is not to bring political actors into law—they are already there. Law remains a language in which governance is written and performed. Even war today is an affair of rules and regulations and legal principles. At the same time, we will want to remember that global governance is—and will likely remain—extremely disorderly, plural and uncertain—a matter of performance and assertion, of argument as much as technique. The world's elites have long learned to inhabit a fluid policy process in which they as often make as follow the law. We must now draw the consequences of that knowledge. They will not be tamed by constitutional schemes. We must look for the politics in the cracks of fragmentation and search for economic possibilities in the choices it enables.

We must remember that things we does not like are also legal institutions and structures of governance. We spend far too little energy understanding the role of law and policy in the reproduction of poverty or the continuity of war in times of peace. We will need to abandon the comforting idea that "international environmental law" concerns only environmental protection and remember that law also offers comfort to the sovereign or property owner who wants to cut down the forest. We must remember what it means to say that compliance with international law legitimates, whether on the battlefield or off. It means, of course, that grinding poverty, terrible inequality, environmental destruction, and the premeditated destruction and death of war have become acceptable.

And we will want to remember that the informal and clandestine, the sacred and the violent, the spectacular, also govern. We push so much off-screen, either back in history or below the waterline of sovereignty. Before Westphalia—religion, empire, conquest as law. Religious confession—and ideological conviction—we say, are matters of national or local concern. Force today the expression and enforcement of right. This is comforting—but it is not accurate. Global governance remains as much a matter of religion, ideology, and war, as of persuasive interaction among the elites we call the "international community" about what is legitimate. It is a terrain for political engagement rather than a substitute for political choice.

Exercising our critical muscles, we can discourage being carried away by the dream of universal values. People disagree about the most fundamental things. Nor will the challenges we face yield to technical expert consensus. They are political. And politics is no more dominated by statesmen and politicians than the economy is directed by "investors" and "multinationals" standing on the commanding heights. Both are far more diffuse and dynamic systems, held together, if at all, by belief, expertise, assertion.

Ultimately, politics is less a matter of structures and agents than of ideas and expertise. After all, if for a generation everyone thinks an economy is a national input/output system to be managed, and then suddenly they all become convinced that an economy is a global market for the allocation of resources to their most productive use through the efficiency of exchange in the shadow of a price system, lots has changed. That is also governance. We rarely have a good picture of the blind spots and biases of expertise. We too often focus on the authority of agents we can see to act within structures we understand. We have paid too little attention to the myriad ways power flows through belief, common sense, affiliation, or the experience of victimization, pride, and shame. All these things move like a virus or a fad, but our epidemiology is weak, our sociology of status, convention, and emulation at the global level rudimentary.

All this is an enormous positive program for thought. While we pursue it, the global order will be remade—indeed, it is already being remade. International lawyers can wait to see what emerges and write it down—or they can embrace the challenge of midwife-ing a new political economy. After all, the global nature of "problems" and the local nature of "government," whether linked to a city, a state, or to the international order itself, is not only a troubling fact to be overcome. It is also the product of a very particular political economy and a historically specific set of institutional arrangements.

Our traditions for thinking about global governance, however, remain surprisingly uninterested in remaking the political economy of the world, in redistributing economic growth and political authority. For all our talk about global governance, the national, local, and transnational institutions that reproduce the problems we deplore remain totemic focal points, objects of a cult-like veneration. No sensible discussion of global governance can begin with the premise that "independent central banks" or the "demands of the market" or "the European project" will need to be swept away or substantially transformed. They simply must be defended. In the United States, an enormous majority can view the government as a dysfunctional part of the problem without anyone seriously proposing to alter anything about it. The government is crazy, but the constitution is sacred.

Perhaps our attitude toward global governance would be quite different if we began with the idea that our world is already governed, but that we are not part of, nor likely to become part of, the governing class. From this perspective, things we do not like, from economic instability, poverty, and warfare to environmental degradation, are not problems which escape governance. They are the byproducts—or even the intended consequences—of our current governance arrangements. Were we to start here, the urgent issue would be precisely to reinterpret and remake of the world rather than seeking to harness existing institutions to new rulership possibilities.

These two perspectives—global governance as the public good we need and the system of power we resent—are at war in contemporary discussions of global public policy. An endless debate between them has been institutionalized, professionalized, and stylized. Indeed, in large measure, debate about the desirability and limits of global governance is what global governance has become, just as international law has become debate about the bindingness of norms, the boundaries of process, the meaning of sovereignty, and so on. Substantive debates about what to do turned into debates about the boundaries of process, power, and norm, or into technical matters to be managed by familiar institutional players. In such debates, global governance appears both as a project and promise and as a frightening and disappointing reality. The promise seems always to recede before us, our fervor to get there fueled by our disappointment in its reality. Starting anew will mean pulling ourselves away from this mesmerizing and repetitive discussion about the governance that might be.

We might turn our attention, instead, to the world—what do we see outside the window? What is the world—how is it arranged, what wars are continued in its settled structures and routines? We might say, for example, that in political economic terms, what is going on in the world today is less the rise of Asia or the internet than a rapid process of factor price equalization and technological assimilation. After all, the last two centuries have been an aberration—characterized, in the wake of the industrial revolution, by one nation, and then a small group of nations, rising to unprecedented levels of prosperity relative to everyone else. It was only a matter of time before the scientific and human technologies which enabled the dramatic rise of the North Atlantic, including the governance arrangements, would become more widespread. Until everyone aspired to a refrigerator, an air conditioner, a car—and until their societies began to provide the means to realize those ambitions.

But relative income equalization, like growth, is an extremely uneven business. It certainly does not mean the elimination of income differentials. On the contrary. Inequality is everywhere. Nor is a global economy a uniform economy. Things turn at different speeds. People are left out. People are dragged down. Economic change is profoundly destructive.

When people turn to their sovereigns for help the results are terribly uneven. Some are too big to fail—others too small to count. Indeed, the public hand everywhere has become a force multiplier for leading sectors, nations, regions. As it was between nations in the colonial era.

As a result, our modern global economy rests on an accelerating social and economic dualism between leading and lagging sectors, economies, nations, and populations. We face a revolution of rising frustrations among the hundreds of millions who can see in, but for whom there seems no route through the screen except rebellion and spectacle. At the same time, we face the restive demoralization of all those whose incomes, economic opportunities, and expectations have fallen—and will likely continue to fall. Indeed, the fundamental organizing framework for global political struggle today is neither ideological hegemony nor great power competition. It is the political economic question of the distribution of growth. How will economic opportunity be distributed between those who lead and those who lag? The wild horse to be ridden now is precisely this dynamic of dualism, the tendency for growth here to impoverish there.

We know that not everyone can be a highest tech, greenest technology leader—any more than everyone can be the lowest wage manufacturer. These are niche market dreams. Justifications for mobilizing resources behind those most likely to lead one way or the other. But the global, political, and economic challenge is to link experimental, leading edge economic dynamism with everyone else. Across cities, within and between nations, in regions, across the world. The central questions today are not political questions—if by that we mean questions to be addressed by governments acting alone or negotiated through conventional diplomatic circuits. Nor, however, are they economic questions—if by that we mean questions to be answered by the operations of markets, guided by the hand of robust competition. They are questions of political economy—and they will be decided in the diffused institutional and regulatory structures which frame the interconnected, fluid, and chaotic operations of political and economic life after globalization.

Once we see this world, it will be hard to avoid the conclusion that the relationship between politics and economics is being remade. And in that effort, law has much to contribute. After all, economic thinking is not only the product of academic economics departments, any more than politics is owned by political science. Legal scholars have generated new economic and political ideas before. Prior to the Second World War, a robust institutionalist tradition was shared between the legal, political, and economic fields. Over the last 30 years, some of the most influential economic ideas were forged in law faculties by the "law and economics" movement. The return of "political economy" will require an alternative, for which the intellectual foundations have already been laid. Heterogenous traditions in social theory, in economic and legal scholarship, have opened a window on the politics embedded in the basic operations of economic life, the nature of political economy in a world of global markets and local rules, the nature of instability and risk in economic activity, and the mechanisms by which inequalities between leading and lagging sectors, nations, and regions are reproduced.

We know that the elements of economic life—capital, labor, credit, money, liquidity—are creatures of law. Law not only regulates these things, it creates them. The history of economic life is therefore also a history of institutions and laws. Economies configured differently will operate differently. We may discover choices among different economic trajectories—among alternative, perhaps even equally efficient, modes of economic life with diverging patterns of inequality. Too often, even scholars sensitive to the interaction of economic and political forces, whether in law, history, political science, or economics, nevertheless treat these domains as distinct, generating accounts of political change sensitive to materialist drives, or registering the impact of political and institutional change on economic life. This work can entrench the assumption that economic and political life follow different logics. The presence of law in the foundations of economic and political life suggests a different path. Not to explore the relationship between "efficiency" and cultural or political commitments, but to understand the concrete forms through which these are each constructed as different and placed in a relationship with one another. Pursuing this path will strengthen our understanding of inequality and dualism in political and economic life.

After three decades of "new approaches," a great deal of intellectual work remains to be done. I hope you will read these essays in that spirit—less a history of new approaches to follow than a record that as the century turned, people tried to shake off the promise of repeated renewals, looked hard at the arrangements of power and the complicity of law. They did not figure it out. These essays reveal no path forward, no recipe for a new world political economy. But we must recall how long it took to invent a national politics and organize the world in nation states. For all the agony that has come with success, building a national public politics across the planet had a strong emancipatory dimension—slaves, women, workers, peasants, colonial dominions obtained citizenship in relationship to the new institutional machinery of a national politics. It will not yield easily. It was equally difficult to build a global economy atop that political order. For all the vulnerability, instability, and inequality wrought by the effort, the global economy has also lifted hundreds of millions from poverty. It will not be unbuilt in a day. Building a new political economy for a global society will be equally difficult. The promise is equally large. The spirit of new approaches is to begin. I hope it does not take as long, nor require as much violence to be born.

David Kennedy
Manley O. Hudson Professor of Law
Director of the Institute for Global Law
and Policy at Harvard Law School
Email: dkennedy@law.harvard.edu

# Contents

# Part I
# History of the Human Rights Movement

# Chapter 1
# Where Does the Critique of International Human Rights Stand? An Exploration in 18 Vignettes

**Frédéric Mégret**

**Abstract** This chapter is an attempt to survey the broad field of critical approaches to international human rights law through a series of "vignettes" that give a sense of the diversity of the critique. Based on a stylized account of that critique's many voices—epistemological, historical, ideological, pragmatic, etc.—it suggests that it has much to contribute to our understanding of a series of challenges that the discipline of international human rights often has a hard time tackling. The chapter finishes by outlining a few leads for what a sustained critical/constructive engagement with human rights could be, one that is neither utopian endorsement nor mere pragmatic detachment but based on a deliberate reactivation of the politics of human rights.

## Contents



The author would like to thank Karen Engle, John Haskell, and Ralph Wilde for very helpful comments.

F. Mégret (✉)
Faculty of Law, Canada Research Chair in the Law of Human Rights and Legal Pluralism, McGill University, Montreal, QC, Canada
e-mail: fredericmegret@gmail.com

J. M. Beneyto and D. Kennedy (eds.), *New Approaches to International Law*,
DOI: 10.1007/978-90-6704-879-8_1,

## 1.1 Introduction

Human rights increasingly occupy a central place within international law. In many ways, they have emerged as one of the key ways in which international law seeks to reinvent itself after the Cold War. The critique of human rights thus is bound to occupy a key place within the critique of international law, one that potentially makes more complicated or even threatens to compromise international law's reconversion into a "law of people" rather than a "law of peoples".

Yet there is no doubt that the last two decades have witnessed, coinciding with the dramatic rise of international human rights law as a force to be reckoned with, the emergence of a significant, sustained, and complex critique of the global reach of human rights. By and large, the "victory" of international human rights in the Post-Cold War era was a victory by temporary default, rather than one that heralded anything like the end of History. Debates supposedly buried by the rise of international human rights have simply (or not quite so simply) re-emerged as debates conducted *within* human rights. At the same time, the post-Cold War has also been a liberating era for a critique that is no longer constrained by or suspected of being simply an emanation of geopolitical interests. The critique is multifaceted and it is not the object of this piece to present an exhaustive portrait of it. However, it is also often misunderstood and caricatured by those who see it as an unmitigated threat to the human rights project.

This chapter seeks to survey the field by engaging in a broad exploration of what might be called "critical international human rights", i.e., a vision of international human rights broadly informed by critical insights. Critical approaches to human rights have their source in something approximating an existential angst about the practice of human rights. David Kennedy is probably the author who has been most forthcoming about the tension between reality and professional roles, as well as a subtle feeling of imposition that can affect even the best meaning, compassionate professional.[1] However, this existential unease also has its source in some of the unavoidable and never resolved dilemmas that are at the very source of human rights as a way of seeing the world as much as a program to change it. As the expression suggests, critical human rights is not a project of hostility to human rights and therefore not to be confused with a long tradition of anti-human rights projects, but it is a project that is, at the minimum, prudent and even skeptical about some claims made relating to international human rights, even as it recognizes the particular place that human rights have come to occupy in our global legal imagination.

Critical approaches to human rights stand in a productive dialectical tension with human rights, and their attitude can best be expressed as one of ambivalence: willing to applaud the accomplishments of human rights when those seem significant, but keen to caution against some of the limitations and even dangers of the discourse—and, most importantly perhaps—dubious that the two can be disentangled. Perhaps the best way to describe that attitude is as agnostic about human rights, although broadly committed to the broad pursuit of some of the ideals that underscore them. There are many strands of the human rights critique, and this article will only deal with the relative few that specifically addressed international human rights law, as opposed to, for example, the general idea of human rights or domestic human rights law, even though the two are connected.

Critical approaches to international human rights should be distinguished from the great diversity of approaches and sensitivities *internal* to human rights that have, at any one point in time, expressed reservations about particular features of human rights. Needless to say, international human rights as a field of practice and scholarship is internally diverse, almost extraordinarily so. One of the difficulties in developing a coherent critique of international human rights as a project is this richness. This makes it easy to confuse a part for the whole, or what is said on behalf of human rights for what the project actually does, or manipulations of rights for "real" rights. It is important for the critique not to target a "straw man"[2] and to construct what it critiques in as fair a way as possible. This article will assume that classical human rights proponents are sophisticated, savvy, and worldly, even perfectly aware of the deeper critiques levelled against them, even if not always willing to engage with them.

Quite central to the idea of a critique is that, for all its diversity, there is such a thing as an "international human rights movement," part idea, part professional field, and part historical project. This project proposes the prospect of a unitary, all-encompassing ideal focusing on the dignity of human beings that transcends the world of states. It has its blind spots, its pet peeves, and a few skeletons in its closet. Although as we will go on to see, part of the challenge is defining who counts as the "international human rights movement", this chapter will primarily focus on the classical international human rights movement as it has emerged

---

[1] Kennedy 1984.

[2] Alston 1996.

principally in the West in the second half of the twentieth century and manifested through the rise of major transnational human rights NGOs and mechanisms within intergovernmental fora.

This chapter is in a broad panoramic and strategic genre that will sacrifice in detail what it hopes to gain in breadth of survey. It aims to offer a broad illustrative rendering of the critique of human rights in its diversity rather than a fully articulated discussion of its tenets. It will proceed to present 18 "vignettes" that each synthesize a crucial critical intuition of the critique of international human rights law whether at the level of theory, explanation, or proposal. I begin by suggesting a stylized portrait of the critique of international human rights as a movement and of its fundamental coherence (1.2). I then suggest a number of concrete ways in which critical approaches to international human rights envisage and shed light on a range of real world issues (1.3). Finally, I propose an outline of what currently seem some of the most fruitful leads to develop a critical sensitivity to international human rights law (1.4).

## 1.2 A Portrait of the Critique as a Movement

Although the critique can appear diverse, it is arguably united by several strands. Three factors, in particular, inform its genesis. First is the perception that, unlike the human rights movement's own self-presentation and its recurrent emphasis on the "victim", human rights are actually in many ways all-powerful, even hegemonic, if only in that they have become the central criterion of the legitimacy of political action in many places (raised equally by the virtuous and not so virtuous). Human rights are what allow the Turkish government to refuse to give a veiled woman her university diploma because she wears a veil, what allows hundreds of human beings torn by shrapnel to be computed in the legal category of collateral damage, or what allows international financial institutions to dictate huge conditions to the attribution of loans. Indeed, it is the very turn from human rights as a revolutionary and vulnerable ideology of contestation to human rights as a rather established mode of governance[3] that opens the stage for the critique.

Second, the movement is based on a frustration with a certain tone of human rights: conquering, millenarian, end-of-History trumpeting, hubristic. The movement is suspected of claiming too much for itself, of portraying itself as a cause of that which it is merely a consequence of, of taking the credit retrospectively for accomplishments that it merely ratified. Indeed, human rights are suspected of being fetishistic, of liking the thing more than what it is made for ("humanism worshipping itself"),[4] of turning human rights into an "object of devotion". The reliance of proponents on the media, on the "cause célèbre" and a certain spectacular rendering

---

[3] Weiler 2001.

[4] Ignatieff et al. 2003, 53.

of the world causes them to be highly selective in their indignation,[5] and to perpetuate a crisis mentality.[6]

Third, the development of critical approaches is also triggered by what one might describe as the post-metaphysical turn in human rights, i.e., the idea that human rights do not really exist in an absolute or metaphysical sense. Critical theorists are not alone in taking that turn more or less for granted, but they take it further than various brands of human rights pragmatists: if human rights are the rights that humans beings decide to give themselves, then this opens up a considerable space not only for instrumental reason, but to think about why we want rights, what for, and even whether we want rights at all. The liberation from the ontology of rights, in other words, opens up much needed space for debates about what we are left with, such as an idea that is less truth-claim and more social practice.

In this context, it must be noted from the outset that the critical movement has profound misgivings about the possibility of transcending the world of states by projecting a global concept of the good life, and a suspicion that this cannot be done genuinely, without manipulation or violence, or without forfeiting things that we should value at least as much as rights. At the same time, critical views of human rights tend to share much of the distaste for oppression, injustice or discrimination that has arguably characterized the human rights movement at its best. Beyond that, critical paradigms are, in fact, a family of approaches that ties together different, sometimes competing and sometimes complementary critical sensitivities. In what follows, I will seek to highlight some of their fundamental coherence.

### *1.2.1 The Critique of Epistemology: of Indeterminacy*

The claim that international human rights law is fundamentally indeterminate or at least inconclusive is one that is quite central to the critical project, although it is also often the most misunderstood. The peculiar indeterminacy of international human rights is both a feature of human rights, and of the international law in which it is embedded. International human rights law is the project to internationally "legalize" human rights. Even as it seeks to reform international law, it has a tendency to fall prey to it, and to the constant oscillations between apology and utopia that Martti Koskenniemi has famously identified.[7] Human rights law today is often a consciously transformative project that sees itself in opposition to classical public international law. It proposes something else to what came before it. Hence, human rights will be grounded in appeals to some higher law, antecedent or superior to the international law of states. However, they can never entirely overwrite the international law in which they are embedded, except at the cost of

5 Mégret and Pinto 2003.

6 Charlesworth 2002a; Starr 2007.

7 Koskenniemi 2005.

irrelevance. They must render their own apologetic tribute, which is not that far removed from that of international law *simpliciter*, recognizing what they owe to the sovereign as a source of legitimacy, power and order. Irrelevance is too high a price to pay even for idealism. However, sticking too much to the reality of the interstate world will result in the project's implosion through excessive apology.

In addition to the indeterminacy of international legal thought, international human rights law has to deal with the inconclusiveness of the concept of human rights itself.[8] This is the sheer indeterminacy of human rights as a body of law that is all principles, that does not even try to have the pseudo rigidity of rules. Here we are in the familiar terrain of even positivist critiques of rights adjudication except that the critique is not based so much on the indeterminacy of words as the embeddedness of human rights legal discourse in intractable liberal dilemmas. As Koskenniemi has argued, the attempt to prioritize "rights" over the "good" is doomed, because the former are constituted by our visions of the latter, and that when it comes to the latter we are notoriously undecided.[9] This manifests itself in rights being forever subject to "reasonable", "necessary" and "proportional" limitations, which only seems to push back the problem and to involve debates about what the function of the state is, and the status of the individual in relation to it—exactly the sort of question that resort to rights language was supposed to have at least significantly resolved. "Reasonableness" either barely conceals a reference to "Reason", which we have reason to be skeptical of, or is a recipe for generalizing the preferences about what is reasonable for whoever happens to be deciding.[10] To answer these difficult questions one cannot safely proceed from rights. One must instead understand what the right was meant to protect and why, but this leads us back to foundational debates and invariably questions the utility of rights.[11]

Moreover, most contemporary rights claims involve the complex weighing of some rights against others. This forces human rights back into the utilitarian calculations that it initially forcefully rejected. The only way human rights reach a degree of determinacy is by referring back to certain community understandings buried deeply behind the veil of rights talk. What is then seen as relative determinacy and routinely credited to rights, is simply the comforting feeling of looking back at oneself. Domestically, such community understandings may exist, although it may just as likely be the imposition of a majority on the minority. The internationalization of rights, if anything, radicalizes the claim of intrinsic indeterminacy, as rights now uncomfortably straddle borders and a vast plurality of cultures. The trouble with inconclusiveness is that it leads straight to the discretion of the judge or the technocrat, a risk that is perhaps even direr in the case of human rights than it was in the case of international law, which at least was substantively uncommitted and bent on process.

---

[8] Tushnet 1983.

[9] Koskenniemi 1990.

[10] Koskenniemi 2000.

[11] Petman 2011.

### *1.2.2 The Critique of History: The Never Ending Civilizing Mission*

What is missing from the relatively theoretical claims made about indeterminacy is a sense of where these ideas come from and, to put things bluntly, *à qui le crime profite*. Much critical work on international human rights is archaeological in nature. To understand the system's biases internationally is to reach back in time substantially for the dawn of the movement. For international lawyers, particularly international human rights lawyers, who consider that international law has moved on once and for all, the invocation of the specter of colonization is a particularly stinging one. But the idea that international law has already purged itself of some of its colonial biases allows it a little too easily off the hook. The colonial moment will not go away that easily because it helped forge some of the very basic concepts of international law and human rights. In particular, the claim that human rights is new to international law and transformative of it and therefore does not come with the baggage associated with the emergence of international law is a point that is remarkably misleading. As Tony Anghie has argued, cardinal concepts of international law did not pre-exist the colonial encounter as readymade rules to be applied to new problems; rather, they were given their specific meaning *through* the colonial encounter.[12] The "standard of civilization," in this respect, was not so much an instrument as a product of the colonial encounter, one that served to vet new entrants on the basis of something remarkably akin to "human rights".

Vitoria believed Indians to have a rationality of sorts, which meant that they could and should abide by the *jus gentium*. But the benefit of reason was granted to Indians only to allow them to extend an open ended invitation to the Spaniards. Moreover, Indians were found not to be quite up to their ontology as rational beings, and thus in need of being brought up to Spanish universal standards, thus arguably making Vitoria one of the founders of humanitarian imperialism.[13] Of course, Vitoria may have been an improvement on many of his contemporaries. His was not the brutal colonialism of the ruthless conquistadores, who would have simply butchered everyone for gold. But it was a particular form of "enlightened" colonialism nonetheless. In due course, the great birth pangs of modern human rights coincided with the perpetuation of slavery and colonization. In the nineteenth century, colonization was justified in part because of the failure of the Africans to abolish slavery.[14] Similarly, the plight of women has consistently been invoked to justify intervention in the affairs of non-European peoples.[15] Later on, international human rights would miss a historical chance to be at the forefront of

[12] Anghie 2005.

[13] Anghie 1996.

[14] Mégret 2012a.

[15] Ahmed 1992.

decolonization, only ratifying self-determination in the structure of international law by the time it had been hard won by peoples.[16]

The ways in which that colonial past expresses itself today continue to haunt international law. Human rights have been associated with processes of "othering," often heavily focused on racial, cultural, or religious markers. Makau Mutua has framed this in terms of a "savages-victims-saviors" metaphor.[17] Female genital mutilation is presented as the most abhorrent of practices, for example, but the West's own long tradition of subjugating the female body, be it in informal and subtle ways, is neglected[18]; the media vividly portrays the Southern despot (Bokassa, Mobutu) as eccentric and the Eastern despot (Hussein, Pol Pot) as uniquely cruel whilst disenfranchisement, fraud, and massive confusion of interest in the North are presented as accidents of democracy; the Middle-Eastern terrorist is presented as nihilist whilst the Western response is presented as political.[19] Human rights law continues to be part of the "standard of civilization", albeit in more subtle ways.[20] International human rights institutions for example are a product and a guarantor of a certain differentiating function, regulating the gates of accession to the EU for example, or deciding which cases are prosecuted internationally or ripe for armed intervention.[21]

### *1.2.3 The Critique of Voice: Who Speaks?*

The critique of "voice" or of the "subject" has perhaps never been as important as in critiquing a movement that famously begins with a "*We* believe these truths to be self-evident". Who is the "we"? What does it hide? Who is speaking in whose name? International human rights' power lies in its ability to portray certain issues as being "human rights" issues and others not, in ways that can leave certain groups profoundly sidelined. Women, children, migrants, workers, the disabled, indigenous groups, or sexual minorities have all at one point or another been presented as raising issues that are not strictly about human rights. There is a strong suspicion among critical voices that human rights' inclusive embrace always comes at the cost of exclusive practices.

In contesting these boundaries, perhaps no strand of thinking about international human rights has been more illuminating than feminism. Gender has proven to be a powerful prism to challenge hierarchies implicit in the international human rights movement. The critique of international human rights law's androcentrism arguably operates at three levels. First, in the way the proclamation of the great

---

[16] Rajagopal 2003; Mégret 2009b.

[17] Mutua 2001.

[18] Tamir 1996.

[19] Mutua 2002.

[20] Donnelly 1998; Fidler 2001.

[21] Mégret 2011.

domestic "men's" rights instruments was seen as compatible with inferior status in private law, denial of the right to vote, violence against women, or a general failure to take issues of discrimination seriously. Second, feminist scholars have highlighted the way human rights law is structured by masculinist assumptions including, most notably, an emphasis on the public sphere of the state as opposed to the private sphere where most women's experience of rights violations occur. Third, feminist analysis has focused on how international law, in which human rights are embedded, is itself deeply indebted to certain schemes of thought—for example, sovereignty as a form of private-sphere writ-large, and which profoundly conditions human rights' development.[22]

Following some of these feminist overtures, critical race theory has challenged the "whiteness" of the dominant narrative and indeed of the human rights movement itself,[23] whilst indigenous people,[24] the gay and lesbian community,[25] and the disabled,[26] have all sought to both challenge and be recognized by the human rights narrative. The relationship between these critiques and human rights however is fraught with tension and raises complex dilemmas about whether liberal human rights can ever accommodate the demands of difference,[27] in a context of sobering reassessments of the contribution of international human rights to women's rights.[28]

### *1.2.4 The Critique of Substance: What Lies Behind Human Rights?*

Against claims that human rights are neutral, critical lawyers have emphasized their core ideological assumptions.[29] The critique of international human rights is based on a strong skepticism of a number of claims that are often made about human rights.[30] First, the critique of universalism. After the global spread of international law, the suspicion is that human rights is a second, deeper stage in Western universalization. The universality of human rights rests on the plausibility of certain minimal criteria for the good life, abstracted from culture, religion or even politics. There is by now considerable and convincing critical literature on the extent to which human rights "expresses the ideology, ethics, aesthetic sensibility and

22 Romany 1993.

23 Lewis 2000.

24 Williams 1990.

25 Sanders 1996.

26 Stein 2007.

27 Brown 2002.

28 Otto 2009.

29 Mutua 1995.

30 Kapur 2006c.

political practice of a particular Western Eighteenth-through Twentieth-Century liberalism".[31]

Second, critical thinkers typically take issue with this other standard of Enlightenment thinking, the idea of Progress. Human rights occupies a very special place in international law's contemporary rhetoric of triumph, it is its *avant garde*, perhaps its best hope for redemption. Progress validates the idea that a project can break loose from its moorings, that there is no curse, no fatality from which one cannot recover decisively. It encourages a developmentalist and convergencialist view of the evolution of societies towards human rights. This sentiment is reinforced by a narrative of progress which always presents the "crowning addition" (a new treaty, a new court) to be just round the corner. Critical views of human rights counter this narrative of progress and renewal by inscribing it against a historical background of repetition and continuity. Every move to liberate has tended to be simultaneously a move to incarcerate. The present is haunted by the ghosts of the past, mental habits die hard, structures even more so. From this perspective, progress as a concept is at best unhelpful at worst, it is a dangerous obfuscation.

Finally, and linked to all of the above, critical theorists take issue with human rights' close association and occasional virtual indistinguishability from the tradition of political liberalism. Rights are criticized for their individualism and its tendency to do violence to the communal nature of human life, even in those societies that have given rise to the individualist archetype (and far more beyond them). Human rights, like modernity, tend to disaggregate the social fabric by making each the keeper of his/her rights. International human rights law has insisted that it is compatible with a range of political regimes, but in practice some clearly attract more of its favors. Although liberalism presents itself as a "thin" and minimalist theory of justice, there is a strong suspicion that its basic foundations individualism, rule of law, democracy, are quite thick, and this becomes particularly apparent in the context of the transnational diffusion of human rights. The suspicion is that human rights are occasionally a sort of Trojan horse for the global expansion of something much broader, including not only liberalism but also democracy, the rule of law, good governance, and market capitalism.

### *1.2.5 The Critique of Means: On Over-Reliance on Law and Lawyers*

The rise of international human rights is the result of a massive investment in law as a regulatory project.[32] In fact, perhaps the defining phenomenon in human rights of the last 60 years globally is the attempt to operate a *rapprochement*, emulating many a domestic constitutional reform, between rights as aspirational rhetoric and

[31] Kennedy 2002.

[32] Meckled-García and Cali 2006.

positive international law. Whilst rights are powerful ways of formulating claims against the powers that be, critical theory has a long-standing issue with their formalism, and not simply because of the problem of indeterminacy. There are dangers to entrusting our most deeply held moral intuitions to lawyers. The legal discourse of human rights can lose us in a meander of debates about whether a norm is customary or not, or whether it has *jus cogens* status or not, or whether a state is actually a party to it, rather than discuss the substance of the norm itself. It can make us believe that what drafters said about a treaty decades ago matters more than the complex issue at hand today. It can lure us into a false sense of safety that certain values are protected because they are embodied in the Law, even as the jurisprudence busily outlines exceptions and limitations to these values. It can make the most important issue hang on whether something called "genocide" was committed or not, even when tens of thousands are killed; or make ratification of a treaty seem like the most important item on a reformist agenda. The law can set up a veil between us and the norms, encouraging us to believe that if we produce "valid" law then we also achieve just outcomes.

The discourse of rights dramatizes oppositions rights are either violated or respected through strident moralization of political discourse, in a way that makes necessary political compromises more improbable.[33] Human rights are said to foreground procedure over substance, elections over meaningful participation, economic rights over economic justice, etc. The prioritization of human rights as opposed to citizens' rights in itself devalues the significance of political associations, suggesting an image of the state as purveyor of rights rather than locus of political association within which all are more than their individuality. At a certain level, rights talk is decried as profoundly anti-democratic (in that popular sovereignty is reduced to an expression of the search for rights), and even anti-political (in that taboo reinforces struggle).[34] The pursuit of a strategy of legalization for human rights is also part and process of a transfer of authority to international technocrats and judges.

In fact, "institutionalization" may be the defining trend in the growth of international human rights rather than simply the amorphous rise of an idea.[35] Inevitably, international human rights law will become caught up in professional projects and the construction of fields of expertise that tend to present themselves as an all-encompassing solution.[36] Internationally, the investment in law may be seen by some as a form of "overlegalization" that in fact does harm to its own purported goals,[37] or stultifies the necessary development of our political and moral intuitions,[38] or more generally sanitizes the radical charge in human rights

[33] Ignatieff et al. 2003, 20.

[34] Gauchet 1980.

[35] Oberleitner 2007.

[36] For a fascinating introduction to the sociology of the movement, see Dezalay and Garth 2006.

[37] Helfer 2002.

[38] Waldron 1993.

through repeated proceduralization. As such, international human rights law raises very problematic questions for the functioning of domestic democracy,[39] or about the absence of an international one.

Critical voices in international human rights seek to explore how the movement has structured itself over time; how its existence as a movement is somehow a reality onto itself that must be understood sociologically; and how the politics of human rights expertise also have hegemonic connotations.[40] The "movement" does not exist outside a web of interests, strategies, funding, etc. It is crucial to understand it as one internally constituted by strong currents of social stratification, for example between "elite" NGOs and their cohorts of lawyers from top global universities, and the boutique operations of grass root movements. The critical sensitivity in human rights asks the hard questions about how the human rights movement is constructed by this dependency: for example, what are the links between global capitalism and the major human rights NGOs? Why is there an ATCA only in the US, and what does its use for the purposes of transnational human rights litigation say about the role of global US legal firepower? Why are there no or very few Southern human rights NGOs doing human rights work in the North? Why is the urge to comment on the ethical record of other nations and governments so intense in the West when it seems so muted in other places? Why do the leading global human rights NGOs seem to have very little to say about economic and social rights, war, or disability issues?

### *1.2.6 The Critique of Praxis: When the Road to Hell is Paved with Good Intentions*

The critical voices in human rights are, finally, often less interested in foundational issues than they are in what might be described as the praxis of human rights. Kennedy has had some memorable passages on the over investment in the language of human rights as a particular lens that generalizes or particularizes, foregrounds or backgrounds too much.[41] Human rights tend to infiltrate all discourses, displace and eventually replace them. There are human rights approaches to development, to corruption, to trade, to the environment, to culture, to the internet. These occupy "the field of emancipatory possibility" and "crowd out other ways of understanding harm and recompense".[42] Human rights tend to be rhetorically absolutist, and risk operating as a sort of fundamentalism.[43] They encourage a culture of indignation and denunciation, rather than adjustment and compromise. They evade questions of History and conflict for the benefit of a

---

39 Gauchet 2000.

40 Guilhot 2005.

41 Kennedy 2002.

42 Kennedy 2002, 108.

43 Kinley 2007.

horizon of commensurable ends. Human rights encourage gradualism, reformism through adjudication, rather than political struggles, disobedience, or revolution. Victories are won every now and then, but at a high cost that distracts from the aggregate effects of injustice. The result might be a massive discounting of the possibilities of politics, as rights assume priority over the pursuit of competing visions of the good society, and strikingly reduce the horizon of what is achievable. Human rights, which were supposed to only set out the minimum conditions for the good life, actually become equated with the good life. The movement also has a tendency to speak in the name of others, often on the basis of dubious mandate or authority, and that may in fact condemn the "other" to obscurity.[44]

International human rights' reign often comes at a considerable cost, that of apology and deferring to the sovereign, even as it presents itself as an ideology of countering sovereignty. Built into human rights is a considerable toleration for state power and the needs, for example, of a "democratic society." Perhaps nothing is more misleading than the Dworkinian image of rights as "trumps." The state seems to stand to have much to lose from human rights in terms of power, yet the modern human rights state is a more difficult state to challenge precisely because it drapes itself in human rights. Human rights law tends to have a very conservative bent, recognizing certain social advances, e.g., in relation to homosexuality only by the time all relevant states have, and conspicuously failing to take a pioneering role. Human rights are routinely quite willing to defer to either a wide domestic "margin of appreciation" or to public international law, e.g., in relation to immunities.[45]

Another dimension of human rights is their implication in patterns of violence. That violence could be the violence of speaking in the name of others, or of speaking for all; it might lie in the unquestioned legitimization of the sovereign[46]; or in the obligation to frame complex, local, irreducible problems in the language of human rights if one wants to be heard internationally at all.[47] Human rights is a form of power, but one that does not recognize itself as such, and has not developed a corresponding vocabulary of the exercise of power.[48] Finally, international human rights' praxis can be seen as part and parcel of processes of exoticization, that draws attention away from local "problems" to "international human rights issues." International human rights has at times become a catch phrase less for universal than for *foreign* human rights.[49] One's "international human rights" students, for example, may manifest a certain displeasure if the

---

[44] Engle 1991.

[45] For example, it was clearly the ECHR that decided to defer to the rule on sovereign immunities in Al-Adsani v. United Kingdom, not, for example, the ICJ. Thomas and Small 2003.

[46] Noll 2003.

[47] Merry et al. 2005.

[48] Evans 1998.

[49] As exemplified in the US by the reference to human rights as always describing the rights of, rather than the *civil* rights of the American demos.

class does not take them on an exotic journey to the Heart of darkness, and instead brings them back to the discomfort of their own neighborhoods, and their role in sustaining them. The field's aspiration to exoticism is reinforced by a number of metaphors that portray the "other" as a far-flung victim.

## 1.3 A Few Illustrations

Critical discourses on human rights have occasionally been criticized, even by those sympathetic to them, as being too abstract or too elusive about their intentions or even their politics.[50] In what follows, I propose to highlight six issue-areas for international human rights, and analyze them from the point of view of "critical international human rights." I suggest that critical approaches can at the very least raise troubling questions about the ordinary operation of international human rights, clarify what it is we actually value about rights, and highlight what may be part of darker legacies that human rights lawyers should be wary of.

### *1.3.1 The Torture Debate*

Perhaps few debates have marked the terrain of human rights more than the contemporary debate on torture. Where human rights seems to be permanently about weighing basic human entitlements against legitimate democratic priorities, torture is the one "deontological" right that is supposedly to be entirely inelastic to social demands. On the face of it, human rights lawyers can indeed point to sources systematically indicating that torture is a non-derogable and non-limitable right. In this context, it should come as no surprise that the international human rights movement rallied against apologists for torture, especially at times when all else seemed to be in flux.

Where international law would in the end fall short of requiring that states disintegrate rather than risk using nuclear weapons, international human rights law would actually demand that torture not be used even in "ticking time bomb" scenarios. The problem is that this position takes flight into utopia whereby it is not likely to be treated very seriously by states, which will be prompted to invoke the language of the human right to life or security, for example, to justify extreme action against suspected terrorists. Human rights lawyers have accordingly searched for ways out of "ticking time bomb" scenarios. One is to say that they never exist in reality in quite the way that their proponents seem to suggest, that things are never that clear. The argument is not very convincing, however, because surely one can think of cases where something very much like a ticking time bomb scenario would occur. An alternative route is to say that there may be "ticking

---

[50] Charlesworth 2002b.

bombs" but that we should proscribe ever allowing them to justify torture because the dangers of abuse are too great. The problem is that this is where a particular kind of robust republican liberalism argues for allowing the use of coercive interrogation techniques under some sort of judicial mandate and supervision.[51]

This leaves human rights lawyers in a quite uncomfortable position. An alternative and quite common route, then, is to say that "torture does not work", and that it in fact almost always fails to yield the information it is meant to obtain. This sort of reasoning avoids the dilemma of deontological v. instrumental rationality by suggesting that "what works" and "what is right" converge, that there is no tragic moral or political choice involved. Surely, however, this promises too much. There will be cases where torture works, and cases where it does not work and if this were the sole deciding factor then the calculation would be one of whether torture was "worth it" in any particular case. More importantly, in anchoring the prohibition to an instrumental justification of its efficiency, those against torture fundamentally weaken their own case by allowing themselves to be led into the realm of costs and benefits, a domain where they can claim no particular expertise.

What the international human rights movement seems to fail to recognize or to refuse to acknowledge is how much the absolute prohibition on torture relies above all on our profound moral intuitions. We feel that allowing torture would perhaps corrupt our souls or would corrupt democracy, in the same way we believe torture is wrong even if we have a hard time convincing a traditional international lawyer of its status as a customary norm under international law given that more than 70 states practice torture, and some do not even seem to be shamed by contrary *opinio juris*.[52] The point is the argument against torture cannot be made unproblematically from within human rights law as if it were a matter of course, especially in view of the fact that human rights law seems to tolerate so much otherwise when it is done for good reason. We are simply, when it comes to torture at least, deontologists and, in that, a straight line runs from Kant to the mainstream of human rights. This is perfectly defensible, it is also more precarious, radical, and even glorious than it is sometimes presented as being.

### *1.3.2 Invasion, Liberal Imperialism, and the Laws of War*

International human rights has a very ambiguous relationship to both old and new problems of international violence. At a certain level, international human rights endorses the regulation of at least certain forms of violence. Yet objectively and perhaps despite its conscious self, the international human rights movement has often been at the forefront of the international interventionist agenda, providing particularly pointed ways to legitimize intervention *on behalf* of the population of

[51] Dershowitz 2001. It is revealing that the proposal, shocking as it may seem, comes from one who is often been presented as a leading human rights lawyer.

[52] Koskenniemi 1990.

the receiving state,[53] notably on behalf of women.[54] There are important questions that need to be asked, of course, from Kosovo to Timor, from Rwanda to Darfur about the occasional need to use force. But the suspicion is that human rights are used to justify violence when not warranted (e.g., the "liberation" of Iraq), yet fail to sway decision makers when some degree of external coercion might be necessary (e.g., Rwanda). It is almost as if, at times, the human rights community had been, more or less unwittingly, furbishing the tools of the military.[55] The subtle orientalization of the "other" through human rights, in particular, has served this powerful interventionist agenda.[56]

Some in the international human rights movement, for example, certainly insisted that the invasion of Iraq for example should not go ahead "in their name".[57] However, the human rights movement was not among the leading voices condemning the invasion, and there has been a tendency to not ask too many questions when it came to the use of force itself perhaps because the movement was subconsciously attracted by the prospect of a "human rights"-oriented reconstruction of Iraq.[58] This is even though the refusal to denounce aggression flies in the face of a tradition at least as old as Nuremberg that sees the use of force as "the mother of all crimes".[59] It is also at odds with a tradition of pacifism that once had much in common with human rights. In Kampala, when the adoption of a definition of aggression for the Rome Statute was mooted recently, human rights NGOs, to the great surprise of many involved in the negotiations, either came out strongly against the adoption of such a definition on the grounds that it might prevent humanitarian intervention,[60] or displayed their indifference. The suggestion that invasion and occupation are valid in this context if they respect international humanitarian law and human rights risks appearing as little more than a whitewash[61]; the emergence of a heavily human rights influenced notion of *jus post bellum* may appear as an attempt to make the best of the spoils of violence[62]; constitutional exercises launched in the midst of chaos seem to be at best the result of ill-timed legalistic thinking.[63] All in all, well-meaning human rights

---

53 Denike 2008.

54 Engle 2007; Cooke 2002.

55 Orford 2003.

56 Abu-Lughod 2002; Bhattacharyya 2008.

57 Roth 2004, 13.

58 Chandler 2001.

59 Luban 1980.

60 Aggression and the international criminal court, letter addressed to the Foreign Ministers attending the Kampala conference, signed by 40 NGOs, May 10, 2010, online: <http://www.soros.org/initiatives/justice/focus/international_justice/news/icc-aggression-20100510/icc-aggression-letter-20100511.pdf>.

61 Mandel 2004, pp 7–8.

62 Nesiah 2009.

63 The Brussels Tribunal, *Open Letter to Amnesty International on the Iraqi Constitution* 7 October (2005), online: Brussels Tribunal <http://www.brusselstribunal.org/AmnestyLetter.htm>

cosmopolitanism may be hard to disentangle from the logic of Empire.[64] If anything, the logic of the "war on terror" has shown the plasticity of human rights discourse, which is today routinely invoked under the guise of protecting that "most important of rights", the "right to security".

The failure to denounce aggression goes hand in hand with a movement to align human rights in armed conflicts with the teachings of international humanitarian law, which represents a huge concession to the violence of the world as it is. Many human rights voices, for example, have surrendered to the idea that international humanitarian law is the *lex specialis* of international human rights. International humanitarian law, for its part, has long made no secret that it considers a large amount of violence against combatants and, collaterally, non-combatants, to be compatible with international law, a fact not missed by the military who have arguably fully internalized the enabling logic of the laws of war.[65] There are specific humanitarian reasons for this humanitarian tolerance of violence, i.e., the need to ensure that the laws of war can operate as an autonomous regime in cases of armed conflict. It is conceivably a legitimate strategy to "humanize" and even "human rights-ize" the laws of war, to try and minimize the killings.[66] Yet from a more fundamental point of view, this approach misses the point that even the killing of combatants in armed conflict could be considered to be a violation of human rights to life, dignity, and peace, especially in situations of aggression.[67] In its effort to "civilize" international law, it also makes an immense concession to the permanence and, to a degree, legitimacy of war.

### *1.3.3 The Veil, Gender, and Minorities*

Few issues have agitated human rights minds recently more than the debate on the Muslim veil and, beyond that, the place of religion in multicultural societies. What has been less noticed is the extent to which arguments *against* the burqa or to prevent the building of new minarets have increasingly absorbed and based themselves on the language of human rights. Indeed, such arguments in France, Belgium, Australia, Italy, or Québec are increasingly specifically framed in terms of the protection of women's rights even, of course, against the clearly expressed wishes of women wearing the veil. For example the Preamble to the Belgium law banning the full "Islamic veil" in any public space refers to concerns for "the dignity of women", in addition to "Belgian values."

The defense of the ban includes feminist activists and some highly contextual and articulate calls not to render women's rights subservient to religious minorities,[68]

---

[64] Douzinas 2007.

[65] Kennedy 2004.

[66] Bennoune 2004; Watkin 2004.

[67] Schabas 2007.

[68] Bennoune 2006.

but also some clearly opportunistic voices.[69] In particular, a number of extreme right parties, not known otherwise for their human rights inclination or for their feminist militancy, have jumped onto the human rights bandwagon and reinvented themselves as the defenders of women's rights.[70] The risk or the intended result is that human rights will be used to "otherize" Muslim immigrant communities accused of human rights "backwardness," reinforcing the construction of exclusive narratives of nationhood with strong islamophobic connotations.[71] Many xenophobic demagogues are, ominously, "human rights populists." What does international human rights law have to offer in the vicinity of such strange bedfellows?

One might think that this was simply a manipulation of human rights, and indeed there has been no shortage of principled civil liberties stands against the proposed bans, but human rights is not entirely innocent of this wave. The ECHR itself has bent backwards to allow countries like Turkey to ban the Muslim veil in certain public spaces, on the basis of relatively specious arguments, including the fact that Turkey faces a Muslim fundamentalist threat.[72] In its rush to understand the issue as one of oppression and women's equality, the movement risks minimizing women's autonomy, while reifying a vision that denies their agency and fostering a sense that they are in need of being saved.[73] The denial of the right to wear certain religious symbols stands oddly with the shrill invocations and fetishization of the right of freedom of expression in the wake of the Prophet cartoons polemic. Conversely, the temptation to protect minorities under the guise of freedom of opinion by deferring to groups' self-understanding risks degenerating into a superficial political correctness and cultural essentialization. In this context, generalizations based on "freedom of expression" or "dignity of women" seem too broad for their own good, helping to construct the debate as one of incompatible absolutes. They risk reinforcing a narrative of the "clash of civilizations" where dialogue, attention to individual cases and a sophisticated understanding of multicultural dynamics seem of the essence.

### *1.3.4 Economic Rights and Poverty*

World poverty is by and large recognized as one of the greatest threats to the enjoyment of human rights. Economic and social rights are in this context, by most accounts, a progressive move. They seek to complement the "bourgeois" nature of civil and political rights. And indeed, in the global panorama of international human rights there is little doubt that economic and social rights represent a sort of

69 Ho 2007.
70 Fekete 2006; Kapur 2006a.
71 Ho and Dreher 2009.
72 Bleiberg 2005.
73 Kapur 2006b.

*avant garde*, associated with pressing demands for food, water, health. Most of the skepticism about economic and social rights has come from libertarians who warn that they will violate negative liberties. But perhaps a more biting critique can be made from traditions inspired by the left. The rhetoric of economic and social rights has increasingly taken over from alternative discourses of economic, social and distributive justice, including those produced by Marxist, socialist and welfare traditions. It frames aspirations to economic and social justice as minimal even in societies where the discussion of social and economic justice could and arguably should be carried much further.

By focusing on the prize rather than the means, it fails to address head-on the distributive implications of securing economic and social equality. The discourse relies on vague notions such as "progressive realization," that lack any clear political tempo, and can easily become mechanisms for endless deferral. To the extent that economic and social rights rely on litigation, they can channel progressist energies away from collective or mass action towards more particularized claims or discourage all but a very select type of activism. This is in a context where we know that the vast majority of welfare advances that have been obtained in industrialized societies have not been secured through economic and social rights, as much as through class struggle, organized labor, or social activism. The discourse also diminishes the emphasis on solidarity or fraternity, even sacrifice, for the benefit of a disincarnated ideology of basic sustenance.

One story waiting to be told, in this respect, is that of how the international labor rights movement has been sidelined from the mainstream of international human rights. Although international labor rights were amongst the earliest to be recognized internationally through the creation of the International Labor Organization, they are strangely absent from the Universal Declaration, except indirectly through the idea of a right "to work" and "freedom of association." Moreover, international human rights mechanisms have by and large stood aside from most significant labor rights developments, and the principal human rights NGOs do not see these as part of their core mandate. This is despite the fact that labor conditions are an absolutely crucial part of the daily life experience of a very large part of humanity, and that much of what counts as grass roots human rights work, involving a real and tangible element of struggle against oppression, is organized labor.[74] Approaches that challenge this conventional separation and have sought to more aggressively mix both agendas,[75] such as the International Convention on Migrant Workers, have been shunned, in particular, by industrialized states. It is hard not to see how such a separation is part of the complex management of a legal framework receptive to the operation of a capitalistic economy.

The international human rights movement has also found itself unwilling to really problematize the international distribution of wealth, except to say that

[74] Gross 2003.

[75] Compa 2008.

states have different levels of obligation towards *their own* population depending on their resources. The movement's infatuation with agency, is also what frequently leads it to discount the importance of *structures*. Because of its embeddedness in the liberal structure of rights, social democratic rights discourse risks succumbing to the public–private dichotomy by focusing on state duties, in ways that fail to challenge dominant private actors or the operation of the market.[76] This renders the movement vulnerable to the accusation that it is deeply complicit in the operation of neo-liberal economic policies.[77] Human rights' very "legalization" through international law serves to elude the extent to which rights violations occur as a result of power relations for example between the North and the South, rather than simply states' inattention to the economic well-being of their populations.[78] In this context, "rights approaches" to economic problems are often little more than humane discourses of capitalistic governance. Challenges to the fundamental inequities engendered by the operation of multinational corporations' are absorbed by the discourse of "corporate social responsibility," arguably an attempt by multinationals to contain the counter-hegemonic potential of more radical discourses.[79] Rights-based-approaches to development may only have gained credence with international institutions because they have distanced themselves from the earlier language of the "right to development" and any direct challenge to international inequality of wealth distribution.[80] Those emphasizing the discourse of human rights to ground duties in the world's rich towards the poor remain on the fringe of the mainstream human rights movement.[81]

### *1.3.5 Jurisdiction and Hegemony*

Behind the rise of international human rights lies a fundamental transformation of the very notion of *jurisdiction*, both prescriptive, adjudicative and enforcement. The international human rights movement has militated for many decades for an expansion of jurisdiction that communalizes the international interest in human rights, and make promotion of rights an interest of all. This has manifested itself in calls for ever greater degrees of, particularly judicial, centralization. Bypassing the limits of traditional inter-state adjudication, specific human rights bodies have been created (the ECHR, the ICC). When those prove insufficient or too slow to bring change, the preferred strategy has been to encourage transnational litigation using the domestic courts of some states (e.g., ATCA, universal criminal

[76] Stammers 1995, 501.

[77] Gathii 1999.

[78] Evans 2005.

[79] Shamir 2004.

[80] Cornwall and Nyamu-Musembi 2004, 1424.

[81] Pogge 2008.

jurisdiction). This has powerfully reshaped the notion that there is a "domaine reservé," an area of competency that is at least residually purely domestic.

The language of the efficacy of "enforcement" and "compliance" has tended to displace discussions about the justice or even the conceivability of interference (e.g, the Declaration on Friendly Relations between States). In encouraging this trend, often uncritically, human rights lawyers have arguably furbished the tools of the hegemon. Human rights concerns are potentially so broad that they can be used to justify interference on any range of issues. Conditionality powerfully reshapes the ability of a state to choose a distinct path in conditions of dependency. Transnational prescription and adjudication involve very significant shifts of the regulatory burden in which, under the guise of human rights, the more or less idiosyncratic preferences of forum states will be imposed on other states. The emphasis on mechanically "enforcing" human rights thus tends to put in the background issues of forum selection, cultural sensitivity and symbolic economy who is judging who, where, and why?[82] It impoverishes the range of ways in which one might respond to human rights violations, typically highlighting the West's own highly specific forms of legal response. Moreover, transnational judicial flows typically follow a North South route, often one strangely reminiscent of former colonial paths.[83]

The urge to extra-territorially apply human rights by some activists, for example in contexts of foreign occupation, is generally presented as allowing foreign nationals to benefit from the "higher" human rights standards of the home state and making that state accountable. Yet it may also be reminiscent of an earlier and justly rejected tradition of extra-territoriality of law's application, or contribute, under the guise of regulating it, to the legitimization of foreign presence. States, victims, stake holders are dispossessed of the application of local law for the dubious benefit of any law being applied. Conversely, international human rights law extra-territorial applicability may be denied, on the basis of an account which, under the pretext of not thrusting cultural norms on others, is deeply indebted to a dubious, orientalist account of the "other".[84] Either way, it seems, international human rights law finds it difficult to escape the temptation of hegemony or differentialism.

Supranational adjudication may be a marginal improvement on the transnational sort in that it more clearly centralizes the triggering of cases. Even in conditions of subsidiarity/complementarity, however, it also involves a very real potential for dispossession of a *contentieux* and the ways to dispose of it, which is implicit in the notion that crimes have been committed "against humanity" rather

[82] Mattei and Lena 2000.

[83] For example, it is quite striking that a great many of the exercises of universal jurisdiction in Europe involved former imperial powers France, Belgium, vis-à-vis former colonies Rwanda, the Congos.

[84] Wilde 2010.

than against a particular people, or particular individuals of flesh and blood.[85] Although the jury is still out on whether truth and reconciliation commissions are compatible with the obligations contained in the Rome Statute to prosecute, there is certainly a strong human rights constituency in the West that militates for an absolutist anti-impunity stand, and is ready to back such an injunction even in the face of renewed conflict or killing, and perhaps even when domestic alternatives have been chosen democratically. Moreover, there is often little understanding or sympathy for traditional means of dealing with crimes, which tend to be gauged on the basis of their ability to conform to rigid international human rights standards, regardless of their local legitimacy. Finally, the centralization of international judicial resources also involves conferring considerable powers no less in the case of international criminal justice than deciding who gets prosecuted to a few international technocrats with little accountability and, more importantly, in conditions where the loose criteria for picking defendants "gravity" invariably appear to be in the eyes of the beholder and take international criminal justice's gaze away from the West and onto Africa.

### *1.3.6 Human Rights and Ecology*

One of the consequences of the domination of the international human rights movement is a tendency to want to make international human rights into a cure for all ills, and to minimize the tension with alternative social and international agendas, in a way that limits our collective ability for hard choices. This is evident in the way every social good can be translated in a "right to" language, and the resulting inflexibilities and exclusions, as well as the way in which the international human rights movement is defined as much by what is part of it than what is not.

One area where a link is currently being made between human rights and a not easily subsumable concern but with potentially very ambivalent consequences is the environment. This encounter has given rise to the idea of a "right to the environment,"[86] a claim particularly formulated in the context of global warming and presented as adding renewed vigour to arguments to curb global carbon emissions. Yet there is also reason to think that the invocation of human rights, for example for the worthy cause of protecting the Inuits and their arctic livelihood,[87] is fraught with hidden tensions. The fundamental intuitions that gave rise to the human rights project, in particular, may have begun to be deeply at odds with some of the challenges to which humanity is confronted. One thing that the international human rights movement can never escape is that it is, viscerally, a humanist movement.

More importantly it is a particular anthropocentric movement profoundly embedded in a form of modernity that has made the total domestication and

---

85 Alvarez 1999.

86 Shelton 1991.

87 Goldberg and Wagner 2004.

control of nature for human needs an article of faith. The unrelenting exploitation of the planet's natural resources began in the eighteenth Century and has culminated in the last decades as the accomplished form of liberation of man by man. Deeply ensconced in the human rights psyche is a sense of entitlements that may derive from nature but that also deeply reify nature. Nor can human rights easily free itself of these biases. As de Sousa Santos has shown, human rights is above all an episteme embedded in a particular Western dissociation between subject and object, human and nature. Hence the suspicion, only beginning to be voiced, that human rights are too "human-centric" for an era profoundly challenged by the catastrophic impact of human activity. The framing of the problem as that of a "right to an environment," whilst it may achieve some tactical goals, risks reinscribing the original and highly problematic pattern of anthropocentric domination over nature in an endless loop. Similar arguments could be made about the complex relationship between human and animal rights.

## 1.4 Reimagining Human Rights as a Critical Project

The temptation of reconstruction in the grand sense is one that the critical project would probably rather avoid, and its forays into something in a less typically critical vein should be seen as more a work of reimagining than reconstruction. Yet precisely because the critique is often pragmatic it must also recognize the huge capital of sympathy from which human rights benefit, and the positive uses that capital can be put to. A part of the critical project is thus devoted to thinking critically about how to actualize both the project and practice of human rights in ways that avoid or at least minimize some of the dangers that have historically beset human rights.

### *1.4.1 Critical Cosmopolitan Horizons*

In seeking to gain an international foothold, human rights law has in some ways conceded too much and too little to the world of states. Too little, because in its rush to universalize it has glossed over the sheer diversity of the world and exposed itself to accusations of imperialism. But also too much because it has too readily accepted that the state is necessarily the ultimate arbiter of justice domestically, neglected the transnational and the interstitial for the benefit of the domestic, and forgotten to really address how the interstate world is its own source of violence and exclusion. International human rights' universalism has often been a thin universalism, one in practice powerfully mediated by—but also highly reliant on the world of states.

Turning a cosmopolitan human rights against public international law is one strategy with serious transformative potential. The cosmopolitanism I have in mind is one in which the benefits of plurality are not paid by the price of isolation and indifference, and the aspiration to commonality is not paid by a glossing over difference. Critical legal voices in that more deliberately reimagining genre have been far and few and sometimes await an unguarded moment,[88] but the work of authors as different as Philip Allott[89] or Patrick Macklem come to mind.[90] Macklem proposes an alternative account of international human rights law, one in which "the legitimacy of international human rights lies in their capacity to serve as mechanisms or instruments that mitigate some of the adverse consequences of how international law organizes global politics into an international legal system".[91] In essence, Macklem faults human rights for its excessive apology of the international legal system of sovereign states, which is an interesting sort of critique since it challenges human rights to be in a sense truer to its promise than it has been. For example, international human rights law is called to account for its role in defining morally relevant political communities, which are typically presumed to exist and unproblematized, at the exclusion of some. These might include the state, the *civitas maxima*, but also various forms of sub-state identification. Rather than reify territorial political arrangements, international human rights law could be about challenging the very distribution of sovereignty as opposed to simply its "unjust" manifestations, for example when it comes to minorities and indigenous peoples.[92]

There is by now a spattering of work of this sort, which is not content with taking the distribution of international authority as neutral from the point of view of human rights. International economic inequality is an obvious target.[93] The state is supposed to guarantee economic rights, but the state's ability to do so is seemingly dissociated from its place in the international system. International human rights law has made moves to better understand how its inability to challenge the very injustice of the international system may occasionally be part of the problem. The right to development is, for example, an uneasy attempt to mediate economic and social rights on the one hand, and the unequal—and morally arbitrary—worldwide distribution of wealth as resulting from the interstate system. Challenges to the interstate system's ability to exclude individuals from circulating freely around the globe, an ability deeply reinforced by the logic of human rights, also seem to have a more radical potential than the liberal concentration on right to asylum for the few.[94] Human rights critiques of the humanitarianism of the laws of war also challenge the extent to which the regulation of war has conceded too much to its reality, and needs

---

[88] Kennedy 2006.

[89] Allott 2002; Allott 2001; Allott 1992.

[90] In many ways this work complements work being done in political theory that seeks to chart possible moves beyond the current limitations of a world of sovereign coexistence. See Nardin 2000.

[91] Macklem 2007.

[92] Macklem 2006.

[93] Chatterjee 2004.

[94] Benhabib 2004.

to rediscover critical energies,[95] rather than consider that the jus ad bellum is an issue of "politics" that is beyond human rights as most human rights NGOs, somewhat sheepishly, do.[96]

### *1.4.2 Decentering the Subject and the Politics of Defining the "Human"*

The critical project is typically less interested in definitive catalogues of rights and their interpretation than it is in the conditions of participation in the human rights movement. What matters is not what human rights are in the absolute, but who gets to participate in the "dialogue" about what they should be, and who defines how that dialogue operates. As Rorty and others have highlighted, perhaps the central dynamics of human rights is the definition of *what counts as human*.[97] "Humanity" has often been described in remarkably narrow ways that benefited whoever was in a position to monopolize that exercise of definition. A great part of the history of human rights has involved the gradual problematization of what it means to be human, and the enlarging of the circle of participants. Under a conventional liberal framework, the first efforts consisted in promoting strong "anti-discrimination" norms. The "right to equality" then gradually gave a more substantive and proactive meaning to the obligations of states reasonable accommodation, positive discrimination, etc., even as it became more central within the human rights edifice.

Increasingly, however, the challenge is not only promoting a norm of equality, but recognizing that being human means different things to different humans, and that we are human in irreducibly different ways. In particular, demands for equality have increasingly led to demands for *inclusion*,[98] in the form of societal acceptance of a diversity of ways of being human and a diversity of "rights experiences." This has led to a fragmentation of international human rights law, underlined the precariousness of univocal claims in the name of human rights, and contributed to loosen some of the intemporal and universal assumptions of human rights discourse. It is interesting to note that this movement has for the most part not come from the mainstream of international human rights. For example, it was not the High Commissioner for Human Rights, or the European Court of Human Rights, or Amnesty International that militated strongly for disability rights as human rights, but persons with disabilities who, vociferously, effectively, and after decades of being ignored, claimed the human rights language for themselves the same thing could be said of most groups that have sought to obtain specific human rights recognition.

---

[95] Bennoune 2004.

[96] Luban 1980.

[97] Rorty et al. 1993.

[98] Collins 2003.

However, it is also important that the demand made by such groups, beyond inclusion, has also been one for *transformation*, that points out some of the inherent deficiencies in rights language for the purposes of accepting all as they are, and not simply as human abstractions. The original concept and catalogues of rights were what they were also because their reference population was relatively narrow, the beneficiaries "knew who they were." When women, indigenous peoples, sexual minorities, migrants, persons with disabilities have sought to claim their rights in specific instruments they have insisted on reframing what human rights mean for *them*.[99] Contemporary human rights are thus increasingly less the solemnity of the Universal declaration and increasingly a patchwork of group, category, and phenomenon-specific instruments.[100] This leads to an endless work of creative destruction, as one's group concept of what it means to have rights is pitted against another group's critique of that concept, etc. Ultimately, more than merely about inclusion within the liberal house of rights, the demands made by various groups are that this house be fundamentally remodeled to accommodate a rich diversity of life-worlds—or indeed that it no longer be a single house at all.

### *1.4.3 Sovereignty, Community, and the Justice of Self-Determination*

A further direction for the critical project in human rights has been to better problematize the relationship of human rights and sovereignty, universalism and pluralism, individual rights and self-determination. This is a central dilemma of the movement that human rights lawyers are keenly aware of, but a certain form of domestic human rights liberalism projected onto the international sphere can have the effect of systematically making sovereignty and community appear as part of the problem rather than the solution. Critical views on human rights, because of their skepticism of universalism and their sensitivity to how human rights can be used to legitimize agendas of intrusion and invasion, seem better suited to understanding the inherent value that lies in forms of collective existence, and the intimate links that exist between individual and collective rights.

This is obviously very familiar to third world critiques of human rights, and international human rights law since the 1960s has nodded to the right of self-determination, even though little has come out of this in terms of interpreting actual rights. In fact, the tensions between a Third World agenda of national liberation and the liberal framework of human rights remain quite glaring and recent historical research has reminded us of how uneasy and unnatural their union was from the start.[101] This may call for a re-exploration of the normative foundations of sovereignty, not simply as a second best solution but as expressing some

99 Mégret 2008a.

100 Mégret 2008b.

101 Moyn 2010.

form of fundamental recognition of value diversity, incommensurability of ends, and aspiration to live in distinct communities. Value pluralism, in that respect, is a richer proposition than relativism, which sounds like it is for ever caught up in indecision or looking for excuses.[102] However, if international human rights law goes down that route, there is no reason why it should stop in midstream, and reserve respect for autonomy to states as particular historically and juridically constituted communities. The margin of appreciation could well become a tool to tolerate human rights variation within a sovereign framework and to rediscover what have been some of international human rights' perennial blind spots: minorities, indigenous peoples, multicultural societies in a world of migrations, etc.[103]

Yet the traditional rights critique that sovereignty and community are always at risk of becoming the tomb of rights also needs to be taken seriously. Rather than simply deferring to an unproblematized "margin of appreciation" that becomes a route to legitimizing the status quo or internal systems of oppression, critical international human rights would use human rights to highlight both the reality and the contingency of communitarian bonds. It would be attentive to the fact that, whilst sovereign oppression no doubt exists, individuals also exercise agency in how they cope with communal demands and that certain forms of "voluntary servitude" are inherent to social life. It would be sensitive to the extent to which radical change, however desirable it may be, has human costs, whilst outsiders with a reformist urge will often not have to bear the brunt of it themselves. It would be committed to the idea that one cannot protect individuals' autonomy against their own autonomy, without at least going against the very idea of human dignity.

Most importantly, critical international human rights would emphasize the impossibility and undesirability of settling the tensions between rights and culture, individuality and community along anything resembling a universal formula. Instead of the "rights of communities," with its considerable potential for reification of culture and existing hierarchies, it would emphasize "communities of rights", i.e., how every human group is not simply a subject but a producer of rights logic that needs to be interpreted hermeneutically and on its own terms before it is dissected for compatibility with a universal framework. Rather than a rights violation framework, it would think in terms of rights compromises, the difficult compromises that human beings make when they accept conditions that others might find hard to accept, for reasons that at least have the merit of being their own. Instead of freeing people from themselves, it would merely offer to side by those involved in their own "arduous struggle to become free"—or whatever else it is they want to become—"by their own efforts."[104]

[102] Danchin 2006.

[103] Mégret 2012b.

[104] Mill 2006.

### 1.4.4 Making the "International" Accountable

One thing that makes the critique of the depoliticizing effect of human rights particularly biting in the international context is that the international system creates very few structures of accountability and debate to sustain a critical practice of human rights. The emphasis is on developing enforcement capability and international human rights mechanisms, at the expense of a true human rights public sphere. Human rights law is therefore not merely tangentially depoliticizing, it is often a *substitute* for an international politics of debate and vision about the role of human rights. None of the existing UN institutions, and certainly not those specializing in human rights, provides the right sort of forum. Diplomatic dialogue caters to fundamentally other needs and the emphasis after adoption of instruments has too often been on rigorous implementation rather than renewed democratic debate.

Only the most recent international human rights instruments testify to a truly significant investment by international civil society but even then in conditions that one would hesitate to describe as democratic. No wonder then that international human rights is routinely decried as sharing some of the worst depoliticizing features of human rights domestically, without any of the normal countervailing forces. Reinventing the international public sphere,[105] or rendering it more democratic,[106] in this context, are critical human rights strategies that seem to have the potential to capitalize on some of the residual energies of the project.[107] There would seem to be a deep logic to the idea that global human rights issues should be debated by those primarily supposed to benefit from them,[108] not only in terms of adopting instruments but also of the many policies that are taken in their name.

Moreover, international organizations generally, including those involved in human rights promotion, typically cannot be made to be accountable for human rights violations. The perception, by and large, has long been of international organizations that "can do no harm" because speaking in the name of a necessarily benevolent "international community." A critical practice of international human rights would see international organizations as just as capable if not sometimes more of committing human rights violations. It would turn the human rights critique on those that promote human rights standards for others. It would challenge human rights INGOs[109] and NGOs,[110] for example, to answer for some of the consequences of the policies they advocate, rather than seeing the state as the only repository of rights obligations. It would also seek to problematize recurring invocations of the "international community" or "Humanity" as fundamentally deresponsibilizing moves that abstract human rights initiatives from their real cultural, political and economic moorings.

---

105 Fraser 2007.

106 Falk 2000a; Falk and Strauss 2001.

107 See also Falk 2000a.

108 Goodhart 2008.

109 Mégret and Hoffmann 2003.

110 Slim 2002; Collingwood and Logister 2005.

### 1.4.5 International Human Rights from Below and Legal Pluralism

For a movement that is philosophically obsessed with individual agency, international human rights law as a practice has also tended to be obsessed with the state. The international human rights paradigm is still largely indebted to a formal positivist concept of the Law. There is a strong association between the project of human rights and the aspiration to a more centralized international legal order capable of backing norms by credible threat of sanctions. International human rights lawyers typically think of international human rights sources as a hierarchy with universal organs superior to regional ones, and regional ones superior to domestic ones. A critical approach to international human rights would seek to transcend this reliance on international and formal organization and instead emphasize the degree to which human rights norms today are produced in a great variety of interstitial spaces, in ways that make the distinction between hard and soft law largely redundant. For example, it would emphasize the degree to which human rights norms are produced as much by NGO reports, domestic and transnational litigation, or even popular culture as by the Human Rights Committee or the Human Rights Council. It would thus contribute to dissociating the aspiration to human rights from the strict legal forms that purport to constrain it.

Against international law's very top-down approach to international human rights, it would emphasize the degree to which human rights are the product of a multitude of not particularly authorized encounters in the state, transnational and global realms.[111] Rajagopal is perhaps the author most associated with the attempt to conceptualize a theory of "human rights from below,"[112] and emphasize the degree to which social movements in particular have appropriated the discourse of human rights to challenge certain dominant features of international law. There are some ambiguities involved in the attempt to reframe the "international human rights movement" as something else than it purports to be, yet this attempt also takes seriously the notion that "human rights" is in a sense nothing else than a struggle over the socially acceptable meaning of the term. It is a narrative that can give their due to social forces, where international law has often been only too happy to take the credit for conquests that were hard won elsewhere. It can focus attention on the idea that it is not rights themselves that have brought about advances in rights, but the willingness of people to invest them with meaning. Nor would a critical approach to human rights mistake the fact that certain actors invoke human rights with the triumph of human rights; rather, it would be attentive to how every use of human rights is an attempt to reframe them for a particular cause.

---

[111] Mégret 2010.

[112] Rajagopal 2006.

In the effort to elucidate the actual meaning of human rights for those actors, it has never been more necessary to understand human rights anthropologically, as a social practice. Both mainstream human rights lawyers and critical ones have at times tended to operate at the level of the ideological superstructure, or of elite discourses about human rights major NGOs, intergovernmental organizations, at the expense of work more rooted in an observation of the actual uses of human rights. More than ever it seems what is needed is to answer the question "what do human rights do?"[113] and to answer it in detail with an eye for the local and the idiosyncratic. The goal should be to better understand, from a legally pluralistic perspective, how rights are produced and reinvented by their holders.[114] Anthropologists have considerably enriched our understanding of human rights by treating them as cultural practices and shown the benefits of a more grounded perspective to understand the potential and the constraints imposed by resorting to human rights language.[115] Legal pluralism can also channel attention to non-legal modes of norm production and the extent to which various forms of resistance, rebellion or civil disobedience are also at heart normative practices.[116]

### *1.4.6 Human Rights: Between Pragmatism, Ethics, and Politics*

Today, it seems, everyone is a human rights pragmatist. Human rights cease to be believed in as "things in themselves", and become merely a tool of politics, albeit an idealist or virtuous politics. Pragmatism, however, is a complicated place from which to proceed. It assumes that we know what the goals are, when what is much needed is a politics of ends. Pragmatism may only work because the pragmatist is speaking to a particular community of reference, one that happens to share his world view, and within which talk of "costs" and "benefits" or distributive effects immediately makes sense. Moreover, pragmatism does not offer us much in terms of assessing competing world views, and can leave human rights pragmatists' either quite isolated or in strange company. Could it not also be said that John Yoo is a "well meaning, compassionate legal professional" who heeded the call to think pragmatically about the law in an age of terror? Moreover, there is a sense in which human rights pragmatism is a political agenda that advances masked, constantly hiding behind an anti-political smokescreen. A politics, even a *realpolitik* of human rights might of course fully acknowledge and accept the movement's aspiration to power. But human rights cynicism hardly seems an improvement on human rights naivety.

Is there room, in seeking to invent a non-hegemonic practice of human rights, for a turn to ethics? A critical ethics of human rights would emphasize how the

---

113 Asad 2000.

114 Nyamu-Musembi 2005.

115 Merry 2006; Goodale et al. 2006.

116 Mégret 2009a.

invocation of rights places the invoker in relation to the "other". It might, for example, shift the gaze of human rights inwards rather than outwards, focusing on rights violations "at home" rather than routinely criticizing the record of others. Bringing the whole of international human rights home more systematically to question one's own practices, rather than using them as an instrument of international projection might expose international human rights less to charges of hypocrisy.[117] It might also encourage the movement to resist the temptation of speaking in the name of others, unless such persons can absolutely not speak in their own name or ask others to do so. There is often an urge to speak for the victims of human rights violations that can end up reducing any meaningful sense of agency on their part, in a way that is deeply antithetical to human rights. Instead, human rights would emphasize an "ethics of invitation". Human rights "interventions" should be at the behest of some significant local human constituency and should learn to not overextend their welcome and not mistake silence for an invitation, not confuse polite curiosity with wholehearted endorsement, and not take an invitation to throw off the tyrant for an invitation to become the new one. An awareness of how human rights can often crowd out and even destroy other competing discourses could surely sensitize to an important hidden cost of rights discourse. A general sense of knowing one's place, of realizing the idiosyncrasy of much of what passes for a universalist human rights discourse, and of acting accordingly is also something with which human rights activists could usefully equip themselves. Finally, problematizing, questioning and ultimately forfeiting some of the unidirectionality of the human rights impetus, e.g., North, South; Center, periphery might also set the stage for a global practice of human rights that centers more. There needs to be space for the logic of *don-contre-don* to express itself, more Southern human rights NGOs visiting Northern prisons, for the global economy of rights not to simply reproduce a geography of rights surpluses and deficits.

Yet there may be something to mild and polite about a mere ethics of rights, a way of rounding corners without challenging rights indeterminacy. A true politics of rights, on the contrary, might emphasize the need to re-politicize rights by foregrounding debate, and process over eternal truths, technocratic rationality, judicialization and universalism. An ability to sense when rights discourse exceeds its welcome and morphs into a tepid, bourgeois superstructure that provides only a gloss of resolution to intractable political dilemmas may in fact be one of the keys to a renewed rights lucidity. A re-policitization of rights would in other words "normalize" rights as values and priorities, and make them amenable to the same sorts of discussions that are characteristic of politics' dialectics of ends and means. The fear of course is that in reducing rights to politics—"not taking them seriously" in Dworkin's famous words—one may be throwing the baby (the sense of some values being sacrosanct) with the baby water (the potentially anti-democratic ethos of rights discourse). Do we really want vigorous political debates on

---

[117] Geer 2000; Saito 2002.

whether torture is permissible? Yet this is partly a scare tactic, one that fails to recognize how all rights conquests were born from major social struggles or democratic developments, and how most of the issues crystallized in rights (aside, precisely, from torture) are eminently amenable to debate. A more "republican" view of human rights as oriented towards citizenship and participation in the polity also dovetails nicely with the sense that the rights narrative needs to be declined much more diversely.

Repoliticizing rights might involve, for example, putting at the heart of rights thinking the issue of the material conditions of its production, and the role that it serves in the sustenance of the ideological foundations of a globalized economy in the post Cold-War *Weltanschauung*. It could serve as a way to combat human rights' subtle depoliticizing effect as a corroder of class solidarities, and the demobilizing effects of "human rights-ism's" fundamentally humanitarian, philanthropist and charitable ideology. It could foreground the degree to which fundamental distributive issues underlie, produce and constrain debates that are presented as merely doctrinal or formal. It could highlight the degree of alienation that rights discourse can produce even among those who seem to embrace it enthusiastically. It could challenge the automatic association between human rights, democracy, the rule of law and the market economy. It could find common cause and seek to forge alliances with those social movements thinking about the sustainability of the dominant economic model for the planet.

## 1.5 Conclusion

Where does skepticism even disillusionment about rights leave the project of internationalizing human rights law? Is there a place from which human rights can operate if not safely from such skepticism, in dynamic tension with it? What does it mean to be an ethical, compassionate professional, as Kennedy, for example, frequently claims to be, in a context where formalist idols are crumbling? If there is no space free from politics, then how can rights still constrain them? Recuperating a place free from the angst about rights seems implausible. Yet median, fluid strategies are constantly opening. One of course does not have to "believe" in human rights in any metaphysical sense to see that they either have a deep mobilizing force with some constituencies and at some junctures or, more realistically, that they are occasionally backed by significant symbolic and real resources. Understanding the potency of rights discourse is also to accept that for most people, including many in the international rights movement, rights have long ceased to be a metaphysics and are already simply a register for political action that builds on a sense of community, history and a particular culture of activism. There is an "as if" character to much of human rights praxis as in, "as if rights existed". Taking that potential seriously even as one remains wary of it, is a first step.

A whole range of positions can be defended from within international human rights law. The point of the above discussion was not in itself to show that international human rights have occasionally reached a number of contestable positions, but that these positions are difficult to disentangle from the web that is human rights discourse. Conversely, positions that might at any one point seem to meet expectations of progress or justice are not "required" or "mandated" by human rights in the way that the too often dominant formalist framework would suggest. Rather, they draw their force from the ethical, social or political projects they embody, which human rights at best help shape and market as political projects. In this perspective, human rights is less the international community's governing agenda than a particular style of reasoning. The problem is that this style of reasoning is not quite law, yet not quite politics or ethics either. As a result, one often gets neither the claimed promises of the rule of law nor the frank confrontation of politics or the questioning of ethics, but a bizarre mix of technocratic rationality, consensual policy, and charismatic authority. Moreover, there is no mistaking that the discourse makes important demands on those who seek to use it including, by and large, that they forsake alternative discourses of emancipation or challenge. This then makes it much harder to contest particular human rights outcomes, and ultimately to challenge established hierarchies.

Part of the misunderstanding about critical approaches to international human rights is a misunderstanding about the nature of the project. The project is not one of destruction, but nor is it principally one of construction. In that, it resists the urge to "propose" solutions as itself a little too indebted to the frenzy of "relevance" and the politics of expertise and as such can of course occasionally be criticized for its passivity. Rather it is a project committed to paradoxical thinking, willing to live to the full the contradictory promise of rights, and accept the ambivalence inherent to them. One of its principal contributions may be a particular tone of guarded disenchantment. Critical approaches to international human rights law can help open eyes to the highly indeterminate and therefore highly contentious and political nature of debates about human rights. They can instil a healthy skepticism about overinvestment in one particular legal discourse, and emphasize the need to see human rights from outside as well as from within. They can unearth the hidden violence that lies at the heart of human rights and often threatens to overtake the project. They can reconcile the human rights movement with a particular form of politics, one that can rely neither on metaphysical certainty about the existence of rights, nor on its second best, legal certainty about their content. As such, critical approaches encourage complex thinking and accountability for choices made under the heading of human rights. They discourage grandstanding, sensitize to cost/benefit analysis, and foster a culture of caution rather than triumphalism.

One of the paradoxes of course is the extent to which the critique has by and large been internalized by the mainstream of human rights. What was provocative during the Cold War is the mainstream after it; what was challenging in the 1990s no longer is today. Yet there is also a part of the human rights program's genetics code that is not as easy to shed, and goes beyond tinkering at the margin with the discourse of human rights. Assuredly, some of the hegemonic drive of the project remains, part of it anchored in the inherent claim of universalism, part of it anchored in the backing of powerful patrons, and part of it crusading enthusiasm of the believers. The international human rights movement does thrive on a certain paucity of alternative projects of international justice, where a critical approach would treat human rights as one emancipatory discourse among several.

Ultimately, critical views of human rights are dependent on what they critique, but reflect what seems like a healthier distance to the project than the human rights movement, which is too dependent on the discourse to be willing to tackle its dark spots head on. The critical project also suggests that there will be no respite from the agony of difficult choices, not even through a reliance on politics, pragmatism or ethics. To speak the "language of human rights" does not make us its servants, and thus does not relieve us of responsibility for the ways in which that language is used in the world.

## References

Abu-Lughod L (2002) Do Muslim women really need saving? Anthropological reflections on cultural relativism and its others. Am Anthropologist 104:783–790
Ahmed L (1992) Women and gender in Islam. Yale University Press, New Haven
Allott P (1992) Reconstituting humanity-new international law. Eur J Int'l L 3:219–252
Allott P (2001) Eunomia: new order for a new world. Oxford University Press, New York
Allott P (2002) The health of nations: society and law beyond the state. Cambridge University Press, Cambridge
Alston P (1996) Human rights law. Dartmouth, Aldershot
Alvarez J (1999) Crimes of states/crimes of hate: lessons from Rwanda. Yale J Int Law 24:365
Anghie A (2005) Imperialism, sovereignty, and the making of international law. Cambridge University Press, Cambridge
Anghie A (1996) Francisco de Vitoria and the colonial origins of international law. Soc Leg Stud 5:321–336
Asad T (2000) What do human rights do? an anthropological enquiry. Theor Event 44:1–33
Benhabib S (2004) The rights of others: aliens, residents, and citizens. Cambridge University Press, Cambridge
Bennoune K (2006) Secularism and human rights: a contextual analysis of headscarves, religious expression, and women's equality under international law. Colum J Transnat'l L 45:367–426
Bennoune K (2004) Toward a human rights approach to armed conflict: Iraq. U C Davis J Int'l L Pol'y 11:171–228
Bhattacharyya GS (2008) Dangerous brown men, exploiting sex, violence and feminism in the War on terror. Zed Books, London
Bleiberg B (2005) Unveiling the real issue: evaluating the European court of human rights' decision to enforce the Turkish Headscarf Ban in Leyla Sahin v. Turkey, 91 Cornell L Rev pp 129–170
Brown W (2002) Suffering the paradoxes of rights. Left legalism/left critique, pp 420–434
Chandler D (2001) The road to military humanitarianism: how the human rights ngos shaped a new humanitarian agenda. Hum Rights Q 23:678–700
Charlesworth H (2002a) International law: a discipline of crisis. Mod Law Rev 65:377–392
Charlesworth H (2002b) Author author: a response to David Kennedy. Harv Hum Rts J 15:127–131

Chatterjee DK (2004) The ethics of assistance: morality and the distant needy. Cambridge University Press, Cambridge

Collingwood V, Logister L (2005) State of the art: addressing the INGO "legitimacy deficit". Political Stud Rev 3:175–192

Collins H (2003) Discrimination, equality and social inclusion. Mod Law Rev 66:16–43

Compa L (2008) Labor's new opening to international human rights standards. WorkingUSA 11:99–123

Cooke M (2002) Gender and September 11: A roundtable: saving brown women, Signs. J Women Culture Soc 28:468–470

Cornwall A, Nyamu-Musembi C (2004) Putting the "rights-based approach" to development into perspective. Third World Q 25:1415–1437

Danchin PG (2006) Between rogues and liberals: towards value pluralism as a theory of freedom of religion in international law. Proc Ann Meet Am Soc Int Law 100:414–416

Denike M (2008) The human rights of others: sovereignty, legitimacy, and "just causes" for the "war on terror". Hypatia 23:95–121

Dershowitz A (2001) Is there a torturous road to justice? Los Angeles Times 8 Nov 2001

Dezalay Y, Garth B (2006) From the cold war to Kosovo: the rise and renewal of the field of international human rights. Ann Rev Law Soc Sci 2:231–255

Donnelly J (1998) Human rights: a new standard of civilization? Int Affairs 74:1–23

Douzinas C (2007) Human rights and empire. Routledge, Cavendish

Engle K (1991) Female subjects of public international law: human rights and the exotic other Female. New Eng L Rev 26:1509–1526

Engle K (2007) Calling in the troops: the uneasy relationship among Women's rights, human rights, and Humanitarian intervention. Harv Hum Rts 20:189–226

Evans T (2005) International human rights law as power/knowledge. Hum Rts Q 27:1046–1068

Evans T (1998) Human rights fifty years on. Manchester University Press, Manchester

Falk R (2000a) Resisting "globalization-from-above" through "Globalization-from-below". In Gills (ed.), Globalization and the politics of resistance, Palgrave, London

Falk R (2000b) Global civil society and the democratic prospect. In: Holden B (ed), Global democracy: key debates, Routledge, New York

Falk R, Strauss A (2001) Toward global parliament. Foreign Aff 80:212–220

Fekete L (2006) Enlightened fundamentalism? Immigration, feminism and the right. Race Cl 48:1–22

Fidler DP (2001) Return of the standard of civilization, Chi J Int'l L 2 pp 137–158

Fraser N (2007) Transnationalizing the public sphere. Theor Culture Soc 24:7–30

Gathii JT (1999) Good governance as a counter insurgency agenda to oppositional and transformative social projects in international law. Buff Hum Rts L Rev 5:107–174

Gauchet M (1980) Les droits de l'homme ne sont pas une politique. Le débat 3:3–21

Gauchet M (2000) Quand les droits de l'homme deviennent une politique, Débat pp 258–288

Geer MA (2000) Human rights and wrongs in our own backyard: incorporating international human rights protections under domestic civil rights law—a case study of women in United States prisons. Harv Hum Rts J 13:71–289

Goldberg D, Wagner M (2004) Human rights litigation to protect the peoples of the arctic, Proceedings of the Annual Meeting American Society of International Law, pp 227–229

Goodale M, Baxi U, Cowan J, et al. (2006) Toward a critical anthropology of human rights. Curr Anthropol 47:485–511

Goodhart M (2008) Human rights and global democracy. Ethics Int Aff 22:395–420

Gross JA (2003) Workers' rights as human rights. Cornell University Press, Ithaca

Guilhot N (2005) The democracy makers: human rights and international order. Columbia University Press, New York

Helfer LR (2002) Overlegalizing human rights: international relations theory and the commonwealth caribbean backlash against human rights regimes. Colum L Rev 102:1832–1911

Ho C (2007) Muslim Women's new defenders: women's rights, nationalism and Islamophobia. In: Contemporary Australia, women's studies international forum

Ho C, Dreher T (2009) Not another Hijab row: new conversations on gender, race, religion and the making of communities. Int Feminist J Pol 11:114–125
Ignatieff M, Appiah KA, Gutmann A (2003) Human rights as politics and idolatry. Princeton University Press, Princeton
Kapur R (2006a) Normalizing violence: transitional justice and the Gujarat riots. Colum J Gender L 15:885–928
Kapur R (2006b) Revisioning the role of law in women's human rights struggles. The legalization of human rights: multidisciplinary perspectives on human rights and human rights law, pp 101–116
Kapur R (2006c) Human rights in the 21st century: take a walk on the dark side. Sydney L Rev 28:665–688
Kennedy D (1984) Spring Break. Tex L Rev 63:1377–1424
Kennedy D (2002) International human rights movement: part of the problem? Harv Hum Rts J 15:101–126
Kennedy D (2004) The dark sides of virtue : reassessing international humanitarianism. Princeton University Press, Princeton
Kennedy D (2006) Sovereignty: responding to Anghie and Aravamudan. Tex Int'l LJ 41:465–468
Kinley D (2007) Human rights fundamentalisms. Sydney L Rev 29:545–576
Koskenniemi M (1990) The pull of the mainstream. Mich Law Rev 88:1946–1962
Koskenniemi M (2000) L'utilisation du "raisonnable" par le juge international: discours juridique, raison et contradictions. Am J Int Law 94:198–201
Koskenniemi M (2005) From apology to utopia: the structure of international legal argument. Cambridge University Press, Cambridge
Lewis H (2000) Reflections on Blackcrit theory: human rights. Vill L Rev 45:1075–1090
Luban D (1980) Just war and human rights. Philos Public Aff 9:160–181
Macklem P (2007) What is international human rights law-three applications of a distributive account. McGill LJ 52:575–604
Macklem P (2006) The wrong vocabulary of right: minority rights and the boundaries of political community. In Sajo A (ed), Abuse: the dark side of fundamental rights, Eleven International Publishing, Utrecht
Mandel M (2004) How America gets away with murder: illegal wars, collateral damage and crimes against humanity how. Pluto Press, London
Mattei U, Lena J (2000) US jurisdiction over conflicts arising outside of the United States: some hegemonic implications. Hastings Int'l Comp L Rev 24:381–400
Meckled-García S, Cali B (2006) The legalization of human rights: multidisciplinary perspectives on human rights and human rights law. Psychology Press, London
Mégret F (2008a) The Disabilities Convention human rights of persons with disabilities or disability rights? Hum Rights Q 30:494–516
Mégret F (2008b) The Disabilities Convention: towards a holistic concept of rights. Int J Hum Rights 12:261–277
Mégret F (2009a) Civil disobedience and international law: sketch for a theoretical argument, Canadian Yearbook of international law, pp 143–192
Mégret F (2009b) Comrades and fellow South Africans…: the end of apartheid and the many strands of an international law "event." In Johns J, Pahuja (eds) Event: the force of international law, Routledge, London
Mégret F (2010) International human rights and legal pluralism: a research agenda. In: Provost, Sheppard (eds.) Human rights and legal pluralism, forthoming
Mégret F (2011) ICC, R2P and the security council's evolving interventionist toolkit, Finnish Yearbook of International Law, forthcoming
Mégret F (2012a) Abolition de l'esclavage et colonisation: de l'ambiguïté de l'œuvre de civilisation facilitée par le droit des gens, African Yearbook of International Law, forthcoming
Mégret F (2012b) Is there ever a right to one's own legal system? Possible rights foundations for legal pluralism, Israel Law Review 45, forthcoming

Mégret F, Hoffmann F (2003) The UN as a human rights violator? Some reflections on the United Nations changing human rights responsibilities? Hum Rights Q 25:314–342
Mégret F, Pinto F (2003) "Prisoners" Dilemmas': The Potemkin villages of international law? Leiden J Int Law 16:467–490
Merry SE (2006) Human rights and gender violence: translating international law into local justice. University of Chicago Press, Chicago
Merry SE, Stern RE, Deveaux M, et al. (2005) The female inheritance movement in Hong Kong. Curr Anthropol 46:387–409
Mill JS (2006) A few words on non-intervention. New Engl Rev 27:252–264
Moyn S (2010) The last utopia: human rights in history. Belknap Press, Cambridge
Mutua M (2001) Savages, victims, and saviors: the metaphor of human rights. Harv Int'l LJ 42:201–246
Mutua M (2002) Terrorism and human rights: power, culture, and subordination. Buff Hum Rts L Rev 8:1–14
Mutua MW (1995) The ideology of human rights. Va J Int'l L 36:589–658
Nardin T (2000) International pluralism and the rule of law. Rev Int Stud 26:095–110
Nesiah V (2009) The specter of violence that haunts the UDHR: the turn to ethics and expertise. Md J Int'l L 24:135–154
Noll G (2003) The exclusionary construction of human rights in international law and political theory. SSRN eLibrary
Nyamu-Musembi C (2005) Towards an actor-oriented perspective on human rights. In: Kabeer N (ed) Inclusive citizenship: meanings and expressions, Institute of Development Studies, Brighton, pp 31–49
Oberleitner G (2007) Global human rights institutions: between remedy and ritual. Polity Press, Cambridge
Orford A (2003) Reading humanitarian intervention: human rights and the use of force in international law. Cambridge University Press, Cambridge
Otto D (2009) The exile of inclusion: reflections on gender issues in international law over the last decade. Melb J Int'l L 10:11–26
Petman J (2011) Egoism or altruism? No Foundations 373
Pogge T (2008) World poverty and human rights: cosmopolitan responsibilities and reforms. Polity Press
Rajagopal B (2006) Counter-hegemonic international law: rethinking human rights and development as a third world strategy. Third World Q 27:767–783
Rajagopal B (2003) International law from below: development, social movements, and third world resistance international law. Cambridge University Press, Cambridge
Romany C (1993) Women as aliens: a feminist critique of the public/private distinction in international human rights law. Harv Hum Rts J 6:87–126
Rorty R, Shute S, Hurley S (1993) On human rights: the Oxford amnesty lectures. Basic Books, New York
Roth K (2004) War in Iraq: not a humanitarian intervention. In: Human Rights Watch, world report: human rights and armed conflict
Saito NT (2002) Asserting plenary power over the other: Indians, immigrants, colonial subjects, and why U.S. jurisprudence needs to incorporate international law. Yale L Pol'y Rev 20:427–480
Sanders D (1996) Getting lesbian and gay issues on the international human rights agenda. Hum Rts Q 18:67–106
Schabas WA (2007) Lex specialis—belt and suspenders—the parallel operation of human rights law and the law of armed conflict, and the conundrum of jus ad Bellum. Isr L Rev 40:592–613
Shamir R (2004) The de-radicalization of corporate social responsibility. Crit Sociol 30:669–689
Shelton D (1991) Human rights, environmental rights, and the right to environment? Stan J Int'l L 28:103–138
Slim H (2002) By what authority? the legitimacy and accountability of non-governmental organizations. J Humanitarian Assist 10:1–12

Stammers N (1995) A critique of social approaches to human rights. Hum Rights Q 17:488–508
Starr S (2007) Extraordinary crimes at ordinary times: international justice beyond crisis situations? Nw U L Rev 101:1257–1314
Stein MA (2007) Disability human rights. Cal L Rev 95:75–121
Tamir Y (1996) Hands off clitoridectomy. Boston Rev 21:21–22
Thomas KR, Small J (2003) Human rights and state immunity: is there immunity from civil liability for torture? Netherlands Int Law Rev 50:1–30
Tushnet M (1983) Essay on rights. Tex L Rev 62:1363–1404
Waldron J (1993) A right-based critique of constitutional rights. Oxford J Leg Stud 13:18–51
Watkin K (2004) Controlling the use of force: a role for human rights norms in contemporary armed conflict. Am J Int Law 98:1–34
Weiler JHH (2001) Human rights, constitutionalism and integration: iconography and fetishism. Int'l LFD Int'l 3:227–238
Wilde R (2010) Compliance with human rights norms extraterritorially: 'human rights imperialism'? Liber Amicorum Vera Gowlland-Debbas. International Law and the Quest for its Implementation, pp 319–348
Williams RAJ (1990) Encounters on the frontiers of international human rights Law: redefining the terms of indigenous peoples' survival in the world, Duke, pp 660–704

# Chapter 2
# Self-Critique, (Anti) Politics and Criminalization: Reflections on the History and Trajectory of the Human Rights Movement

**Karen Engle**

**Abstract** In this chapter, I identify and critically discuss three aspects of the history and trajectory of the human rights movement from the 1970s until today: its increasing tendency toward self-critique, its roots in and ongoing struggle with a commitment to being antipolitical, and its relatively recent attachment to criminal law as its enforcement mechanism of choice. In part, I contend that the latter two aspects work in tandem to defer, even suppress, substantive debates over visions of social justice, even while relying on criminal justice systems of which the movement has long been critical. The chapter pursues this discussion through an in-depth reading of two related works by David Kennedy, the first published in 1985 and the second, which reproduces but also revisits the writing and reception of the first, in 2009. Because the pieces are primarily situated in Uruguay in 1984, it contextualizes them and my own thesis in a 25-year old struggle in Uruguay over whether to grant amnesty to military and political officials for acts committed during the dictatorship that ended in 1985.

*The left lost the war. All we have now is justice.*
Guatemalan Human Rights Activist, 2010

---

Many thanks to José María Beneyto and the Institute for European Studies at the University CEU San Pablo for organizing the conference on the occasion of the publication of the Spanish translation of David Kennedy's, *Rights of Spring*, out of which this chapter grew. I benefitted greatly from the conference discussion, as well as the feedback from a faculty workshop at the University of Florida. I am also grateful to Henry Steiner for his extensive comments on an earlier draft of the article, to Dan Brinks and Ariel Dulitzky for useful conversations, and to Juandrea Bates for outstanding research assistance.

---

K. Engle (✉)
Minerva House Drysdale Regents Chair in Law, Founder and Co-Director, Bernard and Audre Rapoport Center for Human Rights and Justice, University of Texas, Texas, TX, USA
e-mail: KEngle@law.utexas.edu

J. M. Beneyto and D. Kennedy (eds.), *New Approaches to International Law*,
DOI: 10.1007/978-90-6704-879-8_2,

## Contents



## 2.1 Introduction

In 1985, David Kennedy published an article entitled "Spring Break" in the Texas Law Review, chronicling his experiences during a two-week human rights mission to Uruguay in 1984.[1] Sponsored by five scientific and medical associations in the United States, Kennedy played the lawyer in a three-member delegation that also included a physician and a writer. At the time of the trip, Uruguay was in the final months of a military dictatorship. The delegation's mission was to meet with and assess the health situation of political prisoners, especially four medical students who had been arrested the previous year. Such human rights missions were becoming increasingly common in the mid-1980s,[2] but Kennedy's approach was not. His narrative, written as nonfiction but with pseudonyms for the individuals in Uruguay, offered a keen, edgy, and self-reflective approach to the team's personal and professional encounters with both male and female prisoners with whom they met as well as with prison and other governmental officials. It also demonstrated and reflected upon the difficulty of defining the boundaries between the personal and professional. In many ways, the account called into question the innocence and politics (and their mutual imbrication) of the human rights movement, and

---

[1] Kennedy 1985.

[2] That said, Kennedy's delegation was the first private foreign delegation since 1978 allowed into the particular prisons in Uruguay that it visited. Breslin et al. 1984, 2. Although the International Committee of the Red Cross had visited both prisons, its reports were of course confidential. Breslin et al. 1984, 27 note 1. In the report it wrote for its sponsors, Kennedy's delegation described the government as cooperative in terms of supporting its mission to visit the prisoners, and saw such cooperation as one of several then-recent events that "raise hopes for an orderly return to democratic, civilian rule". Breslin et al. 1984, 20.

suggested ways in which the movement itself might be, what Kennedy later termed, "part of the problem".[3]

Kennedy's piece was groundbreaking. Today, such self-reflective accounts of human rights and humanitarian enterprises, as well as other more traditionally scholarly critiques of human rights law and discourse, are plentiful.[4] But in 1985, only a few years after the contemporary human rights movement had come into being,[5] Kennedy's account was unprecedented both in style and in content. As Kennedy later explained, the Harvard Law Review had initially agreed to publish the piece, but then became reluctant because, as Kennedy puts it, "[t]here was something unseemly about uncertainty in the face of suffering. To write about moral ambiguity risked sacrilege".[6] When the Texas Law Review accepted it for publication, the editors asked Kennedy to write an appendix "situating *Spring Break* in contemporary legal scholarship".[7] Apparently, the article was so unusual that it needed an explanation. Telling of the absence of critique of the human rights movement at the time, the appendix situates the work within critical legal studies and the indeterminacy critique; there is no mention of human rights or international law.

In 2009, Kennedy published *The Rights of Spring*, a short book that intersperses the 1985 story (but not the appendix) with Kennedy's musings about what happened to the human rights movement over the subsequent two and a half decades.[8] The book calls for a revisitation of the "common ambivalence and confusion, excitement, boredom, and occasional vague nausea" associated with the human rights movement in the early days from which he first wrote, before what he considers its "spectacular rise and subsequent decline".[9] For Kennedy, the movement's decline is marked by its institutionalization and bureaucratization, and its failure to represent any longer "a common global rhetoric for justice".[10] Although I disagree with Kennedy on the extent to which the movement has

---

[3] Kennedy 2002.

[4] For other self-reflective accounts, see Cain et al. 2004, Fassin 2007, Orbinski 2008, Branch 2011. For a typology of scholarly critiques of human rights more generally, see Mégret 2012 (in this volume), identifying the following critiques, which I have reworded slightly: (1) human rights as indeterminate; (2) human rights as neo-colonial; (3) human rights as privileging already privileged voices; (4) human rights as substantively and problematically biased—in favor of market capitalism, individualism, rule of law; (5) human rights as institutionalized and as governance; (6) human rights as compromised politically—committed to incrementalism and tinkering—rather than revolution.

[5] Although scholars disagree about the roots of the contemporary human rights movement, I basically agree with Samuel Moyn's situation of its founding in the late 1970s, at least in or with regard to the United States, Europe, and Latin America. Moyn 2010.

[6] Kennedy 2009, 9.

[7] Kennedy 1985, 1417.

[8] Kennedy 2009. In this chapter, I cite the book, not the original article, unless some part of the article is not in the book. Still, I try to make it clear whether the part I refer to was originally written in 1985 or 2009.

[9] Ibid., 9.

[10] Ibid., 3.

declined, I do believe that together his 1985 and 2009 texts illuminate a number of significant shifts that have occurred within the movement.

In this chapter, I read "Spring Break" and *The Rights of Spring* to identify three aspects of the history and trajectory of the human rights movement from the 1970s until today, which structure the first three sections of the chapter: its increasing tendency toward self-critique, its roots in and the ongoing struggle with a commitment to being antipolitical, and its relatively recent attachment to criminal law as its enforcement mechanism of choice and for its understanding of justice. In the fourth section, I revisit the last two themes through a study of the 25-year old struggle in Uruguay over whether to grant amnesty to military and political officials for acts committed during the dictatorship that ended in 1985. In part, I contend that the early antipolitics of the movement has reemerged in the criminal justice arena, functioning to defer, even suppress, substantive debates over visions of social justice, even while relying on criminal justice systems of which the movement has long been critical.

## 2.2 Self-Critique and the Human Rights Movement

David Kennedy was not the first person to bring a skeptical eye to the idea of international human rights. From its first entry into international institutional discourse in the mid-1940s through the beginning of its dominance as the basis of a movement in the late 1970s, many had criticized or been wary of international human rights for a variety of reasons: its Western bias, support for property rights and capitalism, interference with local cultures, and concern for rights rather than duties of individuals.[11] Many explicitly eschewed human rights during these years for other forms of politics, namely self-determination.[12] Indeed, according to Samuel Moyn, human rights had less traction than most people assume during this

---

[11] As early as the mid-1940s, scholars had begun to criticize international human rights for these and other reasons. A volume edited by UNESCO published in 1949, based on a 1947 survey that it conducted of scholars from around the world about their perspectives on a declaration on human rights, demonstrates a range of these opinions. See, e.g. Hessen 1949, Laski 1949 and Sommerville 1949 (on Western bias); Hessen 1949, Laski 1949, and Maritain 1949 (on property rights and capitalism); Gerard 1949, Tchechko, 1949 and Northrop 1949 (on influence over local culture); Riezler, 1949, Gandhi 1949, Lewis 1949 and Chung-Shu 1949 (on the emphasis on rights rather than duties). Of course, if one traces the intellectual history of international human rights to the enlightenment, as some have done, critiques abound from as disparate sources as Bentham, Burke, and Marx. *See, e.g.*, Hunt 2007. See Moyn 2010, 11–43, for a challenge to such historiography due in part to its failure to capture the importance of the international aspect of the human rights movement.

[12] See Moyn 2010, 84–120, for an argument that the anticolonialist movement was a self-determination, rather than human rights, movement. For a related argument about this period and later with regard to indigenous rights, see generally Engle 2010.

time, largely because of the dominance of other utopias or visions that drove international and local social movements.

In the 1970s, however, the modern day human rights movement began to emerge, and—by the late 1970s and early 1980s—became the dominant mode of contesting dictatorships and authoritarian regimes, particularly in and regarding Eastern Europe and Latin America.[13] For a variety of complicated reasons that many have hypothesized and which I discuss in greater detail below, much of the left opposition in Latin America shifted its support from revolutionary armed struggle and socialist utopia toward what Moyn identifies as a much more minimalist strategy, that of human rights.[14] That said, Latin America "proved far more hospitable [than Eastern Europe] to the persistence of revolutionary and guerilla utopianism even as human rights took root there".[15] To the extent that some on the left did not fully embrace human rights, they nevertheless deployed it as a strategy, even if they did so alongside other strategies. They therefore learned to separate their "radical claims for social change" from their "human rights activism".[16] But, because they were using human rights, they were also not directly challenging the movement or paradigm.

I think it is fair to say, then, that in 1985, however minimalist the human rights movement might have been, there was little direct liberal or left critique of it, at least in the United States or Latin America. Moreover, there was little self-critique or questioning of what it meant for Eastern Europeans or Latin Americans to have North American or Western European interlocutors. At least in the context of Latin America, it made sense to rely on human rights organizations like Amnesty International and Helsinki Watch, precisely because they were in a position to pressure the United States, which had supported—if not designed—the overthrow of left, democratically elected governments and the rise of authoritarian regimes.[17] (The overthrow of Chilean socialist President Salvador Allende by the coup led by General Augusto Pinochet is often given as a prime and precipitating example.)

---

[13] Many have theorised the reasons for the emergence of the movement at this time and what, if any, relationship there was between the pro-democracy movements in the two regions. Most trace the movement to the formation of Helsinki Watch and its many affiliates, following on the Helsinki Final Act of 1975 and the Helinki process beginning in 1977. See, e.g., Keck and Sikkink 1998, Lauren 2001, Youngs 2002, Mertus and Helsing 2006. In contrast, Moyn points to the large amount of philanthropic money poured into the cause in 1977, contending that the strength or appeal of the movement would not have been predicted in 1975: "When [the Helsinki Final Act] had been signed, no one could have predicted that Eastern bloc dissidents would mobilize in such numbers or that an American president would throw himself into the cause". Moyn 2010, 172. For discussions of the relationship in the movements between Eastern Europe and Latin America, see Moyn 2010, 133–167.

[14] Moyn 2010, 141.

[15] Ibid.

[16] Ibid., 142 (quoting Markarian 2005, 141).

[17] As Markarian puts it in the context of Uruguayan exiles, many "reevaluated the role of international organizations formerly conceived as 'tools of U.S. imperialism' such as the OAS and of allegedly 'apolitical' organizations such as AI". Markarian 2005, 177.

Many Latin American activists thus put their hope in that governmental and non-governmental activity in the United States which relied heavily on human rights. The stakes seemed too high to question the movement, the strategy or the way in which one went about participating in it.

Given this backdrop, it is both surprising and not that when Kennedy's piece first appeared in 1985, few human rights scholars or activists made mention of it. On one hand, it posed a significant challenge to the apparent consensus that had congealed around human rights practice as a strategy not to be criticized. On the other hand, there was little scholarly discussion of human rights to which he might have addressed his critique. Recall that in the appendix to the article, Kennedy himself situated the piece in critical legal studies, and not in international legal thought. Those who engaged with it in the immediate years following its initial publication did so for its use of narrative and other contributions it made to critical legal thought and methodology;[18] no one discussed it for the lessons it might teach human rights advocates or scholars. Scholars and activists working on and in Uruguay also had little apparent reason to engage with it. By the time it was published in May 1985, civilian rule had returned to Uruguay, with democratically elected President Julio Maria Sanguinetti having taken office on March 1 of the same year.

I have taught "Spring Break" to my human rights students nearly every year since 1992. For most of those years, the piece provoked intense debate. For reasons that should become clear in the ensuing discussion, some identified the piece as "daring", "refreshing", "important self-criticism", or "humanizing". Others saw it as "narcissistic", "disrespectful", "sexist", or "dehumanizing". Class debates were not about whether the piece was accurate (it was after all Kennedy's account of his own thought process, something one would be hard-pressed to challenge), but about whether he should have thought what he wrote and, more importantly perhaps, whether he should have written what he thought.[19]

Around five years ago, at least in my classes, it seems the debate stopped. Students generally agree today that the piece is riveting and an accurate reflection of tensions they themselves have experienced or that, if they were human rights advocates, they imagine they would and maybe even should experience. Kennedy identifies a similar trend in reactions to his own telling of the story:

> In the pressure cooker of academic identity politics, the whole story often seemed to be about my sexism. Torture, along with self-consciousness, faded from view. In subsequent

---

[18] See, e.g., Frankenberg 1988, Freeman 1988, Minda 1989, Singer 1989, Oetken 1991, Purvis 1991, Goodrich 1993. Not until the mid to late 1990s did scholars even begin to consider the work in the context of international law and human rights. See, e.g., Spahn 1994, Carrasco 1996, Abbott 1999, Howland 2004.

[19] Apparently my students were not alone in this reaction. Reflecting in 2009 on one of his own lines in "Spring Break" ("I feared that my desire to see the women prisoners, to cross the boundary guarded by these men, shared something with [the guards'] prurient fascination for our [female] guide"), Kennedy asks, "Was it wrong to think that?...In the intensity of identity politics, the flash of feminist anger that shot through the campus in the following years, I was told I should not have thought it". Kennedy 2009, 17–18.

> years, as the bloom came off the rose of human rights, whenever I taught the story, our trip seemed to foreshadow what many then were discovering about the dark sides of human rights advocacy.[20]

Perhaps, then, Kennedy's account of human rights advocacy resonates more than ever today, over two and a half decades since it was first published. But why does it not provoke in the way that it used to?

For Kennedy, the explanation is expertise. As the field became professionalised, it learned to manage and respond to the uncertainties that earlier advocates might have expressed. Advocates began to "remind one another to analyze, strategize, keep our powder dry, weigh and balance".[21] In other words, while advocates acknowledge having similar reactions to their work today as Kennedy had in 1985, they are not puzzled by them in the same way that he or others might have been in the early days. Kennedy returns to his spring break narrative in 2009, he tells us, to recall the "uncertainty, hesitation, or worry" of the early, pre-professional, days".[22] He "hope[s] that in those befuddled moments we might catch a glimpse of the elusive and heady experience of human freedom and of the weight which comes with the responsibility of moments like that", of having "the mysterious feeling of being free and responsible right now, of making it up for the first time".[23]

Having directed three human rights delegations with students over three consecutive spring breaks, from 2007–2009, I am less convinced than Kennedy about the extent to which some of those doing human rights work, at least for the first time, no longer experience those heady moments of freedom and responsibility. I find that when student delegations are involved in the "fact-finding" process, they experience the uncertainties of having entered into a world they know they will never know, of trying to make sense of conflicting narratives they hear, and of attempting to figure out how what they are listening to fits within a "human rights framework" and why it needs to. Over the course of a week of fieldwork, they oscillate between many of the feelings toward themselves, their work, and their relationships to the "victims" and "perpetrators" they meet that Kennedy so aptly describes.

That said, they also struggle with the fact that they need to find a way to write a collective report about the issues on which they are conducting fact-finding. The need to write the report often causes them, particularly as the end of the trip nears, to repress the gaps, tensions, and ambiguities within and between accounts they have heard. They find it hard to acknowledge or appreciate conflicting information from those they have come to see themselves as representing or in convincing explanations offered by government officials. They therefore become focused on collecting testimony and data that can make sense of the inconsistent information

[20] Kennedy 2009, 97.

[21] Ibid., 98.

[22] Ibid., 99.

[23] Ibid., 102.

they have already gathered. Inconsistency and lack of clarity are no longer "facts" to be discovered in their "fact-finding missions", but problems to be resolved or explained.

To the extent that the delegation members cannot find a way to express their uncertainties and worries in the form of a human rights report, Kennedy's account of the effects of professionalism on the field seems accurate. But Kennedy in 2009, I think, might underestimate the human rights professionalism that was in fact already quite present in 1985. While human rights reports might not have been as ubiquitous or standardized at that time as they are now, a number of NGOs were engaged in the process of writing them.[24]

Although Kennedy's delegation was charged with writing an account of its trip for its sponsors, the specter of the report does not seem to have played as significant a role for that mission as it does for my students.[25] Kennedy 2009, 89–90. In part, that might be because the report the delegation eventually wrote, unlike other reports at the time and like most today, offered few recommendations to the United States or Uruguayan governments, international or regional organizations, or even the sponsoring organizations. While today many reports begin with such recommendations (and, even then, reports often used bullet points to highlight the recommendations), the report issued by Kennedy's team buries suggestions—not quite recommendations—in a conclusion. And the authors begin from a relatively optimistic perspective about the likelihood of change in the country, even while noting that "the process of democratization in Uruguay remains fragile". The latter conclusion leads to something like a recommendation, albeit not a very strong one: "The institutions involved in the mission, and others concerned about Uruguay, must continue to watch events there closely". They should also aim to support democracy by "strengthening their ties with their sister organizations in Uruguay".[26]

Regardless of the final content of the report, did its sheer existence—the formal account of the trip—permit Kennedy to write his own, self-critical account? If so,

---

[24] Based on the reports that Human Rights Watch includes in its historical database, the organization published at least forty-two reports between 1979 and 1986. Human Rights Watch Publications 2011. Likewise, according to its digital library of reports, Amnesty International issued at least twenty-five reports during the same period. Amnesty International Report Library 2011.

[25] That said, one of his few references to it would be familiar to my students:

So many people had told us their stories, looked to us for help, asked us to take on their struggle, to work when we got back. Even those who understood the limits of our context spoke with both resignation and hope about 'international public opinion' whose symbol we three became, if only for an instant. We kept saying that our institutions would 'remain concerned,' that we would write a report, that we would carry their story back. But three individuals cannot fulfill the promise implicit in the words 'foreign,' 'American,' 'professional,' 'authority,' 'witness'.

[26] Breslin et al. 1984, 20.

perhaps Kennedy's intervention is, if unwittingly, an early example of a particular type of splitting that now seems acceptable within the movement. That is, today, it seems perfectly appropriate for a human rights advocate to reflect critically on her work—in writing or in other ways—as long as it is done in an appropriate forum, one that does not interfere with the "real" work on behalf of marginalised individuals and groups that needs to be accomplished.[27]

## 2.3 (Anti) Politics of the Human Rights Movement

For many supporters of the human rights movement in its early days, the movement's strategy of minimalism and its insistence on being antipolitical were two of its greatest strengths. The two understandings were often connected. Speaking of the dramatic rise in membership in Amnesty International between the early and late 1970s and its principal activity of engaging in letter-writing campaigns to seek the release of individual political prisoners in Eastern Europe and Latin America, Moyn concludes that its minimalism was part of the appeal. At least initially, he contends, a small act of mailing a card was part of a larger move of "leaving behind political utopias and turning to smaller and more manageable moral acts".[28] That the movement largely grew up in reaction to left-wing regimes in Eastern Europe as well as right-wing regimes in Latin America meant that human rights had to provide a language that could be used to criticize states at both ends of the political spectrum. For those inside both regions, according to Moyn, human rights emerged in response to "the failure of more maximal visions of political transformation and the opening of the avenue of moral criticism in a moment of political closure".[29] Both Prague, Czechoslovakia in 1968 and Santiago, Chile in 1973, for example, suggested that revisionist socialism was no longer viable in either the Soviet or American spheres.

As already mentioned, Moyn does note that a human rights framework existed alongside the possibility of armed revolution for some time, at least in Latin America: "While human rights proved more lasting, utopia would remain 'armed' in the region through the end of the Cold War, if not beyond".[30] Instructively, he offers Uruguay as an example of a country with a persistent active left that refused minimalist and antipolitical approaches and instead called for a revolution in which "those who are exploited open up the doors of the jails".[31]

[27] I have described elsewhere a similar splitting, in the context of strategic essentialism and in what is often referred to as "activist scholarship". Engle 2010, 10–13.

[28] Moyn 2010, 147.

[29] Ibid., 141.

[30] Ibid.

[31] Ibid., 142 (quoting Markarian 2005, 99).

Markarian, the historian on whom Moyn relies for much of his analysis of the Uruguayan left's approach to human rights, claims that much of the left in Uruguay resisted the human rights ideology because of its entrenchment in liberalism, even after significant repression had begun in the country in the late 1960s.[32] Moreover, she contends that the left actively resisted a victim-centered approach to torture until after the 1973 coup, when the majority of those in exile began to align with the international human rights movement to seek outside condemnation of the right-wing regime. Some in exile rejected what they considered "humanitarian laments" as incapable of "advancing our objectives", and called instead for political confrontation based on class struggle.[33] Yet, "the realization that space for radical activism was dwindling not only in [Uruguay] but also in Chile and Argentina, led to a slow but clear change in leftist politics, setting human rights violations at the top of their agendas".[34]

Based on Markarian's and Moyn's analysis, by the time that Kennedy visited Uruguay, the left, if it had not conceded its larger political aims, had subordinated discussion of them to human rights claims. As such, Kennedy's narrative is instructive of what was happening at the time more generally and also foreshadowed what was yet to come: human rights discourse would provide a way for liberal and left activists to oppose right-wing dictatorships without insisting or relying on the left's larger, redistributive, economic, and political agenda. Focusing on the embrace of human rights by Uruguayan exiles in search of those who could put pressure on Uruguay from the outside, Markarian says they ended up moving "from endorsing a socialist view of rights as only attainable in a revolutionized socioeconomic horizon to accepting the concept of universally held rights".[35] Speaking years later about the politics of this depoliticising move more generally in human rights,[36] Kennedy notes:

> [T]the human rights intervention is always addressed to an imaginary third eye—the bystander who will solidarise with the (unstated) politics of the human rights speaker

[32] Markarian 2005, 4 (noting in general that the Latin American left "had previously rejected [a human rights] approach as 'bourgeois' and often opposed the main tenets of political liberalism"); 65 (describing a 1971 meeting organized by the National Convention of Workers and the national university on the relevance of human rights in Latin America and noting that "[d]espite being the subject of the conference, the great majority of the Uruguayan participants ignored the language of human rights used by international organizations.... In the final proceedings, the participants expressed that the 'real implementation of human rights will be only possible through a fundamental structural change and the exercise of power by the popular classes'".).

[33] Ibid., 99. She quotes here the Stockholm chapter of the Committee for the Defense of Political Prisoners of Uruguay, which also stated in the same document Moyn quotes above, "The problem of the political prisoners should be confronted politically, positioned in terms of class struggle".

[34] Ibid., 102.

[35] Ibid., 178.

[36] I use this terminology instructively, to emphasize that depoliticisation is a political strategy, if not ideology.

> because it is expressed in an apolitical form. This may often work as a form of political recruitment—but it exacts a terrible cost on the habit of using more engaged and open ended political vocabularies. The result is professional narcissism guising itself as empathy and hoping to recruit others to solidarity with its bad faith.[37]

This view is resonant with some of the same critique he expressed, albeit in different form, in "Spring Break" in 1985.

Despite the Uruguayan left's shift in strategies, it seems that Kennedy was able to glimpse some aspects of a pre-antipolitical project that were soon to disappear. Looking back from 2009, he notes some atypical aspects of his delegation in 1984, particularly in terms of its connection to scientific organizations: "In those days, scientific institutions often resisted engaging in human rights work because they feared it would diminish their scientific neutrality—ironically the very neutrality that might enable and legitimize their human rights work".[38] Thus, Kennedy reminds us that, despite the explicitly apolitical, even antipolitical, ideology of the human rights movement in the mid-1980s, "[i]t was not yet clear that human rights was ideologically safe, spoken in the name of a universal quite widely acceptable to their peers".[39] The scientific sponsors of Kennedy's delegation, he notes, overcame their doubts "through reliance on well-worn norms of professional responsibility to limit and channel what could be done, against the background of a rising confidence in the universality of human rights ideology". They began to see, for example, that "torture was, has always been and must always be, a matter of public health".[40]

The report the delegation submitted to its sponsors demonstrates how the delegation attempted to assuage the organizations' fears. It does so by borrowing from the antipolitical posture of human rights, which Wendy Brown describes as "manifesting itself in a moral discourse centered on pain and suffering rather than political discourse of comprehensive justice".[41] Indeed, the report makes clear that it is not meant to constitute "political advocacy". It insists that the delegation's positioning of itself as associated with "scientific and medical organizations having a humanitarian concern for human rights" was "one key to our success".[42] The report relies on medical ethics standards regarding the participation of medical personnel in torture, and on the codification of those ethics in United Nation documents. In what comes closest to the recommendations section of the report, the conclusion states "that precise ethical standards exist and must be applied".[43]

---

[37] Kennedy 2002, 121.

[38] Kennedy 2009, 27.

[39] Ibid.

[40] Ibid., 28.

[41] Brown 2004, 453.

[42] Breslin et al. 1984, 21.

[43] Ibid., 20 (citing World Medical Association, Declaration of Tokyo: Guidelines for Physicians Concerning Torture and other Cruel, Inhuman or Degrading Treatment or Punishment in Relation to Detention and Imprisonment (1975).

Those ethics are not seen as political; to the contrary, they are standards that should be disseminated through the "non-political exchange [of] professional, scientific, and academic information", such as by having greater attendance of Americans and Europeans in Uruguayan conferences and vice versa.[44]

I do not mean to suggest that the report was not a negotiated and strategic instrument; it clearly was. Its strategy to bring scientific organizations on board and then use their authority to attempt to take advantage of a possible opening in Uruguay[45] relied upon the performance of a type of antipolitics. The report, by walking a fine line between appealing to these organizations through the denial of any political purpose and harnessing their authority for what would be difficult to deny were political purposes, provides important insight into a moment when the movement was not yet, as Kennedy puts it, "ideologically safe".

Kennedy's narrative account of his team's meeting with the warden at the women's prison makes clear how the delegation used the scientific nature of its sponsors to make themselves seem less threatening: "We explain that our concern is scientific and our motivation humane. We are interested in public health, not public policy".[46] He then adds a parenthetical with his own doubts about that distinction: "I wonder as I make that bald assertion what it could mean in such circumstance to say that public health and public policy are distinct. On the other hand, if our institutions did not think we could keep them separate, would they have sent us on this mission?"[47]

Perhaps the sponsors, and even at times the delegation, could become convinced that the work was not political. But at least two of the prisoners with whom the delegation met offered a different perspective. Although they, as with all of the prisoners interviewed, described horrific torture they had experienced, Kennedy describes these two prisoners—whom he calls Ramon and Francisco—as political and as fighters. Both, he notes, "focused on the political context of our visit and told of their torture rather matter-of-factly".[48] Specifically of Ramon, he says: "He seems to have used his body, deployed it, spent it. He is also an activist".[49]

Markarian identifies a similar approach to torture—as political and as a part of the battle—in her description of the resistance of many on the left to identifying as victims in the late 1960s and early 1970s, when torture was becoming a common tactic of the Uruguayan government. Indeed, she contends, "[e]nduring any suffering ranked high among the attributes of these militants". She offers the

---

[44] Ibid., 21.

[45] The delegation seemed more positive about the possibility of an opening with the Uruguayan government than with the U.S. embassy, about which it was remarkably critical. Ibid., 7 ("[D]espite a request by the Bureau of Human Rights and Humanitarian Affairs that the United States embassy in Montevideo help us secure appointments and permission to visit the prisons, the embassy remained aloof and declined to help us in any way"). See also ibid., 8 ("The meeting was cordial in tone but empty of content").

[46] Kennedy 2009, 20.

[47] Ibid.

[48] Ibid., 65.

[49] Ibid., 64.

example of an anonymous Tupamaro guerilla member who "declared that 'torture was a good experience,' since 'it contributed to self-knowledge, to know how much you can resist'".[50] She also considers a 1973 letter from Communist Party leader Rodney Arismendi to a militant who had been tortured, which reads, "[a]uthentic communists behave like you did", and indicates that those who do not "win over [torture]...cannot keep on the breast the badge of the party".[51] In sum, she says, "[t]he communists and the Tupamaros expressed two common ways of talking about torture among leftists: as a badge of revolutionary commitment and as an enriching experience".[52]

While Kennedy's interviewees certainly did not talk about torture as having been enriching—and would not have because, by the time he interviewed them, human rights provided the dominantly accepted framework for considering torture and also for his mission—they had not fully given up the sense that they were in a battle, if only a political one. There was something about the posture of Ramon and Francisco that, at least to Kennedy, made their politics, as well as their torture, legible. It also made them less in need of a human rights mission:

> Ramon and Francisco seemed to carry themselves as temporarily defeated warriors in a greater political struggle, and that is how they seemed to view their stories of capture, torture, and imprisonment. Imprisoned warriors like Ramon and Francisco seemed our equals; they needed no rescue. To them we were comrades, coparticipants in a political struggle.[53]

Ironically perhaps, as the victims transformed into comrades, Kennedy notes that this connection to them "diminished my purpose".[54]

The human rights purpose reemerged when the team met with another medical student prisoner, Victor, who Kennedy describes as "a naive and sensitive man". In contrast to Ramon's and Francisco's understanding of the political need to describe their torture to the human rights delegation, "Victor seems more interested in pleading his defense, more embarrassed to be seen".[55] Victor complained

---

[50] Markarian 2005, 63 (quoting María E. Gilio, "Entrevista a un tupamaro", *Marcha*, May 9, 1969, 12–13).

[51] Ibid., 64 (quoting Letter from Arismendi to Sócrates Martínez, September 1973, in R. Arismendi, Uruguay y América Latina en los años 70, 229).

[52] Ibid. For Markarian, it is important that denunciations of torture did not draw on human rights language. Rather, these attitudes were part of "a heroic language" employed by the left, which "made abuses part of their expected political experience and eluded legalistic references in order to privilege social and economic explanations". Ibid., 65. For a detailed description of the Tupamaro National Liberation Movement from 1962 to 1972, its leftist ideology and style of guerilla warfare, see Porzecanski 1974. For a discussion of the history of the Tupamaros, including their reemergence as a part of the *Frente Amplio* in the 1980s, see Weinstein 2007. Uruguay's current president, José Mujica, was a founding member of the Tupamaros. As I discuss below, he has been strongly in favor of prosecuting former military and police under the dictatorship.

[53] Kennedy 2009, 66.

[54] Ibid.

[55] Ibid., 65.

about the process by which charges were brought against him and insisted that he was not a Communist: "Sheepishly, he describes his own political acts: attending a rally, voting against the military in a recent referendum".[56] It is then that Kennedy is reengaged. He explains, "Victor, the passive victim, awakens my indignation and motivates me to act…Victor, pleading legal procedure and propriety, rekindles our involvement, somewhat dampened by our abstract political solidarity with his fellows".[57] For Kennedy, it is Victor's lack of politics, not the pain he endured, that set him apart from the others: "[His] pain comes through plainly as he details the familiar mix of blows, shocks, and other tortures. Victor, a man without politics, suffers under the harsh prison regime".[58] That same lack of politics enabled Victor, the delegation, and the Uruguayan government to act out their roles as victim, savior, savage, as Makau Mutua would describe the actors in the human rights movement over fifteen years later.[59]

If Ramon and Francisco had an opportunity to break out of the victim role—through politics—female prisoners, it seems, were not afforded the same possibility. With important insight, Kennedy notes the difficulty that the delegation members had in seeing female prisoners as political activists in the same way as they saw Ramon and Francisco. He tells of meeting Ana, Ramon's girlfriend, in the women's prison (before the delegation has met Ramon). As she described the conditions of her and Ramon's arrest, he says, "I begin to think of Ana as a student activist; her calm willingness to speak seems to reflect a self-assured politicization".[60] But as Ana began to tell the details of her torture, Kennedy distanced himself, "find[ing] her personal story too intimate and shocking to relate to".[61]

The team met with five other female political prisoners, who also described some of the torture they had endured. And, in the process of the encounters, the delegation experienced moments of solidarity with them. Yet, after the subsequent meetings with the male prisoners and while driving back to Montevideo to meet with (male) government and military officials in the capital, Kennedy considered how gender differentiation allowed the all-male delegation to exploit the spatial and temporal distance between the female prisoners and the officials: "In prison we had been with the women, the victims, and we were returning to the men, the victimizers, in Montevideo. This spatial difference was partly sustained by contrasting the sacred woman with the profane man and partly by contrasting the female victim with the male avenger".[62]

Although, as Kennedy notes, the delegation had made "elaborate efforts to connect with Ana as a person, a politico sympatico", those efforts were lost or

56 Ibid.

57 Ibid., 66.

58 Ibid., 67.

59 Mutua 2001.

60 Kennedy 2009, 41.

61 Ibid., 43.

62 Kennedy 1985, 1404. The first sentence can also be found at Kennedy 2009, 70–71.

forgotten not just when meeting with the "avengers", but with male political prisoners as well. The delegation later "reimagined Ana's torture as an abomination", making it "possible to relate more objectively to Ramon's tales. Ramon seemed subjugated, not violated. His pain was instrumental, his body political. Ana had been trespassed upon, Ramon punished".[63] As Kennedy states elsewhere in the narrative, Ana's pain seemed "extra, gratuitous, imposed".[64] She would not, it seems, ever be able to don her battle marks in the same way as Ramon; yet, that very inability made her more capable of being represented as a human rights victim.[65]

If Kennedy attends to the different possibilities for gendered victimhood under a human rights rubric, Markarian identifies differences in the approach to male and female torture victims in an earlier period. She points out that, although there was little attention to gender issues during the revolution, "women did play an important role in leftist politics and were often imprisoned, tortured, and killed".[66] Yet, "[d]enunciations of abuses against women were different to those of similar practices against men: their nakedness before police or military personnel was considered particularly outrageous and insults to motherhood were often referred [to] as especially vicious offenses".[67] Women who had been tortured did not have access, she contends, to the language of left heroism that facilitated an understanding of torture as either a sign of revolutionary commitment or an enriching experience, as described above. That is, "[i]f men had their honor to defend in public, women had to preserve their virtue from shameful exposition".[68]

If Kennedy and Markarian are right, it seems that women might have been uniquely poised to be ideal human rights victims—once the language of heroism gave way to the apolitical discourse of victimhood. Yet, as many feminists have argued, the early human rights movement did not pay particular attention to women as victims of human rights violations or to the gendered aspects of women's victimisation. Human rights NGOs claimed to treat women who were tortured or improperly detained as human rights victims in the same way as they treated men. But they were not interested in pursuing the gendered or sexual meanings of the types of torture they experienced or of acts that might have been perpetrated by non-state actors.

I would contend, however, that, as the movement has grown, sexual violence against women has come to represent one of the quintessential violations of human rights. Human rights NGOs, intergovernmental organizations, and states alike

---

[63] Kennedy 2009, 72.

[64] Ibid., 63.

[65] In 1985, Ana seemed a stand-in for all the female prisoners in this regard. In 2009, however, Kennedy points out that "[t]hinking about it later, I realized we also imagined our forty-four-old [one of the other five female prisoners] as a spent warrior, different from Ana". Ibid., 72.

[66] Markarian 2005, 63.

[67] Ibid.

[68] Ibid.

condemn, at least at a rhetorical level, sexual violence against women, particularly in armed conflict. One manifestation of this condemnation, which I and others have critically analyzed elsewhere, can be found in the treatment of sexual violence in international criminal law which, as the next section notes, has become one of the primary focuses today of the human rights movement.[69]

## 2.4 Criminalization and the Human Rights Movement

In 1985, in "Spring Break", Kennedy discusses a meeting between the delegation and the warden of the women's prison where Ana was held. He portrays the warden, Kleber Papillon, as a staunch defender of the high-security prison of which he was in charge and which he considered to house violent prisoners. Yet, he let the delegation in, "an admission that belied his defense".[70] In one of the passages that provoked students for many years, Kennedy describes his own attempt during this encounter to imagine the warden and Kennedy outside of their professional roles: "David and Kleber relaxing around the piano. Sherry. Wives lounging on the couches. Servants spreading dinner. My effort at empathy had placed us in a television miniseries…because I, the foreign lawyer, would never find him revealed, no longer the warden".[71]

In 2009, Kennedy continues to fantasize the warden's personal life, and—as in the 1985 account—he recognises its inseparability from Kleber's professional life. In his weaving of this fantasy, Kennedy writes a damning critique of transitional justice that voices doubts about transitional justice mechanisms that few express today:

> Twenty years on, I wonder what became of our warden. Did some transitional justice procedure educate him to our universal perspective, offer him some peace? Was he made to suffer, that he might be released from suffering? This man, this manager: perhaps he was hoisted up, hair shorn, before his enemies. Did they go too far? Or perhaps he moved to the suburbs, sold furniture, raised his family, retired, died. Did he remain, in all the years that have passed, the same self, any more than I? If he was brought to account, by his son, his neighbors, by Ana and her parents, her boyfriend, something in me wishes him well. Whether he offered apologies, felt regret, or stuck with timid self-justification, rigidity, and professionalism, it all now seems to slip through my fingers, so paltry as an accounting of responsibility, the product of a later story, a later audience. Responsibility was for then. As for the strange way all of us are separate, if he can live with it, I can too.

[69] See, e.g., Engle 2005; Halley 2008.

[70] Kennedy 2009, 34.

[71] Ibid., 33. In discussing the oscillation he experienced between relating to the warden in the warden's professional and personal roles, Kennedy notes that he was likely to place the violence in the institution when they connected in their professional roles, but in the warden personally when they were sipping coffee together (even if inside the prison). "Working with this ambiguity…I avoided both blaming the prisoners for the violence against them and openly rebuking Warden Papillon's account of their suffering". Ibid., 34.

> I hope, given the chance, I would choose not to take responsibility for desiring his confession, his punishment, his enlightenment.[72]

Kennedy's paragraph goes against a near-universal consensus among human rights activists and scholars today on the centrality of impunity to the protection of human rights. For a number of reasons I consider below, it is instructive that Kennedy did not write this paragraph in the mid-1980s. Indeed he could not have done so; it simply would not have made sense. In 1984, prosecutions were going forward against former military leaders in Argentina, and then-opposition party members in Uruguay were engaged in conversations over whether, post-transition to democracy, those in the military and police would be tried for criminal actions committed during the dictatorship.[73] But, as I discuss in more detail in the next section, the issue had largely been deferred in public negotiations between the parties. Moreover, "transitional justice" was not a term used at the time, and there were no international criminal tribunals or courts in existence.[74]

By 2009, however, both the state of the human rights movement and the state of Uruguay had changed significantly from the mid-1980s. The remainder of this section considers some of the shifts in the human rights movement. The next section turns more specifically to Uruguay.

Today's human rights movement places the fight against impunity at its center. This focus is the culmination of a governance project in which the movement has been engaged for close to two decades that puts an enormous amount of attention on and faith in criminal justice systems—international, transnational and domestic. In *The Rights of Spring*, Kennedy makes a similar observation from the vantage of 2009, when considering some of the questions the delegation had in 1985 about the effectiveness of the mission. ("After we had found the facts, would our institutions return like avenging angels? Would the 'international community'? Was history on our side? What had our warden to fear?"[75]) For Kennedy, these types of questions provided the impetus for the criminalization we see today: "In the years since, the urgency of these questions has led human rights practitioners to construct an entire Potemkin village of international courts and tribunals, stage props to instill the fear of retribution when activists speak in the name of norms".[76]

Moyn considers transitional justice as one of several examples of a "transformation from antipolitics to program" that has taken place over the years.[77] That perspective seems to accord with Kennedy's observation that "activists speak in the name of norms". At some level, I agree. The transitional justice movement does appear to be a much more maximalist—and programmatic—project than the

---

[72] Ibid., 23–24.

[73] Markarian 2005, 160–169.

[74] For a genealogy of the term "transitional justice", which places its earliest use in 1992, see Arthur 2009, 329–330.

[75] Kennedy 2009, 31.

[76] Ibid., 31–32.

[77] Moyn 2010, 221.

early human rights movement. Yet, I hope to show, in the context of Uruguay in the next section and Guatemala in the conclusion, that the fight against impunity reflects and promotes an antipolitical stance that mirrors that of the early movement. In some instances, it seems to be leading to acquiescence in, if not support for, the prosecution of former state and non-state actors alike. In the context of those two countries, that means that former guerilla members might be subject to the same investigation as former military and police officers.

On one hand, this new reliance on criminal justice is a big shift from where the human rights movement started. Recall that Amnesty International's (AI) initial letter-writing campaigns in the 1960s were largely aimed at *releasing* political prisoners. And, although it almost seems too obvious to mention, *amnesty* was central to its mission. By the 1970s, AI had begun to work more broadly on the treatment of prisoners in custody, challenging detentions without trial, and ensuring the right to fair trial.[78] While some criminal justice systems might have been more suspect than others, all were considered as capable of abusing power. Today, AI consistently opposes amnesty laws for those responsible for human rights violations and, to my knowledge, the organization has not challenged the treatment of prisoners accused of gross human rights violations in either domestic or international criminal justice systems.[79] Thus, if AI is representative, the same human rights movement that has long been critical of criminal justice systems is now dependent on criminal punishment for enforcement.

On the other hand, the change might not be as great as it seems. While the early international human rights movement's focus was on issues of imprisonment and detention, it was largely concerned with those who had been wrongfully detained, or detained for reasons for which one ought not to be detained. "Common criminals" have rarely been the focus of the human rights movement, with the exceptions of consideration of the death penalty and of general prison conditions.[80] Thus, to be a human rights victim is largely to be innocent. As the discussion of Kennedy's treatment of torture in the previous section suggested, it has often been only the innocent who are seen to suffer the indignity worthy of victimhood.

As the human rights movement has become increasingly focused on criminalization, particularly by advocating for the application of universal jurisdiction and the development of international criminal law regimes, it has gone after perpetrators with a vengeance. It also has opposed, as an international legal matter, most amnesties, and has pressured transitional countries to prosecute former human

---

[78] Clark 2001.

[79] For examples of opposition to amnesty laws, see Amnesty International 2011a (Uruguay), Amnesty International 2011d (Yemen), Amnesty International 2011c (Libya), Amnesty International 2010b (Sudan), Amnesty International 2010a (Chile).

[80] For reports on the death penalty in the United States, see Amnesty International 2011b (United States), Amnesty International 2010a (United States), Amnesty International 2007 (United States), Amnesty International 2003 (United States). For a recent report on prison conditions, see Amnesty International 2011e (United States).

rights violators. While, during the 1990s the legality and political sensibility of both international and domestic prosecutions (and whether the former should be encouraged or required when the latter has failed to occur) were debated *within* the human rights community, today that debate has largely waned.[81] South Africa's Truth and Reconciliation Commission, for example, in which amnesty was exchanged for truth, was once seen by a sizeable number of human rights advocates and institutions as an acceptable form of amnesty, in part because it constituted neither self-amnesty nor blanket amnesty.[82] Over time, however, those distinctions have largely become eroded, with most NGOs, international institutions and courts having moved away from the position that any amnesties are compatible with human rights.

The jurisprudence of the Inter-American Court of Human Rights is instructive here. In 2001, it issued its decision in *Barrios Altos v. Peru,* which was considered path-breaking for its finding that self-amnesty laws, such as those in Peru, are "manifestly incompatible with the aims and spirit of the [American] Convention [of Human Rights]" because they "lead to the defenselessness of victims and perpetuate impunity".[83] In a subsequent case involving what the Court considered to be self-amnesty in Chile, the Court began to suggest that its analysis would extend to other types of amnesty as well.[84] In 2010, in a case against Brazil, the Court found it unnecessary to consider whether the challenged amnesty could or should be considered self-amnesty. The case posed a new challenge because the Brazilian Federal Supreme Court had upheld the law, in large part on the ground that it represented "a political decision [in] a moment of conciliatory transition in 1979".[85] The Court responded: "In regard to [arguments] by the parties regarding whether the case deals with an amnesty, self-amnesty, or 'political agreement,' the Court notes…that the

[81] For a sense of this debate through the 1990s, see Roht-Arriaza 1990, Cohen 1995, Zalaquett 1995, Cassese 1998, Scharf 1999, Minow 1999.

[82] For a lively debate over the nature of South African amnesty, see Meintjes and Mendez 2000, 88, arguing that South African amnesty "is a significant step in the evolution of domestic efforts to deal with the past in a manner that satisfies the requirements of international law," and Rakate 2001, 42, responding that South Africa's Truth and Reconciliation Commission was "totally unsatisfactory, but that it is what South Africans had to accept, because no other solution was politically or materially conceivable", and contending that victims received nothing in the way of compensation and that the perpetrators remain convinced of their innocence. For a counter to Rakate, see Meintjes and Mendez 2001.

[83] Inter-Am Ct. H.R. 2001, Case 75, *Barrios Altos* v. *Peru,* Judgment, para 43.

[84] Inter-Am Ct. H.R. 2006, Case 12.057, *Almonacid Arellano* et al. v. *Chile*, para 120 ("[E]ven though the Court notes that Decree Law No. 2.191 basically grants a self-amnesty, since it was issued by the military regime to avoid judicial prosecution of its own crimes, it points out that a State violates the American Convention when issuing provisions which do not conform to the obligations contemplated in said Convention….[T]he Court…addresses the *ratio legis*: granting an amnesty for the serious criminal acts contrary to international law that were committed by the military regime").

[85] Inter-Am Ct. H.R. 2010, Case 11.552, *Gomes Lund* v. *Brazil*, Judgment, para 136 (quoting Vote of the Rapporteur Minister in the Non-Compliance Action of the Fundamental Principle No. 153 resolved by the Federal Supreme Court).

non-compatibility with the Convention includes amnesties of serious human rights violations and is not limited to those which are denominated, 'self-amnesties'".[86]

With this position established, if arguably only in dicta, the Court was poised to face the issue squarely in 2011 in *Gelman v. Uruguay*. As I discuss in more detail in the next section, the 1985 democratically elected government in Uruguay was responsible for the 1986 amnesty law (called "*Ley de Caducidad*", or "Expiry Law"),[87] which was challenged under the American Convention in this case. Unlike in other countries in Latin America, the question whether the law should be repealed had been put to voters through public referenda, in 1989 and again in 2009. Both times, voters refused to repeal the law, placing Uruguay in a unique position among those states defending amnesty laws. In its decision, the Court reiterated its view that the prohibition on amnesty is not limited to self-amnesty.[88] It makes clear that the referenda do not constitute an exception: "[T]he protection of human rights constitutes a[n] impassable limit to the rule of the majority, that is, to the forum of the 'possible to be decided' by the majorities in the democratic instance".[89]

Some have argued that the Court's strict position against amnesty in Latin America is due to the particular circumstances of the history of military dictatorships there, and that it should therefore not necessarily be applied to those outside the region.[90] Yet, the Inter-American Court insists that its position is in compliance with other international and domestic fora. In the *Gelman* case, for example, the Court considered a variety of other institutional decisions to claim the following relatively uniform view: "This Court, the Inter-American Commission on Human Rights, the organs of the United Nations, and other universal and regional organs for the protection of human rights have ruled on the non-compatibility of amnesty laws related to serious human rights violations with international law and the international obligations of States".[91] That said, in several of the documents and decisions the Court cites, the concern seems primarily to be about amnesties that preclude investigation, not simply prosecution, of crimes. And some scholars do continue to argue that amnesties that are an important part of the truth process, such as in South Africa, are or should be permissible under international law.[92] Still, to the extent that there continue to be debates about the reconcilability of amnesties and international

86 Ibid., para 175.

87 El Senado y la Cámara de Representantes de la República Oriental del Uruguay, Ley N° 15.848 *Ley de caducidad de la pretensión punitiva del estado,* 1986.

88 Inter-Am Ct. H.R. 2011, Case 221, *Gelman v Uruguay*, Merits and Reparations, para 229.

89 Ibid., para 239.

90 See, e.g., Seibert-Fohr 2009, 108–109.

91 Inter-Am Ct. H.R. 2011, Case 221, *Gelman v Uruguay*, Merits and Reparations, para 195.

92 See, e.g., Mallinder 2007.

law, they are largely positioned as questions about the permissibility of exceptions to a background presumption against amnesty that is rarely contested.[93]

## 2.5 Uruguay and the Battles Over Amnesty

Given this near consensus against amnesty among human rights advocates and institutions, Kennedy's (2009) comment on transitional justice is particularly provocative. Ironically, one place in which it might have lacked shock value in 2009 is in Uruguay, given that in that year voters defeated by six points an attempt to repeal the same amnesty law that was later challenged in the *Gelman* case discussed above.[94]

Amnesty in Uruguay has a long and complicated history, and Uruguay is exceptional for the progression of its laws regarding amnesty for political prisoners as well as for the military, its (failed) referenda in 1989 and 2009 to repeal the 1986 Expiry Law, the way that some prosecutions have gone forward despite the law, and the legislature's recent eventual repeal of the law in 2011. The story of the birth and death of the Expiry Law sheds light on both the antipolitics ideology of the human rights movement discussed in the second section of this chapter and the movement's drive against impunity addressed in the third section.

As I have already mentioned, even before Sanguinetti was elected president of Uruguay in 1985, discussions had been taking place among representatives of various political parties and of the military—as a part of transition talks—about whether those in the military regime who had engaged in human rights violations should be subject to criminal liability for their actions. At the same time, parties on the left were largely focused on a different type of amnesty—the release of political prisoners. The two issues were intertwined in a variety of ways.

Markarian traces left support for amnesty for political prisoners back to the early 1970s, before the 1973 coup, and notes that the understanding of amnesty for some on the left was relatively broad, as "some kind of amnesty and even an implicit mutual forgiveness [were seen] as necessary steps to open negotiations among parties, the military, and guerilla groups".[95] She points to the 1971 platform of the *Frente Amplio* (a then new coalition of left-wing parties), which called for using amnesty "as a tool to reincorporate all sectors of society to legal political life…[It will] comprise all those who committed political offenses…with the aim

[93] For an example of a recent argument in favor of amnesty on utilitarian grounds, see Freeman 2010. A review of the book suggests how unusual any argument for amnesty is today. "International popular opinion now stands firmly in opposition to amnesty and transitioning societies are generally expected to aggressively prosecute individuals responsible for human rights violations". Minogue 2010, 307.

[94] 52.64 percent voted against repeal. Corte Electoral de Uruguay 2009.

[95] Markarian 2005, 133.

of transforming current political, economic, and social structures".[96] That said, Markarian notes that in the ensuing years, with increased government repression against left opposition, the left began to turn away from use of the term "amnesty". By the time of the 1973 coup, she notes, the left referred only to "political prisoners", avoiding the word "amnesty" so as not to suggest reciprocal forgiveness".[97]

In the late 1970s, however, Uruguayan exiles in Europe began to use the term again by, for example, forming the *Secrétariat International de Juristes pour l'Amnistie en Uruguay* (SIJAU) in 1977 in Paris.[98] When they did so, the meaning of the term was not clear. For instance, some connected to amnesty groups in Europe supported asylum (which would effectively constitute amnesty) for a former military official who fled Uruguay for Europe claiming that he had been punished for refusing to torture, others did not. As Markarian notes, the debate over this issue foreshadowed later discussions on what would be called "transitional justice".[99]

Although during various stages of transition negotiations in the early 1980s, amnesty both for political prisoners and for military and police involved in human rights violations were on the table, the issue of amnesty for the military and police was ultimately deferred. At least in open meetings, there was little discussion of it, in large part because it was a hot-button issue.[100] Meanwhile, even before elections in November 1984 and before Sanguinetti's term began on March 1, 1985, some political prisoners were released. Yet, proposals from both the right and the left attempting to enact legislation regarding their release had failed.

When Sanguinetti came to power, he successfully pushed for what is commonly referred to as the *Ley de Pacificación Nacional* (National Pacification Law), although its official title is "amnesty law". That law decreed amnesty for political crimes committed since the beginning of 1962.[101] While Sanguinetti had originally proposed a law that would exclude those jailed for violent crimes from the amnesty, he was unable to get the support he needed for such an exclusion. Nevertheless, the law fell short of what many on the left had called for in that it included a review of cases and a possible sentence reduction for early release, rather than unconditional amnesty, for those who had committed intentional

[96] Ibid. (quoting the *Frente Amplio* platform).

[97] Ibid., 134.

[98] Ibid.

[99] Ibid., 136–137.

[100] There has, however, been much speculation that, behind closed doors, an agreement had in fact been made in which Sanguinetti, with the acquiescence of some on the left, agreed to grant amnesty for the military. While the agreement—called the Naval Club Pact—"had not included explicit assurances of impunity, such an outcome was allegedly arranged". Barahona de Brito 2001, 129.

[101] El Senado y la Cámara de Representantes de la República Oriental del Uruguay. Ley N° 15.737 *Se aprueba la ley de amnistía*, 1985.

homicide.[102] Still, the National Pacification Law did more for most political prisoners than grant amnesty; it also attempted to ensure their reintegration into civic, political and economic life.[103]

Importantly, the law specifically excluded "those members of the police or military, whether on duty or working on their own, who were the perpetrators, authors or accessories to inhumane, cruel or degrading treatment or to the detention of people who disappeared, or who have concealed any such conduct".[104] Once most political prisoners were released, therefore, many had assumed that prosecutions against the military would begin. Although charges were brought in a number of cases, they were stalled for a variety of reasons, including that military officers often refused to appear in person before civilian courts (sometimes at the behest of the defense minister), and that military courts challenged civilian court jurisdiction over members of the military. When Sanguinetti eventually responded by proposing two different laws that would grant unconditional amnesty for the military (either during certain periods or for all but the gravest crimes), opposition parties on both sides balked. After a series of alternative proposals and a Supreme Court decision upholding civilian court jurisdiction over the military, Sanguinetti convinced a majority of legislators (though none from the Christian Democrats or the *Frente Amplio*) to pass the Expiry Law.[105]

The Expiry Law essentially prevented the prosecution of members of the military or police for human rights violations committed prior to March 1, 1985. Although investigations or prosecutions would be permitted to proceed in very limited circumstances, the executive would be required to agree to pursue them, which is something that no president took seriously for twenty years.[106] The new

[102] Ibid. at Articles 1, 8–10. For discussion of these provisions and of the law that Sanguinetti initially proposed, see Mallinder 2009, 30–33.

[103] Mallinder 2009, 34–35 (discussing articles 12 & 13 of the law). The law also returned all seized property and assets of those imprisoned or in exile, created the *Comisón Nacional de Repatriacón* (National Commission for Repatriation) to support returning exiles and ensured that public officials who had been dismissed because of their political beliefs could regain their former jobs or that their relatives would receive their pensions. Ibid., 35–36 (discussing Articles 24 and 25).

[104] El Senado y la Cámara de Representantes de la República Oriental del Uruguay, Ley N° 15.737 *Se aprueba la ley de amnistía*, 1985, Article 5 ("Quedan comprendidas en los efectos de esta amnistía todas las personas a quienes se hubiera atribuido la comisión de estos delitos, sea como autores, coautores o cómplices y a los encubridores de los mismos, hayan sido o no condenados o procesados, y aun cuando fueren reincidentes o habituales").

[105] This general history is relatively well-known and can be found, with some differences in emphases and detail, at Mallinder 2009; Markarian 2005; Barahona de Brito, 1997; Skaar 2011; Inter-American Commission on Human Rights 2010, Case 12.607, *Gelman* et al. v *Uruguay*, Application, paras 81–85.

[106] See El Senado y la Cámara de Representantes de la República Oriental del Uruguay, Ley N° 15.848 *Ley de caducidad de la pretensión punitiva del estado,* 1986, Articles 3 & 4. For a discussion of various efforts by President Tabaré Ramón Vázques Rosas, elected in 2005, to pursue investigations, partly by interpreting narrowly the scope of amnesty provided for in the Expiry Law, see Mallinder 2009, 65–68.

government argued that such amnesty had been assumed in the 1984 transitional agreement between the military and those political parties that participated, often referred to as the Naval Club Pact.[107]

According to Elin Skaar, "[t]he human rights community was appalled at the law and its negative consequences for the pursuit of legal justice".[108] In response, a number of human rights groups successfully mobilized alongside trade unions and politicians opposed to the amnesty to collect signatures for a public referendum on the repeal of the law. The referendum was held in 1989, and it failed by over thirteen points, with 56.7 percent voting against and 43.3 percent voting for repeal. Many explanations have been given for the outcome, from fear of military retaliation to the desire to put the past behind for a variety of reasons. As Skaar notes, however, "[s]ince no systematic academic work has been done on the political, cultural, or psychological motivations driving the outcome of the referendum, nothing conclusive can be said about why the people approved the law".[109]

Given international debates during this time period over the best means to achieve peace and democracy in transitional societies, the ambivalence in Uruguay is not surprising. And the ambivalence was perhaps deeper, even among some involved with the human rights movement, than Skaar suggests. While human rights groups might have supported repeal of the law in 1989, many on the left, including some who had employed human rights discourse during the dictatorship, in fact had concurred—implicitly if not explicitly—with the amnesty that was codified in the Expiry Law. Indeed, Markarian sees the 1984 transitional agreement's failure to ensure human rights prosecutions against the military as stemming from a series of compromises. Such compromises were made because for many people, including many on the left who had adopted human rights in exile but returned to a country where the discourse had not developed or prevailed, "finding a rapid way out of the current situation was considered more important than demanding truth and justice for human rights violations committed by the outgoing regime".[110] Ironically, the very language of human rights that the left in exile had adopted (which she equates with both truth and justice) was now "often deemed too radical to fit the leftist coalition's negotiating approach to transitional politics in Uruguay".[111] In contrast, "human rights language, once toned down and bereft of radical claims for accountability, became a useful tool for presenting the left as a reliable political actor—one that had not only endured the bulk of

[107] Indeed, the law itself states that it results from "the logic of events originating in the agreement between the political parties and armed forces in August 1984". El Senado y la Cámara de Representantes de la República Oriental del Uruguay, Ley N° 15.848 *Ley de caducidad de la pretensión punitiva del estado,* 1986, Article 1 ("como consecuencia de la lógica de los hechos originados por el acuerdo celebrado entre partidos políticos y las Fuerzas Armadas en agosto de 1984").

[108] Skaar 2011, 145.

[109] Ibid., 147.

[110] Markarian 2005, 167.

[111] Ibid., 168.

repression by the military but that was also willing to give up on revenge and embrace democratic politics".[112]

Whatever the motive might have been for some to negotiate away criminal accountability, Uruguay was not unique in passing amnesty laws during this period. In its region, Argentina, Chile, Brazil, and Peru passed similar laws.[113] While in ensuing years, some of those countries repealed their amnesty laws—through legislation or as a result of constitutional or Inter-American Court decisions (or a combination)—Uruguay continued to put the question of repeal to popular vote. Indeed, Uruguay seems to be "the only case in world history in which the people of a democratic country have ratified a law granting the military impunity through a referendum".[114] When it did so for the second time in 2009, it was clear that the consensus among human rights NGOs and institutions was that the law violated international law. Yet, the majority of the electorate voted against repeal, in part because, since 2005, President Tabaré Vásquez, former Tupamaro and the first president elected from the *Frente Amplio*, had—unlike any other president—been approving the launching of investigations under the exception in the law discussed above.[115] Indeed, former president Juan Maria Bordaberry (1971–1976) and former head of the military junta and de facto president General Gregorio Alvarez (1981–1985) had both been arrested and prosecuted for crimes committed during their rule.[116]

Still, that voters rejected repeal came as a surprise to many, particularly because in the same year voters elected the *Frente Amplio*'s candidate, José "Pepe" Mujica, as their president. Mujica is a former Tupamaro guerilla leader, and he opposed the 1986 Expiry Law.[117] Moreover, the Supreme Court had recently unanimously

---

[112] Ibid., 175–176. The refusal to push for accountability during the Naval Club Pact reappeared in the electoral campaign that elected Sanguinetti in 1985. According to Barahona de Brito, "although expressing sympathy with accountability, [the Blancos and the *Frente Amplio*] did not consistently or determinedly champion it". Barahona de Brito 2001, 127.

[113] For Argentina, see El Senado y Cámara de Diputados de La Nación Argentina, Ley 23.492 *Ley de punto final*, 1986 and El Senado y Cámara de Diputados de La Nación Argentina, Ley 23.521 *Ley de obediencia debida*, 1987. For Chile, see La Junta de Gobierno de Chile. Decreto Ley 2.191 *Decreto ley de amnistía*, 1978. For Brazil, see Congresso Nacional do Brasil. Lei 6683 *Lei da anistia*, 1979. For Peru, see El Congreso Constituyente Democrático, Ley 26.479 *Conceden amnistía general a personal militar, policial y civil para diversos casos*, 1992 and El Congreso Constituyente Democrático, Ley 26.492 *Interpretación y alcances de la ley de amnistía*, 1995.

[114] Skaar 2011, 146.

[115] See discussion of Article 4 of the law in *supra* note 106 and accompanying text. Although Vásquez opposed repealing the law, he did so on the ground that he could and would continue to pursue convictions under Article 4. Mallinder 2009, 65–66.

[116] For discussion of the bases of the charges and convictions, see Galain Palermo 2010, 607–609, 616. Bordaberry died in July 2011 under house arrest after having been sentenced in 2010 to thirty years.

[117] Skaar 2011, 185.

found the law unconstitutional in a case that the (previous) president had not pursued because he contended it did not fit under an exception provided in the law. The ruling, however, only applied to that particular case, and did not overturn the Expiry Law.[118] The task of repealing the law, it seemed, would be left to the voters.

I have already revealed at least part of the end of the story. In February 2011, in the *Gelman* case discussed in the previous section, the Inter-American Court of Human Rights found the Expiry Law to violate the American Convention, notwithstanding the democratic vote supporting it. In May 2011, however, a subsequent Supreme Court decision, in contrast to the direction the Court seemed to have been heading, handed a defeat to those who were pushing for prosecutions. The Court refused to classify forced disappearance as a crime against humanity or a gross human rights violation and also found it barred from consideration as a common crime because it was not listed as a crime in the criminal code until 2006.[119] In late October 2011, President Mujica signed legislation that effectively repealed the law. Had the legislation not been passed or signed, some were concerned that the Supreme Court might use the statute of limitations on common crimes to bar further prosecutions after November 1, 2011.[120] The new law responds to this and other concerns by reinstating the possibility of prosecution for all crimes committed as acts of State terrorism before March 1985, and by declaring that such crimes constitute crimes against humanity under international law treaties to which Uruguay is a party.[121]

As Uruguay moves forward, in step with international standards against impunity, a number of questions are raised that have implications more broadly for the meaning of transitional justice. In one of the first news releases of the eventual repeal of the Expiry Law, the following was reported:

118 Ibid., 183-84 (referring to Suprema Corte de Justicia de Uruguay, *Nibia Sabalsagaray Curutchet*, Sentencia no. 365/09 (October 19, 2009)). Two subsequent decisions of the Court, one in October 2010 and another in February 2011, also found the application of the Expiry Law unconstitutional. Brunner 2011, note 19 (citing cases) and accompanying text.

119 Brunner 2011, notes 20–22 and accompanying text (discussing Suprema Corte de Justicia de Uruguay, *Gavazzo Pereira, José Nino y Arab Fernández, José Ricardo*, Sentencia no. 1501 (May 6, 2011)). For Brunner, the recent Supreme Court cases as a whole suggest that "[t]he Uruguayan judiciary's approach to cases involving human rights abuses committed during the dictatorship appears to be as equivocal as that taken by the executive".

120 Ibid., notes 23 and 24 and accompanying text.

121 El Senado y la Cámara de Representantes de la República Oriental del Uruguay, *Ley de Imprescriptibilidad*, 2011, Article 1 ("Se restablece la pretensión punitiva del Estado para todos los delitos cometidos en aplicación del terrorismo de Estado hasta el 1° de marzo de 1985); Article 3 ("Declárase que, los delitos a que refieren los artículos anteriores, son crímenes contra la humanidad de conformidad a los tratados internacionales de los que la República es parte").

> Retired Colonel William Cedrez president of the Military Club, cautioned if amnesty was eliminated the military was ready to denounce former Tupamaros, an armed movement in which Mujica was involved, as many of them never went to trial for their crimes because they either fled the country or were not prosecuted.[122]

What will or should be the position of the human rights movement on whether to investigate former members of the guerilla? If it takes an antipolitical stance, might it need to support such investigations and perhaps even repeal of the 1985 amnesty law for political prisoners as well? Where would the cycle end?

One one hand, it seems that criminal prosecutions on both sides would strip both the right and the left of their historical and ongoing political positions. The drive against impunity, as with human rights discourse more generally, often serves to submerge the reasons why on side initially engaged in revolutionary struggles as well as why the other side might have found the oppositional ideas so threatening.[123] On the other hand, were those on the left to attempt to revisit issues of distributional justice, might there be a way to do so without simply representing themselves as victims of human rights violations? If they were to be reclassified as potential perpetrators through the prospect of criminal investigations against them, might that paradoxically provide them a way to articulate the aims of their struggles and consider the extent to which even former guerillas in power today might have lost sight of the distributional aims that originally motivated them?

With regard to criminal justice, how should the prosecutions move forward? Is there a way in which they might avoid what Daniel Pastor has identified as *neopunitivismo*, "the renewed messianic belief that criminal power *can and should* be extended to all corners of social life, to the point that it completely obscures the civil and constitutional protections in favor of criminal law".[124] In an article speaking mostly of post-amnesty-repeal trials in Argentina, but also of the jurisprudence of the Inter-American Court of Human Rights in striking down amnesty provisions, Pastor contends that "[w]e have elevated "the penal" to a level of a social "painkiller" the likes of which have no precedence".[125] He is particularly concerned about what he calls the "'relaxation' of the restraints on the penal

---

[122] La Voz Interior, 28 Oct 2011. In the days following the repeal, numerous newspapers in Latin America and the United States repeated Colonel William Cedrez's words. But, since then, no other member of the military has publically dencounced former Tupamaros and no cases have been filed against them.

[123] In contrast, Markarian discusses how, in the early 1980s, many leftists gave testimonies that, rather than identifying those responsible for human rights abuses, "pursued...goals somewhat independent from the issue of criminal prosecutions". Some of these appeals, she contends, differed from human rights language "in highlighting the ideological and political attachments of those who endured abuses, as well as in connecting human rights claims with their fight for further political and social change". Markarian 2005, 169–170.

[124] Pastor 2006, 1. ("*Neopunitivismo*, entendido ello como corriente político-criminal que se caracteriza por la renovada creencia mesiánica de que el poder punitivo *puede y debe* llegar a todos los rincones de la vida social, hasta el punto de confundir por completo, como se verá más abajo, la protección civil y el amparo constitucional con el derecho penal mismo".).

[125] Ibid.

system", in which those accused of grave crimes get less protection than other criminal defendants.[126]

After noting that "[t]he criminal justice function of human rights as of late has been entirely inverted in that the protection of the accused has ceased to be a point of attention",[127] Pastor contends that "uncontrolled and unlimited, 'the penal' has disrupted and transformed the human rights movement, discrediting it completely".[128] Although I do not agree with him that the human rights movement is in fact discredited by *neopunativismo* (to the contrary, I think it is a way in which it has legitimized itself within the international legal sphere), I do agree with Pastor's observation of the inversion of positions. Given the wide documentation of the injustices that flourish in nearly every criminal justice system in the world, particularly for already disadvantaged groups, why would the human rights movement rely on such a system?

## 2.6 Conclusion

I conclude with two accounts of justice and transition that I believe illustrate a number of the tensions I have described above. The first centers around current events in Guatemala. The second comes from Kennedy.

At the end of 2010, I met with family members of a number of those disappeared during years of state repression in Guatemala. Many of them are now working with Guatemalan prosecutors to investigate the disappearances of their loved ones. Unlike Uruguay's Expiry Law, Guatemala's 1996 National Reconciliation Law, which grants some forms of amnesty, specifically excludes crimes that violate fundamental human rights. It lists genocide, torture and forced disappearance as examples of such violations.[129] Yet, for many years, there was little political will to engage in such investigations and little assurance of protection for those who investigated, prosecuted, judged or served as witnesses. Moreover, when there were prosecutions, courts would often find that the prosecutions did not fit the exceptions to amnesty granted in the law. As in Uruguay, after the left (leaning) government was elected, in this case in 2007, the number of prosecutions increased. Moreover, the Constitutional Court rejected claims to

---

[126] Ibid., 3. Other scholars have also begun to make observations about the illiberality of international criminal law more generally. See, e.g., Robinson 2008, 927 (specifically asking: "How is it that a liberal system of criminal justice—one that strives to serve as a model for liberal systems—has come to embrace such illiberal doctrines?").

[127] Pastor 2006, 2.

[128] Ibid., 3.

[129] El Congreso de la República de Guatemala, Decreto N° 145–196 *Ley de reconciliación nacional*, 1996, Article 8.

amnesty in important cases.[130] And, as in Uruguay, the human rights community in the country rallied around such prosecutions.

I spoke with an activist who was considering opening a case against the National Police for the torture of one of his siblings who had fought with the guerilla. I asked him whether he was concerned that transforming his brother into a victim might take away from the very politics for which his brother had been willing to fight and die. As we began to talk about the substantive agenda of the (old) left in Guatemala, and about its aim of a massive redistribution of wealth that is still so badly needed in the country, the activist made clear he understood my question. But his response was clear. "The left lost the war. All we have now is justice". By justice, he meant individual prosecutions.

Less than one year after this conversation, former General Perez Molina was elected president of Guatemala on a right-wing platform. Given his background and connection to many former military and police officers whose prosecution has been sought or was underway, human rights activists feared he would attempt to put the brake on the prosecutions.

Even before Perez Molina took office, however, he announced his public support for Attorney General Claudia Paz y Paz, who had been responsible for many of the prosecutions under the previous administration. Within Perez Molina's first two weeks in office, Guatemala appeared to be moving forward on a path against impunity. A judge had ordered former military dictator Efraín Ríos Montt to appear in court on an investigation of genocide charges, and it seemed that the new president would make no effort to interfere in the case. Moreover, legislators from the president's conservative party initiated Congress's ratification of the Rome Statute, which means that Guatemala has now consented to the jurisdiction of the International Criminal Court.

It would appear, then, that in Guatemala (at least at the time of the writing of this chapter—at the end of January 2012), the idea of criminal prosecutions for human rights violations has gained mainstream, even right-wing, support. To the extent that human rights has become the *lingua franca* of political discourse both domestically and internationally, so has the fight against impunity.[131] And, as in Uruguay, it might cut both ways in Guatemala. At the end of 2011, family members of former military personnel and businessmen in Guatemala brought criminal complaints against former guerillas, including relatives of Attorney General Paz y Paz, for crimes they say were committed during the war.[132] They accused the Attorney General of bias in her investigations and prosecutions, maintaining that crimes had been committed on all sides. Perez Molina's support

[130] See, e.g., Impunity Watch 2009 (reporting the Constitutional Court's decision regarding the El Jute massacre to reject the appeal of Guatemalan army officer Marco Antonio Sanchez Samoa, who claimed he was entitled to amnesty under the 1996 law).

[131] That said, also at the time of writing of this chapter, Judge Baltasar Garzón was being tried in Spain for investigating crimes perpetrated by the Franco regime during the Spanish Civil War that were covered by a 1977 general amnesty.

[132] Valladares 2011.

for Paz y Paz was important with regard to the bias allegations, but indications are that she might counter such accusations by ordering investigations into the actions of the former guerillas. Prosecutions are the new site of political struggle; what type of justice they are likely to exact, and for whom, is yet to be seen.

After fantasizing the life of the prison warden in 2009 and the effect that transitional justice might have had on him, Kennedy turns back to Ana, one of the prisoners under the warden's control. He imagines the relationship between her well-being and the warden's punishment, and writes:

> I hope Ana has found peace, love, power. Though I must say, she seemed remarkably at peace when we met, in love, her life transformed by her exercise of power. I would not want to freeze her in a story of suffering that could be unlocked only by some confession from the man who was once her warden. Doing so would make her live her time in prison forever, would render our warden a strange frog-prince, alone able to grant her closure and set her free.[133]

Kennedy reminds us of some of the reasons that many once gave, including in the human rights movement, for amnesty, for moving on. If, after all these years, the state were to decide to prosecute the prison warden, should Ana be given a meaningful choice about whether and how to participate? Would a refusal on her part to assist with the investigation be considered a political act? Would it mean that she were against justice?

## References

Abbott K (1999) International relations theory, international law, and the regime governing atrocities in internal conflict. Am J Intern Law 93:361–379

Amnesty International (2003) United States of America: death by discrimination: the continuing role of race in capital cases. Amnesty International Publications, London

Amnesty International (2007) United States of America: death and democracy. Amnesty International Publications, London

Amnesty International (2010a) Chile: no immunity for crimes against humanity. Amnesty International Publications, London

Amnesty International (2010b) Bringing power to justice: absence of immunity for heads of state before the International Criminal Court. Amnesty International Publications, London

Amnesty International (2011a) Uruguay amnesty vote a missed opportunity for justice. Amnesty International Publications, London

Amnesty International (2011b) United States of America: an embarrassment of hitches: reflections on the death penalty, 35 years after Gregg v. Georgia, as states scramble for lethal injection drugs. Amnesty International Publications, London

Amnesty International (2011c) Libya urged to investigate whether Al-Gaddafi death was a war crime. Amnesty International Publications, London

Amnesty International (2011d) Yemen: no immunity for serious violations under president Saleh. Amnesty International Publications, London

[133] Kennedy 2009, 23–24.

Amnesty International (2011e) United States of America: the cruel and inhumane treatment of Albert Woodfox and Herman Wallace. Amnesty International Publications, London

Amnesty International Report Library (2011) Amnesty International Library Search Results Reports 1979-1986. In: Search Results. http://www.amnesty.org/en/ai_search?keywords =&show_advanced=true&title=&ai_index=&sort=date&start_date5Bdate5D=1979-01-01 &end_date5Bdate5D=1986-12-30&region5B5D=**ALL**&issue%5B%5D=**ALL**& language5Ben5D&document_types%5Breports%5D=reports&form_build_id=form-898b5a 3427f7c2a54f0b5e3813d1407c&form_id=amnestysearch_filters_form&op=Search. Accessed 3 February 2012

Arthur P (2009) How "transitions" reshaped human rights: a conceptual history of transitional justice. Hum Rights Q 31:321–367

Barahona de Brito A (1997) Human rights and democratization in Latin America: Uruguay and Chile. Oxford University Press, New York

Barahona de Brito A (2001) Truth, justice, memory, and democratization in the Southern Cone. In: Barahona De Brito A, González Enríquez C, Aguilar P (eds) The politics of memory: transitional justice in democratizing societies. Oxford University Press, New York, pp 119–160

Branch A (2011) Displacing human rights: war and intervention in Northern Uganda. Oxford University Press, New York

Breslin P, Kennedy D, Goldstein R (1984) Report on mission to Uruguay. New York Academy of Sciences, Committee on Human Rights, New York

Brown W (2004) "The most we can hope for…": Human rights and the politics of fatalism. South Atlantic Q 103:451–463

Brunner L (2011) Is Uruguay foundering on the path to accountability? The aftermath of the Gelman decision of the Inter-American Court. American Society of International Law. http:// www.asil.org/accountability/summer_2011_3.cfm

Cain K, Postel H, Thomson A (2004) Emergency sex and other desperate measures: a true story from hell on earth. Miramax, New York

Carrasco E (1996) Opposition, justice, structuralism, and particularity: intersections between LatCrit theory and law and development studies. U Miami Inter-Am L Rev 28:313–336

Cassese A (1998) On the current trends towards criminal prosecution and punishment of breaches of international humanitarian law. Euro J Intern Law 9:2–17

Chung-Shu L (1949) Human rights in the Chinese tradition. Human rights: comments and interpretation: a symposium edited by UNESCO. 185–190

Clark AM (2001) Diplomacy of conscience: Amnesty International and changing human rights norms. Princeton University Press, Princeton

Cohen S (1995) State crimes of previous regimes: knowledge, accountability, and the policing of the past. Law Soc Inq 20:7–50

Corte Electoral de Uruguay (2009) Elecciones nacionales, 25 de octubre de 2009. http:// elecciones.corteelectoral.gub.uy/20091025/SSPMain.asp

Engle K (2005) Feminism and its (dis)contents: criminalizing wartime rape in Bosnia and Herzegovina. Am J Intern Law 99:778–816

Engle K (2010) The elusive promise of indigenous development: rights, culture strategy. Duke University Press, Durham

Fassin D (2007) Humanitarianism as a politics of life. Publ Cult 19:499–520

Frankenberg G (1988) Down by law: irony, seriousness, and reason. Northwest Univ Law Rev 83:360–390

Freeman A (1988) Racism, rights and the quest for equality of opportunity: a critical legal essay. Harvard Civil Rights-Civil Libert Law Rev 295:295–413

Freeman M (2010) Necessary evils: amnesties and the search for justice. Cambridge University Press, New York

Gandhi M (1949) Letter to the director-general of UNESCO. Human rights: comments and interpretation: a symposium edited by UNESCO, 3–4

Gerard RW (1949) The rights of man: a biological approach. Human rights: comments and interpretation: a symposium edited by UNESCO, 209–214

Goodrich P (1993) Sleeping with the enemy: an essay on the politics of Critical Legal Studies in America. 68 University Law Review, New York 416–419
Halley J (2008) Rape at Rome: feminist interventions in the criminalization of sex-related violence in positive international criminal Law. Mich J Intern Law 30:1–123
Hessen S (1949) The rights of man in liberalism, socialism and communism. Human rights: comments and interpretation: a symposium edited by UNESCO, 108–142
Howland T (2004) UN human rights field presence as proactive instrument of peace and social change: lessons from Angola. Hum Rights Q 26:1–28
Human Rights Watch (2011) Human Rights Watch publications report titles by year: 1980-2004
Hunt L (2007) Inventing human rights: a history. W.W.Norton, New York/London
Impunity Watch (2009) Guatemalan constitutional court decision paves the way for El Jute trial. http://www.impunitywatch.org/en/publication/36
Keck M, Sikkink K (1998) Activists beyond borders: advocacy networks in international politics. Cornell University Press, Ithaca/London
Kennedy D (1985) Spring break. Tex Law Rev 63:1377–1423
Kennedy D (2002) The international human rights movement: part of the problem? Harv Hum Rights J 15:101–125
Kennedy D (2009) The rights of spring: a memoir of innocence abroad. Princeton University Press, Princeton
Laski H (1949) Toward a universal declaration of human rights. Human rights: comments and interpretation: a symposium edited by UNESCO, 78–92
Lauren PG (2001) The evolution of international human rights: visions seen (Pennsylvania Studies in Human Rights), 3rd edn. University of Pennsylvania Press, Philadelphia
Lewis J (1949) On human rights. Human rights: comments and interpretation: a symposium edited by UNESCO, 43–58
Mallinder L (2007) Can amnesties and international justice be reconciled? Intern J Trans Justice 1:208–230
Mallinder L (2009) Uruguay's evolving experience of amnesty and civil society's response. Transitional Justice Institute Research. Available at SSRN: http://ssrn.com/abstract=1387362 or http://dx.doi.org/10.2139/ssrn.1387362
Maritain J (1949) On the philosophy of human rights. Human rights: comments and interpretation: a symposium edited by UNESCO, 72–77
Markarian V (2005) Left in transformation: Uruguayan exiles and the Latin American human rights network, 1967–1984. Routledge, Abingdon
Meintjes G, Mendez J (2000) Reconciling amnesties with universal jurisdiction. Intern Law FORUM Du Droit International 2:76–97
Meintjes, G., Mendez, J (2001) Reconciling amnesties with universal jurisdiction– A reply to Mr. Phenyo Keiseng Rakate, Intern Law FORUM Du Droit International 3:47–49
Mégret F (2012) Where does the critique of international human rights stand? an exploration in 18 vignettes in this collection new approaches to international law: lessons from the European experience
Mertus J, Helsing J (2006) Human rights and conflict: exploring the links between rights, law, and peace building. United States Institute of Peace, Washington
Minda G (1989) Jurisprudential movements of the 1980s. Ohio State Law J 50:599–619
Minogue O (2010) Peace vs. justice: the utility of amnesties. Criminal Justice Ethics 29:306–316
Minow M (1999) Between vengeance and forgiveness: facing history after genocide and mass violence. Beacon, Boston
Moyn S (2010) The last utopia: human rights in history. The Belknap Press of Harvard University Press, Cambridge
Mutua M (2001) Savages, victims, and saviors: the metaphor of human rights. Harv Intern Law J 42:201–245
Northrop F (1949) Toward a bill of rights for the united nations. Human rights: comments and interpretation: a symposium edited by UNESCO, 181–184
Oetken JP (1991) Form and substance in Critical Legal Studies. Yale Law J 100:2209–2228

Orbinski J (2008) An imperfect offering: humanitarian action for the twenty-first century. Doubleday, Canada
Palermo G (2010) The prosecution of international crimes in Uruguay. Intern Crim Law Rev 10:601–618
Pastor D (2006) La deriva neopunitivista de organismos y activistas como causa del desprestigio actual de los derechos humanos. Revista Jurídica: Nueva Doctrina Penal 1:73–114
Porzecanski A (1974) Uruguay's Tupamaros: the urban guerrilla. Praeger Publishers, Santa Barbara
Purvis N (1991) Critical Legal Studies in public international law. Harv Intern Law J 32:81–128
Rakate P (2001) Reconciling amnesties with universal jurisdiction in South Africa: a response to Garth Meintjes and Juan Mendez. Intern Law FORUM Du Droit International 3:42–46
Riezler K (1949) Reflections on human rights. Human rights: comments and interpretation: a symposium edited by UNESCO, 145–148
Robinson D (2008) The identity crisis of international criminal law. Leiden J Intern Law 21:925–963
Roht-Arriaza N (1990) State responsibility to investigate and prosecute grave human rights violations in international law. Calif Law Rev 78:449–513
Scharf M (1999) Amnesty exception to the jurisdiction of the international criminal court. Cornell Intern Law J 32:507–527
Seibert-Fohr A (2009) Prosecuting serious human rights violations. Oxford University Press, New York
Singer J (1989) Should lawyers care about philosophy? Duke Law J 1989:1752–1783
Skaar E (2011) Judicial independence and human rights in Latin America: violations, politics, and prosecution. Palgrave Macmillan, New York
Sommerville J (1949) Comparison of the Soviet and Western democratic principles with special reference to human rights. Human rights: comments and interpretation: a symposium edited by UNESCO, 139–144
Spahn E (1994) Waiting for credentials: feminist theories of enforcement of international human rights. Am Univ Law Rev 44:1053–1083
Tchechko B (1949) The conception of the rights of man in the USSR based on official documents. Human rights: comments and interpretation: a symposium edited by UNESCO, 149–174
Valladares D (2011) Military allies take ex-guerillas, journalists to court. Inter Press Service, http://ipsnews.net/news.asp?idnews=106314
Weinstein M (2007) The left's long road to power in Uruguay. In: Deonandan K, Close D, Prevost G (eds.) From revolutionary movements to political parties: cases from Latin America and Africa. Palgrave MacMillan, New York, 67–80
Youngs R (2002) The European Union and democracy in Latin America. Latin Am Politics Soc 44:111–139
Zalaquett J (1995) Confronting human rights violations committed by former governments: principles applicable and political constraints. In: Kritz N (ed) Transitional justice. United States Institute of Peace Press, Washington, pp 3–31

# Chapter 3
# National Responses in Latin America to International Events Propelling the Justice Cascade: The *Gelman* Case

**Yolanda Gamarra**

**Abstract** This chapter offers an overview of the decisions taken by international human rights bodies with regard to the eradication of amnesty laws which impede the investigation and prosecution of those suspected of grave breaches of human rights. The chapter focuses on three principal questions. First, it addresses the growing interest in recent decades in seeking justice in supranational courts for cases of human rights violations. Second, the chapter attempts to identify those cases in which the obligation to respect human rights prevails because it is considered hard law. And, third, the chapter considers the resistance put up by national parliaments against modifying laws contrary to international obligations contracted in the area of human rights. In conclusion, the chapter argues that there is a strong international legal basis for the claim that amnesties that allow impunity in cases of serious violations of human rights are incompatible with international law. Although, there is no broad consensus with regard to affirming that the prohibition of these types of amnesties form part of customary law, it can be said that these amnesties violate states' obligations derived from customary law.

> *"Si para todo hay término y hay tasa y última vez y nunca más y olvido, ¿quién nos dirá de quién, en esta casa, sin saberlo, nos hemos despedido?"*
>
> Jorge Luis Borges, "Límites", El Otro, El Mismo.

The author greatly appreciates the insights, shared knowledge, and assistance of Alejandra Vicente and Mariana Mota. This study was carried out under the Government of Aragon (Spain) Research Group S 102, "Nuevas vías de participación política en democracias avanzadas".

Y. Gamarra (✉)
Assistant Professor of International Law, Faculty of Law, University of Zaragoza, Zaragoza, Spain
e-mail: gamarra@unizar.es

J. M. Beneyto and D. Kennedy (eds.), *New Approaches to International Law*,
DOI: 10.1007/978-90-6704-879-8_3,

*If there is a limit to all things and a measure. and a last time and nothing more and forgetfulness, Who will tell us to whom in this house. We without knowing it have said farewell?*
[Translation by Alastair Raid].

## Contents



## 3.1 Introduction

When I visited the Parliament of Uruguay in May 2011 to give a series of lectures, I found myself in a divided country. Some representatives supported modifying the *Ley de Caducidad*[1] thereby permitting the courts to proceed with investigations opened into human rights violations presumed to have been committed by members of the armed forces. Other representatives opposed the reforms, seeking to block calls of justice to take its course, which might stir up the past.

In states which have experienced authoritarian and dictatorial regimes, such as Chile, Argentina, Peru, Brazil, Uruguay, or Spain, there has been renewed discussion of the legality and validity of amnesty laws, particularly those approved with the coming of democracy as measures designed to encourage its consolidation.[2] Arguments often used by those who favor maintaining the amnesties include claims that they are based on principles of "legal certainty", "non-retroactivity of criminal law", and "national security", and that they serve as a guarantee of

---

[1] It is a law signed by the Uruguayan Parliament in 1986 under the democratic Government of President Sanguinetti.

[2] Majzub 2002, 247.

"social peace". It is also frequently mentioned that, in a good number of cases, such amnesties have permitted a peaceful transition to democracy—e.g. Spain is offered an example in this regard.[3]

Nevertheless, international courts and organizations have repeatedly, especially in recent years, reaffirmed the incompatibility of amnesty laws with the principles and obligations of human rights law to which states are bound by their ratification of international treaties.[4] For example, the United Nations Commission on Human Rights[5] and its Sub-Commission for the Prevention of Discrimination and Protection of Minorities have concluded that amnesty is a major reason for continuing human rights violations throughout the world.[6]

With the internationalization of human rights and humanitarian law and the emerging democratic principle in international law, the international community has shown its repulsion against human rights abuses, and its preference for prosecuting the perpetrators of crimes over granting them amnesty.[7] This preference for prosecution is reflected in certain legal instruments, such as the Genocide

---

[3] Spain opted to give priority to the transition to democracy via a general amnesty Act, with the agreement of all parties, rather than judge those responsible for atrocities committed during the Civil War and Franco's dictatorship, and to reconstruct the past and the truth. Proposals for the reconciliation of the Spanish people and integration of everyone into political life without any type of discrimination were embodied in a series of political measures, both actual and symbolic, that meant the rehabilitation, albeit partial, of the vanquished. This rehabilitation was not complete, not only because of the time that had passed since the Civil War (nearly 40 years), but also because of the willingness to forget that existed at the time. First, actual political measures were passed, such as the pardon decreed by the King, or the recognition of pension rights for the vanquished and equality with the victors. It is significant that in the preamble of the pardon granted by the King, there was a relatively clear statement of intent in which the idea of the Monarchy was linked to the reconciliation of the Spanish people. Second, a series of symbolic measures of reconciliation with the past was adopted, such as recognition of the bombing of Guernica, the transformation of the Victory Parade into the Day of the Armed Forces, the erection of a monument to all of the fallen, and the recognition of the Civil War as being the 'war of the madmen', the period of 'collective madness' par excellence in the history of Spain. A bill was approved for the recovery of historical past in December 2007 (BOE, 27 December 2007).

[4] Orentlicher 1995; Meintjes and Méndez 2000, 76; Young 2002–2003, 216.

[5] United Nations Human Rights Commission, "Basic principles and guidelines on the right to a remedy and reparation for victims of violations of international human rights and humanitarian law", Final Report of the Special Rapporteur, Cherif Bassiouni, submitted pursuant to Resolution 1999/33, E/CN .4/2000/62, 25.

[6] See Report on the Consequences of Impunity, United Nations Commission on Human Rights, UN Doc. E/CN.4/1990/13.

[7] See Penrose 2000, 193 et seq. Professor Penrose advocates the enactment of prosecutorial rules and urges the international community and states in particular to take the necessary steps to try the perpetrators.

Convention of 1948,[8] the Geneva Conventions of 1949,[9] the International Convention on the Suppression and Punishment of Crime of Apartheid of 1973,[10] and the Convention against Torture and Other Cruel, Inhuman or Degrading Treatment or Punishment of 1984,[11] as well as in international institutions, such as the Inter-American Court of Human Rights—henceforth, IACHR –,[12] and the European Court of Human Rights—henceforth, the ECHR –,[13] and the United Nations Human Rights Committee.[14]

The IACHR and the Inter-American Commission of Human Rights have held that amnesties granted by several Latin American countries are incompatible with the American Convention on Human Rights. Nonetheless, a compromise between the international demand for prosecution of international crimes and the national appeal for a political compromise involving amnesty can in some cases be achieved by recognizing a distinction between permissible and non-permissible amnesties and giving international acceptance to the former only.[15]

Thus in the years 2010 and 2011, the IACHR declared the amnesty laws of Brazil and Uruguay to be incompatible with the American Convention on Human Rights. By doing so the IACHR ruled on the only two amnesty laws that remain in force on the American continent. The jurisprudence of the IACHR is thus of great importance for international law given that, unlike the ECHR, the history of Latin America has obliged it to examine massive human rights violations that occurred

---

[8] Article 4 of the Genocide Convention of 1948 states that "(p)ersons committing genocide or any of the other acts enumerated in article III shall be punished, whether they are constitutionally responsible rulers, public officials or private individuals".

[9] Article 146, para. 1 of the IV Geneva Convention of 1949 relative to the Protection of Civilian Persons in Time of War goes further when the contracting parties are committed to "enact(ing) any legislation necessary to provide effective penal sanctions for persons committing, or ordering to be committed, any of the grave breaches of the present Convention", and para. 2 states the obligation that "shall bring such persons, regardless of their nationality, before its own courts. It may also, if it prefers, and in accordance with the provisions of its own legislation, hand such persons over for trial to another High Contracting Party concerned, provided such High Contracting Party has made out a prima facie case".

[10] Article V of the International Convention on the Suppression and Punishment of Crime of Apartheid of 1973 states that "Persons charged with the acts enumerated in article II of the present Convention may be tried by a competent tribunal of any State Party to the Convention which may acquire jurisdiction over the person of the accused or by an international penal tribunal having jurisdiction with respect to those States Parties which shall have accepted its jurisdiction".

[11] Article 5 paras. 1 and 2, and Article 7 of the Convention against Torture and Other Cruel, Inhuman or Degrading Treatment or Punishment of 1984 deal with similar engagements that the International Convention on the Suppression and Punishment of Crime of Apartheid.

[12] Barrios Altos, Chumbipuma Aguirre et al. versus Perú, Judgment, IACHR,14 March, 2001, para. 41.

[13] Streletz, Kessler and Krenz versus Germany, Judgment, ECHR, 22 March 2001, para. 103.

[14] General Commentary No. 20 of the United Nations Committee for Human Rights.

[15] See the comparison between the experiences of Chile and South Africa noted by Dugard 1999, 1001 et seq.

during periods of great political convulsion experienced on its continent, including cases where the states concerned did not recognize its jurisdiction.[16]

This study adopts an inductive and a critical approach to this debate in the context of contemporary international law with the aim of examining the culture of human rights, justice, and rule of law, especially to what extent the work of the IACHR has been effective in the national reconciliation processes of the Latin America Republics evolving from the end of the "war on terror". The thesis of this study revolves around decisions taken by the IACHR with regard to the eradication of amnesty laws which impede the investigation and prosecution of those suspected of grave violations of human rights. I will focus on three principal questions. First, I will address the growing interest in recent decades in seeking justice in supranational courts for cases of human rights violations. Second, I will attempt to identify those cases in which the obligation to respect human rights prevails because it is considered hard law. And, third, I will examine the resistance put up by national parliaments against modifying laws contrary to international obligations contracted in the area of human rights. There is no doubt that the influence of politics in the execution of judgments of international human rights bodies in national jurisdictions impedes progress in the proceedings against perpetrators of human rights violations. Moreover, Latin America's experience in eradicating amnesty laws may well serve other regions that wish to follow a similar path.[17] Time, international pressure —by NGO's, International Organizations, think tanks or lobbies—, and willingness to reform are necessary in order for national courts to make progress in the relevant criminal proceedings.

## 3.2 The Nature and Use of Amnesty

Amnesty laws, and other exculpatory measures focused on responsibility, try to leave egregious violations of human rights committed during armed conflicts or other situations of political turmoil unpunished, such as crimes of torture, forced disappearances, extrajudicial killings, sexual violence and ever gave violations constituting war crimes, genocide, or crimes against humanity. In response, United Nations has adopted a policy that approved peace agreements can never include amnesties for crimes of genocide, war crimes, or grave violations of human rights.[18] This ban includes both legislation and norms and regulations that *de facto* prevent the investigation and punishment of certain crimes.

---

[16] Deodhar 1988, 284; Zuppi 2007, 195.

[17] See Lutz and Sikkink 2001.

[18] The Rule of Law and Transitional Justice in Conflict and Post-Conflict Societies, Report of the Secretary General of 23 August 2004. S/2004/616.

### *3.2.1 Forced Disappearances as Continuing Crimes*

The practice of forced disappearance, widely recognized as a crime against humanity, stains the history of the American continent.[19] The IACHR has been a pioneer in its treatment of forced disappearances from the first case it examined in 1986[20] to the 2006 *Goiburú* case where the court determined that

> the prohibition of the forced disappearance of persons and the correlative duty to investigate and punish those responsible for it have achieved the character of *jus cogens*.[21]

The gravity, but also the nature of these crimes, endows it with a series of characteristics of great importance when it comes to analyzing the duty of states to investigate and punish those responsible. This is because the continuing character of the crime of forced disappearance means that the crime continues to be committed from the moment of its initial commission to the moment when the state identifies the whereabouts of the victim, and identifies his or her mortal remains. The continuing nature and gravity of the crime means that it cannot be subject to any statute of limitations, and bars states blocking implementation on the basis that the crime was committed during a political-historical now closed.

The IACHR has always been unambiguous in this regard to affirm that forced disappearance is a "multiple and continuing violation" of various rights recognized in the American Convention on Human Rights.[22] These principles are reaffirmed in the Preamble and Article III of the Inter-American Convention in order to prevent and punish the crime of forced disappearance. The multiple nature of the crime means that when such crimes occur,[23] it involves a violation of the right to personal integrity, personal liberty, life, and the legal status of the victim.[24] Its permanent nature, as has already been pointed out, arises from the fact that the disappearance continues until the whereabouts of the victim is found and his or her identity established with certainty.[25] Both the jurisprudence of the IACHR and resolutions of the main organs of the United Nations have likewise recognized the continuing

---

[19] See OAS General Assembly Resolution 666 (XIII-0/83), adopted the 18 November 1983.

[20] Velasquez Rodríguez versus Honduras, Judgment, IACHR, 29 July 1988. Serie C, No. 4.

[21] Goiburú et al. versus. Paraguay, Judgment, IACHR, 22 September 2006. Serie C No. 153, para. 84.

[22] Velásquez Rodríguez, op. cit., para. 156.

[23] Medina Quiroga 2003, 128–129.

[24] Also, see Gelman versus Uruguay, Judgment, IACHR, 24 February 2011. Serie C No. 221, paras. 92–101; Gómez Palomino versus Perú, Judgment, IACHR, 22 November 2005. Serie C No. 136, para. 92.

[25] Gelman versus Uruguay. op. cit., paras. 72 and 73; Radilla Pacheco versus México. Preliminary Exceptions, Merits, Reparations and Costs. Judgment, IACHR, 23 November 2009. Serie C No. 209, para. 138; Ibsen Cárdenas e Ibsen Peña versus Bolivia Case. Merits, Reparations and Costs, Judgment, IACHR, 1 September 2010. Serie C No. 217, para. 57.

nature of the crime of forced disappearance.[26] This means that the crime continues to occur until the bodies of the victims appear. In the case of forced disappearances, neither statutes of limitations nor other principles of criminal law apply.[27]

The obligation to investigate forced disappearances exist regardless of whether or not a complaint has been made given that in these cases, international law and the general duty of guarantee impose the obligation to investigate the case *ex officio*, without delay and in a serious, impartial, and effective manner. The investigation must be carried out by all legal means available and be directed at finding out the truth. Furthermore, all state authorities, civil servants, or individuals who have knowledge related to the forced disappearance most make an appropriate formal complaint as soon as possible.[28]

### 3.2.2 The Imprescriptibility of Crimes Against Humanity and Grave Violations of Human Rights

As well as forced disappearance, there are other imprescriptible violations of human rights, such as torture, rape, and other crimes against humanity,[29] where *jus cogens* is applicable and states thus obliged to investigate. Various treaties exist, which prohibit crimes against humanity, including the statutes of all international criminal tribunals. Of a more general character, the Preamble to the Statute of the International Criminal Court (ICC) recognizes them as the "most serious crimes of concern to the international community", and holds that they must not go unpunished. It further establishes that states must take all necessary measures to guarantee that these crimes be punished.

War crimes committed in internal and/or international conflicts are contrary to the 1949 Geneva Convention and its 1977 Protocols, which determine that states must take all necessary measures to determine the penalties applicable to persons responsible for their commission. Furthermore, the International Committee of the Red Cross has established that there exists international jurisprudence that allows for the conclusion to be reached that war crimes must not be subject to amnesty laws.[30]

---

[26] Gelman versus Uruguay, op. cit., para. 64, and Guerrilla do Araguaia versus Brasil, op. cit. n. 55 *infra*, para. 101.

[27] See, also the case against the former President of Perú, A. Fujimori, Corte Suprema de Perú, Judgment. 7 April 2009, available in http://blog.dhperu.org/?p=2896.

[28] Gelman versus Uruguay, op. cit. n. 24 *supra*, para. 186 et seq.

[29] Almonacid Arellano et al. versus. Chile, Judgment, IACHR, 26 September 2006.

[30] Henckaerts and Doswald-Beck 2007, 693.

The obligation to investigate and punish the crime of genocide has acquired the status of customary international law.[31] The 1948 Convention on the Prevention and Punishment of the Crime of Genocide imposes the commitment on states to punish the international crime to which the title of the convention refers even when those responsible are "government leaders, civil servants or private individuals".[32]

More recently, the monitoring bodies of the international human rights treaties have established that victims of any violation of rights protected by them must have an effective remedy and reparation[33] available to them. These violations not only include those mentioned before, but also such crimes as extrajudicial killings, cruel, inhuman and degrading treatment, slavery and sexual violence.

### *3.2.3 The Obligation to Investigate and Punish Human Rights Violations*

The obligation to investigate and punish serious violations of human rights is established in international law and has been reinforced by statements made by the organs dedicated to the protection of human rights.[34] In this context, for example, the Human Rights Committee of the United Nations has established the duty of states to investigate, in good faith, the violations of rights recognized in the International Covenant on Civil and Political Rights.[35]

Even in those cases in which the human rights violations occurred before the signing of an international treaty by states, some international organs have established that states, though they have no responsibility for events prior to the signing of the treaty, do have international responsibility if, where necessary, they do not

[31] See Convention on the Prevention and Punishment of the Crime of Genocide of 1948, and Rule of Law Tools for Post-Conflict States. Amnesties, Office of the High Commissioner for Human Rights. New York, 2009, 12.

[32] See Articles I and VI of the Convention on the Prevention and Punishment of the Crime of Genocide of 1948.

[33] Treaties such as the International Covenant on Civil and Political Rights, and its optional protocols; American Convention on Human Rights; African Charter on Human and Peoples' Rights; European Convention for the Protection of Human Rights and Fundamental Freedoms. See Right to the Truth, Report of the Office of the High Commissioner for Human Rights, UN Document A/HRC/5/7, 7 June 2007, para. 152.

[34] Qani Halimi Nedzibi versus Austria. Communication No. 8/1991. United Nations Comité against Torture (CAT), Report of 30 November 1993, para. 13.5; Impunity. Resolution 2005/81, United Nations Human Rights Committee. 61 Session, U.N. Doc. E/CN.4/RES/2005/81, 21 April 2005; Final Rapport of Cherif Bassiouni, U.N. Doc. E/CN.4/2000/62, 18 January 2000; Aksoy versus Turkey. Application No. 21987/93, Judgment, ECHR, 18 December 1996, para. 98.

[35] Larrosa versus Uruguay. Communication No. 88/1981, Inter-American Commission of Human Rights, Directive, 25 March 1983, pár. 11.5; Gilboa versus. Uruguay. Communication No. 147/1983, Inter-American Commission of Human Rights, Directive, 1 November 1985, para. 7.2.

investigate them and punish the guilty, both those responsible for the planning of the crimes and their execution.

In the *Almonacid Arellano* case, the IACHR held that according to Article 1, Paragraph 1 of the American Convention on Human Rights states are obliged to investigate violations of human rights.[36] Also, in the *Cantuta* case, the IACHR deemed "inadmissible those dispositions of amnesty and inadmissible those dispositions regarding proscription and the establishment of responsibility which seek to impede investigation and punishment".[37] In summation, there exists a general duty to investigate grave violations of human rights that have been the object of specific judgments.

One important function of justice is to create a detailed historical record of the events and atrocities committed in order to have knowledge of what happened, who was responsible, why it should be condemned, and to prevent it from happening in the future.[38] For families who do not know what happened to their loved ones, truth is an essential part of meaningful accountability. Thus, making public the truth about what happened will help to discredit the policy applied and the regime that applied it.

Creating a detailed historical record was an important function of the Tokyo and Nuremberg Tribunals. The Chief Prosecutor at Nuremberg, R. Jackson, noted that the most important legacy of the trials was the documentation of Nazi atrocities "with such authenticity and in such detail that there can be no responsible denial of these crimes in the future".[39] To accomplish the objective of establishing the truth and creating an accurate and comprehensive historical record, it is incumbent upon institutions of justice to ensure that they investigate and make public at the appropriate time all relevant information concerning the nature of the atrocities or crimes committed during the political crisis. The international justice body should also disseminate the documents, not only in the crisis area but also internationally.

The IACHR is contributing to that end in a noteworthy manner by collecting witness testimonies and other evidence, as well as analytical studies, investigations, and other information regarding the crimes committed against the civilian population. Moreover, the Court's jurisdiction and prosecutorial practices fail to cover many smaller -but nevertheless important from the victims' point of view —incidents during the crisis. In addition, procedural or legal technicalities may lead to information being withheld from the public, in order to protect witnesses or

---

[36] Almonacid Arellano versus Chile, op. cit. n. 29 *supra*, para. 160.

[37] Cantuta versus. Perú Case, Judgment, IACHR, 30 November 2007, para. 152.

[38] Note Santayana's famous phrase: "Progress, far from consisting of change, depends on retentiveness... Those who cannot remember the past are condemned to repeat it". George Santayana, "Life of Reason or the Phases of Human Progress", 5 vols., Charles Scribner's Sons, 1936.

[39] See, Report of Robert Jackson, U.S. Representative to the International Conference on Military Trials 432 (Dep. Of State, Pub. 3080, 1949).

for other reasons.[40] At the end of the day, establishing a truthful record of atrocities and their perpetrators and causes can be an essential part of building a better future by communicating a consensus that certain conduct occurred and should not be repeated.

## 3.3 Recognizing Amnesty as Inconsistent With Human Rights

Amnesty laws and other exonerations from liability have been used by states as mechanisms to prevent and hinder the investigation and punishment of persons responsible for serious human rights violations. There exist, for instance, many statements from different United Nations bodies on the incompatibility of amnesty laws with human rights law.

The Secretary General of the United Nations in 2004 reiterated that "peace agreements approved by the United Nations can never promise amnesty for genocide, war crimes or crimes against humanity or gross violations of human rights".[41]

In this regard, the United Nations High Commission for Human Rights has found that amnesties and other exonerations from responsibility promote impunity and are an obstacle to achieving the right to the truth of the victims, as they prevent the investigation of the facts.[42] This body has also clearly signaled that amnesties with the following characteristics are forbidden:

a) That prevent the prosecution of persons who may be responsible for war crimes, genocide, crimes against humanity or gross human rights violations, including crimes that specifically affect women and gender violence;
b) interfere with the right of victims to an effective remedy, including compensation; or
c) limit the right of victims and societies to learn the truth about violations of human rights and humanitarian law.[43]

These statements were reiterated in the "Updated Set of Principles for the Protection and Promotion of Human Rights Through Action to Combat Impunity", which the United Nations Commission on Human Rights took note of in 2005.[44]

---

[40] By way of example, the Judges normally dismiss the case if the defendant dies before judgment is issued, with the result that the court's findings of fact and law are never publicly pronounced. This was the case of Slavko Dokmanovic, who died while in detention awaiting judgment. See the ICTY Press Release, Completion of the Internal Inquiry into the Death of Slavko Dokmanovic, UN Doc. CC/PIU/334-3, 23 July 1998.

[41] See "The rule of law and transitional justice in conflict and post-conflict societies", Report of the Secretary General, UN, Document S/2004/616, paras. 10 and 32.

[42] Right to the Truth, Report of the Office of the High Commissioner for Human Rights, UN Document A/HRC/5/7.

[43] Rule of Law Tools for Post-Conflict States. Amnesties, op. cit. n. 31 *supra*, 11.

[44] United Nations Commission on Human Rights Resolution 2005/81. Impunity, para. 20.

Principle 24 explicitly states that perpetrators of serious crimes against international law may not benefit from amnesties unless those responsible are brought before a competent national or international court.

At the same time, the General Assembly of the United Nations adopted a resolution in 2005 titled, "Basic Principles and Guidelines on the Right to a Remedy and Reparation for Victims of Gross Violations of International Human Rights Law and Serious Violations of International Humanitarian Law".[45] These principles establish the obligation of states to investigate and punish in cases of gross violation of international law[46] and to ensure that the victims have appropriate resources to play their part in this process.[47]

In the same vein, the United Nations has also established that even when internal amnesties exist related to violations of human rights this cannot interfere with the prosecution of those responsible before foreign or international courts.[48] Truth, reparation, and the declaration of responsibility are essential principles of justice compatible with peace. It has been said that justice is related to truth, fairness, rectitude, and retribution.[49] In order to apply justice, it is important to know the truth, to record and find the causes of murders, rapes, or tortures perpetrated by repressive regimes, and to determine who is responsible for what. In the context of reconciliation process, truth relates to an accurate understanding and recording of the causes of a political crisis, as well as of which parties are responsible for which actions, and which parties, including individuals, may be characterized as the victims or the aggressors. This exercise is better undertaken by a third party that is able to show fairness and impartiality. Impartiality in this context means that once the facts are known by the third party, they are not misrepresented in order to maintain artificial impartiality, but are incorporated into the decision-making process. Fairness also means that negotiators do not seek to find an agreement at the expense of the victims, forcing them to accept concessions against their will or judgment. Although concessions by one party may be effective for achieving an agreement avoiding human suffering in the short term, they may not help to reach lasting peace in the area.[50]

In sum, amnesty laws are incompatible with the protection of human rights. The practical aspects of this issue are dealt with in the following section which

---

[45] Resolution A/RES/60/147 of the General Assembly of United Nations, Basic Principles and Guidelines on the Right to a Remedy and Reparation for Victims of Gross Violations of International Human Rights Law and Serious Violations of International Humanitarian Law, 21 March 2006.

[46] Ibid. para. 4.

[47] Ibid. para. 3(d).

[48] Right to the Truth, Report of the Office of the High Commissioner for Human Rights, UN Doc. A/HRC/5/7, paras. 29 and 30.

[49] More information on the retributive justice approach in Pinto 2003, 698–703.

[50] Estrada-Hollenbeck argues that "(t)o resolve, of course, is to do more than stop the violence. To resolve is to leave the conflicted parties with institutions and attitudes that favour peaceful interactions", Estrada-Hollenbeck 2011, 69.

examines two recent cases which demonstrate the incompatibility of amnesty laws with international human rights law.

## 3.4 Interface of National Politics and International Obligations

### *3.4.1 An Immediate Precedent: The* Guerrilha do Araguaia *Case*

In the *Guerrilha do Araguaia* case, the IACHR ruled on an amnesty law passed after the return of democracy, and on the basis of which fact the government of Brazil argued that it could not be annulled. In Brazil, there not exists the will to implement and fully comply with the decision of the IACHR.

The *Guerrillha do Araguaia* was a movement of resistance against the military dictatorship that ruled Brazil from 1964 to 1985. It aimed to fight against the regime by forming a people's liberation army.[51] Between 1972 and 1975, the *Guerrilha do Araguaia* was the object of arbitrary detentions and later the elimination of its members. By the end of 1974, the group had no surviving members.[52] In 1995, the Brazilian state passed a law recognizing its responsibility for the murder of opposition politicians during the dictatorship, the forced disappearance of sixty members of the *Guerrilha do Araguaia*. In response to these events, the law established the right to reparations of their families.[53]

On the 28th of August 1979, Law Number 6.683/79 was enacted in Brazil having been previously approved by Congress. This law granted an amnesty to all persons between 1961 and 1979, identified

> [to have] committed political or related crimes, electoral crimes, those who had their political rights suspended and direct or indirect servants of the state, servants of foundations related to the state, servants of the legislative and judicial authorities, members of the armed forces and leaders and representatives of trades unions sanctioned on the basis of institutional and complementary actions.[54]

Thus, Brazil's amnesty law covered not only public servants such as the police and members of the armed forces who committed crimes against the civilian population but also those who committed political crimes during the military dictatorship, which included members of the opposition and resistance groups.

On the 29th of April 2010, the *Supremo Tribunal Federal do Brazil*, the nation's highest court, declared inadmissible a petition which sought the

---

[51] Gomes Lund et al. ('Guerrilha do Araguaia') versus Brasil, Judgment, IACHR, 24 November 2010. Serie C No. 219, para. 88.

[52] Ibid, paras. 89 and 90.

[53] Ibid, paras. 91 to 93.

[54] Article 1 of the Law 6.683/79.

annulment of the amnesty law. The court ruled that the law was a result of the process of transition to democracy and the democratization of the country and that it was not a self-amnesty.[55] So, in the opinion of the judges making up the *Supremo Tribunal Federal do Brazil*, they did not have the authority to question a law that had been duly approved by the legislative branch.[56]

At the time of this ruling the case was already before the IACHR. This fact was used by Brazil to claim a preliminary objection to the effect that the IACHR lacked the competence to review decisions taken by the highest authorities of the state. In this regard, the IACHR responded firmly stating that it was, not being called upon to examine the amnesty law in relation to the National Constitution [of Brazil], a matter for internal law and beyond its competence [...], but rather to examine the alleged incompatibility between that [amnesty] law and Brazil's international obligations arising from the American Convention on Human Rights.[57]

The importance of prosecuting crimes after a repressive regime, and the impact prosecution has on reconciliation, cannot be discussed without making reference to other approaches aimed at reconciliation. In effect, in the last century, the international community went from accepting amnesty laws as the standard way of securing peace, to considering that punishment before national or international courts was a preferred solution for achieving justice and reconciliation. Meanwhile, a third alternative is emerging with characteristics of both—the truth commission, or truth and reconciliation commission.[58]

In Brazil, the first step was done in November 2011, when the President of Brazil, Dilma Rousseff, dictated a law who created the Commission of Truth. This Commission intended to inquire into and document torture, murders, and other human rights violations that otherwise would be denied and covered up by repressive regimes. This approach constitutes a new form of dealing with the past that might be situated between amnesty laws and international or national tribunals. Moreover, the Commission could not adjudge individual legal culpability for those who supported or tolerated the previous oppressive government.

By now, the Commission of Truth in Brazil is seen as a successful transitional mechanism to deal with the past, and it has been taken into consideration in many debates when dealing with reconciliation. However, there remains no alternative for Brazil but to modify or repeal its amnesty law in order to comply with its international obligations. The IACHR needs to be vigilant in this respect,[59] and pressure is also necessary from inter-governmental organizations and NGOs that work in the area of the defense of human rights.

---

[55] Gomes Lund et al. ('Guerrilha do Araguaia') versus Brasil, op. cit., n. 51 supra. para. 44.

[56] With the vote of the Minister Rapporter in the Acción de Incumplimiento de Precepto Fundamental No. 153 resolved by the Supremo Tribunal Federal do Brazil.

[57] Gomes Lund et al. ('Guerrilha do Araguaia') versus Brasil, op. cit., n. 51 supra. para. 49.

[58] For a general point of view, see Rotberg and Thompson 2002. Truth Commissions have been described by P. van ZYL as the 'third way', see van Zyl 1999, 647 et seq.

[59] Gamarra and Vicente 2010, 85.

### *3.4.2* The Gelman *Case: Can a Democratic Majority Adopt Decisions Contrary to International Law?*

The *Gelman* case arose from the 1976 disappearance of Maria Claudia Iruretagoyena de Gelman, daughter in law of the Argentine poet Juan Gelman at a time when she was heavily pregnant. Maria Claudia was held captive in Buenos Aires at the clandestine detention center known as *Automotores Orletti*, and later moved to Uruguay—part of *Operación Condor*. In Uruguay, she was held in another clandestine detention center until she gave birth to her daughter María Macarena Gelman. She then disappeared again and her whereabouts are unknown to this day. Her daughter Maria Macarena was given up for adoption in Uruguay.[60]

The IACHR already had occasion, in other cases, to pronounce on the scope of *Operación Condor*. This involved cooperation in the 1970s between authoritarian Southern Cone governments who on the basis of the doctrine of national security carried out repressive activities against people considered to be "subversive elements" and common enemies without regard to nationality.[61]

In the *Gelman* case, the IACHR had to deal with one of the most despicable practices carried out during *Operación Condor*, the removal of babies—often born in captivity—from their mothers so that they could be given to couples from the police and armed forces to raises as their own.[62]

In its analysis of the forced disappearance of Maria Claudia, the IACHR held her being pregnant at the time as constituting "a condition of special vulnerability", and that the facts of her disappearance "revealed a particular conception of women's bodies hostile to their right to have babies when they wish, which forms an essential part of their free development of their personality".[63] Thus, the IACHR concluded, the allegations,

> may be categorised as one of the most serious and reprehensible forms of violence against women [...], which seriously affected their personal integrity and were clearly based on their gender;.[64]

The IACHR also examined the suppression of the real identity of María Macarena Gelman and ruled that it amounted, in the legal sense, to forced disappearance from the moment she was taken from her mother until the discovery of her real identity in 2005. According to the IACHR, the suppression and substitution of the identity of María Macarena as a consequence of the detention and disappearing of her mother had the same purpose as that detention and disappearance—that is, to leave a

---

[60] Gelman versus Uruguay, op. cit. n. 24 *supra*, paras. 79 to 90.

[61] Goiburú et al. versus Paraguay Case. Merits, Reparations and Costs, Judgment, IACHR, 22 September 2006. Serie C No. 153, párrs. 61.5 to 61.8; and Gelman versus Uruguay. op. cit. n. 24 *supra*, para. 44 et seq.

[62] Gelman versus Uruguay. op. cit.n. 24 *supra*, paras. 60 to 63.

[63] Ibid, para. 97.

[64] Ibid, para. 98.

question mark regarding her fate and whereabouts and to refuse to recognize her disappearance.[65] The IACHR further determined that the Uruguayan state violated María Macarena's rights to life, personal freedom, status as a person before the law, her rights as a child, her nationality, her name, and her right to a family, the last three making up the right to identity protected by the Convention on the Rights of the Child.[66]

The other peculiarity of the *Gelman* case is the existence of the *Ley de Caducidad*. This law was a response to a political crisis occasioned by complaints made against members of the armed forces with regard to human rights violations. In the view of a sector of the population, these complaints endangered the then recent return to democracy. In order to preserve the recently established rule of law, a pact of impunity was drawn up, which silenced the right of victims and their families to know the truth and seek justice for violations of their human rights. The amnesty law, which never described itself as such, therefore established the expiration "of the exercise of the punitive action of the state with regard to crimes committed up to the 1st of March, 1985 by military and police personnel".[67]

The amnesty law has twice been subjected to a national referendum seeking its annulment and its constitutionality has been examined by Uruguay's *Suprema Corte de Justicia* [Supreme Court of Justice]. The first referendum took place in 1989 when a group of citizens and family members of victims obtained a sufficient number of signatures. On this first occasion, only 42.4 % of the votes cast were in favor of annulling the law, so the law remained in place. The second referendum took place in October 2009 when the law was subjected to public consideration through the mechanism of a "popular initiative", which amounted to a project of constitutional reform that would have involved the introduction of a specific provision declaring the amnesty law invalid and abolished Article 1 and Article 4. On this second occasion the initiative to annul the amnesty law received 47.7 % of the vote, a quantity still insufficient to bring the measure into effect.

With regard to the examination of the amnesty law's constitutionality, in 1988 the Supreme Court of Justice held it to be in conformity with the Constitution.[68] However, in more recent cases the Supreme Court of Justice has changed its point of view. Thus in October 2009, just days before the second referendum, the Supreme Court of Justice ruled in the *Sabalsagaray* case and held that Article 1, Article 2, and Article 4 of the amnesty law were in conflict with the Constitution, and therefore were not applicable in this particular case.[69] The Supreme Court of

---

[65] Ibid, para. 132.

[66] Ibid, paras. 122 to 131.

[67] Article 1 of the Law 15.848 or *Ley de Caducidad*.

[68] Supreme Court of Uruguay, Case "Detta, Josefina; Menotti, Noris; Martinez, Federico; Musso Osiris; Burgell, Jorge s/inconstitucionalidad de la ley 15.848. Articles 1, 2, 3 y 4", Judgment No. 112/87, Resolution of 2 May, 1988, pp 2256 to 2318.

[69] Supreme Court of Uruguay. Case "Sabalsagaray Curutchet, Blanca Stela –Denuncia de Excepción de Inconstitucionalidad", Judgment. No. 365, 19 October 2009, pp 2325 to 2379.

Justice confirmed this decision in another case some days after the referendum in which it confirmed the unconstitutionality of the law.[70]

In this case, despite of the favorable rulings of the Supreme Court of Justice in 2009, the IACHR faced a number of challenges. The first difficulty concerned the fact of having to rule on a law approved by a democratic parliament as a measure of transitional justice. The second concerned the necessity to decide whether the decision of a majority of a society, against the principles of international law, could prevail against the rights of the victims and their families under the American Convention on Human Rights.

With regard to the *Ley de Caducidad* as an amnesty law, the IACHR confirmed its previous jurisprudence based, not only on the American Convention on Human Rights, but also on numerous statements by national and international organizations. Given its manifest incompatibility with the American Convention on Human Rights, the provisions of the *Ley de Caducidad* which impede the investigation and punishment of grave violations of human rights have no legal effect and, as a result, cannot continue to represent an obstacle to the investigation of the events of the present case and the identification and punishment of those responsible, nor can it have an equal or similar impact with respect to other cases of grave violations of human rights enshrined in the American Convention on Human Rights that may have occurred in Uruguay.[71]

The IACHR explicitly ruled on the value of the referendums held on the *Ley de Caducidad*, and affirmed the fact that the *Ley de Caducidad* had been enacted by a democratic regime and ratified by the people on two occasions "does not automatically, nor on its own, confer it with legitimacy under international law".[72] Furthermore, the IACHR held that the two referendums regarding the law were events attributable to the state, and that they therefore enacted its international responsibility.[73]

Finally, the IACHR examined the fact that the law had been approved by a democratically elected government—an argument, as we have already seen, that is frequently used by those states which still have amnesty laws in force. In this regard, the IACHR stated the following: the democratic legitimacy of specific acts or events in a society is limited by international norms and obligations related to the protection of human rights recognized by the American Convention on Human Rights. Thus the existence of a truly democratic regime is determined by both its formal and substantial characteristics so that, particularly in cases of grave breaches of International Human Rights Law, the protection of human rights constitutes an absolute limit to majority rule, that is to say to the sphere of what is "open to

[70] Supreme Court of Uruguay. Case "Organización de los derechos humanos—denuncia —excepción de inconstitucionalidad—Articles 1, 3, 4 of the Law No. 15.848—Ficha IUE 2-21986/2006, Judgment No. 1525, 29 October 2009, pp. 5205–5207.

[71] Gelman versus Uruguay, op. cit. n. 24 *supra*, para. 232.

[72] Ibid, para. 238.

[73] Ibid.

decision" by majorities arrived at by democratic mechanisms, mechanisms in which the priority should be given to a "monitoring of conventionality" which is the function and task of any public authority and not only that of the Judicial Branch.[74]

Thus, the IACHR confirmed that states cannot violate their international obligations regarding grave violations of human rights, even where there exists norms and laws adopted in democracy or by the will of a majority. The IACHR also established a fundamental point that even in cases where the state does not recognize the inapplicability of amnesty laws, the various branches of the state, including judges and civil servants, are obliged as representatives of the state to comply with its international obligations. Amnesty Laws were, therefore, not enforced and allowed the legitimate rights of the victims and their families to the truth and justice.

Unlike the case of Brazil and the implementation of the judgment in the *Guerrilla de Araguaia* Case, in Uruguay there exists the will to implement and fully comply with the decision of the IACHR. In spite of this, the adoption of the internal measures necessary to annul the *Ley de Caducidad* is not an easy task, especially when one takes into account the polarization which exists in Uruguayan society with regard to this matter. President José Mújica has himself maintained a position of detachment and neutrality with regard to a decision he knows will have political costs in some sectors of society, and which have already generated a reaction from those retired members of the armed forces who see the possibility of cases being opened against them.

The Supreme Court of Justice has, for its part, pronounced the law to be unconstitutional,[75] and the first domestically initiated cases against members of the armed forces are beginning to resolve themselves. Thus, on the 28th of November, 2010, General Miguel Dalmao, the head of the Army's IV Division, became the first serving member of the armed forces to be formally accused of violations of human rights during the dictatorship—this kind of crime was specifically a charge of "aggravated murder" in the *Salbasagaray* case.

In addition, anticipating the decision of the IACHR on the *Gelman* case, the Chamber of Deputies of Uruguay passed a bill in October 2010 that sought to annul the *Ley de Caducidad*. The passage of the bill was achieved with the votes of the ruling *Frente Amplio* party and in the face of opposition from the other three parties represented in the lower house of parliament. On the 12th of April 2011, after the publication of the decision of the IACHR, the Uruguayan Senate passed,

---

[74] Ibid, para. 239.

[75] On the 1st November 2010, the Supreme Court of Justice declared unconstitutional the Ley de Caducidad in relation with a case who implicated to former President Bordaberry by 20 murders. On the 11 February 2011, the Supreme Court of Justice declared unconstitutional the Ley de Caducidad, by the third time in less than a year, for the case of murders of 5 members of the guerilla tupamaros kidnaped in Argentine, in 1974, and murders near the Montevideo, in the Soca city.

by a vote of 16 to 15, a bill that annulled the three unconstitutional articles of the *Ley de Caducidad*, and leaving it inapplicable in practice.

The amended bill was sent back to the Chamber of Deputies for its approval. The vote in the lower house was a tie—with 49 for and 49 against—so the bill could not be sent to the Executive for ratification. New alternatives are currently being studied to resolve the impasse at which the partial repeal of the contemporary amnesty law. The challenge now is to study what measures to adopt so that the Uruguayan judiciary can comply with international standards and with the verdict of the IACHR in the many pending criminal prosecutions for serious human rights violations in Uruguay.

## 3.5 Conclusions

The traditional approach to the intersection of peace and justice was the amnesty law, by which outgoing authorities granted themselves, or negotiated the granting of, amnesty. Not surprisingly, this mechanism has been abused many times in the past by repressive military or other regimes seeking impunity for their crimes before relinquishing power to successor governments. Democratic transitions to peace have been made without amnesty provisions when such provisions seemed to be the only possible solution for a political crisis or conflict. At certain points in history, amnesty was the only approach for smoothly reaching a democratic transition after a repressive regime, and thus may have represented the best available option to victims as well as perpetrators. As the ostensible purpose of amnesty laws is to create an atmosphere of reconciliation -often at the expense of victims of crimes, but in the interests of the larger community—, amnesty is a political act were the element of "justice" in a judicial sense does not figure.

However, in recent years, a cascade of cases has managed to modify amnesty laws as a result of the influence of international bodies dedicated to the protection of human rights. This has happened in such places as Chile, Peru, or Argentina. The mission of international human rights bodies is not to indentify who bears individual criminal responsibility, but rather to identify the violations of human rights committed by the state. It is the responsibility of the state to modify or annul those laws, such as amnesty laws, which violate the most basic rights of every individual. In any case, National Courts have to prosecute the perpetrators in their own jurisdictions and under their own judicial system.

On the basis of this study, it can be seen that there is a strong international legal basis for the claim that amnesties that allow impunity in cases of serious violations of human rights are incompatible with international law. Although there is no broad consensus with regard to affirming that the prohibition of these types of amnesties form part of customary law, it can be said that these amnesties violate states' obligations derived from customary law.[76]

## References

Antowiak Th M (2001–2002) Truth as right and remedy in international human rights experience. Mich J Int Law 4:977–1013

Arsanjani MH (1999) The International Criminal Court and national amnesty laws. Am Soc Int Law Proc 65–67

Bennouna M (2003) Truth, justice and amnesty. In Vohrah L Ch et al (eds) Man's inhumanity to man. Essays on international law in honour of Antonio Cassese. The Hague, Kluwer Law International, pp 136–178

Blumenson E (2006) The challenge of a global standard of justice: peace, pluralism, and punishment at the international criminal court. Columbia J Transnatl Law 44:801–874

Boed R (2000) The effect of a domestic amnesty on the ability of foreign states to prosecute alleged perpetrators of serious human rights violations. Cornell Int Law J 33:297–329

Bohl K (2006–2007) Breaking the rules of transitional justice. Wis Int Law J 24:557–585

Bowring B (2010) The Russian federation, Protocol No. 14 (and 14bis), and the battle for the soul of the ECHR. Goettingen J Int Law 2:589–617

Cassese A (2007–2008) Clemency versus retribution in post-conflict situations. Columbia J Transnatl Law 46:1–13

Cerna CM (2002) Introductory Note to IACHR: Barrios Altos Case (Chumbipuma Aguirre et al. *vs.* Peru). Int Legal Mater 41:91–92

Colangelo AJ (2008–2009) Universal Jurisdiction as an international "False Conflict" of laws. Mich J Int Law 30:881–925

Deodhar NS (1988) Recent development in international organizations. First contentious cases before the Inter-American court of human rights. Am Univ J Int Law Policy 284–297

Dockery T (1995–1996) The rule of law over the law of rulers: the treatment of *De Facto* laws in Argentina. Fordham Int Law J 19:1578–1635

Donoho J (2008–2009) Minimalist interpretation of the jurisdictional immunities convention. Chi J Int L 9:661–684

Drucker L (1988–1989) Governmental liability for "Disappearances": a landmark ruling by the Inter-American Court of Human Rights. Stanf J Int Law 298–322

Dugard J (1999) Dealing with crimes of a past regime. Is amnesty still an option? Leiden J Int Law 12:1001–1015

Estrada-Hollenbeck (2001) The attainment of justice through restoration, not litigation: the subjective road to reconciliation. In Abu Nimer M (ed) Reconciliation, justice and coexistence. Oxford, Lexington Books, pp 66–93

Franck Th (1997) Fairness in international law and institutions. Oxford University Press, New York

Gamarra Y, Vicente A (2010) El discreto control de los órganos políticos sobre las decisiones de las instituciones judiciales: un análisis comparado de los sistemas americano y europeo, en Fernández Sánchez, PA (ed) El espacio jurídico común del Consejo de Europa (En Conmemoración del 60 Aniversario del Consejo de Europa), Sevilla, ed. Gandulfo, pp 73–107

[76] See Right to the Truth, Report of the Office of the High Commissioner for Human Rights, op.cit.n. 48 *supra*, paras. 11 and 12.

Garro AM (1993–1994) Nine years of transition to democracy in Argentina: partial failure or qualified success? Columbia J Transitl Law 1–102

Goldstone R (1997) Assessing the work of the United Nations war crimes tribunals. Stanf J Int Law 2–8

Greiff P de (2001–2002) Deliberative democracy and punishment. Buffalo Crim Law Rev 5:373–403

Haldemann F (2008) Another kind of justice: transitional justice as recognition. Cornell Int Law J 41:675–37

Henckaerts J-M, Doswald-Beck L (2007) El Derecho internacional humanitario consuetudinario. Int Comm Red Cross

Henkin AH (2000) Honouring human rights. Kluwer Law International, The Hague

Henkin AH (ed) (2002) The legacy of abuse, confronting the past, facing the future. The Aspen Institute, Washington

Hobbs CM (2010) The conflict between the Alien Tort statute litigation and foreign amnesty laws. Vanderbilt J Transnatl Law 43:505–532

Jowdy G (1997) Truth commissions in El Salvador and Guatemala: a proposal for truth in Guatemala. Boston Coll Third World Law J 17:285–330

Kaplan N (2002–2003) A failure of perspective: moral assumptions and genocide. Boston Coll Third World Law J 23:359–418

Kelly M (2004) *Aut Dedere Aut Judicare* and the death penalty extradition prohibition. Int Leg Theory 53–81

Laplante LJ (2008–2009) Outlawing amnesty: the return of criminal justice in transitional justice schemes. Va J Int Law 49:915–983

Lau H (2005–2006) Rethinking the persistent objector doctrine in international human rights law. Chi J Int Law 495–510

Lavrov S (1999–2000) The Russian approach: the fights against genocide, war crimes, and crimes against humanity. Fordham Int Law J 415–428

Lutz E, Sikkink K (2001) The justice cascade: the evolution and impact of foreign human rights trials in Latin America, 2. Chi J Int Law 1:1–33

Majzub D (2002) Peace or justice? Amnesties and the International Criminal Court. Melb J Int Law 3:247–279

Matas D (1989–1990) Prosecuting crimes against humanity: the lessons of World War I. Fordam Int Law J 13:86–104

Medina Quiroga C (2003) La Convención Americana: Teoría, y Jurisprudencia. Vida, Integridad Personal, Libertad Personal, Debido Proceso, y Recurso Judicial, Centro de Derechos Humanos Facultad de Derecho, Universidad de Chile

Meintjes G, Méndez JE (2000) Reconciling amnesties with universal jurisdiction. International Law Forum du droit international 2:76–97

Neier A (2003) Accountability for State crimes: the past twenty years and the next twenty years. Case W Res J Int Law 35:351–362

Newman DG (2004–2005) The Rome Statute, some reservations concerning Amnesties, and a distributive problem. Am Univ Int Law Rev 20:293–357

Norris H N (2010), Closer to Justice: Transferring Cases from the International Criminal Court. Minn J Int Law 201–239

O'Brien R (2005) Amnesty and international law. Nordic J Int Law 74:261–278

O'Shea A (2002) Amnesty for crime in international law and practice. Kluwer Law International, The Hague

Okun H (2006–2007) The role of international criminal justice in peace negotiations. Penn State Int Law Rev 779–790

Orentlicher D (1995) Addressing gross human rights abuses: punishment and victim compensation. In: Henkin L, Hargrove JL (eds) Human rights: an agenda for the new century. Polity Press, Cambridge

Osuna JP (1988) Amnesty in the immigration reform and control act of 1986: policy rationale and lessons from Canada. Am Univ J Int Law Policy 3:145–196

Pinto MCW (2003) Truth and consequences or truth and reconciliation? Some thoughts on the potential of official truth commission. In: Vohrah L Ch et al (eds) Man's Inhumanity to man. Essays on International Law in Honour of Antonio Cassese. Kluwer Law International, The Hague, pp 698–715

Rabkin J (2005) Global criminal justice: an idea whose time has passed. Cornell Int Law J 38:753–777

Rakate PK (2001) Reconciling Amnesties with Universal jurisdiction in South Africa- a response to Garth Meintjes & Juan Méndez. International Law FORUM du droit international, 3:42–46

Ratner SR, Abrams JS (2001) Accountability for human rights violations in international law: beyond the Nuremberg legacy, 2nd edn. Oxford University Press, Oxford

Robinson D (2003) Serving the interests of justice: Amnesties, truth commissions and the International Criminal Court. EJIL 14:481–505

Robinson M (2006–2007) Rule of law and international human rights in challenging times. Penn State Int Law Rev, 833–853

Rogers SB (2007–2008) The World Bank Voluntary Disclosure Program (VDP): A distributive justice critique. Columbia J Transnatl Law 46:709–731

Roht-Arriaza N (1998) Truth commissions and amnesties in Latin America: the second generation. Am Soc Int Law Proc 313–315

Rose C (2008) Looking beyond amnesty and traditional justice and reconciliation mechanisms in Northern Uganda: a proposal for truth-telling and reparations. Boston Coll Third World Law J 345–400

Ross BG (1986–1987) Federal tax amnesty: reflecting on the states' experiences. Tax Law 145–184

Rotberg RI, Thompson D (eds) (2002) Truth v Justice, The morality of truth commissions. Princeton, Princeton University Press

Schabas W (2004–2005) Amnesty. The Sierra Leone truth and reconciliation commission and the Special Court for Sierra Leone. Univ Calif Davis J Int Law Policy 146–170

Scharf MP (1999) The amnesty exception to the jurisdiction of the international criminal court. Cornell Int Law J 507–527

Scully L (2007–2008) Neither justice, Nor Oasis: Algeria's Amnesty Law. Brook J Int Law 975–1035

Sebert-Fohr A (2005) Human rights as guiding principles in the context of post conflict justice. Mich St J Int Law 179–196

Seyedin-Noor S (2000) The Spanish Prisioner: understanding the prosecution of senator Augusto Pinochet Ugarte Davis J Int Law Policy 41–104

Shamsey J (2001–2002) 80 years too late: the International Criminal Court and the 20th century's first genocide. J Transnatl Law Policy, 327–383

Sikkink K, Walling CB (2006) Errors about trials: the emergence and impact of the justice cascade. Paper presented at the Princeton International Relations Faculty Colloquium. Princeton NJ, March 27 2006

Slye RC (2002–2003) The Legitimacy of amnesties under international law and general principles of Anglo-American Law. Is a Legitimate amnesty possible? Va J Int Law 43:173–247

Slye RC (2004) The Cambodian amnesties: beneficiaries and the temporal reach of amnesties for gross violation of human rights. Wis Int Law J 22:99–123

Stahn C (2001) Accommodating individual criminal responsibility and national reconciliation: the UN Truth Commission for East Timor. Am J Int Law 95:952–966

Sterio M (2006) Rethinking amnesty. Denver J Int Law Policy 373–400

Theidon K, Laplante LJ (2006–2007) Transitional justice in time of conflict: Colombia's *Ley de Justicia y Paz.* Mich J Int Law 49–108

Wash JL, Suagee DB (1988) Conference report. The Inter-American human rights system: into the 1990s and beyond. Am Univ J Int Policy 517–565

Weisma N (1972) A history and discussion of amnesty. Columbia Hum Rights Law Rev 529–540

de Wet E (2004) The prohibition of torture as an international norm of *ius cogens* and its implications for national and customary law. Eur J Int Law 15:97–122

Wippman D (1999–2000) Atrocities, Deterrence, and the limits of international justice. Fordham Int Law J 473–88

Young GK (2001–2002) Amnesty and accountability. Davis Law Rev 427–482

Young GK (2002–2003) All the truth and as much justice as possible. Univ Calif Davis J Int Law Policy 9:209–246

Zyl P (1999) Dilemmas of transitional justice: the case of South Africa's truth and reconciliation commission. J Int Aff 52:647–667

Zyl P (1999b) Dilemmas of transitional justice: the case of South Africa's truth and reconciliation commission. J Int Aff 52:647–667

Zuppi AL (2007) Swinging back and forth between impunity and impeachment: the struggle for justice in Latin America and the international criminal court. Pace Int Law Rev 19:195–222

# Part II
# New Theoretical Approaches in International Law

# Chapter 4
# Engaging History in International Law

**Thomas Skouteris**

**Abstract** This paper points to the intimate relationship between international legal writing and history. It typifies modes of engagement with history in international law in order to contrast, rather impressionistically, a traditional approach with a set of present-day critiques. It proposes that the distinction between professional historiography and legal work proper is in some way misleading: while there are significant differences in terms of their respective objectives and styles, legal work inevitably requires a positioned engagement with the past, thus producing (or contributing to the production of) historical knowledge (Sect. 4.2). Second, it argues that modern international law histories tend to share specific, albeit often unregistered, assumptions about the past that raise unsettling questions about the legitimacy of the axiomatic narratives of the discipline (Sect. 4.3). Third, it samples some alternative modes of engagement with history as evidenced in the "historical turn" and, in particular, in Critical histories of recent years (Sect. 4.4). The closing section identifies some starting points for reckoning with the role of history in international law work (Sect. 4.5).

The author would like to thank Juan Amaya-Castro and Alexandra Kemmerer for reading and commenting on early drafts of this paper.

T. Skouteris (✉)
LawDepartment, The American University in Cairo,
New Cairo, Egypt
e-mail: tskouteris@aucegypt.edu

J. M. Beneyto and D. Kennedy (eds.), *New Approaches to International Law*,
DOI: 10.1007/978-90-6704-879-8_4,

## Contents



## 4.1 Introduction

International lawyers prefer to do history rather than talk about it. Historical narrative entwines legal writing so seamlessly that it almost passes unnoticed. International law's normativity resides, at least partly, in the historical past and a flight to history appears necessary in order to establish it. Think of how we write about law creation, the evolution of human society, the role of law in social progress, key events in the discipline's development, the changing content of doctrines, the origins and development of institutions. As an end in itself or to support more pragmatic, problem-solving enquiries, international law is replete with historical argument.

By contrast, there is very little talk among international lawyers about how to engage history as a discourse and the past as a constant presence in legal texts. The silence is generally considered unproblematic. One common rationalization is that international law's interface with history comes in two distinct forms, namely professional legal historiography on the one hand, and legal work proper on the other. Professional historiography designates the work of salaried legal historians (or others self-identified with the genre), whose labour is to make sense of the past and produce knowledge about it. In legal work proper, by contrast, the role of the lawyer is not to produce historical knowledge but merely to make use of historical facts for the production of legal argument.

This division of labor leads to a paradox. While international law discourse is awash with historical analysis, there is very little discussion about the role of history in legal argument. Add the momentous transformation that the discipline of history has endured for the past half-century, the cutting edge of which is incredulity toward the very possibility of knowledge of the past in some objective way.[1] This paper points to the intimate relationship between international law writing and history. It draws up a preliminary account of the ways in which international lawyers engage history today with the following objectives in mind. First, it proposes that the distinction between professional historiography and legal work proper is in some way misleading: while there are significant differences in terms of their respective objectives and styles, legal work inevitably requires a positioned engagement with the past, thus producing (or contributing to the production of) 'historical knowledge' (Sect. 4.2). Second, it proposes that modern international law histories tend to share specific, albeit often unregistered, assumptions about the past that raise unsettling questions about the legitimacy of the axiomatic narratives of the discipline (Sect. 4.3). Third, this essay samples some alternative modes of engagement with history as evidenced in the "historical turn" and, in particular, in Critical histories of recent years (Sect. 4.4). The closing section identifies some starting points for reckoning with the role of history in international law work (Sect. 4.5).

## 4.2 International Legal Historiography Today

The distinction between professional legal historiography and legal work proper is understated but salient. The term 'professional' usually serves as a qualifier to connote the writing of proper History, the purpose of which is to discover the truth about the past by means of historical method.[2] The originalism of professional historiography is contrasted with 'amateur' or 'enlisted' historiography. These latter forms are the end-result of the setting aside, or abuse, of methods and techniques of professional historiography—the kind of historiography that is sometimes written by international courts, international organizations, Foreign Offices, law firms, or academics in their everyday work. 'Amateur' history, the story goes, fails to apply good historical method due to lack of training. 'Enlisted' history, to make matters worse, instrumentalizes history to produce truth-effects in the service of positioned legal argument, often at the cost of the truth. Such seems to be the case with 'law office history' or with historical evidence creatively re-interpreted to serve legal argument before a court.[3] Such concerns about poor quality history are only meaningful against the backdrop of the claim that historiography, if done well, yields knowledge the accretion of which incrementally improves our collective skills in social engineering or our approximation to truth. Done badly, however, historiography can obscure the truth and, in its enlisted version, is handmaiden to power.

---

[1] For a few 'new classics' see, a.o., Jenkins 1991; White 1987; Munslow 2006; Jenkins 2009.

[2] See, the argument in Lesaffer 2007, 27–42; Bederman 2002, 42–63.

[3] Bederman 2002, 45–48; Lesaffer 2007, 37–41.

Professional international legal historiography is traditionally observed to exist in short supply.[4] In recent years, the literature has surveyed the poor state of affairs yet again.[5] The few existing monographs constitute today a relatively narrow field of study.[6] In their scarcity, they have become canonical: they make compulsory reading and receive abundant academic review. The majority of this scholarship belongs to the genre of history of ideas (intellectual history) and, to a lesser extent, to the history of facts, doctrines, processes, or institutions. With some notable exceptions, and until very recently, there has been little emphasis on the epistemology of international legal history as such.[7]

The scarcity of professional international legal historiography is explained away by evolutionary justifications according to which, traditionally, a number of systemic obstacles hindered professional reflection. Several variants of this view can be found in recent literature: (a) the turn to pragmatism in the aftermath of WWII steered the profession toward functionally oriented tasks and, consequently, away from theoretical analysis[8]; (b) the tardy professionalization of international law as an academic discipline set different scholarly priorities[9]; and (c) traditional positivist influences divided experts into two separate professions, international lawyers, and historians, thus obstructing inter-disciplinary dialog.[10] Recent developments are claimed to have lifted some of these constraints and to have unleashed new possibilities of cross-disciplinary historical work. The "increased political possibility connected with the end of the Cold War" and "the breakdown of the modernist frame of politics that used to provide a rather optimistic and above all universalistically inclined interpretation of the international world" are at least two of the parameters that may have enabled an "atmospheric change".[11] For others, a certain democratization of research was brought about by the "progressive incorporation of new technologies and a trendy rising demand of international lego-historically oriented work from the publishing side."[12] To take it a step further, one could argue that the 'End of History' discourse and the prevalence of a bourgeois, capitalist market economy based on relative value may have nurtured and finally succeeded in corroding traditionally restrictive professional practices, making room for relativism, even cynicism, but also for new

[4] Several generations of scholars have lamented this. See, e.g., Verzijl 1968, 400, as cited in Lesaffer 2007, 27; Schwarzenberger 1962, as cited in and Kemmerer 2008.

[5] Hueck 2001; Koskenniemi 2004. See also Galindo 2005; and Kemmerer 2008.

[6] For a few old and new best-sellers in English *see* Maine 1861; Nussbaum 1954; Verzijl 1968/1998; Neff 1990; Grewe 2000; Koskenniemi 2002; Bederman 2002; Janis 2010. For a review of the literature in German, French and Italian, see Hueck 2001, 199–203.

[7] See Kennedy 1999. It is Koskenniemi's *Gentle Civilizer* that re-instated history as a conscious way of talking about international law for the main part of the European academic audience.

[8] Koskenniemi 2004, 661; Galindo, 2005, 548; Hueck 2001, 207.

[9] Hueck 2001, 201–204

[10] Galindo 2005, 548.

[11] Koskenniemi 2004, 63.

[12] de la Rasilla del Moral 2009.

terms of engagement. To use a David Kennedy snippet, far from having become a 'postmodern fandango where everything is up for grabs', chunks of international law discourse can arguably be destabilized today more easily than before. The very reflexivity that led early modernism to ask radical questions about the role of reason and the production of knowledge may have now led to the postmodern condition, in which international law reluctantly begins to acknowledge with a modest 30-year delay: postmodernity as the corollary of modernity. Or, one could choose to be less wordy. If novelty and innovation seems no longer possible, turning to the past may at least bring some imaginative space: "the limits of our imagination are product of a history that may have gone another way".[13]

Regardless of your chosen etiology, the last two decades witness a marginal but spirited engagement with international legal history. The phenomenon is described perhaps over-enthusiastically as a "turn to history".[14] The "turn" refers to the growing need on the part of international lawyers to review the history of the discipline and "establish links between the past and present situations".[15] This renewed interest in 'talking history' is reflected demographically in a small but perky body of literature[16] and collaborative research projects[17] that try to unravel the complex relationship between the disciplines of history and international law, work that could be classified as belonging to the philosophy of legal history. The "turn to history" comes to international law a few years later than similar moves in domestic law.[18]

It has to be noted, however, that most surveys continue to understate the fact that international lawyers actually 'do history' all the time, even when they say they don't, a point that I would like to pursue a little further. Craven identifies at least three different modes of engagement with history: (a) history *of* international law, or history in narrative form describing the evolution of the discipline as such; (b) history *in* international law, or debates about the role of historical events or persons in the development of the substance of the law; (c) international law in history, or understanding how international law and lawyers are involved in the

---

13 Koskenniemi 2002, 5; Craven 2007, 3.

14 E.g., Craven 2006, 3; Galindo (Turn), at 541.

15 Galindo 2005, 541.

16 The Journal of International Legal History is a relatively new project that seems to adopt a wide angle on the subject. In its seven years of operation, it has nevertheless hosted a handful of articles that squarely take on questions of theory and epistemology. See, e.g., Allott 1999; Hueck 2001; Onuma 2000. The *European Journal of International Law* and the *Leiden Journal of International* Law have both launched intellectual history projects during the last 5 years about events or individual scholars and their contribution in international law. See also the work redefining the relationship between memory, history, and the representation of past atrocities in the context of post-conflict reconciliation. See, e.g., Todorov 2009; Hinton and O'Neil 2009.

17 For a review of such projects in Europe *see* Hueck 2001; Kemmerer 2008, 76.

18 This has been especially the case in North America. See, e.g., Gordon 1984; Fisher 1996–1997.

creation of history in a wider sense (i.e. outside disciplinary history).[19] It is proposed here that, regardless of one's typology, any intellectual process of narrativizing the past is always positioned. Historical accounts, even those made in passing or as a sidekick to legal work proper, require assumptions and choices (e.g. which facts to mention, how to tell the story, whose common knowledge to use, etc.) that are far from natural, mechanical, or neutral. By denying the label of History in uppercase and through repetition, such 'everyday' histories perform a central ideological role in the construction of what George Steiner would call the "axiomatic fictions" of our field, namely contemporary and overwhelmingly dominant assumptions about what constitutes historical knowledge.[20]

This is not a minor point. The crucial difference between 'professional' and 'everyday' historiography is that the former is expected to bring to the fore the conceptual device that determines the conditions for knowing the past. The latter typically suppresses to the deep structure of the text such conditions, where they continue to serve as a hidden but decisive apparatus that sets limits in the production of meaning. While there is nothing necessarily wrong with the latter, this mode of doing history should also be called to the fore so that we can look more clearly at the ways in which it constructs orthodoxies about the past some of which are described as common knowledge. To demonstrate the point, what follows is the close reading of a sample of well-known 'everyday' legal work, namely the introductory paragraph of Prof. Malcolm Shaw's classic textbook on public international law.

> In the long march of mankind from the cave to the computer a central role has always been played by the idea of law—the idea that order is necessary and chaos inimical to a just and stable existence. Every society, whether it can be large or small, powerful or weak, has created for itself a framework of principles within which to develop. What can be done, what cannot be done, permissible acts, forbidden acts, have all been spelt out within the consciousness of that community. Progress, with its inexplicable leaps and bounds, has always been based upon the group as men and women combine to pursue commonly accepted goals, whether these are hunting animals, growing food, or simply making money. Law is that element which binds the members of the community together in their adherence to recognized values and standards. [...] And so it is with what is termed international law, with the important difference that the principle subjects of international law are nation-states, not individual citizens.[21]

One may presume that the author does not consider this to be 'professional' legal historiography but rather a general introduction to a legal text that refers to historical events that are real, well known, and verified elsewhere. The first sentence places the reader in the context of the historical evolution of humankind: a story about how things were before, how things are today, and what is the distance traveled; or, to put it differently, a narrative with a beginning, a middle, and end. In Shaw's excerpt, humanity has had a "long march from the cave to the

[19] Craven 2007, 6.

[20] Steiner 1998, 144.

[21] Shaw 2003, 1.

computer", leading to the present day. With a single strike the reader is interpellated, summoned from afar, and placed within a concrete and clearly defined context: a historical continuum (humanity's development) and a social group (a universal community of human beings). The reader is also informed that humanity's progression (*our* progression) was long and arduous ("long march"). It has resulted, however, into definite progress. On the one hand, it has evolved from technologically primitive life ("the cave") to modern technological advancement ("the computer"); on the other, from a primitive social state ("chaos") to an advanced social state ("order"). In Shaw's text, this statement receives no further elaboration and is taken as self-explanatory: our modern era *is* a much better time for humanity than its primitive past because of these advances.

Law, we are also told, has played a "central role" in this transformation. This central role was performed "always" and in "every society, whether it be large or small, powerful or weak". The idea of law that Shaw alludes to is universal, perennial, and transcendental. Law embodies the idea of order and is the element that binds the community of humans together and enables progress. Progress has "always been based upon the group as men and women combine to pursue commonly accepted goals". International law is finally introduced in the closing sentences as something similar to law at large, with the same effects and sharing the same history. The founding difference is that nation-states and not individuals are its principal subjects. At the end of Shaw's passage, the student is assured that the history of humanity unequivocally demonstrates that law existed in every society and has always done well. In this account of progress, the "I" of the author is absent. Shaw adopts the posture of a dispassionate, neutral, objective chronicler that merely records events as they "are", from a seemingly external point of view.

After reading Shaw's passage, the reader hits the road running. She is introduced to the study of international law with the conviction that this body of rules and its supporting scientific discipline has always been a progressive agent for humanity. History's sadder moments are severed from international law or silenced altogether. It is the historical account that legitimizes, for the purposes of an introduction to a student textbook, the virtue of public international law. At the same time, there are no footnotes or references to 'professional' histories. One assumes that the author has, rightly, avoided extensive references for the sake of narrative economy. Or, one assumes that the story presented is so obvious or well known that speaks itself and requires no proof. Either way the author's story about the past *becomes* the past for international law with no gaps or discontinuities. Regardless of whether one agrees with Professor Shaw, one wonders whether human evolution occurred *really* or *only* along the lines described. This is a crucial question: if the truth of the account is destabilized, and if a multiplicity of alternative histories of equal plausibility are allowed, then the background for his approach to international law should be more nuanced, since different lessons should be learned from the past. If one was able to demonstrate, for argument's sake, that life in today's world is not necessarily 'better' than the one in a previous era, one would then have to adopt a more ambivalent posture toward the social function of international law than the one implied in Shaw's text. The book would have to explain, for example, how international law might have to list international law's failures or examples where international law was part of the problem instead of part of the solution. One may wonder about the epistemic basis on which such an account of human progress has been constructed, as well as its political, cultural, ideological, gender, race, class, and other properties. No historical narrative can be compiled without an external point of view that offers itself as a filter, which helps distinguish events worth being recorded from others that are not. A simple list of events, listed by date or genre, is never sufficient to describe what happened and, besides, what is an appropriate event to include in such a list? What are the alternative accounts which have been set aside? What has been foregrounded and what has been relegated to the background?

## 4.3 Four Assumptions About History

This Section seeks to outline the starting assumptions of a dominant style of historical argument in international law work today. Any attempt to reduce a large body of scholarship into a repertoire of positions is doomed to be impressionistic and needs to make generalizations that some will not recognize but will hopefully engage. The four assumptions about history presented here are intertwined with other assumptions about law, humanity, society, and change, which cannot be fully explored in the confines of this brief paper. With these caveats in mind, it is proposed that international legal writing endorses a set of assumptions about history, the past, and the capacity of the international lawyer to know it, which go as follows.

### *4.3.1 Assumption #1: International Legal History is About the Search for Truth*

The first assumption is that international legal history is concerned with the truth about the past. Proper History is method-based scientific work, whose purpose is ontological, i.e. to reveal how historical facts took place. This assumption is not naïve in the sense of simplistically considering the past as an object that can be readily uncovered and recorded. It is, however, defined by the conviction that, ultimately, History is distinguishable from ideology or fiction on account of its ability to discover truth. This credo finds its roots in the empiricist and re-constructionist tradition that dominated the mainstream of the science of history in the nineteenth and early twentieth centuries, and in the tradition of legal positivism that postulated sharp divisions between social sciences. Along these lines, and under conditions, the truth about the past can be revealed through empirical-sensory experience and the study of its traces and evidences. Inferences from and interpretation of evidence needs to be done 'correctly' by means of applying good method that removes distortions and subjectivism (bias, situationality, ideology, etc.). The professional historian is the custodian of good history: a forensic expert that toils for the excavation of artifacts from the surrounding debris. Under such conditions, good History can become synonymous with the past. History can only be useful to law if it can lead to truths about law's content, normativity, social function, or evolution; knowledge that, when accrued, can be converted to more accurate conclusions and, ultimately, scientific progress.

Historical explanation is textually constructed in narrative form, a discursive formation with a "contextualizing and backward look", "a referential text in which temporality is represented".[22] Everyday international law historiography tends to take the past to reveal itself to the observer in the form of stories in which events and situations exist in a cause-and-effect relationship. Literary embellishments are tolerated for stylistic purposes and the sources should speak for themselves. Historiography must not entertain but report. Proper history must be disinterested, dispassionate, and objective. The rational, sequential structure of the narrative helps organize the past and explain it. This way the dominant view sets aside one of Hayden White's central claims that the narrative, aside from a form is also "content": it is the narrative form itself that produces the truth of the story about the past.[23]

The entire truth about the past cannot always be known, since only fragments can be found. Processing them can be an immensely complicated process and sometimes not enough primary materials can be acquired. This, however, does not reduce the legitimacy of the endeavor. When the evidence is scarce the legal historian must admit inability to know the truth. It is a problem of evidence and not of epistemology.[24] An historical account may therefore be right or wrong, but should never be fictional. This is a rather absolute position that has become somewhat softened in the aftermath of the 'linguistic turn' and the challenge of structuralist, poststructuralist, deconstructive, postmodern, and other critiques during the last half-century. A range of 'neo-objectivist' positions now accepts some relativity in the reading of evidence but only up to the point that the object of study does not dissolve in the process. Ultimately, facts and legal relationships between them do exist and can be determined.

> Academic historians are, typically, only too happy to embrace a sort of "non-extreme relativism" on the basis of a liberal-pluralistic, domesticated *perspectivalism* of phenomena on the basis that while we all read things "from our own perspectives", nevertheless this potential multiplicity of perspectives does not lead to subjectivism because we can all agree what we have different perspectives *on*.[25]

---

[22] Ducrot & Todorov 1979. See, generally, White 1987.

[23] White 1987, xi.

[24] On this point *see*, e.g. Elton 1991, 29.

[25] Jenkins 2003, 13.

Commitment to history-as-truth appears as a no-brainer, as the only way to secure firm historical ground to derive correct conclusions about the law. The promise of eventual truth is enticing when the alternative is despair.[26] If you endorse the opposite view, i.e. that history is what historians write without a quality filter; if history can be based on shaky evidence, and if every interpretation goes, then you may wonder what is the point in doing history at all. Indeterminacy appears a terrible place for a scholar to be in and hardly a good basis for academic work. Committing oneself to further improving our techniques of discovering the truth about the past seems like the right way ahead.

### 4.3.2 Assumption #2: Using Historical Knowledge is Different from Writing History

As demonstrated in the Shaw excerpt earlier on, some law texts perform a very popular rhetorical move: they distinguish the use of historical data from the writing of history. The distinction makes sense intuitively and is perhaps understandable on functional grounds. Responsibility for establishing the truth about the legal, political, social, economic, cultural, or other past belongs to professional historians (legal or others), whose findings are reviewed by a learned community of peers. Comparative advantage and academic division of labor make it counter-productive for, say, legal practitioners to have to verify every piece of historical knowledge and have to reckon with all relevant epistemological questions in the course of their ordinary legal work.

The distinction has important methodological consequences. For one thing, it defers responsibility for the validity of historical knowledge to named or unnamed professional historians while setting aside the need to bring to the surface the conditions for knowing the past. The distinction assumes that there is a 'core center' of historical facts that can be established beyond doubt (objectively) and therefore can be used as axiomatic. It also assumes that there is such a thing as a decisive historical method that can guarantee the truth of conclusions about the past. This way, everyday legal histories, such as Shaw's account above, become naturalized (natural), universalized (universal), and dehistoricised (timeless) on account of repetition and professional practices of cross-referencing augmented by the invocation of the authority of professional history. 'Everyday' history is removed from the purview of critique together with the agency of the jurist-author in the process.

[26] The expression is borrowed from Berman 1993.

### 4.3.3 Assumption #3: Law Has a Definite Relationship to a Social Context

According to the third assumption, legal events are the product of, or a response to, a wider context that may be legal, political, diplomatic, cultural, historical, economic, and so on. One of the tasks of legal history is to figure out the precise causal relationship between the two for a variety of reasons, ranging from interpreting correctly a legal event to understanding longer processes of systemic change and the role of law. Prof. David Bederman describes his method as aiming to place international law in the "correct context" and to avoid "premature generalizations".

> "Correct context" means, I would suppose, that statements made about notional rules of State conduct in international relations are weighed against the available historical record of State behavior in antiquity. It is not enough, of course, that States may have *said* that they observed a particular rule of international law. It is quite another matter to see whether they, in fact, did so. My survey will attempt, wherever possible, to ascertain the actual observance of these norms of state conduct.[27]

Such law-in-context enquiries have resulted in historical explanations of legal events of varying levels of persuasiveness, detail, and sophistication. So, in recent literature the so-called proliferation of international tribunals is often described as a phenomenon catalyzed primarily by the end of the Cold War. Similarly, the necessary premise for the development of the present international system is the rise of the modern national states between the fifteenth and seventeenth centuries. While globalization is a process that started a long time ago, it was slowed down by economic protectionism in the first part of the twentieth century and was precipitated by postwar economic liberalization; and so on.

Law-in-context enquiries usually have different views on the degree of autonomy that a legal event may retain from its context[28] but agree that their relationship can ultimately be determined. For most international lawyers, a "contextual study" of law[29] is necessary in order to understand the reasons leading to a legal event, its original purpose, or the original intent of the entities involved. But this is mere background to legal work proper, which is rather concerned with assessing the event in terms of its legal significance only. Regardless of why a norm, institution, or process, may have come into existence, its normativity or legal effects can only be determined on the basis of the relevant rules of international law, and without recourse to ideology, politics or any other extra-legal concerns that may have produced it. Legal history can explain the cause-and-effect relationships that led to the United Nations and the adoption of Article 2(4) of the

---

[27] Bederman 2002, 5.

[28] See, the distinction between 'formalist' and 'realist' variants of law-in-context studies drawn by Gordon 1984, 64–67.

[29] See, e.g. Nijman 2004, 17–25.

UN Charter, i.e. as a response to World War II and as embodying a particular worldview about how to manage postwar international politics. The legal meaning of Article 2(4), however, has to be determined on the basis of the relevant rules of treaty interpretation, rules that are technical-legal, internal to international law. Historical analyses of this sort focus mostly on judicial decisions, travaux preparatoires, official documents and instruments, or any other fact that could be relevant to legal analysis proper.

### *4.3.4 Assumption #4: Humanity's Path is Evolutionary and International Law is an Agent of Social Progress*

The final assumption sees international law as evolving in a linear fashion, caught up in humanity's historical necessity for progress.[30] This is not to suggest that evolution has always been linear, that mankind has always done the right thing, or that law has always been an agent of progress. Unhappy moments in the history of law, however, are seen either as aberrations 'never again' to be repeated or are ascribed to forces external (e.g. nationalism, passion) and hostile to the progressive core (and course) of the discipline. Ultimately, sadder moments are reread as confirmations of the teleology, as exceptions that confirm the rule. Thus, in Shaw's account, humanity's evolution from the cave to the computer is the overarching historical necessity, like Ulysses' journey to Ithaka whose end-point is real and inevitable, while lateral narrative plots are recounted as trials-and-errors that helped discover the right way home. International legal history of this sort looks for continuities, events and landmarks in the past that confirm the procession from one stage of development to the next. The manner in which progress occurs varies from author to author: some speak of epochs; others of paradigm shifts; of scientific revolutions; others of tributaries flowing into the grand river of evolution; others of a marketplace of values where the best survive through a process of natural selection in episodes that mark the important turning points. Sometimes progress happens in single bursts, in grand leaps forward, other times by means of longer, invisible, processes of slow evolution. Either way, international law, the international community, or even humanity, ultimately follows a teleological trajectory that takes us from the past through the present towards a future defined by the promise of a better world. Once we reach a turning point, past trials and tribulations are continuously re-assessed as episodes in the evolutionary course of history till, one day, we are able to reconstruct the entire story. Progress is attributed to factors in the real world that are exogenous to the "I" of the historian. The historian needs to adopt the posture of a dispassionate, neutral, objective chronicler that merely records events as they unfold before her sight or through the traces and evidences of the past.

---

[30] On this point see Skouteris 2010, esp. Chap. 1.

## 4.4 Critical Responses

This dominant style of international legal historiography has met substantial critique during the recent "turn to history". This is not to suggest that the dominant style described above has been a static affair. Methodological reflection, however, has always been marginal to the discipline's central occupation with more pragmatic, problem solving priorities. Conscious and systematic engagement with history is the trademark of the work of Critical Theory-inspired scholars since the late 1980s that have become associated with a range of intellectual movements such as New Approaches to International Law (NAIL),[31] Third World Approaches to International Law (TWAIL),[32] feminist international law,[33] Critical Race Theory,[34] and so on. The intellectual claims of these movements have been mapped elsewhere and need not be repeated here.[35] It is important to note, however, that this body of work should not be seen as 'new approaches to history,' but rather as scholarship that re-deploys history as a technique of criticism and as part of a larger intellectual project of 'reinventing' international law. This project of 'reinvention' is done in many ways, one of which is to disentangle the assumptions that rest in the inner structure of international legal argument and bring to light their rhetorical patterns, ambivalences, paradoxes, bias, and distributive effects. Critical histories comprise an enormous and diverse body of work that has been received with anything from enthusiasm to outright suspicion and hostility by different professional groups. Different authors state a variety of reasons for engaging with history, such as to liberate the field from the grip and structural bias of hegemonic historical narratives; to write back into history what is excluded; to re-write history; to explain the discursive role of historical argument in law; to read law as a 'text'; to create imaginative space for new forms of politics; to provoke loss of faith in mainstream accounts, to reveal the structural bias of existing doctrines and institutions, and so on. By regarding history not as the search for truth but 'merely' as a technique of criticism critical histories sometimes intersect with "turn to history" scholarship, but other times part company with it. Regardless of how successful critical scholars have been, their extensive occupation with history places them at the heart of contemporary debates. For the sake of the present narrative, critical histories are re-arranged on the basis of three propositions that go as follows.

---

[31] For an early overview, see Kennedy 1988; Kennedy and Tennant 1994.

[32] E.g. Chimni 2006.

[33] E.g. Charlesworth and Chinkin 2000; Charlesworth et al. 1991.

[34] See, e.g., the contributions in the Symposium Critical Race Theory and International Law: Covergence and Divergence, 45 Villanova Law Review 827–1220 (2000).

[35] Cass 1996.

### *4.4.1 Proposition #1: International Legal History as a Discourse*

In the antipodes of the first assumption (History as the quest for truth), critical scholars propose that, while historical work may be method-based, international legal history can never reflect the truth about the past in the sense of recounting what *really* happened in a decisive or final way. The distinctions between proper History on the one hand and amateur/enlisted history/fiction on the other are unstable: while differences can be found in their respective methods and styles, all are constructed and positioned literary modes of speaking or thinking about the past. This is because most critical work in history approaches history as a discourse[36] and, in fact, as one of many discourses that tries to make sense of the world. This view goes hand in hand with the work of structural linguistics, semiotics, ideology critique and the intellectual movements of structuralism, post-structuralism, postmodernism that stridently entered the field of the social sciences in the second half of the twentieth century. It rests on the basic idea, which by now has become epistemological commonplace between these movements,[37] that the word and the world are two separate categories[38]: knowledge and representations about how the world is 'out there' are not mere reflections of the world but products of certain ways of categorizing the world. Truth, or rather a truth-claim, is a discursive construction. The past, the object of enquiry of the science of history, has already occurred, it is gone, and it is brought to us not as actual events but as historiography, i.e. as the work of historians. History and the past are therefore two different things. The same historical fact can be read differently by different discourses (e.g. law, history, sociology, economics, art, history), while within each discourse there are different readings over space and time, none of which are decisive.

Critical histories do not doubt that certain events 'occurred'. Historical records, such as official public records, can certify the reality of some events. Critical approaches, however, underline the fact that disputes about history, at least in their

---

[36] Discourse is understood as "a particular way of talking about and understanding the world (or an aspect of the world)": Philips and Jørgensen 2002, 2. See also Paltridge 2007; Widdowson 2004; Fairclough 1995. In this colloquial sense, we speak of medical, political, economic, or legal discourse to refer to the different ways (or the different vocabularies) in which a doctor, political scientist, economist, or jurist would speak in their professional language about the same topic. It is therefore even more to the point to take Michel Foucault's definition, whose "archeology" was the defining moment for discourse studies: "We shall call discourse a group of statements in so far as they belong to the same discursive formation; [...] [Discourse] is made up of a limited number of statements for which a group of conditions of existence can be defined. Discourse in this sense is not an ideal, timeless form [...] it is, from beginning to end, historical—a fragment of history [...] posing its own limits, its divisions, its transformations, the specific modes of its temporality rather than its sudden irruption in the midst of the complexities of time." Foucault 1972.

[37] For the Relationship between these movements and critical international law writing see e.g. Kennedy 1986.

[38] Steiner 1989, 95.

majority, do not concern the reality of facts but the selection of facts included in the historical account and the relationships between them. Knowing what happened does not tell you what it means. Historical narrative is impossible without a filter that identifies some facts as worth being mentioned and/or draw relationships between them. Historians create the descriptive categories for reading and talking about the past, i.e. create a discourse. No historical narrative can fully recover the past because the past did not happen in the form of a story. As a consequence, history remains a personal construct. The form of historical narrative is not the only way of doing history either. As Hayden White explains, notable masters of modern historiography have preferred non-narrative or anti-narrative modes of representation, such as meditation, the epitome, or the anatomy.[39] Proper and rigorous historical method cannot recover the originality of the past because the problem remains as to what method to choose from. From the empiricists to the Marxists and the postmoderns, there is a range of methods that stand the test of professional peer review but would lead to entirely different histories.

With these starting points in mind, critical modes of engagement use a variety of overlapping techniques to bring out the instability of history's claim to truth. A first set of techniques, emblematic for the early years of the various critical movements, treat histories about international law not as formal statements about the evolution of the law but as replications of variations of a closed set of argumentative positions.[40] Using structuralist technique, they identify oppositions, 'doubles', or other discursive formations in the deep structure of the argument in order to demonstrate "what rules govern the production of arguments and the linking of arguments together in such a familiar and conventionally acceptable way and why is it that no definite resolution of standard problems has been attained".[41] A second set of techniques goes beyond identifying the deep structure of the argument in order to unmask the 'hidden bias' within that structure. Such work explains how legal histories tell stories about the past that conceal interests and bury inequalities that naturalize, perpetuate, and universalize relationships of power, exclusion, and domination.[42] The purpose of this analysis may be to write back into history what has been excluded or enable strategies of resistance or emancipation. A third set of techniques sees historiography as 'text' thus blurring the dividing line between history and literature. The idea here is to demonstrate that legal histories employ specific literary plots, literary styles and aesthetic forms

---

39 See White 1987, 2.

40 The classic example here is the 'structuralist' phase of the work of David Kennedy and Martti Koskenniemi whose re-casting of international legal argument into soft/hard and ascending/descending positions was a watershed for the literature in the years that followed. See Kennedy 1987; Koskenniemi 2005.

41 Koskenniemi 1989, 8.

42 The classic reference point here is the work of postcolonial scholarship. See, e.g. Tony Anghie's work that demonstrates how the doctrine of sovereignty and its associated doctrines reflect the inequities of colonialism behind a mask of equality. See, e.g. Anghie 2005. See also Okafor 2000; Gathii 2007; Chimni 2004.

that acquire their meaning in the context of a wider cultural, philosophical or social context.[43] Some scholars, for example, read legal events alongside with fiction[44] or drama[45] to point to forms of emplotment that are not unique to law and can therefore be read, understood and analyzed through the techniques of literary criticism.[46] Another technique re-reads the history of international law not as the progression between doctrines, institutions or processes but as a set of individual professional commitments and projects.[47] Here the disciplinary unity of international law is exploded into numerous individual projects, suggesting that there may be as many 'international laws' as international lawyers.[48] Legal arguments are read alongside the positioned lifework of the authors, often in the form of intellectual portraits, finding uncanny resonance between what they write and their personal-ideological stakes. This way the limitation of possibilities for change presented by history can be re-read as produced by a particular combination of such commitments.

### *4.4.2 Proposition #2: International Law's Relationship to Context is Underdetermined*

In the antipodes of the third assumption above (law has a definite relationship to a social context), recent approaches to history claim that the relationship between a legal event and its context is in fact underdetermined: even if all possible facts surrounding a legal event are listed, one would still not be able to determine cause-and-effect relationships between them in a final way.[49] In order to ascertain such relationships, one needs a method for the identification of relevant factors. There is however no way of choosing between multiple methods. If there exist processes that control the production of legal events at all, these processes are complex, multi-layered and influenced by numerous factors. The point is not academic: certain etiologies are privileged at the cost of others that are denigrated or removed from sight.[50] In trying to assess legal relationships the jurist cannot avoid the

---

43 See, e.g., Berman 1992; 1993; 2004.

44 Morgan 2001.

45 See, e.g. Kennedy 1993; Morgan 1988.

46 See, e.g. Knop 2011.

47 The classic here is Koskenniemi 2002. But also Landauer and Brierly 1993; see also the various contributions to the Special Issue (2006) of the Leiden Journal of International Law—The Law and Periphery Series: Alejandro Álvarez, 17 Leiden Journal of International Law 857–1040.

48 E.g. Kennedy 1999.

49 Allott writes that "After five centuries of intrinsic and extrinsic histories of international law, five centuries of the negotiating of an idea of itself and an idea of its place within international society, there is still no functional integration of a theory of international law with a theory of international society": Allott 1999, 2.

methodological conundrums of contemporary history. The fact that the object of study is 'law' does not mean that legal technique alone can provide the answer. Take, for example, the question of ascertaining the intent of a state in a given situation. Tony Carty claims that it is impossible to determine exactly how public international law is being interpreted, applied, followed or ignored at a given moment. Knowledge of state intent is intertwined with various other parameters, such as security and power, that cannot be dissected from the question of intent. It is not only a question of evidence (e.g. state secrets that may prevent knowledge of what really happened); it is rather that, among other things, "self understanding is limited to an analysis of the extent of the power of the sovereign, measured geo-politically".[51] Another author re-reads judgments and international instruments that are normally read as leading to the formation of the right to self determination as "successive encounters with marginalized groups and their perspectives on international law", thus undermining the conventional narrative about how the right to self determination 'emerged' and what was its content.[52] A third set of techniques of destabilizing law-in-context enquiries is to describe 'everyday life' experience with the law in order to juxtapose multiple readings of the same legal 'event', none of which is decisive.[53] The claim here is that law, ultimately, cannot retain its autonomy as an object of study from, say, a social, political, personal or other context. This leads to multiple histories in the lowercase, each one of which constitutes a separate non-decisive reading. While this may not reveal the truth of the relationship to be determined between a legal event and its context, it can propose explications usually excluded from dominant histories. This leads to a rejection to the preoccupation of dominant approaches to history with the idea that change is 'caused' by something in particular. And this leads us to the slightly overlapping final proposition.

### *4.4.3 Proposition #3: Humanity Does Not Follow a Evolutionary Path*

Taking its cue from the underdetermined relationship between law and context and the absence of a decisive cause, critical histories also reject the assumption that humankind or social life are subject to linear and evolutionary change. For mainstream histories, the direction in which change occurs can be perceived as leading towards a goal that may even be unknown to the actors involved but is somehow inherent in the various stages in which history evolves. Critical histories

[50] See, e.g., the argument in Koskenniemi 2006.

[51] Carty 2006.

[52] Knop 2002.

[53] E.g. Tallgren 1999; Kennedy 1985; 1993.

argue that (a) inscribed in the notion of progress and the pattern of history's evolution are philosophical political and other assumptions which are difficult to sustain[54]; (b) such histories "reduced a complex world into hierarchical blocs, following each other in a more or less monotonous parade headed by laws of interdependence, Great power policies,"[55] and so on; (c) they fail to account for the role of individual international lawyers in the process; (d) they ultimately fail to account for how we got here. Critical histories prefer to focus on the conditions that may be dispersed in society, culture, and legal discourse that make a particular explanation about humanity or legal development seem as a compelling reality. Instead of seeing the past as made of continuities, epochs, stages of development, they look for ruptures, discontinuities and the uniqueness, rather than teleological nature, of legal phenomena. To this effect, one set of strategies brings genealogical method[56] to legal texts to re-read legal events not as manifestations of continuity and historical necessity, but rather as contingent and unique events that have become accepted through a totality of forces at play.[57] Genealogy focuses on relations of power rather than relations of meaning as causing change, not in order to discover the truth about these relations, but to undermine them. Another set of strategies explain how dominant legal historiography reads historical processes as 'the present unfolding in the past': conventional history focuses on some aspects of the past that contribute to elements that come to form the present while down-playing aspects judged not to be significant in the present.[58]

## 4.5 Engaging History in International Law Work

Previous Sections typified modes of engagement with history in international law in order to contrast, rather impressionistically, a dominant approach with a set of present-day critiques. Critical histories have put forward a significant body of criticism by using common strategies and themes of analysis and, as a consequence, raise some important questions of their own which we can begin to outline here.

The first set of questions asks whether the self-reflexivity and, in some cases, irony of critical histories towards method ultimately produces 'better' history.

[54] Skouteris 2010.

[55] Koskenniemi 2002, 6.

[56] On Foucault's genealogical method and legal analysis see, a.o., Golder 2008; de la Rasilla de la Rasilla del Moral 2009.

[57] The work of Nathaniel Berman is most characteristic here. See, in particular, the essays collected in Berman 2008.

[58] E.g. Kennedy 1997.

Despite disavowals of a strict attachment to method,[59] critical histories often make conventional use of evidence and narrative forms, dramatization and emplotment, sequential narrative, cause-and-effect reasoning, ontological statements, and so on. Locating, for example, the production of meaning in the narrative form or to textual structures (as opposed to a reflection of the world) may appear as suspect of a constructionist imposition as originalist history is. One can begin to ask whether the self-reflexivity about the limits of method really makes a difference. Not unexpectedly, the answer comes in the negative. Critical histories do not offer 'superior' methods or techniques of doing history, i.e. they do not necessarily provide more reliable, objective, legitimate, persuasive knowledge of the past compared to traditional empiricist and re-constructionist approaches. If history is what historians write, it is impossible to speak about 'good' and 'bad' (critical) history without a reference to a methodological template of choice. Some new histories also seem to care about internal (critique of internal coherence) and external critique (critique of external validity). This also seems suspect of a very ironic use of method. As historian Georg Reisch writes, the main development in the philosophy of history during the last generation may have been the proposal that history's primary cognitive device may reside in its power of narration.[60] One reason may therefore be that the use of conventional forms of historical discourse and the search of formal coherence are necessary for critical histories to acquire professional validity. Narrative, non-narrative, anti-narrative forms may be equally plausible techniques of doing history methodologically, but some forms can be less or more persuasive than others in specific contexts. Critical histories, like mainstream histories, need to rely on a set of professional practices for peer-validation: they need a form that legitimizes their content. This form could be tracked down to established group practices and supportive references from neighboring social sciences. The primary goal is the critique of 'axiomatic fictions' and not the production of 'better quality' history.

If all the above is true, if one cannot know the past in a decisive way, a second set of objections emerges that questions the point of doing legal history at all. Would it not be more useful to give up on history altogether and write about present experience with the law instead? Critical scholars signal in their work the end of History in the uppercase and the arrival of multiple histories in the lowercase. Viewed positively, this multiplicity of voices creates emancipatory space: even the most marginal and underwritten of histories can now be told, even if they never become dominant. From postcolonial, race and gender histories to the role of new social movements and new readings of the creation of doctrines and institutions, this polyphony is already empowering for many. Needless to say, not all

[59] Koskenniemi 2002 Civilizer, 9–10, describes the book as "a kind of experimentation in the writing about the disciplinary past in which the constraints of any rigorous 'method' have been set aside in an effort to create intuitively plausible and politically engaged narratives about the emergence and gradual transformation of a profession that plays with the reader's empathy".

[60] Reisch 1991, 1.

will like the outcomes of this process.[61] There is no guarantee that one's politics will be gratified by the subaltern histories that will be told and the new forces that emerge. At the same time it is fair to say that rumors about the demise of the dominant historical narratives of international law are rather exaggerated.

Seen negatively, critical histories make historiography look futile. They feel subversive and leading to a discipline without a past, and to a present with multiple readings. If every idol has clay feet, if the authority of every single piece of historical knowledge can be subverted, how does this contribute to social progress? The chopping, relentless grind mill of deconstructive analysis seems to raze everything in its path, even the good stuff. It seems to lack humility and empathy for the dilemmas of everyday life as a jurist, where actual decisions have to be taken. Reluctance to find oneself in a position of relativism is understandable. It seems to dissolve any possible ground for assessing the historical past and seems to undermine the possibility of performing much of the work that any jurist is expected to perform in her everyday tasks. How can you establish the presence of state practice or opinio iuris if every fact's validity is suspect?

Between the two extremes, originalism on the one hand and relativism on the other, there may be quite a bit of middle space. In this space, engaging history can allow new insights to make a huge difference for a lot of people and for a long time even within the present paradigm of liberal democratic political discourse. Rather than a flight from decisionism, writing into history what has been excluded, and the writing of new histories, generates imaginative space with immediate re-distributive impact.[62] If all history, professional or everyday, is constructed anyway, some of these new modes of doing history have a head start in choosing to bring to the fore their own constructed character. This is not necessarily anti-history, nihilism, or cynicism; it may well stem from acceptance of history as what it is, namely as a narrative composition about the past written here and now that acknowledges the importance of its form as a way of producing content that can be socially relevant. One can write history *and* point to its limits in conscious awareness. The "I" of the author is back in business, at the center of the quest for a new international law. This quest accepts that re-writing history is both part of the problem and part of the solution. In this sense, the author agrees with the suggestion that what would now seem needed by international legal history is "to contextualize the legal ideologies or concepts within the intellectual, social, and political environment in which they have operated".[63] This way we regard our own enquiries as everyday participation in intellectual projects that seek to figure out the processes that create stories about the past. Whether this is a confirmation

---

[61] Charlesworth 1993.

[62] Charlesworth and Chinkin 2000, esp. 308–335, describe the transformative potential of feminist readings of international law. See also the call for strategies of resistance stemming out of postcolonial critiques of international law: Chimni 2006; and Rajagopal 2003.

[63] Koskenniemi 2004, 65.

of the modernist idea that knowledge of the past is intrinsically useful,[64] or whether this is a new form of knowledge production, are questions distinct from the distributive impact of engaging history this way.

## References


Allott P (1999) International law and the idea of history. J Hist Int Law 1:1–21

Anghie A (2005) Imperialism sovereignty and the making of international law. Cambridge University Press, Cambridge, UK

Bederman D (2002) International law in antiquity. Cambridge University Press, Cambridge, UK

Berman N (1992) Modernism, nationalism, and the rhetoric of reconstruction. Yale J Law Humanit 4:351

Berman N (1993) 'But the alternative is despair!' European nationalism and the modernist renewal of international law. Harv Law Rev 106:1792

Berman N (2004) 'The appeals of the orient': colonized desire and the war on the riff. In: Knop K (ed) Gender and human rights. Oxford University Press, Oxford, UK, pp 195–230

Berman N (2008) Passions et Ambivalences. Le Colonialisme, le nationalisme, et le droit international. A. Pedone, Paris

Carty A (2006) Distance and contemporaneity in exploring the practice of states: the British archives in relation to the 1957 Oman and Muscat incident. In: Craven M, Fitzmaurice M, Vogiatzi M (eds) Time, history and international law. Martinus Nijhoff Publishing, Leiden, pp 243–244

Cass D (1996) Navigating the newstream: recent critical scholarship in international law. Nord J Int Law 65:341–383

Charlesworth H (1993) Alienating Oscar: feminist analysis in international law. In: Dallmeyer D (ed) Reconceiving reality: women and international law. American Society of International Law, Washington, DC, pp 1–18

Charlesworth H, Chinkin C (2000) Boundaries of international law: a feminist analysis. Manchester University Press, Manchester, UK

Charlesworth C, Chinkin C, Wright S (1991) Feminist approaches to international law. Am J Int Law 85:613–645

Chimni BS (2004) International institutions in the making: an imperial global state in the making. Eur J Int Law 15:1–37

Chimni BS (2006) Third world approaches to international law: a manifesto. Int Commun Law Rev 8:3–27

Craven M (2007) Introduction: international law and its histories. In: Craven M, Fitzmaurice M, Vogiatzi M (eds) Time, history and international law. Martinus Nijhoff Publishing, Leiden, pp 1–26

de la Rasilla del Moral I (2009) International law in the historical present tense (review essay). Leiden J Int Law 22:629–649

Ducrot O, Todorov T (1979) Encyclopedic dictionary of the sciences of language (trans: Porter C). John Hopkins University Press, Baltimore, pp 297–299

Elton GR (1991) Return to essentials: some reflections on the present state of historical study. Cambridge University Press, Cambridge, UK

Fairclough N (1995) Critical discourse analysis: the critical study of language. Longman Group, Essex


[64] Allott speaks of humanity's empowerment by means of history, in the direction of reaching potential previously unreached; Allott 1999, 20–21.

Fisher WW (1996–1997) Texts and contexts. The application to American legal history of the methodologies of intellectual history. Stanf Law Rev 49:1065
Foucault M (1972) The archaeology of knowledge. Pantheon Books, New York
Galindo GRB (2005) Review essay: Martti Koskenniemi and the historiographical turn in international law. Eur J Int Law 16:539
Gathii JT (2007) Imperialism, colonialism and international law. Buffalo Law Rev 54:1013–1066
Golder B (2008) Foucault and the incompletion of the law. Leiden J Int Law 21:747–763
Gordon R (1984) Critical legal histories. Stanf Law Rev 36:57
Grewe WG (2000) The epochs of international law (trans: Byers M). De Gruyter, Berlin, New York
Hinton AL, O'Neil KL (eds) (2009) Genocide: truth, memory and representation. Duke University Press, Durham
Hueck I (2001) The discipline of the history of international law—new trends and methods on the history of international law. J Hist Int Law 3:200
Janis M (2010) The American tradition of international law: great expectations 1789–1914, vol I. Oxford University Press, New York
Jenkins K (1991) Re-thinking history (London/ New York: Routledge)
Jenkins K (2003) Re-thinking history/with a new preface and conversation with the author by Alan Munslow, Routledge, Abingdon
Jenkins K (2009) At the limits of history: essays on theory and practice. Routledge, London
Kemmerer A (2008) The turning aside: on international law and its history. In: Miller R, Bratspies R (eds) Progress in international law. Martinus Nijhoff Publishers, Leiden, pp 71–93
Kennedy D (1985) Spring break. Tex Law Rev 63:1377
Kennedy D (1986) Critical theory, structuralism, and contemporary legal scholarship. New Engl Law Rev 21:209
Kennedy D (1987) International legal structures. Nomos, Baden Baden
Kennedy D (1988) A new stream of international legal scholarship. Wis Int Law J 7:1–49
Kennedy D (1993) Autumn weekends: an essay on law and everyday life. In: Sarat A, Kearns S (eds) Law in everyday life. University of Michigan Press, Ann Arbor, p 191
Kennedy D (1997) International law and the 19th century: history of an illusion. Quin Law Rev 17:99–136
Kennedy D (1999) The disciplines of international law and policy. Leiden J Int Law 12:9–133
Kennedy D, Tennant C (1994) New approaches to international law: a bibliography. Harv Int Law J 35:417–460
Knop K (2002) Diversity and self-determination in international law. Cambridge University Press
Knop K (2011) The Tokyo women's tribunal and the turn to fiction. In: Johns F, Joyce R, Pahuja S (eds) Events: the force of international law. Routledge, Abingdon, pp 145–164
Koskenniemi M (1989) From apology to utopia: the structure of international legal argument. (Helsinki: Lakimiesliiton Kustannus)
Koskenniemi M (2002) The gentle civilizer of nations: the rise and fall of international law, 1870–1960. Cambridge University Press, Cambridge
Koskenniemi M (2004) Why history of international law today. Rechtsgeschichte 4:61–66
Koskenniemi M (2005) From apology to Utopia: the structure of international legal arguments, reissue with epilogue. Cambridge University Press, Cambridge
Koskenniemi M (2006) Review of M. Janis.The American tradition of international law. Am J Int Law 100:266–270
Landauer C, Brierly JL (1993) The modernization of international law. Vanderbilt J Transnatl Law 25:881–917
Lesaffer R (2007) International law and its history: the story of an unrequited love. In: Craven M, Fitzmaurice M, Vogiatzi M (eds) Time, history and international law. Martinus Nijhoff Publishing, Leiden, pp 27–42
Maine H (1861) Ancient law: its connection with the early history of society and its relation to modern ideas. Dent & Sons, London
Morgan E (1988) Retributory theater. Am J Int Law Policy 3:1

Morgan E (2001) The other death of international law. Leiden J Int Law 14:3–24
Munslow A (2006) Deconstructing history, 2nd edn. Routledge, London
Neff S (1990) Friends but no allies: economic liberalism and the law of nations. Columbia University Press, New York
Nijman J (2004) The concept of international legal personality: an enquiry into the history and theory of international law. T.M.C Asser Press, The Hague
Nussbaum A (1954) A concise history of the law of nations, 1947, 2nd edn. Macmillan, New York
Okafor OC (2000) Redifining legitimate statehood: international law and state fragmentation in Africa. Kluwer Law International, Dordrecht
Onuma Y (2000) When was the law of international society born?—an enquiry of the history of international law from an intercivilizational perspective. J Hist Int Law 2:1–66
Paltridge B (2007) Discourse analysis: an introduction. Continuum, London
Philips L, Jørgensen M (2002) Discourse analysis as theory and method. Sage Publications, London
Rajagopal B (2003) International law from below: development, social movements and third world resistance. Cambridge University Press, Cambridge, Cambridge
Reisch GA (1991) Chaos, theory and narrative. History and Theory 30:1–20
Schwarzenberger G (1962) The frontiers of international law. Yb World Aff 6:251
Shaw MN (2003) International Law. Cambridge University Press, Cambridge
Skouteris T (2010) The Notion of progress in international law discourse. T.M.C. Asser Institute, The Hague
Steiner G (1989) Real presences. Faber, London
Steiner G (1998) After Babel—aspects of language and translation, 3rd edn. Oxford University Press, Oxford
Tallgren I (1999) We did it? The vertigo of everyday life at the diplomatic conference on the establishment of an International Criminal Court. Leiden J Int Law 12:683–707
Todorov T (2009) Memory as remedy for evil. J Int Crim Justice 7:447–462
Verzijl JHW (1968–1998) International law in a historical perspective. 12 Volumes, Leyden, Sijthoff
White H (1987) The content of the form: narrative discourse and historical representation. John Hopkins University Press, Baltimore
Widdowson H (2004) Text, context, pretext: critical issues in discourse analysis. Blackwell Publishing, Oxford

# Chapter 5
# Hugo Grotius in the Contemporary Memory of International Law: Secularism, Liberalism, and the Politics of Restatement and Denial

**John D. Haskell**

**Abstract** The specter of Hugo Grotius remains an important reference point within the conceptual vocabulary of international law. In this paper, I provide a brief analysis of how Grotius' legacy functions within the rhetoric of international legal texts via lessons from the 'New Approaches to International Law' tradition (e.g., David Kennedy, TWAIL), as well as other heterodoxical sources that found a place within international legal scholarship through advances by the 'critical studies' movement more generally (e.g., Alain Badiou, Judith Bulter). In particular, the paper critically takes up the rhetoric of Grotius in relation to two mainstream claims: first, that modern international law is 'secular', and second, that international law, in relation to this turn to a secular orientation, is committed to some cosmopolitan ethic of 'tolerance'. Offering alternative readings of Grotius in light of these claims, I conclude the paper with some brief suggestions about how we might participate in a new tradition of remembering Hugo Grotius.

I am deeply grateful to the generosity, encouragement, and thoughts of first and foremost Peter Fitzpatrick and Mark Janis, as well as Jason Beckett, Jose Maria Beneyto, Bill Bowring, Stephen Chan, Justo Corti, Matthew Craven, Catriona Drew, Florian Hoffmann, David Kennedy, Rob Knox, Boris Mamlyuk, Susan Marks, Anne-Charlotte Martineau, Ugo Mattei, Scott Newton, Reut Paz, Ignacio de la Rasilla del Moral, Akbar Rasulov, and Joseph Singer. I also wish to express my thanks to the Institute for Global Law and Policy (IGLP), the International University College, Turin (IUC), the Centre for the study of Colonialism, Empire and International Law (CCEIL), the Erik Castrén Institute of International Law and Human Rights (ECI), the Institute for the study of Political Economy and Law (IPEL), the editorial staff at Emory International Law Review (where an earlier but similar version of this paper was published in 2011), and my colleagues at Durham Law School and Mississippi College School of Law. The views expressed in this article are, of course, solely my own.

J. D. Haskell (✉)
Mississippi College School of Law, 151 East Griffith Street, Jackson, MA, USA
e-mail: johndhaskell@gmail.com

J. M. Beneyto and D. Kennedy (eds.), *New Approaches to International Law*,
DOI: 10.1007/978-90-6704-879-8_5,

## Contents



## 5.1 Introduction Grotius as Narrative

Hugo Grotius (1583–1645) frequently occupies the title, 'father of international law'. While the origins of professional lineage were a source of professional and personal conflict for jurists in the nineteenth century, scholars today tend to treat Grotius as either a symbolic marker of changing historical thought, or the symbolic figure of a style or school of global governance.[1] In the first instance, Grotius is important because he is said to have made a methodological leap in one form or another from a theological to a secular frame of jurisprudential thinking, and in so doing, characterizes the dilemmas of governance in terms familiar to modernity.[2] For other authors, the legacy of Grotius is not directly this shift from ecclesiastic to secular authority, but rather that his efforts are remembered to spark the political aspiration, implied to be at the core of international law itself, toward a more liberal tolerance of difference and a sentiment of restraint toward over-aggrandizing political agendas.

These two contemporary streams of remembrance operate within a dense background of assumptions about the nature and possibilities of the global order, which raise at least three sets of curiosities. First, in light of nuanced scholarship of Grotius' primary materials in recent decades, what does an emphasis on the actual content of Grotius' work impart about the character of his times, and through what

[1] In the 1870s, international jurists entered into heated contests over who deserved the right to be claimed the 'father' of international law. For instance, a group of jurists, including T. Asser, T. Holland, G. Macinni, and T. Twiss, drafted a resolution and formed a committee to erect a national monument in honor of A. Gentili. Pilgrimages were made to Gentili's hometown, and the Italian government officially requested the U.K. for his remains (the grave, however, was unable to be located). Others, such as A.J. Levy objected, arguing that Grotius should have the honor of having his statue erected first. An English committee was formed in 1875 to add their weight, with Prince Leopold sitting as the honorary president (Phillimore carrying out the actual presidential duties). See der Molen 1937, 63.

[2] In the nineteenth century, Grotius was primarily remembered for a theory of human sociability whereby cosmopolitan society stood in for the 'state of nature'. In the twentieth century, Grotius is often recalled as a narrative devise to capture what is seen as the historical shift from the insulated hierarchical authority of the Church and Emperor to a rapidly expanding international system of formally equal sovereign states based on normative rules of general agreement.

lens should we organize our understanding (e.g., political, juridical, theological, and so on)? Second, what inspires the almost cyclical (or perhaps more perversely, fetishistic) attraction to Grotius in the fields of international law and politics, and how might this help us better understand both the psychological and structural underpinnings of contemporary practice, or even the nature and trajectory of the profession in a broader sense? And third, in lieu of any findings, what if any possibility does this attraction to Grotius open up for future strategic, or even imaginative engagement? In sum, what stories do the Grotius rhetoric allow us to tell about the international legal order, and do such stories carry any political, if not personal, impact?[3]

It is these questions that I attempt to grapple with in this paper in the hopes of providing a concise synthesis of the various engagements within the Grotian tradition to better understand the imaginative contours of our contemporary professional vocabularies and reflect on any emancipatory possibilities this might open up. What seems particularly striking is while ever more scholarship exposes a strong empirical dissonance in respect to the memory of Grotius, such representations continue to exercise powerful sway over ongoing discussions about the past, present, and future of global governance. In response, I have organized the paper into three themes, which overlapping in some respects, are nevertheless helpful in parceling out the various approaches and motivations at work in the literature. The first and second sections provide an overview and then a revisionist account of the claims to what might be labeled the turn to 'the secular' and 'liberal tolerance'. In the third section, the paper moves to reflect more broadly upon the implications of this attraction, attempting particularly to deduce some possible motivations for the continuous misreading of Grotius' actual work. In conclusion, I briefly trace out some initial suggestions about an alternative future toward the legacy of the Grotian tradition, what might be characterized as a shift from a *politics of restatement and denial* to a *politics of truth*.

## 5.2 The Secularization of International Law

In the first contemporary stream of argument, Grotius is viewed as setting forth a secularized restatement of natural law whereby political ethics now become capable of articulation independent of any theological premise. In the first half of the

[3] Without playing into any post-modern angst, it is productive, I think, to keep in mind David Kennedy's injunction that the very act of analyzing the past (not to mention casting judgment) is to do violence to the doctrinal and theoretical content of earlier scholarship, and can often misguide us to think that our vision is somehow more sophisticated and less contradictory. See Kennedy 1986, 98.

twentieth century, though still prevalent in the mainstream literature,[4] this claim was typically supported by pointing to an early quotation from *De Iure Belli ac Pacis*: '[w]hat we have been saying would have a degree of validity even if we should concede that which cannot be conceded without the utmost wickedness, that there is no God, or that the affairs of men are of no concern to Him'.[5] More recent scholarship has radically undermined this line of argument, pointing out that Grotius' intent here was not to push Christendom toward some agnostic reappraisal of political order, but quite paradoxically, to silence the seventeenth century Pyrrhonic skepticism of God's existence by demonstrating that Christianity was left unscathed even through the use of human 'right reason'.[6] In addition to his voluminous work in the field of Christian apologetics and tragedy dramas based on Biblical figures,[7] scholars have typically pointed to the very next line following Grotius' famous passage as proof of his religious conviction: 'The very opposite of this view [that there is no God, or that the affairs of men are of no concern to Him] has been implanted in us partly by reason, partly by unbroken tradition, and confirmed by many proofs as well as by miracles attested by all ages...[so that] it follows that we must without exception render obedience to God as our Creator.'[8] In response,

---

[4] See e.g., Baumgold 1993, 9; see also Kunz 1961, 951–52 (stating that "[t]he Protestant Grotius, who wrote the first treatise on international law, was still strongly influenced by the traditional natural law, but he secularized it by stating that natural law would be valid even if there were no God. This secularization profoundly changed the character of natural law... the Catholic natural law is ... discovered by man's recta ratio—a term stemming from the Stoics... [yet] necessarily presupposes the Christian faith in the Creator... with Grotius this right reason becomes the basis of natural law"); Nussbaum 1947, 105 (claiming that "Grotius made an important step toward the emancipation of international law from theology by his famous pronouncement [about] the law of nature"); Nussbaum 1943, 466 (stating that Grotius "claimed in earnest that the law of nations and international law derived there from could subsist without a divine foundation"); and Pound 1925, 686 (arguing that Grotius, along with other Protestant jurists, helped severe theology from jurisprudential thought).

[5] See Grotius 1925, para II.

[6] See George 1999, 605 (providing a useful overview of the various positions and issues without falling into more traditional misreadings of Grotius, and situating Grotius within a larger return of interest in international legal history and religion); see also Kennedy 1986, 79; Schneewind 1998, 66–81.

[7] Among Grotius' religious work, include the tragedies, The Exile of Adam (1601) and The Passion of Christ (1608), his Commentaries on the Old Testament (1644) and New Testament (1641–50), and his Christian apologetics, On the Satisfaction of Christ against Faustus Socinus (1617) and The Truth of the Christian Religion (1627).

[8] See Grotius 1925, para II. In fact, this mode of argument did not originate with Grotius, but was a common technique for earlier Catholic jurists. For instance, in making his case for the theologian as the authoritative final word of the law of nature, Suarez writes, "that even if God did not exist, or if He did not make use of reason, or if He did not judge of things correctly, nevertheless, if the same dictates of right reason dwelt within man, constantly assuring him, for example, that lying is evil, those dictates would still have the same legal character which they actually possess because they would constitute a law pointing out that evil exists intrinsically in the object." See Schneewind 1998, 60 (quoting Francisco Suarez's 1612 On Law and On God the Lawgiver).

scholars that mark off Grotius as a "great pioneer of modern thinking" maintain that these various appeals to Christianity are not confessions of deep religiosity, but an agnostic strategy to win over Christian populations and their leaders.[9] For legal historians, such as Richard Tuck, Grotius' work falls within the humanist tradition and its emphasis upon the inescapability of the aggressive and self-interested nature of humanity, and in fact, was therefore by no surprise largely motivated by Grotius' personal commitments to Dutch colonialism (which, in its expansion, was increasingly coming into contact with foreign cultures) and his own families' economic advantage (Dutch shareholders in the East Indies' Company).[10]

To some extent, at least at first glance, Grotius' minimal Christianity does seem an agnostic effort to find a common settlement between societies with competing jurisdictions, laws and religious doctrines. In laying out the fundamental tenets of Christianity, Grotius shies away from all sectarian doctrines that might upset relationships between Dutch Protestants and Spanish and Portuguese Catholics whereby in place of any talk about the Trinity or the need for redemption, all that remains are a relatively tame set of tenets: there is a single God that actually cares for all humanity and sits unseen in judgment over their behavior, that Jesus is the resurrected Son of God, and that the faithful will enjoy everlasting life after death, while the wicked will be punished.[11] Moreover, his theorizing on the laws pertaining to warfare do not follow the scholastic tradition of limiting (or even prohibiting) war, but on the contrary, seems to argue adamantly for rather cynical, almost amoral principles of behavior for both individuals and states: states and individuals aspire to sociability, but are equally prone to violent clashes of self-interest; the possession of natural rights allows for autonomous free will, but also the legitimacy of contracting oneself or community into slavery; and though Christian sovereigns are to refrain from barbarity in their military hostilities with one another, in a move foreshadowing later French colonial justifications, they have both the divine and natural sanction to invade and conquer foreign territory by whatever means necessary under the pretext of the 'benefit of human Society'. Thus, Grotius' willingness to discover natural law in the practices of sovereigns, the subjectivizaton of just cause rationale in warfare, as well as his prolific use of ancient classical authorities to arrive at conflicting opinions, suggest on some level that his ultimate decision to locate normative authority in a universal, divinely

[9] This is a common implicit and explicit theme taken up by a great number of authors. See e.g., Cassirer 1946, 172; see also Koskenniemi 2005, 95–108; Schneewind 1998, 65–81; Tuck 1999, 78–108.

[10] See Tuck, 1999, 78–108. Others have also adopted more cynical readings of Grotius, arguing that his reasoning was not founded on any ideological, intellectual, or ethical basis, but more directly, to serve his own material and political interests. See e.g., Schwarzenberger 1990, 301–312.

[11] For a useful, but concise overview of Grotius' religious tenets, see Schneewind 1998, 65–81.

willed framework was less his agreement with prior scholastic theologians and jurists, than it was the afterthought of a humanist to make his theories palpable to a Christian-colored political order.[12]

Upon closer inspection, however, to claim Grotius as some 'avant-garde of secular jurisprudence' is forced to suppress the overall tenor of his writings and personal beliefs, as well as miss strong thematic linkages between his 'secular' work and the "profoundly Christian" traditions of the Protestant humanists and late medieval Catholic jurists.[13] First, the minimal Christianity he expounds in both his political polemic concerning warfare, *De Iure Belli ac Pacis*, and his Christian apologetics, *The Truth of the Christian Religion*, is not simply the work of an agnostic strategically wooing Christian states, but very much in keeping with his own personal religious convictions as a Remonstrant and a pupil in Leiden under Arminius. As both a diplomat and theologian by professional calling, and politically repressed along with other Remonstrant members by Calvinist forces in the Netherlands and condemned to life imprisonment (though his wife engineered his daring escape, being smuggled out of prison in a suitcase), Grotius' avoidance of points of doctrine was not conceived as a neutral position, but firmly understood to be a religious polemic in favor of a broad understanding of Christendom.[14]

Second, Grotius' rather 'thin' conception of human sociability—whereby human nature wars between the desire for rational order amongst each other and conflicting self-interests—was not some nascent twentieth century 'realpolitik' that he applied evenly across the global spectrum, but aimed particularly at accentuating the difference between Christian and non-Christian societies in accordance with the Protestant and Catholic humanist traditions from the late medieval and Reformation/Renaissance eras. In the Catholic tradition, the propaganda campaign for the anti-Turkish Crusades carried out by Pope Leo X (1513–21) produced a robust corpus of humanist jurisprudence that condemned warfare between Christian powers while justifying unrestrained warfare upon non-Christian societies.[15] Humanist jurists by the early sixteenth century viewed

---

[12] The humanist, or 'oratorical', tradition 'drew most extensively on the literary and rhetorical writings of the ancient world', and, in a skeptical register, commonly employed the rhetorical technique of 'leaving the reader rather unclear about where the author stood'. See Tuck 1999, 16–17 (referencing Seigel's 1968, Rhetoric and Philosophy in Renaissance Humanism: The Union of Eloquence and Wisdom, Petrarch to Valla). See generally Tuck 1977.

[13] See generally Grewe 2005; see also Kennedy 1986, 79.

[14] See e.g., Janis 2004, 121–126; see generally Stompf 2006.

[15] For instance, Erasmus is remembered as a passionate advocate for peace, but in fact espoused a militant antipathy to non-Christians. "France alone remains not infected with heretics, with Bohemian schismatics, with Jews, with half-Jewish marranos, and untouched by the contagion of Turkish neighbours." See Tuck 1999, 30 (quoting from Vol. 4 of Erasmus' Collected Works). In relation to a war against the Turks, Erasmus adopts a Machiavellian tone, "[I]f war… is not wholly avoidable, that kind would be a lesser evil than the present unholy conflicts and clashes between Christians. If mutual love does not bind them together, a common enemy will surely unite them after a fashion, and there will be a sort of a common purpose, even if true harmony is lacking." Ibid.

inter-Christian warfare as potentially just for both Catholic and Protestant camps, falling into an almost Darwinian explanation of Providence's design—the humanist jurist, François Connan, for instance, echoing his master, Andrea Alciato that "you can investigate and speculate all you like, but you will find no other reason ... [than that] by a tacit law of nature the weaker give way to the more powerful; from which single principle all the laws of war derive."[16] In other words, Grotius' distinction between just and formally legal wars was not by any means a 'significant' leap from a unified conception of faith to a subjective agnosticism,[17] but actually a popular technique among Christian jurists and theologians to unify the populations and leaders around an external enemy, thereby preserving the balance of power within Christendom itself and guarding against any revolutionary uprising within its own territories. Legitimate warfare to dismantle the status quo was bracketed outside of the domestic realm of Europe, whereas internal conflict could be characterized as illegitimate violence that demanded immediate police action to preserve what was in fact some mythical homogeneous stability (though keeping open the possibility of exceptions, e.g., the Dutch toward the Spanish).[18]

It is within his passages concerning the justifications and conditions of warfare, especially in relation to foreign non-European territories, that Grotius is perhaps most often misread to announce the dawning of the modern secular regime of international law. In a characteristic excerpt that touches on some of the more popular themes said to point toward a secular understanding of politics and law, Grotius writes:

> Kings, and those who are invested with a Power equal to that of Kings, have a Right to exact Punishments, not only for Injuries committed against themselves, or their Subjects, but likewise, for those which do not peculiarly concern them, but which are, in any Persons whatsoever, grievous Violations of the Law of Nature or Nations. For the Liberty of consulting the Benefit of human Society, by Punishments, which at first, as we have seen, was in every particular Person, does now, since Civil Societies, and Courts of Justice, have been instituted, reside in those who are possessed of the supreme power... we follow [the tradition of writers] who hold that War is lawful against those who offend against Nature; which is contrary to the Opinion of Vitoria, Vasquez, Azorius, Molina, and

[16] See Tuck 1999, 33 (quoting from Andrea Alciato's 1571 Paradoxorum Juris Civilis Libros).

[17] See Koskenniemi, 2005, 103–104.

[18] See e.g., Wight 2005, 29–62 (covering a number of seminal themes in Grotius' work, and describing Grotius' conception of an inner and outer conception of political identity: the outer circle that which embraces all humanity under natural law, and an inner circle of the corpus Christianorum bound by laws of Christ, and at least in part defined in their unity against Turkish populations). Though not typically brought together, Grotius' understanding and strategy of political identity seems to bear a close relationship to Carl Schmitt, another figure who has become a trendy academic figure of study over the past two decades. See e.g., Schmitt 2005; see also Schmitt 2003.

> others, who seem to require, towards making a War just, that he who undertakes it be injured in himself, or in his State, or that he has some jurisdiction over the Person against whom the War is made. For they assert, that the Power of Punishing is properly an Effect of Civil Jurisdiction; whereas our Opinion is, that it proceeds from the Law of Nature.[19]

The passage carries a distinctly modern feel a la Clausewitz: warfare is not simply a necessary evil that comes with humanity's sinful nature as would be the case with Hobbes, rather it is the very continuation of law by other means.[20] War is litigation, or at the very least, wrapped up in juristic exercises—what David Kennedy has discussed in the modern context of the American military as 'lawfare'.[21] Moreover, the rejection of the neo-scholastic tradition suggests both a prima facie rejection of faith in the hierarchies and dogma of medieval Christendom, and at least a hesitant step away from any overarching normative natural order toward a positivist regime of subjective reciprocal rights held by competing sovereign entities.[22] To be sure, the 'law of nature' is still referenced, but it is now coterminous with the 'law of nations', and in the place of ecclesiastic authorities imposing the wishes of the divine, sovereignty now seems to take an anthropological turn whereby it is left to secular rulers to mete out material punishments on behalf of the 'benefit of human society'.

This, however, does not seem to actually be the case; the turn to subjectivity and the emphasis on state sovereignty had nothing to do with any atheistic or agnostic turn in intellectual disposition, but in fact orthodoxies of the Protestant Reformation initiated by Luther and his jurist comrades. Concerning subjectivity and the distancing from ecclesiastic authority, Luther argued against the Church as mediator between the sinner and God to instead present the laity itself as the living Church, and each believer their own priest. On the one hand, this meant that each individual, as their own "lord", was granted "the splendid privilege" of "inesti-

---

[19] See Grotius 1925, para II, 20.40.

[20] See generally Clausewitz 1989.

[21] See generally Kennedy 2006; see also Berman 2004, 1.

[22] 'Grotius' most important contribution to modern theory was his theory of rights… Instead of being something… a person has… [t]he concept becomes subjectivized, centered on the person…'. See Haakonssen 1985, 240; see generally Tuck 1977.

mable power and liberty".[23] Drawing here upon the tradition set by thirteenth and fourteenth century Catholic theologian reformers,[24] Luther anticipates Grotius (if not Kierkegaard), to celebrate the subjective Christian experience of "the inner man" who nurtures faith away from the sinful crowd. In this sense, the Lutheran movement (and which would be carried further in Calvinism) swept away the Church as the locus and vehicle of the sacred with its emphasis on the necessity of salvation through a wholehearted personal adhesion. On the other hand, however, the priestly calling brought not only freedom, but also the responsibility to imitate the example of Christ in everyday life, a duty of sociability and positive reciprocal care. "Christ has made it possible for us, provided we believe in him, to be not only his brethren, co-heirs, and fellow-kings, but also his fellow-priests," reminds Luther, "A man does not live for himself alone, he lives only for others"—and not only for the living, but also to owe fidelity, an almost Aristotelian sociability so famous in Grotius' own legacy, to all the Christian believers who had already died, the "saints in heaven".[25] Thus, while the church itself had lost is central mediating role, salvation continued to be at least implicitly premised on connections to a wider order, only the sacramental life was now brought into the daily vocations and relationships of the citizenry and its government whereby our understanding of 'the good' would only be discoverable within human life.

By denying the distinction between the sacred and profane, the anthropological turn that we begin to witness coming into focus more fully with Grotius, therefore,

---

[23] See Witte Jr. 2002, 95; see generally Berman 2003.

[24] At least as early as Norman Anonymous and John de Salisbury, various more critical theological traditions within Catholicism (and in early Protestant with the writings of authors like Johann Oldendorp who would provide detailed lists of instances where the citizen's conscience might require disobedience of civil authorities) emphasized the role of the citizen in both political and religious life. See generally O'Donovan and O'Donovan 1999; see also Berman 1983, 1–3. In the dominant historical and legal literature, the rise of the individual is conveniently located somewhere in the fifteenth or sixteenth century, helping us to mark the transition into the modern era of some emancipated existence (whether that is articulated on the formal horizontal equality of sovereign states or the subjectivity of personal experience that undermines any objective normative order). When scholars do talk about the pre-modern era, the concepts of the individual and community are said to be largely non-existent, either suppressed beneath an imperial-religious logic or simply not yet even within the imaginative framework to be grasped in the first place. However, what we in fact witness in the pre-modern period is not only an awareness of both individual and social components of political life, but a militancy that feels shockingly radical to standard liberal democratic notions of civil society, at least since the aftermath of the French and American Revolutions. While individuals were to submit to the authority of their leaders, even when they strongly disagreed, they also had the divine obligation to excommunicate their leadership, body, and/or soul, under a variety of conditions. Emphasizing seventeenth century notions of social contract (e.g., Locke, organic political theory) or placing absolute sovereign authority in the nation state (e.g., Bodin, Hobbes) potentially robs the vitality and agency given to people in older, more radical traditions of individualism and social consciousness.

[25] See Witte 2002, 98 (citing Luther, and referencing Paul Althaus' 1966 The Theology of Martin Luther). In some respects, this seems to anticipate later jurists in the nineteenth century who claimed their work as part of an organic heritage of the dead, the living, and future generations.

does not mark a turning away from Christian thought, but rather its interpenetration into the routine activities of this life. Instrumental rationality takes on fresh importance as the very act of coming to God, as well as the marker of actively belonging to a shared political community.[26] As Kennedy observes, Grotius' willingness to 'find natural law in the practices of sovereigns' is not so much any 'relocation of normative authority from divine to sovereign will' but that 'natural law accords with and is binding as a matter of divine law' whereby the sovereign may be the source or vehicle, but by no means the origin of the law of nations.[27] Writing during what was in many ways the tail end of the Protestant Reformation, the turn to secular authorities in Grotius' text again displays a characteristically Lutheran tenant: that the specific practices and rules of the territorialized secular administrations were in fact the albeit imperfect manifestation, or 'mask', of God's will.[28] Breaking from the scholastic tradition that human reason could prove the divine sanctity of moral propositions, Luther's colleague, the eminent Philip Melanchthon argued that God has implanted certain 'elements of knowledge', whereby humanity could use reason to discern the general principles of God's will, but only imperfectly. For Melanchthon, the state had the duty "of transforming the general principles of natural law into detailed rules of positive law" that could meet the 'practical considerations of social utility and the common good', what he called nothing other than 'rational positive law'.[29] In other words, 'rational positive law' straddled the line between earth and heaven: on the one hand, the divine will of God manifest through the deliberate labor of the faithful; on the other hand, carried out under the limitations of humanity's sinful nature, an always

[26] This all looks increasingly familiar to our own contemporary period: sober, disciplined production and an attitude of civility that makes possible a life of commerce and acquisition now replace the aristocratic celebration of undisciplined ease and the warrior ethos of seeking personal glory. For studies that circle around this theme in relation to capitalism and religion, see generally Goodchild 2002; see also Hilton 1991; Piggin 1985 (arguing that missionaries played a significant role in the Enlightenment confidence in human reason and the ethical value of efficiency and usefulness); Tawney 1926 (tracing the rise of capitalism back to the medieval era); Taylor 1989, 211–247; Weber 1905; Wright 1988.

[27] See Kennedy 1986, 79.

[28] For Luther, God is 'hidden' in the earthy kingdom and only appears to humanity through the 'masks' of human reason and will, the rule of law and its political officers, and in the conscientious work of believers. The civil law, therefore, not only expresses the natural limitations and needs of humanity, but also serves, in the words of St. Paul, as "our schoolmaster to bring us unto Christ", teaching and coercing us both to civil and spiritual morality. See Witte 2002, 92–175 (discussing these ideas in the teachings of Luther, Melanchthon, Eisermann, and Oldendrop).

[29] Melanchthon was perhaps the leading jurist of the Reformation, drafting the chief declaration of Lutheran theology, the Augsburg Confession and its Apology, and a co-author of the Scmalkaldic Articles, along with writing dozens of instruction books and biblical commentaries. For a discussion of Melanchthon's legal theory, see Berman 2003, 77–87, 405–411; see also Witte 2002, 121–141.

incomplete quest for perfection, which could only seek the eternal through its preoccupation with the "political, economic, and social needs in given times and places".[30] Thus, for the Protestant lineage of jurists, including Grotius, the violation of the fundamental laws of nature or of nations is therefore not an end in itself, but rather an extension of some violation against the divine foundation of existence.

## 5.3 The Rise of Political Liberalism

In the second stream of argument, Grotius earns the title "father of international law" for advocating what is said to be a liberal universalism that embraced diverse religious and political forms (often claimed nowadays as a central tenet of modern international law), sometimes called the 'Grotian tradition'. In this vision, the losers are the medieval res publica Christiana, symbolized by the Holy Roman Empire and the Catholic Church, as its "objective hierarchy of normative meaning" gives way to a pristine European order of nation-states premised on "sovereign equality, religious agnosticism and balance of powers."[31] In a classic description of this claim in relation to Grotius' political liberalism, Hersh Lauterpacht writes in the immediate aftermath of the Second World War:

> [Let us] explain the significance ... of the Grotian tradition in the history of the law of nations. He secularized the law of nature. He gave it added authority and dignity by making it an integral part of the exposition of a system of law which became essential to

[30] Reut Paz's study of early twentieth century and interwar Jewish-German jurists provides an interesting discussion of the idea of international law as a 'ladder' between humanity and God, drawing persuasively upon a mix of Jewish religious thought, philosophy, and socio-historical archival materials—and more generally, innovative in its focus on the relationship between Judaism and modern international law. See generally Paz 2008.

[31] See Koskenniemi 2005, at 71–157 (encoding a series of linear movements, from the ancient to the modern, from belief to rationality, from objectivity to subjectivity, from hierarchical to democratic/plural models of authority, and so on). For an emphasis on a similar set of founding positions, see also Grewe 2005, 20–29, 143, 170, 291 (noting the importance of the balance of power, formal equality and religious tolerance in de-centering the authority of the Pope and Emperor); Schmitt 2005, at 140–154 (focusing on the 'detheologization of public life" in response to "creedal civil wars" through a horizontal organization of formally equal territorial European states intent to maintain a balance of power).

> civilized life... distinguished not only by the fact of its recognition of a source of law different from and, in proper cases, superior to the will of sovereign states... [but] largely based on and deduced form the nature of man as a being intrinsically moved by a desire for social life, endowed with an ample measure of goodness, altruism, and morality, and capable of acting on general principles of learning from experience... [desiring] peaceful and organized life according to the measure of his intelligence ...[32]

In what must have felt particularly relevant to a European landscape torn asunder by nationalist passion and violent superstitions, Lauterpacht sees the Grotian spirit of international law to function as a restraining influence on political aggression, as well as the source and articulation of morality ('endowed with ... goodness, altruism and morality') and knowledge ('learning from experience'). Here, Lauterpacht adopts the traditional narrative that Grotius "secularized" the law of nations, which in turn, provides the groundwork for claiming international law as a detached process of peaceful resolution. In light of our discussion so far, we might be suspicious about Lauterpacht's claim that international law emerged in the waning twilight of religion as a neutral, deliberative process devoid of religious or political prejudices. However, other scholars have specifically appealed to the religious, or at least spiritual character, of the Grotian tradition to claim international law as a tolerant, universalizing project in otherwise strikingly similar terms to Lauterpacht's image. Writing only a few years after Lauterpacht, the British jurist and legal historian Arthur Nussbaum emphasizes the close link between the spiritual and liberal character of Grotius' work:

> A cognate trait of great importance was Grotius' tolerance... Grotius a pious Protestant writing at the time of the most savage of religious wars, refrained from any word which might have offended Catholic feeling... want[ing] to find a synthesis for Protestant and Catholics alike... [and thereby] opened a new path by the doctrine of what he called the temperament of warfare ... urg[ing] moderation for reasons of humanity, religion and farsighted policy... From [his writing] emerges the picture of a man absorbed in his ideals, of a devout seeker after truth and right, and of a passionate and unswerving advocate of humaneness and conciliation—a picture borne out of his life. The spiritual light shining through the fabric of his work explains the success of his undertaking... His work has remained a living force... the essence of his thought has passed into the conscience of the civilized world. His name has become a symbol of justice in international relations.[33]

The claim being made here, I believe, is more radical that what Lauterpacht proposed, though it equally results in support of the idea that international law

---

[32] See Lauterpacht 1946, 24–25. Resurrecting the Grotian tradition of Hersh Lauterpacht, Martti Koskenniemi has characterized it as "a morality of attitude ... of seriousness... a morality of tolerance and of personal and professional virtue... a morality of scales, controlled by the attempt to balance right with duty and freedom with reason... a morality of control and self control, for which the greatest desire is the end of desire... [taking] for granted the intrinsic rationality of a morality of sweet reasonableness, the non-metaphysical doctrine of the golden middle." See Koskenniemi 1997, 215; see also Jeffery 2006, 223–250 Hersh Lauterpacht, the Realist Challenge and the Grotian Tradition in twentieth century International Relations, 12 European Journal of International Relations 223–250 (2006).

[33] See Nussbaum 1947, 105–112.

expounds a universalizing faith that can tolerate religious and political diversity. The argument is not the traditional claim made by international lawyers that the discipline became secular over time, and thereby was able to engage with religious passions in a detached, more enlightened way. Rather, in Nussbaum' strain of argument, international law is part of a living Christian lineage, but it is now this very religiosity itself which is now seen as one of the key elements in international law's ability to embrace a more universalist vision of emancipation and brotherhood. In more recent years, the American legal historian Mark Janis has eloquently argued for this version of the Grotian tradition:

> It was the imprisonment and exile of this religious and political liberal that both provided the time to write and inspired the theme of De Jure Belli ac Pacis... Trained and famed as a theologian as well as a jurist, Grotius unashamedly brought the Bible to the law of nations. It is important to note that Grotius brought religion to the discipline not to exclude other religious groups (be they Calvinists, Catholics, Jews or Moslems), but to show that his religion, a liberal and universal faith, proved that the law of nations was meant to include all peoples... His... [a] liberal Arminian universalism... [at] a time of religious wars among fiercely conservative faiths... was a more forgiving faith, but a faith nonetheless, that could tolerate religious diversity. Grotius employed this liberal religion as a critical source for proof of legal principles which could tolerate both religious and political diversity among the nations.[34]

At first glance, the secular and religious version of the Grotian tradition of international law as a tolerant, civilizing force upon global governance seems to be affirmed in selective passages from *De Jure Belli Pacis*. Within the more secularist version of the tradition, Grotius seems to occasionally sweep away the primacy of the entire Christian normative order in favor of a formally equal, yet divergent array of sovereign authorities:

> Just as, in fact, there are many ways of living, one being better than another, and out of so many ways of living each is free to select that which he prefers, so also a people can select the form of government it wishes; and the extent of its legal right in the matter is not to be measured by the superior excellence of this or that form of government, in regard to which different men hold different views, but by its free choice.[35]

Likewise, this same sort of liberalism also seems to crop up in more religious readings of the Grotian tradition, especially in his polemics in favor of the legitimacy of agreements between Christian and heathen states:

> Do we perhaps believe that we have nothing in common with persons who have not accepted the Christian faith? Such a belief would be very far removed from the pious doctrine of Augustine, who declares (in his interpretation of the precept of Our Lord whereby we are bidden to love our neighbors) that the term 'neighbors' obviously includes every human being... Accordingly, not only is it universally admitted that the protection of infidels from injury (even from injury by Christians) is never unjust, but it is furthermore maintained, by authorities who have examined this particular point (including Vitoria) that alliances and treaties with infidels may in many cases by justly contracted, for

---

[34] See Janis 2004, 121–126.

[35] See Schneewind 1998, 73 (quoting Grotius).

> the purpose of defending one's own rights, too. Such a course of action was adopted (so we are told) by Abraham, Isaac, David, Solomon, and the Maccabees...[36]

It is tempting to read these passages (as so many do) as the initial soundings of liberal political thought, sowing the first kernels of what have become the familiar ethics of disengaged, subjective rationality and formal equality of sovereign nation-states so important nowadays in the daily posture of international law. This temptation contains some validity, for Grotius was in some regards original in reconciling the nominalist tradition of William of Occam and Duns Scotus (arguing that the normative order originates in the will rather some natural order) with the Thomist tradition espoused by late medieval scholastics (that the law of nature was absolutely perfect and did not allow for even divine derogation).[37] In Grotius' solution, the normative order still originates in the willed actions of the sovereign, but the will itself is now constrained to a procedural conception of reason and consent. However, we should be careful not to read this anachronistically through some modern liberal democratic conviction. On the one hand, Grotius' passage advocating the freedom of society to choose its form of government was conditioned upon the understanding that society was premised on 'rational order', which was almost exclusively reserved to the practice and customs of Christian states (e.g., Dutch federation of states, the French state). Thus, for instance, if a foreign territory did not structure land distribution around recognizable forms of industry and private property, Grotius argued the legal, if not moral, right of a conquering power to seize and use that land:

> [O]ur natural needs are satisfied with only a few things, which may be easily had without great labor or cost. As for what god has granted us in addition, we are commanded not to throw it into the sea (as some Philosophers foolishly asserted), nor to leave it unproductive, nor to waste it, but to use it to meet the needs of other men, either by giving it away, or by lending it to those who ask; as is appropriate for those who believe themselves to be not owners of those things, but representatives or stewards of God the Father.[38]

On the other hand, the argument that Christian states could enter into alliances and even protect infidels from violations against the laws of nature/nations was not a novel gesture of benevolent universalism, but firmly rooted within the Catholic humanist tradition (in direct contrast to the Thomist/Aristotelian/Lutheran argument for smaller communities) that came to prominence with the papacy of Leo X. As Richard Tuck has unearthed, at the Colonial Conference of 1613 at London, an English diplomat sardonically noted in the margins of a pamphlet prepared by Grotius containing this very same argument, 'we think it very honest

---

[36] See Tuck 1999, 94 (quoting Grotius).

[37] See generally O'Donovan 1999; see also Tuck 1999, 78–108.

[38] See Tuck 1999, 105 (Grotius' 1627 The Truth of the Christian Religion). "If there by any waste or barren Land within our Dominions, that also is to be given to strangers, at their Request, or may be lawfully possessed by them, because whatever remains uncultivated, is not to be esteemed a Property, only so far as concerns Jurisdiction, which always continues the Right of the ancient People." See Grotius 1925, II.2.17.

to defend oppressed people… against their wills'.[39] Indeed, for Grotius, not only could Christian nations conquer foreign lands for their own use, but also enslave them for their own good. '[Aristotle is correct] when he says that certain persons are by nature slaves,' Grotius argues, '[N]ot because God did not create man a free being, but because there are some individuals whose character is such that it is expedient for them to be governed by another's sovereign will rather than by their own'.[40] While Grotius contemplated that these liberties were reserved primarily in relation to European sovereign powers over non-Europeans, and especially Islamic populations, the rights of domination were not geographically delineated, and applied to non-Christians within the domestic borders of a nascent Western Europe.

In *The Truth of the Christian Religion*, Grotius presents a detailed series of arguments specifically condemning the religious and political systems of 'Heathenism', Judaism, and Islam. When Grotius turns to the 'Heathen' religions, for instance, he justifies the superiority of Christianity on the basis of its rationality, virtue and civility—to deny Christianity in favor of Heathenism, therefore, is to choose crude barbarism over a "delightful" and refined civility, wickedness over goodness, and ignorance over reason.[41] In similar measure, the Jews and Islamic populations are seen as dissonant, if not outright dangerous, elements within the emerging sovereign order of nation-states that must be routinized, if not eradicated.

The Jews, in his view, were 'a people of so obstinate a disposition', and their laws, archaic and absurd, to have 'taken so deep root in the minds of all the Hebrews, as never to be faced out'.[42] Observing that 'they have been driven out of their country, [that] they have continued vagabonds and despised, no prophet has come to them, no signs of their future return; their teachers, as if they were inspired with a spirit of giddiness, have sunk into low fables and ridiculous opinions, with which the books of the Talmud abound', Grotius argues that the reason the Jews are not "heard [by God]… we must of necessity conclude one of these two things, that either that covenant made by Moses is entirely dissolved, or that the whole body of the [J]ews are guilty of some grievous sin, which has continued for so many ages: and what that is, let them tell us themselves; or, if they cannot say what, let them believe us, that that sin is the despising the Messiah, who came before these evils began to befall them'.[43] In other words, the systematic persecution of Jews carried throughout the history of the res publica Christiania—whether under the guise of the Roman Catholic Church, the Emperor, Protestant princes, or the emerging state entities—did not reflect its own moral failing, but due to the internal chemistry of

39 See Tuck 1999, at 94.

40 Ibid. at 89 (quoting Grotius).

41 See Grotius 1925, 173–181.

42 Ibid. at 20–21.

43 Ibid. at 212–213.

both the Jewish psychology and institutional/cultural heritage, which bore the stain of God's curse.

Grotius professed a similar disdain for Islam, 'the Mehometan Religion'. To Grotius, Islam 'was bred in arms, breathes nothing else; and is propagated by such means only… many times very unjust[ly]… against a people who no ways disturbed them, nor were distinguished for any injury they had done; so that they could have no pretence for their arms, but religion, which is the most prophane thing that can be, for there is no worship of God, but such as proceeds from a willing mind'.[44] Here, we could juxtapose these comments to Grotius' early justifications for Christian nations to conquer and subjugate foreign people, for violating laws of Nature or Nations. On the one hand, Grotius might have cynically been maintaining a rather crude double standard whereby regular Christian warfare was nevertheless an unrelated aberration to its core tenets and only mobilized when absolutely necessary to maintain what was a by and large peaceful communal existence. On the other hand, the turn to 'naturalizing' Christian doctrine as 'secular' may also have allowed him to differentiate between 'religious' injury (which was not an acceptable pretext) and injury against the laws of Nature and Nations. Whatever the case, for Grotius, 'Mahomet' himself was not only 'a long time … robber, and always effeminate', who only attracted 'men void of humanity and piety', and orchestrated a false religion, 'which was plainly calculated for bloodshed, delights much in ceremonies, and would be believed, without allowing liberty to inquire into it…'.[45] Just as Grotius' disposition toward the Jewish populations intimates the violent logic that would manifest itself in mutated form in Hitler's death camps, many of the prejudices toward Islam in Grotius' work seem to bear a resemblance to the rhetoric surrounding the ongoing 'war on terror', and more generally, the struggle for liberal democratic governments throughout Islamic countries: the idea that Islamic forms of government possess an almost innately violent character, the juxtaposition between liberal democratic models and intolerant totalitarian regimes, or alternatively secularism versus rigid dogmatisms, and so on.[46] In this sense, perhaps writers like Lauterpacht and Nussbaum are right when they assert that the Grotian tradition lives on at the spiritual core of international law, but in a more perverse manner than either would care to openly contemplate.

---

[44] Ibid. at 100–101, 241.

[45] Ibid. at 235, 238–240.

[46] In contemporary global governance, this theme is addressed by authors across a wide spectrum of academic disciplines, from international relations scholars (e.g., Elizabeth Hurd), to social anthropologists (e.g., Talal Asad) and philosophers (e.g., Alain Badiou). See e.g., Hurd 2007; see also Asad 2003; Badiou 2007. Institutions within American foreign policy have also started to recognize this as an imminent strategic concern—what goes by the coinage, the 'God Gap'. See Waters 2010..

## 5.4 The Politics of Restatement and Denial

The 1999 inauguration of the Grotius Lecture Series by the American Society of International Law opened with a speech by the Vice President of the International Court of Justice, Judge Christopher Weeramantry, reflecting on the purpose of the lecture series and its namesake.[47] In turning to recap the current atmosphere of the Grotian tradition, and turn to assessing its limitations and possibilities, it is worthwhile to reflect a moment upon a longer passage from this event:

> The inaugural Grotius lecture ... is an occasion of deep reflection on the fundamentals of our discipline... A moment to attempt to recapture the spirit of inspiration that moved this great pioneer of our discipline to struggle out of the limitations of the thought-frame of his times and carve out new pathways for international relations in the unchartered waters lying ahead...Grotius rose to the occasion—a towering intellect with a passionate vision of an ordered relationship among states—a relationship based not on the dogma of religion or the sword of conquest, but on human reason and experience... For Grotius' contribution, all succeeding generations are in his debt. The new world order of European states that Grotius envisaged became a reality ... The nation-state system took over the world... It was an eminently successful system for those nation states, but it was dangerous. Some would misread Grotius' system as prescribing a lighted area of law and order for those within and fold, and an area of outer darkness for those without... That is now a past chapter. We are left with the aftermath of empire and task of cleaning up its problems... Like Grotius, we are seeking the friendly association of states and the peaceful resolution of disputes; we are also searching for principles of stability amidst the chaos of competing state interest... like Grotius, we are experiencing a sudden expansion of knowledge and power never seen before...[48] Colonialism was a dark chapter in global history and it has fortunately ended. After the long twilight struggle of dying empires, we must prepare ourselves ... international lawyers, to rise to the task... [and] sail beyond the sunset of that world order and into the sunrise of a new world order of justice, peace and reconciliation.[49]

The text above is a brilliant synthesis of traditional and contemporary feelings to explain the almost fetishistic hold of Grotius on the imagination of international

[47] See Weeramantry 1998a, 1515–1520. Both Weeramantry and Berman situate their conversation of international law in the tradition of Third World Approaches to International Law (TWAIL) scholars.

[48] Ibid. at 1515–1520.

[49] Ibid. at 1569.

lawyers. In Judge Weeramantry's depiction, Grotius stands as a shining example of what international lawyers are at their best—drawing upon human reason, intelligence, and experience to civilize the 'dogma of religion' and the 'sword of conquest' through a 'friendly association' of nation-states. This figure embodies the 'sweet reasonableness' that Koskenniemi ascribed to Lauterpacht's depiction of Grotius—the Victorian political reformer, armed with knowledge and compassion, searching out a 'golden middle' between the vagaries of apology and utopia.[50] At the same time, however, the traditional emphasis on curbing 'natural' anarchy through the self-enlightened cooperation and regulated intercourse of rules, norms, and institutions of sovereign nation-states is moderated by the shame and horrors of European imperialism, the 'dark chapter is global history'.[51] The importance of Grotius, therefore, is to remind international lawyers that the responsibility of the profession is to balance the contradictory needs of freedom and order, at once promoting political ambitions toward greater sociability (e.g., a fully inclusive global cosmopolitan order) while checking the excesses of political ambition (e.g., cultural or material imperialism)—just as Grotius stood against the tides of religious fundamentalism and violent political ambition, so too must international lawyers today transcend the allure of any form of zealous certainty (whether religious, national, and so on). Grotius comes to international lawyers

[50] See Koskenniemi 1997, 215. Koskenniemi's resuscitation of a Victorian reading of the Grotian tradition seems to self-consciously situate itself as the heir to the eclectic British jurist, Thomas Baty. 'We are slipping into some state of anarchic practice… The task of any modern prophet of International Law… should seek to repeat for our age the achievement of Grotius… [though it is] immeasurably harder than his… The modern Grotius can find no… irrecusable authorities to which to appeal… There is no vision. The world lies in twilight. International law… rests on the world's common convictions… If that twilight is not to deepened into dusk and darkness some unifying principle must be found… Shall we be wrong in saying that Sweetness, Beauty and Honour make as wide an appeal to the common mind as anything else today?' See Baty 1954, 9–1515. Baty cites the reader interested in following this theme to the work of his alter-ego, Irene Clyde, who wrote extensively on Victorian manners (e.g., the unseemliness of not only nudity or scant dress, but even sex of any persuasion) and the importance of a feminine ideal for personal and political governance. See generally Clyde 1934.

[51] TWAIL scholars, as well as their counterparts in the field of international relations, have followed upon the postcolonial literary tradition to bring the issue of cultural antagonism and ongoing forms of colonialism/imperialism to the forefront of international legal theory. See e.g., Anghie and Chimni 2003, 77; see also Anghie et al. 2003; Craven 2008; Fidler 2003, 29; Fitzpatrick and Darian-Smith 1999; Gathii 2000, 263; Keene 2002; Mickelson 2008, 355; Mutua 2000, 31; Wilde 2008. At the same time, however, the genre is plagued by ambivalence toward the nature of its critique and the way forward—in particular, whether the issue is inclusion/exclusion from the current global order, or instead, some more fundamental structural critique. Here, post-development studies have for the most part remained neglected int the literature, though post-development itself has failed to offer an alternative proposal. See e.g., Sachs 1999 (frequently criticized itself for not offering a programmatic/systemic alternative vision of global order). In relation to TWAIL, these tendencies are perhaps in part due to an over-reliance on European versus non-European antagonisms rather than looking at how the idea of Europe itself has historically always covered over deep 'internal' hegemonic rivalries and competing ideological visions. But see Harvey 1972, 1–13.

who are searching for guidance like the voice of God out of the wilderness, giving clarity to past, present, and future, and calling upon the profession to restate its (almost messianic) mission in an ever-ascending progression upwards, 'into the sunrise of a new world order of justice, peace and reconciliation'.[52] At the end of the day, though not above the messy realities of human frailty and desire, international law is remembered in the dominant account of the Grotian tradition as a universalizing force of renewal and progress.[53]

And yet, in light of the unearthed realities of Grotius' positions, the curiosity remains: why does the literature of international law repeatedly fasten around his figure, continually misreading his efforts and his legacy in a consistent story of professional hope and affirmation? Indeed, if the Grotian tradition advocates international law as a politics of emancipation and restatement, it does so only by maintaining a politics of denial, not only concerning Grotius himself, but more importantly, about the nature and track record of its liberal cosmopolitanism project. To borrow from Lacanian terminology, we might say that the symbolic order that colors our argumentative patterns and imagination—the secular order and its professed formal agnosticism toward competing hegemonic claims[54]—is itself a response to some underlying trauma, that something which resists symbolization: namely, a non-eclipsed background that not only threatens western rationalities by 'heightening contradictions and suppressions involved in their construction',[55] but more perversely, takes on the role of the Freudian death-instinct, compelling international law into an endlessly repetitive circular movement around a constitutive object that it dares not speak.[56] Here, law functions as a sort of feedback loop that allows society to rationalize and sustain the violence and failures of its past and present, as the necessary limitations of human understanding, while holding on to the belief that its principles are fundamentally sound and coherent, a veritable standard to understand ourselves in the world.[57] In such a Lacanian understanding of the rule of law, the Grotian tradition is nothing short of the symbol of the

---

[52] See generally Skouteris 2010.

[53] See Berman 1989–1990, 1521 (juxtaposing a 'critical genealogist' voice to the standard progress narrative expounded by the 'renewer/restater').

[54] See e.g., Laclau 1996; see also Koskenniemi 2001, Chap. 6; Koskenniemi 2005.

[55] See Fitzpatrick 1992, 13. For Fitzpatrick, a founding figure in the British Critical Legal Studies movement, the effort to bring out these sublimated traumas are political acts of "internal decolonization" against the "white mythology" of mainstream international law. Ibid. at x, 13. There is, however, both a contemporary and historical challenge to this aspiration. See Danchin 2008 (arguing persuasively that liberalism is founded on illiberal historical core of genocide and expulsion in the creation of sovereign nation-states); see also Orford 2007, 353 (pointing out more or less often in her work generally how the violence often decried in poor, or non-Western countries, is often the very sort of violence that European nation-states found instrumental in their formations).

[56] See Butler et al. 2000; Butler 2003, Butler 2005, 25–27, 95–100; Freud 1990 (discussing the 'death instinct'); Lacan 1993)(introducing the idea of the 'forced choice'); Zizek 2001, 103–105.

[57] I am grateful for the many conversation on the topic with Akbar Rasulov, and his useful guidance in understanding these ideas—what he has called, the 'Feuerbach effect'.

existential anxiety among international lawyers over the complex array of human (and more importantly, Western) limitations, both personal and at large.

What makes this trauma so difficult to disclose? I believe the answer contains both a material and symbolic element. On the one hand, the emergence of international law cannot be discussed as a professional, modern discourse without turning to the nineteenth century experiences of both internal (domestic) and external (foreign) colonialism: at home, the violent suppression of working class needs,[58] the brutality described by William Blake within industry's 'satanic' mills, famines and bloody intercontinental warfare[59]; and abroad, the imperial conquest of foreign land through superior warfare technology and resources,[60] the sanctimonious genocide of defeated populations,[61] colonialists and missionaries racked with disease in pursuit of fantasies.[62] For international legal theorists and historians, like Nathaniel Berman and Antony Anghie, the same international law that we typically hold out as the protector of cultural respect and to check political aggression was itself forged in the fires of colonial conquest,[63] far too savage and absolute to allow for any wishful reconciliatory redemption.[64] Here, this nightmarish awakening is not only that we recognize the horrors committed by and upon our fathers and grandfathers, nor that its legacy lingers on despite our best efforts of structural adjustment and ethical denunciation—the trauma that we are almost compelled to

[58] See e.g., Thompson 1963; see also Zinn 1980.

[59] See e.g., Allen 1994; Hobsbawm 1962. In contrast to these texts, the dominant trend in historical literature—both legal and otherwise—is to stress the relatively peaceful, at least 'stable' character of the early to middle nineteenth century, which contributes to a pacified version about the coming together of the Western European system—a sort of 'mythic' Europe that distances any critiques of endemic, or systemic violence at the core of the European state-order.

[60] See e.g., Anaya 2000; Spicer (1962).

[61] See e.g., Hochchild 1998.

[62] See e.g., Oren 2007.

[63] "Sovereignty emerged out of the colonial encounter... Colonialism was central to the constitution of international law in that many of the basic doctrines of international law... were forged out of the attempt to create a legal system that could account for relations between the European and non-European worlds in the colonial confrontation... these origins create a set of structures that continuously repeat themselves." See Anghie 2005, 2–3; see also Berman 1989–1990, 1521–1554.

[64] Drawing upon Edouard Glissant's writings about Caribbean history, Berman argues for a "fierce, even brutal honesty, refusing all redemptive consolations", which rejects all "heroic", "foundational" myths in favor of a "naked self-examination". "Can international law, written by history's victors," he asks, "muster the courage to look frankly, painfully, at the horrors of its own past?" See Berman 1989–1990, 1554.

disavow is that this past is not simply to be shunned, but also exists as our most intimate, secret dream:

> Colonialism is never the other, never the past, it is always with us ... because it has made the world we live in, both in the ex-metropoles and the ex-colonies. Our culture, our economy, our very languages are imbued with the colonial past. With us, because trauma of destruction or of guilt never really leaves an individual or a culture. And finally, with us, because colonialism is not only the shame of the West, it's violent, shadow side, but rather it also expressed some of Western culture's highest ideals that even today we cherish. This is the real challenge... The horror and the dream.[65]

The violence here carries an overt materialist content, its scandalous political ramifications (e.g., structurally sustained gross inequality, cultural imperialism/ genocide, policing actions, and warfare) the very stuff that everyone from neo-colonial critics and human rights activists to global policy makers and bureaucrats seek to (often very self-consciously) struggle against on one level or another.[66] Yet, what we are also touching upon is a more insidious form of violence, a symbolic violence, which is both more elusive, and which actually enlists and assigns our own desires by telling us what can and cannot be said and accomplished.[67] In other words, the rules and historical manifestations of authority, behavior, and beliefs that we live by may very well be experienced as the taken for granted, axiomatic necessity of objective reality, but are in fact culturally arbitrary

---

[65] See Nathaniel Berman, The Alchemy of Empire, or Of Power and Primitivism, inaugural lecture for the Centre for the study of Colonialism, Empire and International Law (CCEIL) at the School of Oriental and African Studies (SOAS) transcribed recording of the lecture on file with author, and any errors solely my fault.

[66] See Kennedy 2001, 463–497.

[67] Symbolic violence is particularly apt in the context of law, which may be itself in some respects the concrete objectification of our anxieties—what the German philosopher Ernst Cassirer called, a "metamorphosis of fear". Unlike Spencer's law of nervous discharge where we enjoy release from a sudden explosion of physical reaction, this metamorphosis into law may actually defer, and thereby intensify, our anxieties. Thus, the Goethe-like tendency to retreat into law to establish order—the "tendency to turn into an image...everything that delight[s] or trouble[s]" us—does not rectify our conceptions to the external world but actually incarnates, and heightens through repetition, our instincts of fear. See Cassirer 1946, 46–48.

phenomena in that they have no privileged connection to some natural or transcendent/universal truth.[68] These circumscribed moments are thereby transmitted to us through both historical baggage (diachronically) and our everyday discourses (synchronically) as an almost unconscious background logic of understanding compelling us to act and speak not so much unwillingly (for it is exactly our inability to separate our knowledge and desires from these conditions) as unwittingly.[69] What makes it so difficult to locate these moments is that they appear immediately 'naturalized' through stylized acts of repetition that are reciprocated, and ultimately lead to the appearance of an essentially ontological core.[70] In short, our understanding of what we ought to do and the parameters we work within are aesthetically determined: less a matter of what actually exists, than how we perform and experience the various forms, images, tropes, perceptions, and sensibilities that we identify with international law.[71]

In this sense, the anxiety that repeatedly draws international lawyers to Grotius is an underlying feeling of being caught in a catch-22 of fears. On the one hand, international lawyers labor under the 'anxiety of influence', that our vision and projects cannot live up to the creative victories of our ancestors, that global governance has become far too complex and uncertain to imagine any truly new

---

68 The term itself, symbolic violence, was coined by Pierre Bourdieu, the late French sociologist and theorist, to denote how impositions of systems of symbolism and meaning (e.g., culture) upon groups and classes would be accepted as legitimate. Bourdieu was particularly interested in the role of 'pedagogic action' in the French university system, which he believed functioned to perpetuate the advantages of privileged class relationships through inculcating students into processes of self-limitation and self-censorship. See Bourdieu 1990; see also Bourdieu and Wacquant 1992, 65–259; Jenkins 1992; Shusterman 1999.

69 Diachronic refers to the historically constituted, or developed, nature of meaning and interpretation. Synchronic denotes meaning produced by a system at any given point in time. See Eagleton 1996, 96–97. For many authors, these two approaches go hand in hand. See e.g., Bakhtin 1997. For a legal discussion of the synchronic play of structuralists, and how it may be engaged in legal analysis, see Kennedy 1985–1986, 248–266 (also providing an extensive list of relevant materials for further research).

70 This idea is indebted to the notion of the American philosopher and cultural/feminist theorist, Judith Butler's idea of 'performativity'. See Bulter 1990. In her 1993 book, Bodies That Matter, Judith Butler links the idea of performativity to the idea of 'iterability' in the work of French literary theorist and philosopher, Jacques Derrida. "Performativity cannot be understood outside of a process of iterability, a regularized and constrained repetition of norms," writes Butler. "[T]his repetition… constitutes the temporal condition for the subject … [and] implies that performance is not a single act… but ritualized production, a ritual reiterated under and through constraint, under and through the force of prohibition and taboo, with the threat of ostracism and even death controlling and compelling the shape of the production, but not… determining it fully in advance. See Butler 1993, 95; see also Derrida 1988.

71 See Schlag 2002, 1047. Schlag takes care to distance himself from an understanding of aesthetics as "the appreciation of art and beauty" to offer four 'aesthetic' models which account for the various ways American lawyers perceive and arrive at outcomes in law, which he believes acts as a formal enterprise whereby 'ethical dreams and political ambitions … do their work'. Ibid. at 1050–52.

world order.[72] On the other hand, even if such a possibility existed, the lessons of the past are not completely lost in the subconscious of the discipline, that any political order, whether it expresses itself as totalitarian or liberal, is dependent on some original (and maintained) condition of violent, exclusionary force. Tolerance, in this respect, is not so much a virtue or goal, as it is the condition of a particular situation of comfort or authority, the rationalization of how violence will be organized and directed once a system disclaims its propensity to violence. In response to these anxieties, international lawyers have sought Grotius to either 'obscure the historically exclusionary origins of the Western liberal state' by emphasizing his magnanimous advocacy of liberal tolerance and formal equality, or alternatively, decried his theory as self-serving justifications for empire, thereby eliciting a subtle polemic for an acceptance of the status quo one or two degrees to the left, some cautious politics of piecemeal reform and mutual distrust.

## 5.5 Conclusion: A Politics of Truth[73]

And yet, in the wake of what would otherwise look like false celebration or grim resignation, the words of Judge Weeramantry still carry a portion of hope. To remember Grotius is, for Weeramantry (and I hope for the rest of us), a 'moment to recapture the spirit of inspiration ... to struggle out of the limitations of the though-frame of [one's] times and carve out new pathways... in the unchartered waters lying ahead...'[74] And so here, I would like to conclude by offering two brief suggestions for how we might seize upon this appeal and answer the Grotian tradition in a new light. First, rather than shy away from the partisan nature of Grotius' convictions, we might instead accept them as the very conditions of any

---

[72] See generally Bloom 1973; see also Bloom 1975.

[73] This might be juxtaposed with the various calls of 'radical democracy' (e.g., Ernesto Laclau), or their legal equivalent, the 'culture of formalism' (e.g., Martti Koskenniemi). At its most appealing, the call for a 'culture of formalism' challenges the international legal community to rise above the 'politics of the possible' to embrace a higher standard, though like its American humanitarian rule of law counterpart, carries the tendency to recognize itself as a restraining, or gentle, civilizing force outside the auspices of power, and more specifically, war. Instead, what I am searching for here is something more akin to a 'politics of truth', which seems to occasionally manifest both within and outside of legal theory—in nineteenth century European political philosophy (Giuseppi Mazzini), in the nineteenth and twentieth century American pragmatic 'can-do' ethos (as drawn out by authors within international law, particularly Mark Janis and David Kennedy), in the liberation struggles in Latin America (Gustavo Gutierrez Merino) and anti-colonial struggles of the twentieth century (emphasized in legal work particularly by TWAIL authors), and in more recent years, within the philosophical writings of authors such as Alain Badiou and Alberto Toscano.

[74] See Weeramantry 1998a, 1515–1520.

emancipatory politics.[75] No victory, no good, came to any group of humans without what was most often passionate and protracted struggle, usually with countless and unsung casualties. That there will be losers and excluded parties are not an unfortunate by-product of the political world, but the very purpose of struggle: to fight for some condition that will change the distribution and well-being of particular individuals and communities always comes as theft and sacrifice to others. To open up patents on necessary drugs to poor countries, for instance, will mean the loss of a particular form of property and profit for shareholders invested in the pharmaceutical industry. Let us say, so be it. As progressive international lawyers committed to a better world, let us leave the comforts of the condemnation of warfare and venture forward into some battle, whatever that might be.[76]

Second, contemporary international lawyers sympathize with Grotius' eclectic use of sources (e.g., nowadays under the rubric of inter-disciplinarity), but too often 'appear both ashamed of their inability to propound doctrine in the imperious tone of tradition texts' and 'proud of having avoided the [methodological] difficulties plaguing each traditional scheme of authority'.[77] While international law should by no means lose sight of the lessons and (partial) victories against oppression (e.g., whether that was expressed as child labor, homophobia, racism, sexism, and so on), too often the condition of accepting any principle only when methodologically defensible leads to a retreat into some politics not simply of humility, but deferral.[78] In contrast, for Grotius, authoritative diversity was neither virtue nor vice, but simply a fact of life. To put this in a more contemporary register, any principle or truth is ultimately unanswerable according to any empirical or rational basis, but simply 'evident' to its adherents. Instead of remaining caught in the spurious infinity of negation that haunts the post-foundational landscape of politics and law, the memory of Grotius and his eclectic boldness directs international lawyers to proclaim a fidelity to a truth without apology.[79] The Grotian tradition calls us to shake off the Victorian pieties that shackle the emancipatory potential of our discipline so that we might return to what our ancestors understood: that to be part of

[75] See generally Kennedy 2006 (drawing out an ethical appeal for a partisan courage to face the 'dark sides' of progressive struggle as the very basis of personal and political freedom); see also Badiou 2003; Toscano 2006.

[76] Ibid.

[77] See Kennedy 1986, 5–7.

[78] This politics of deferral seems to me less constructed on a sentiment of humility but resignation, and which tacitly accepts the 'false necessity' about the nature and outcomes of global governance. See Unger 2004; see also Meillassoux 2008. Arguing against Kantian subjectivity, Meillassoux argues provocatively for us to accept arbitrariness as the sole and necessary absolute of existence—what he terms, a 'radical contingency'. 'We are no longer upholding a variant of the principle of sufficient reason… but rather the absolute truth of a principle of unreason. There is no reason for anything to be or to remain the way it is; everything must, without reason, be able not to be and/or be able to be other than it is.' Ibid. at 48–49, 60. For an experiment to bring Meillassoux's argument into legal human rights theory, see Bowring 2008, Chap. 5; but see Marks 2009.

[79] See generally Badiou 2003; see also Badiou 2009.

the world in our times and to struggle for righteousness is to wager upon some current impossibility that seems against all empirical odds and against all reasonable hope. It is in this faith that I hope we can begin to more fully join together.

## References

Allen T (1994) The invention of the white race: the origin of racial oppression in Anglo-America, vol I. Verso Books, London

Anaya S (2000) Indigenous peoples of international law. Oxford University Press, Oxford

Anghie A (2005) Imperialism, sovereignty and the making of international law. Cambridge University Press, Cambridge

Anghie A, Chimni BS (2003) Third world approaches to international law and individual responsibility in internal conflicts. CJIL 2:77–103

Anghie A, Chimni BS, Mickelson K and Okafor O (eds.) (2003) Third world and international order: law, politics and globalization. Martinus Nijhoff Publishers, Leiden

Anne Orford (2007) Reading Humanitarian Intervention: Human Rights and the Use of Force in International Law (Cambridge Studies in International and Comparative Law)

Asad T (2003) Formations of the secular: christianity, islam, modernity. Stanford University Press, Stanford

Badiou A (2003) St. Paul: the foundation of universalism. Stanford University Press, Stanford (Engl. ed.)

Badiou A (ed) (2007) The century. Polity, Cambridge Engl. ed.

Badiou A (2009) Theory of the subject. Continuum, London (Engl. ed.)

Bakhtin M (1997) The Bakhtin reader: selected writings of Bakhtin, Medvedev, Voloshinov. Bloomsbury Publishing PLC, London

Baty T (1954) International law in twilight. Tokyo Maruzen Company, Tokyo

Baumgold D (1993) Pacifying politics: resistance, violence, and accountability in seventeenth-century contract theory. Political Theory 21:6–27

Berman H (1983) Law and revolution: the formation of the western legal tradition, vol I. Harvard University Press, Cambridge

Berman N (1989–1990) In the wake of empire. AUILR 14:1521–554

Berman H (2003) Law and revolution: the impact of the protestant reformation on the western legal tradition, vol II. Harvard University Press, Cambridge

Berman N (2004) Privileging combat? Contemporary conflict and legal construction of war. CJTL 43(1)

Bloom H (1973) The anxiety of influence: a theory of poetry. Oxford University Press, Oxford

Bloom H (1975) Kaballah and criticism. Continuum International Publishing Group Ltd., London

Bourdieu P (1990) Homo academicus. Standford University Press, Stanford (Engl. ed.)

Bourdieu P, Wacquant L (1992) An invitation to reflective sociology. University of Chicago Press, Chicago

Bowring B (2008) The degradation of the international legal order?: The rehabilitation of law and the possibility of politics. Routledge-Cavendish, New York

Butler J (1990) Gender trouble. Routledge, New York

Butler J (1993) Bodies that matter: on the discursive limits of sex. Routledge, New York

Butler R (2003) Zizek: live theory. Continuum, London

Butler J, Laclau E, Zizek S (2000) Contingency, hegemony, universality: contemporary dialogues on the left. Verso Books, London

Cassirer E (1946) The myth of the state. Yale University Press, New Haven

Clyde I (1934) Eve's sour apples. Urania, London

Craven M (2008) The decolonization of international law: state succession and the law of treaties. Oxford University Press, Oxford
Danchin P (2008) The emergence and structure of religious freedom in international law reconsidered. JLR 23:455–534
Derrida J (1988) Limited Inc. Northwestern University Press, Evanston (Engl. ed.)
Eagleton T (1996) Literary theory: an introduction. Blackwell Publishing, Malden
Fidler D (2003) Revolt against or from within the west? TWAIL, the developing world, and the future direction of international law. CJIL 2:29–76
Fitzpatrick P (1992) The mythology of modern law. Routledge, London
Fitzpatrick P, Darian-Smith E (1999) Laws of the post-colonial. University of Michigan Press, Ann Arbor
Freud S (1990) Beyond the pleasure principle. W.W. Norton and Company, London (Standard Edition ed.)
Gathii J (2000) Alternative and critical: the contribution of research and scholarship on developing countries to international legal theory. HILJ 41:263–275
George W (1999) Grotius, theology, and international law: overcoming textbook bias. JLR 14:605–631
Goodchild P (2002) Capitalism and religion: the price of piety. Routledge, New York
Grewe W (2005) The epochs of international law. Walter de Gruyter GmbH and Company, Berlin (Engl. ed. )
Grotius H (1925) De Jure Belli ac Pacis Libri TresIn. In: Scott JB (ed.) The classics of international law. Carnegie Institution, Oxford-London
Haakonssen K (1985) Hugo grotius and the history of political thought. Political theory 13:239–265
Harvey D (1972) Revolutionary and counter revolutionary theory in geography and the problem of ghetto formation. Antipode 4:1–13
Hilton B (1991) The age of atonement: the influence of evangelicalism on social and economic thought 1785–1865. Oxford University Press, New York
Hobsbawm E (1962) The age of revolution: Europe 1789–1848. Weidenfeld and Nicholson Ltd, London
Hochchild A (1998) King Leopold's ghost: a story of greed, terror, and heroism in colonial Africa. Houghton Mifflin Company, New York
Hurd E (2007) The politics of secularism in international relations. Princeton University Press, Princeton
Janis M (2004) Religion and the literature of international law: some standard texts. In: Janis M, Evans C (eds) Religion and international law. MartinusNijhoff, Leiden, pp 121–126
Jeffery R (2006) Hersh Lauterpacht, the realist challenge and the grotian tradition in 20th century international relations. EJIR 12:223–250
Jenkins R (1992) Key sociologists: Pierre Bourdieu. Routledge, London
Keene E (2002) Beyond the anarchical society: grotius, colonialism and order in world politics. Cambridge University Press, Cambridge
Kennedy D (1985–1986) Critical theory, structuralism and contemporary legal scholarship. NELR 21:248–266
Kennedy D (1986) Primitive legal scholarship. HILJ 27:1–98
Kennedy D (2001) The politics of the invisible college: international governance and the politics of expertise. EHRLR 5:463–497
Kennedy D (2006) Of war and law. Princeton University Press, Princeton
Koskenniemi M (1997) Lauterpacht: the Victorian tradition in international law. EJIL 2:215–263
Koskenniemi M (2001) The gentle civilizer of nations: the rise and fall of international law 1870–1960. Cambridge University Press, Cambridge
Koskenniemi M (2005) From apology to Utopia: the structure of international legal argument, 2nd edn. Cambridge University Press, Cambridge
Koskenniemi M (2007) Formalism, fragmentation, freedom: kantian themes in today's international law. J extre_m Leg Positivism, No Foundations, pp 7–28
Kunz J (1961) Natural law thinking in the modern science of international law. AJIL 55:951–958

Lacan J (Engl. ed. 1993) Book III: The Psychoses, W.W. Norton and Company, New York
Der Molen GHJ (1937) Alberico Gentili and the development of international law: his life, work and times. H.J. Paris, Amsterdam
Laclau E (1996) Emancipation(s). Verso Books, London (Engl. ed.)
Lauterpacht H (1946) Grotian tradition in international law. BYIL 23:1–53
Marks S (2009) False contingency. Current Legal Problems 62:1–21
Meillassoux Q (2008) After finitude: an essay on the necessity of contingency. Continuum, London (Engl. ed.)
Mickelson K (2008) Taking stock of TWAIL histories. ICLR 10:355–362
Mutua M (2000) What is TWAIL? AJIL 94:31–39
Nussbaum A (1943) Just war: a legal concept? MLRev 42:453–479
Nussbaum A (1947) A concise history of the law of nations. Macmillan Company, New York
O'Donovan O, O'Donovan J (1999) A sourcebook in christian political thought: from Irenaeus to Grotius. Wm. B Eerdmans Publishing Company, Grand Rapids
Oren M (2007) Power, faith and fantasy: America in the Middle East 1776 to the present. W.W Norton and Company, New York
Paz R (2008) A gateway between a distant god and a cruel world: the contribution of 20th century Jewish German speaking scholars to the professionalism of international law (unpublished dissertation)
Piggin S (1985) Making evangelical missionaries 1789–1858: the social background, motives and training of British protestant missionaries to India. Sutton Courtenay Press, Abingdon
Pound R (1925) Grotius in the science of law. AJIL 19:685–688
Sachs W (1999) The development dictionary: a guide to knowledge as power. Zed Books, London
Schlag P (2002) The aesthetics of American law. HLR 115:1047–1118
Schmitt C (2003) Nomos of the earth in the international law of Jus Publicum Europaeum. Telos Press Publishing, New York
Schmitt C (2005) The concept of the political. University of Chicago Press, Chicago (English ed.)
Schneewind JB (1998) The invention of autonomy: a history of modern moral philosophy. Cambridge University Press, Cambridge
Schwarzenberger G (1990) The Grotius factor in international law and international relations: a functional approach. In: Bull H, Kingsbury B, Roberts A (eds) Hugo Grotius and international relations. Clarendon Press, Oxford, pp 301–312
Seigel J (1968) Rhetoric and philosophy in renaissance humanism: the union of eloquence and wisdom, Petrarch to Valla. Oxford University Press, Oxford
Shusterman R (1999) Bourdieu: a critical reader. Blackwell Publishers, Oxford
Skouteris T (2010) The notion of progress in international law discourse. T.M.C Asser Press, The Hague
Spicer E (1962) Cycles of conquest: the impact of Spain, Mexico, and the United States of the Indians of the southwest 1533–1960. University of Arizona Press, Tuscon
Stompf C (2006) The Grotian theology of international law: Hugo Grotius and the moral foundations of international relations. Walter De Gruyter Inc., Berlin
Tawney RH (1926) Religion and the rise of capitalism. Hazell, Watson and Viney, London
Taylor C (1989) Sources of the self: the making of modern identity. Cambridge University Press, Cambridge
Thompson EP (1963) The making of the English working class. Penguin Books, New York
Toscano A (2006) Fanaticism: a brief history of the concept. http://www.eurozine.com/authors/toscano.html. Accessed 1 Mar 2010
Tuck R (1977) Natural rights theories: their origin and development. Cambridge University Press, Cambridge
Tuck R (1999) The rights of war and peace: political thought and the international order from Grotius to Kant. Oxford University Press, Oxford
Unger R (2004) False necessity: anti-necessity: anti-necessitarian social theory in the service of radical democracy, vol 1. Verso Books, London

Waters D (2010) The ‘god gap’ impedes U.S. foreign policy, task force says. http://www.washingtonpost.com/wp-dyn/content/article/2010/02/23/AR2010022305103.html. Accessed 1 Mar 2010
Weber M (1905) The protestant ethic and the spirit of capitalism. Courier Dover Publications, New York
Weeramantry C (1998–1999a) Opening tribute to Hugo Grotius. AUILR 14:1516–1520
Weeramantry C (1998–1999b) A response to Berman: in the wake of empire. AUILR 14:1555–1569
Wight M (2005) Four seminal thinkers in international theory: Machiavelli, Grotius, Kant and Mazzini. Oxford University Press, Oxford
Wilde R (2008) International territorial administration. Oxford University Press, Oxford
Witte J Jr (2002) Law and protestantism: the legal teachings of the Lutheran reformation. Cambridge University Press, Cambridge
Wright W (1988) Capitalism, the state, and the Lutheran reformation. Ohio University Press, Athens
Zinn H (1980) A people’s history of the United States: 1492-present. Pearson Education Ltd, Essex
Zizek S (2001) On belief. Routledge, London

# Chapter 6
# New Approaches to International Law: Images of a Genealogy

**Akbar Rasulov**

**Abstract** Where did NAIL 'come from'? How did it start? How did it evolve? What has been its legacy and what is its pertinence today? For most of us who entered the field of critical international legal studies in the last 15 years, asking such questions seems to have become a virtually indispensable part of our shared disciplinary identity. To be sure, no one self-identifies as a 'NAIL person' anymore, and even the

An earlier version of this essay was presented at the Glasgow Conversations in International Law workshop in February 2010. Like most other such projects, it has gone through many different drafts since. My co-panellists—Michelle Burgis, Rose Parfitt, Robert Knox and Owen Taylor—saw and kindly commented on most of them. To say that I am thankful for that would be a radical understatement. Without those comments, it is safe to presume, the argument presented in these pages would not have turned out anywhere near as coherent, detailed, or nuanced as it eventually has. Nor would it have turned out as balanced and focused without the shockingly generous feedback I received on it both before and after the Glasgow workshop from John Haskell, Alejandro Lorite Escorihuela, and Umut Özsu, who through their rigorous questioning and relentless counter-interpretations have helped to mould my understanding of the NAIL enterprise and its evolution so much more than any statement of acknowledgement could ever convey. In trying to work out the basic trajectory of NAIL's history and its current perception by the different NAIL generations, I have drawn quite liberally on various conversations and email exchanges I have had over the years with David Kennedy, Arnulf Becker Lorca, Thomas Skouteris, Martti Koskenniemi, Antony Anghie, Scott Newton, Catriona Drew, Paavo Kotiaho, Reut Paz, Hani Sayed, Karen Knop, Susan Marks, and Michael Fakhri. More generally, my understanding of this subject has also benefited from conversations and exchanges with Duncan Kennedy, B. S. Chimni, Sundhya Pahuja, Emilios Christodoulidis, Nathaniel Berman, Fleur Johns, Andrew Lang, Grietje Baars, Tanya Monforte, Matthew Craven, China Miéville, Irina Ceric, Mai Taha, Christian Tams, Antonios Tzanakopoulos, Itsuko Higashiuchi, Vishaal Kishore, Boris Mamluke, Ileana Porras, Jörg Kammerhofer, Matthew Happold, Robert Cryer, Iain Scobbie, and Ignacio de la Rasilla. All errors and omissions are mine alone.

A. Rasulov (✉)
School of Law, University of Glasgow, Scotland, UK
e-mail: akbar.rasulov@glasgow.ac.uk

J. M. Beneyto and D. Kennedy (eds.), *New Approaches to International Law*,
DOI: 10.1007/978-90-6704-879-8_6,

NAIL moniker itself has long since been retired. And yet our interest in the subject does not go away. From Boston to Helsinki, London to Toronto, Cairo to Melbourne young critically minded international law scholars keep coming back over and over again to the same question: what is NAIL to us? What was the meaning of NAIL as a disciplinary phenomenon? What did it 'represent'? What did it mean to be a part of NAIL in the late 1980s? How did this change by the turn of the century? What was the logic behind this transition? This essay represents an attempt to explore some of the answers to these questions as seen from the vantage point of this new generation of critical international law scholars.

## Contents



## 6.1 Introduction

What do the 1990s mean to us today?

Much in the same way in which the 'long nineteenth century', as Eric Hobsbawm has repeatedly reminded us, was not just a century in the history of Western capitalism,[1] so, too, one might say, the 'long 1990s' were not just a decade in the history of the international legal discipline. In a lecture given some 6 months after the September 11 events, Harold Koh, a then soon-to-take-office dean of Yale Law School, described the period that 'began in November 1989 with the collapse of one structure, the Berlin Wall; and ended on September 11, 2001, with the collapse of another structure, the World Trade Center' as the 'age of global optimism'.[2] It seems safe to assume not everyone who lived through that

1 Hobsbawm 1989, 8–9.

2 Koh 2003, 318.

period would agree with that characterization. Most Bosnians, Chechens, Tajiks or Rwandans—and Cuban factory workers and East Ukrainian coal miners too—would probably disagree with it quite forcefully, and it should not be difficult to see how one could use this as the platform from which to build a stinging critique of the various regional, ideological, cultural and class biases that weave through Professor Koh's worldview. And yet, in some basic sense, all of this is somewhat beside the point. Because what matters here, ultimately, is not how convincing or defensible one finds Koh's vision of contemporary history—the idea that 'between these two collapses we have passed almost literally out of the light and into the dark side of the age of globalization' sounds, at best, a little too melodramatic—but rather the fact that he and those around him have one.

For however many gaps and blind spots one might find in its underlying argument structure, the very fact that it exists and enjoys an obvious degree of popularity suggests that this theory of the long 1990s as the 'age of global optimism' must work perfectly well for its exponents. That is to say—because every historical model, ultimately, is only a useful fiction that helps us to distinguish 'what really matters' and thus, in effect, to determine what is right and good and beautiful—although it could make a certain strategic sense in some cases to challenge that theory in terms of its elementary accuracy, in the wider context it would be a fundamentally pointless exercise. The reason for this is that one would have to assume that theories of such kind come into being and survive solely according to their own intrinsic merits determined in reference to the entirely objective laws of logic and neutral, dispassionate inquiry and that whatever political or economic struggles might consume otherwise the lives of their proponents remain completely unrelated to this process, whereas, in fact, if there is anything one could learn from the modern critical tradition it is that it seems to be precisely the opposite that holds true.

Put differently, rather than taking up each such theory on its own terms, our first reaction should always be to ask about its underlying politics. What mode of political being-together must characterise the life of this particular group of people for such a model of history to have become meaningful enough for its members to start articulating it 'in the open'? What sort of economy of power relations, in other words, must have come into existence among them for it to begin to suggest itself as a sufficiently viable instrument by which they might try to mediate the immediate contradictions of their social existence?

I do not know, I must confess, how one can best answer this question in the case of those who, like Koh, view the long 1990s as the 'age of global optimism'. Partly, that is because I do not know enough about their politics or the conditions of their productive relations with one another, but mainly because it seems to me that what occurred during those years was far too provocative, messy, and ambivalent to be reduced to the imagery of some ill-defined quasi-Hegelian march of global moods, which, given what I have just said, probably reveals a lot more about my own biases and prejudices than it does about the justness of my objective disagreement with that approach, but, oh well, what can you do, nobody's perfect.

More importantly, it also seems to me that in tackling questions like 'what do the 1990s mean to us today?', the starting point should never be with the grand, 'global' subjects, such as the 'international community' or 'international law'. Rather, every such inquiry should always begin with the investigation of the immediate social context of that particular 'we' on behalf of and in conversation with which it is presumed to be carried out.

That 'we' in the present case consists of a group which, alas, is not very easy to define or describe. As a disciplinary phenomenon, it has, as yet, neither a name nor a commonly agreed representation. It has not been formally recognised in any accepted nomenclature of intradisciplinary configurations, and its existence as such in many ways will probably be denied by those whom this essay would otherwise propose to regard as its members. The idea of calling it a 'we' should not therefore be taken to suggest that every member of this group necessarily shares in some common vision, participates in a common project, or sticks to the 'general party line'. What makes it a group, rather, is a great deal more complex than that.

One way to explain how this complexity plays out in practice would be to draw a parallel with the traditional Marxist theory of class formation: the question of the objective existence of any given class, from the traditional Marxist point of view, depends, in the final analysis, neither on the immediate contents of its members' apparent shared consciousness nor on their capacity to undertake any kind of coherent group action, but solely and exclusively on the objective structure of the historically created system of productive relations in which they collectively participate.[3]

In a similar vein, one might say, what underpins the ontological foundations of this collectivity on behalf of and in conversation with which I imagine the present exercise to take place should not be understood in terms of any kind of collective spirit or common agenda but solely in terms of the fundamentally *material* objectivity of its members' common position in the internal economy of power/production relations expressive of the contemporary discipline of international legal studies.

The relevance of these last few points may not seem immediately evident, but what all these explanations are meant to clarify is the essential motivation and purpose behind this essay. To put it in a slightly formulaic fashion, its *ultimate objective* is to help assemble the starting analytical platform for a much broader investigative project the core of which consists of a critical-historiographic inquiry into the general evolution of international law taken both as a modality of governance and a social-normative order over the course of the long 1990s. Its *essential task*, considering this backdrop, can be defined as the attempt to elucidate the basic ideological stakes characterising that specific disciplinary context from within which this investigative project is meant to unfold. Its *immediate focus of inquiry*, consequently, is to reconstruct the intradisciplinary genealogy of that

---

[3] See Wright 1998, 278–300; Poulantzas 1978, 17–18.

particular conjuncture in which this disciplinary context finds itself today so as to prepare the ground for a more effective determination of the constituent stakes.

A different way of putting all this would be to say, that my principal aim in these pages is to explore and illuminate the historical trajectory of one very specific segment of the international legal discipline as it evolved over the course of the long 1990s, from the vantage point of an ideological conjuncture determined essentially in terms of the basic economy of intradisciplinary power/production relations which surrounds that collectivity on behalf of and in conversation with which the broader investigative project into the contemporary history of international law is meant to occur.

And from that point of view, it seems relatively safe to presume, whatever else the long 1990s might have been, it was definitely *not* an age of optimism, joy, and all-round cheerfulness. The invisible but not for all that any less real conflicts that had split the discipline's internal social space during those years repeatedly reached such levels of intensity and complexity as had never been previously experienced in the discipline's living memory. Unresolved and unregretted, many of these conflicts persist to this day, relentlessly reshaping the discipline's internal landscape and political culture.

By far, the most important of these conflicts—a conflict that in the discipline's collective memory is now remembered to have been fought as much over the grand questions of political philosophy as over the far more 'trivial' matters of personal style and self-presentation—has been the battle between what has been variously called the 'new stream of international law scholarship', 'international law CLS' and the New Approaches to International Law (NAIL) movement and what its associates somewhat summarily dubbed the 'mainstream'.

It is the memories of this battle, its legacies, and its continuing impact on the economic potential of the new generation of critically minded international law scholars that constitute the main subject of this essay.

## 6.2 The Challenge of NAIL

But what exactly was this NAIL thing? What was its meaning as a disciplinary phenomenon? What did it represent? What sort of things stood behind that label? Was it a movement? A tradition? A school? Or would it be more appropriate to describe it 'only' as a 'sensibility'? (Could it be all three?) Where did it come from and how did it start? How did it evolve? What was its basic trajectory and why did it unfold in that particular way in which it did? What are the implications of this today? What was exactly that 'new' bit in 'NAIL'? What was the relationship between NAIL and CLS and what was its relationship to other international law traditions? From Boston to Helsinki, from London to Toronto, from Cairo to Melbourne, dozens of young critically minded international law scholars of my generation keep raising these questions over and over—in different contexts, using different vocabularies, placing different emphases, but invariably in the same steadily anxious tone. The reasons for which, of course, are not at all self-evident. For the 'idea' of NAIL, as the conventional wisdom tirelessly insists, has long since expired. Whatever may have been its exact disciplinary status, as a coherent disciplinary phenomenon NAIL has simply run itself into the sand. No one calls themselves a 'NAIL person' anymore, flies a NAIL flag or tries to fight the NAIL corner at general international law conferences. There is no such thing as a NAIL corner anymore. Even the NAIL moniker itself has been officially retired.[4] Like critical legal studies before it, NAIL, it seems safe to say, is now absolutely and irreversibly 'dead'.[5] Which unavoidably leads to the question: so what's with this whole NAIL nostalgia then?

If 'fin de NAIL' was officially declared already as far back as 1998, why should so many of us who were not even 'part of the field' at that point continue to 'obsess about all things NAIL' in 2012? Some of us, undoubtedly, must be motivated by sheer elementary curiosity. Others, it appears, keep coming back to *'l'affaire NAIL'* because they want somehow to 'learn from NAIL's mistakes'. Most of us, though, it seems to me, keep asking these questions because we are anxious. Anxious to learn as much as we can about what that theoretical edifice we are about to make our disciplinary home was used for before; what sort of ideological baggage we are looking automatically to inherit by simply identifying ourselves as 'critical'; what the people that we look up to in the present may have been up to in the past; where the train we have jumped on, in short, may be coming from and where it may be going. Because, as Terry Pratchett once said, 'if you don't know where you come from, then you don't know where you are, and if you don't know where you are, then you don't know where you're going. And if you don't know where you're going, you're probably going wrong.'[6]

Every generation in reconstructing its genealogy inevitably comes to commit a certain kind of injustice against the preceding generations' own sense of legacy and achievement. This essay is not going to be an exception in this regard. What I am looking for in these pages is a way to express what I believe the NAIL legacy *looks like* from the vantage point of the new generation of critically minded international law scholars—half junior academics, half graduate students, most lawyers by training, some with a little background in practice or activism, typically multilingual, practically atheist, socially liberal, knee-jerkishly ironic—the generation of the 'double collapse', 'derision pre-emption', and the 'end of history'.[7]

To use the language of 'vantage points', 'believing', and 'looking like', on reflection, may have been a little unfortunate. It seems to suggest that this essay is going to become an exercise in some sort of phenomenology or that it is going to result in some kind of a manifesto. Let me disabuse you of that notion straight away. What I am looking for here is a sense of the internal structure of a certain

[4] See Skouteris 1997; Kennedy 2000, 492–500.

[5] Tushnet 2005, 99.

[6] Pratchett 2011, 423.

[7] See De Toledo 2008, 7–11.

ideological conjuncture, that is to say, the *object of knowledge* that is pursued in these pages has an essentially non-phenomenological character. I will explain later how exactly the study of such kind of structures relates to the operative logic of phenomenological inquiry. For now let me just register this very significant distinction—and use it also to emphasise the all-important difference between the logics of *inquiring into the contents of subjective experience* (phenomenology) and *studying the make-up of the inter-subjectively held 'unconscious' assumptions* (critique of ideology).

An exercise so conceived, it would be safe to assume, is not going to be to everyone's liking. There is a good chance some of my readers will find the conclusions I draw and the stories I tell here wholly counterintuitive and 'not at all reflective of what people like us experienced, really'. If this happens to you, there is not much, I am afraid, I will be able to offer by way of a meaningful response. Perhaps, you should share your own stories about NAIL so we could all learn how it looked from your end (and what ideological stakes informed your experience).

There also seems to be a very good chance that those of my readers who may have thought about the same kinds of questions that I attempt to tackle in this essay before will take up issue with my 'method'. The argument can be made in any number of ways: 'There is far too much generalization and reification in this story. The image of NAIL that you project in these pages leaves out too many important details. It feels like a caricature.' Or: 'Well, *of course*, if you represent the tradition *this* way, you are going to get this totally outlandish vision of it. But what makes you think it was right to represent it this way?' Or: 'You haven't protected yourself against the selection effect. What you present here is not a story of NAIL but only a projection of your own blind spots.' Or: 'Has it not crossed your mind that people constantly move in and out of disciplinary fields, and so it may not be at all the case that, say, "at some point semiotics just disappears" but rather that "at some point the semiotics crowd moved into comparative law"? Of course, all of your tables and maps, with their public-international-law-centric bias, cannot catch on to this fact.' Or: 'What is the politics of this whole exercise? I feel perturbed/insulted/Oedipally threatened/bored by it. So do all of my friends and students.' Or: 'Where is Derrida in all of this?'

I am not sure, again, how one could best react to such kind of responses. On some basic level, it feels tempting simply to say 'yeah, sure, I agree' or 'I don't agree' or 'my aim was just to provoke a debate, really' or 'this is only a work in progress, don't be too harsh.' But it seems, on reflection, it would be a little too disingenuous and too much of a copout to resort to any of these classical exit strategies. It also seems to me that if such banalities actually do work for you, then perhaps there is a good reason for why you are now feeling so upset by my 'method'. But then, of course, that would not make for a good response tactic either. So let me just say this instead: Yes, it *is* true that the tables and maps I have drawn here reflect an essentially 'PIL-centred' perspective. That is because I came to NAIL from a PIL-centred background. I am pretty certain I am not alone in that.

No, it is not true that the story these tables and maps project is only a story of my own personal prejudices. What went into the drawing of these maps came about as the result of numerous conversations, email exchanges, interviews, and discussions carried out over a number of years and in many different social and institutional settings. Most of my interlocutors in these conversations and exchanges, admittedly, also came to NAIL from a PIL-centred background, but many of them didn't, and many others would never describe themselves as 'international lawyers'.

What follows below is *not* an account of what I think 'actually happened' with/to NAIL. It is an account of what I think many in my generation *believe* happened (and what that belief means to us). If you think we got our picture wrong, feel free to correct it. But don't get too hung up on it otherwise. It is (probably) not your fault.

## 6.3 First Image: Oral Histories

Everything begins with oral histories. Some of us think of it as nothing more than idle pub conversations or silly gossiping. Others regard it as some kind of intra-disciplinary mythology. The NAIL lore is certainly rich in gossips and idle pub chats. But it is also rich in mythologies, and what all mythologies have in common—and gossips do not—is that they tend to project narratives designed to educate. The moment one realises this is the moment one also grasps that to be on the receiving end of such narratives often means turning into an integral element of their practical operation.

Listening is becoming: the more we are exposed to the field's ever-expanding mythological canon, the more clearly we begin to detect our own place within each of these narratives. Sometimes we do this consciously; in most cases, however, we just tend to internalise the 'implicit message'. To follow the oral histories 'of the field' becomes in this sense virtually indistinguishable from *becoming (a part of) the field*[8]—and not just because that is how interpellation always works, but because on some fundamental level the intellectual space of the NAIL tradition operates essentially as a field of restricted cultural production, which is to say that it is an integral part of the design of the NAIL lore that it constantly moves in a self-perpetuating cycle of simultaneous production-consumption-critique, where the enactors always double as the recipients, the readers are writers, and the actors make one another's audience.[9]

Naturally, each of us in the end goes on to develop our own individual NAIL experience. It would be pointless to deny that just as it would be pointless to try to predict what each of these experiences will eventually turn out like. But it would also be unwise to forget that a large part of what 'having a NAIL experience' involves seems to revolve in practice around being told about that experience:

---

[8] I owe this point to Alex Lorite.

[9] See Bourdieu 1993, 115–116. 'No one has ever completely extracted all the implications of the fact that the writer, the artist, or even the scientist writes not only for a public, but for a public of equals who are also competitors'. (Ibid.) Cf. infra n.38.

what it is supposed to represent, how one should react to it, what one ought to be able to take away from it, and so on and so forth.

The received wisdom at the heart of the NAIL lore today typically projects a mythological structure organised around three main themes: (i) the history of NAIL is a history both of a *movement* and an *intellectual tradition*; (ii) the logic of NAIL's relationship with the rest of the international legal discipline is that of a continuous revolution/rebellion; (iii) although the NAIL movement was formally brought to an end in the late 1990s, the NAIL tradition continues to this day, albeit it in a somewhat different organisational form. The overall pattern that emerges as the result of such a configuration seems to project in turn a relatively rigid model of historical evolution built around an implied temporal sequence whose essential structure of constantly alternating stages of contraction–expansion/crisis–respite appears to reproduce the standard encoding formula of the traditional Heroic Quest narrative.[10] Given the basic logic of that formula—the Hero, struggling against various challenges, works slowly towards discovering and (re)claiming some highly esteemed Prize, while constantly drawing on support from his loyal Helpers and encountering vicious resistance from the malevolent Villains—the immediate question that arises at this point unmistakably points towards the implied identity of the presumed hero figure: just who exactly is meant to be the hero in the NAIL story? The moment one finds the answer to that question, the rest of the answers automatically follow. Hero: the NAIL movement—Prize: new disciplinary mode of production; Helpers: the movement's members but also their institutional, cultural, and organisational sponsors; Villains: the disciplinary orthodoxy. Hero: the NAIL tradition—Prize: the Truth/'grace'/'after empire'; Helpers: old and new generations of critical scholars; Villains: liberalism, conceptualism, legal fetishism, the 'dead and the wrong', etc. Hero: a certain group of people within the movement—Prize: the movement itself; Helpers: the group's strategic allies, their acolytes, and institutional and organisational sponsors; Villains: the rival factions within the movement and their hangers-on.

Seen from this angle, the general story one tends to pick up through NAIL's oral histories, if one were to try to draw up a thematically integrated account, seems to acquire a pattern the basic structure of which can be gleaned from Table 6.1 (p. 185–186 infra).

What was the ontology of NAIL? Where did NAIL start? How did it evolve and what was the overall shape of its trajectory? Like most other Heroic Quest narratives, the standard account of NAIL's history at the heart of the NAIL lore bases its mythopoetic momentum around two main focal points: the movement's 'pre-history stage' (Hero's life before he leaves home) and the story of its 'golden age' (Hero's main victory, feats, and triumph over adversity).

In the first case, the general thrust of the narrative seems to be shaped by the interplay of two basic storylines. Firstly, there *was* in fact a group of founding figures behind NAIL (the project did not emerge spontaneously) who came to

[10] See Booker 2004, 69-86.

share their common critical impulse through a *disciplinarily complete* experience. Secondly, even at the moment of its initial inception, neither as a movement nor as a tradition was NAIL 'only' a Harvard phenomenon or 'just' a continuation of CLS. Naturally, it would be pointless to deny that in both of its practical hypostases the 'idea' of NAIL took off for the first time at Harvard and that all throughout their early years both the NAIL movement and the NAIL tradition remained closely affiliated with the US branch of the CLS enterprise. But the first formative experiences that prepared the stage for NAIL's emergence almost certainly took place on the opposite side of the Atlantic and the basic ideological framing they evolved in quite unmistakably derived from a completely different intellectual context than the US CLS. A good decade before anyone even began using the NAIL label, three of its four founding figures—Philip Allott, Martti Koskenniemi and Anthony Carty—had already started their first explorations in critical international legal theory. All three of them proceeded in their endeavours by drawing on a decidedly European tradition of critical-theoretic inquiry. All three, furthermore, lived and worked in Europe and openly identified themselves as *cultural* Europeans. None of them, in the final analysis, had managed to find the magic solution that would bring NAIL into existence, and so it was only when the fourth founding figure, David Kennedy, brought all their different breakthroughs together—while adding also a tremendous amount of his own original work—that the pieces finally started to fall into place. And yet note that Kennedy too before he established himself at Harvard had moved first to Europe to spend some time there as a visiting researcher at various continental institutions and to work in Geneva. It was there and then, during those European years, that he eventually met Allott and Koskenniemi. It was there and then also that he published his first genuine NAIL work.[11]

To be sure, there may not have been any clearly identifiable institutional basis behind the new disciplinary initiative that he began forming then, or any sense of a common discursive identity, let alone a common theoretical agenda. But whether one thinks of it in terms of its broader cultural temperament or even in terms of its most common tropological habits, there seems to be no doubt that this new initiative was fundamentally 'European' in every one of its defining features. What is more, however much it would go on in the later years to evolve into a purely academic phenomenon, in those early years the critical impulse that drove NAIL's formation derived its animating dynamics as much from the abstract theoreticism of Wittgenstein, Derrida, and the Frankfurt school as from the 'endlessly real' lived experiences of a disenchanted international law practitioner. Both Allott and Koskenniemi entered the project, having come from an extensive diplomatic background, and Kennedy, too, even though he was principally based in academia, had spent a considerable part of that decade 'in the field', working with various human rights and refugee projects.

[11] See Kennedy 1980.

What exactly should be considered the timeline of NAIL's golden age, predictably enough, does not (yet) appear to have been fully settled. Nevertheless, the general consensus, inasmuch as one can make it out, seems to suggest that (i) the golden age almost certainly ended with the official dissolution of the NAIL movement in the late 1990s; (ii) a large part of what made the golden age golden and gave the movement its essential character came from the introduction in the early 1990s of the so-called Dighton writing workshops. Everything that the NAIL enterprise has managed to achieve, runs the implied argument, it achieved through and because of the experiences it acquired and generated during those weekend retreats at Dighton. In a way, indeed, it would probably not be an exaggeration even to suggest that if there has ever been such a thing as the 'essential core' of the NAIL enterprise, the keys to uncovering it no doubt would have to be sought in those Dighton weekends. (To draw a somewhat liberal parallel, if Kennedy's general international law course at Harvard was NAIL's equivalent of what Aaron Director's course on antitrust at Chicago had been for law-and-economics some 40 years earlier,[12] the Dighton weekends would be its equivalent of George Mason Law School and the John Olin programmes all rolled into one.[13])

Now, all of that may look fine and well, but note now how the first cracks start to emerge in the narrative's implicit logic. If it should indeed be true that those institutional formulae which were first developed at Dighton in the mid-1990s[14] did in fact acquire the function of NAIL's chief organisational form of practical self-realisation, that is to say, if they have indeed become the principal site for its material articulation of its fundamental ideological core, then it seems obvious that: (i) not only the NAIL tradition *lato* sensu but also the NAIL *movement* safely survived the dramatic events of the late 1990s and still continues to function even today; and (ii) the essential logic of NAIL's relationship with the rest of the international legal discipline does not actually have that much of a rebellious/revolutionary theme. Bracket out the immediate content of the substantive discourse and the remaining institutional formula—short-term small-scale workshops in which carefully selected academic participants gather to present and comment on one another's recent writings, works-in-progress, and canonical texts by 'external thinkers', all with a view to cultivating the habit of writing-with-one-another-in-mind-as-one's-target-audience—will look as orthodox and traditional as anything one would typically find in other, more 'mainstream' disciplinary contexts.

What should one make of this? None of us, frankly, can be sure how to answer that, but two logical possibilities generally seem to suggest themselves at this point. In the first place, if the conventional wisdom is correct in identifying the Dighton formula as the central defining element in the organisational structure of the NAIL enterprise, then it would seem to follow from this that, despite the

[12] See Teles 2008, 93–95.

[13] Ibid. 101–132; 181–207.

[14] For a more or less detailed description of which, see Kennedy and Tennant 1994, 417–430.

popular perception, the NAIL project does not actually entail any deep commitment to any form of disciplinary rebellion or revolution. Rather, it appears, we should consider it as just another regular intradisciplinary enterprise, one among many others. In the second place, if the conventional estimation of the systemic importance of the Dighton formula is, in fact, incorrect, then it seems there must be a whole lot more about NAIL's golden age that the narratological structures of the current NAIL lore are preventing us from learning about than one might normally expect otherwise.

## 6.4 Second Image: Patterns of Discourse

In the work of every historian, writes Hobsbawm, there exists always a certain twilight zone—what one might call an epistemological 'no-man's land'—in which the order of history proper morphs ever so imperceptibly into the order of individual memory, erasing every standard distinction between the private and the public experiences, the factual and the emotive, the logic of subjective recollection and the logic of the objective, dispassionate inspection. The ultimate extent of this zone, of course, varies from case to case. But for every historian it is always there and sooner or later each of us has to confront its consequences.[15] Leaving aside the various mythopoetic complications sketched out in the previous section, one of the main problems with NAIL's oral history tradition from the standpoint of the new generation of critical international law scholars is that there just seems to be too much 'memory' and not enough 'history' in it.

And, of course, there may in fact be nothing wrong with that: what else would you expect from an oral history if not a celebration of the personal, the individual, and the emotive? Or maybe that is exactly what one should expect from an intergenerational divide: the young feel that the old are dwelling too much on their past glories and triumphs, recycling long-expired hopes and regrets instead of giving facts and hard evidence; the old feel that the young are too naïve about knowledge and that they might be missing the whole point about what is important in life and in science and one day they will come to regret that. And maybe this sense of irritation and discontent says in the end far more about 'us' than it says about 'them', and maybe also what it says to 'us' does not make any sense to 'them' and that is how it was always intended to be, even if nobody likes it. I am not sure any of us really knows what to make of this conundrum. But it seems to me pretty self-evident that there exists today a rather widespread feeling of exasperation that many in my generation have come to share and the central theme behind this exasperation comes from the conviction that the 'old generation' perhaps have not done a very good job traversing their Hobsbawmian twilight zone when it came to explaining the history of the NAIL enterprise.

---

[15] See Hobsbawm 1989, 3-5.

And, of course, one could say, this might be a wholly unjustified reaction. For is it not true that it was, in fact, one of the main goals of the NAIL tradition to bring home the idea that history can never be told in a de-subjectivised mode; that 'events' and 'feelings about events' are actually indistinguishable from one another; that if knowledge is power and the ultimate thing about power is that it would always be best to exercise it while recognising that we act in a state of radical uncertainty, then it must follow, logically, that knowledge, too, is always best experienced and exercised in this mode of radical uncertainty; and that each of us, moreover, is a delicate and unique human person, full of feelings and emotions, and it would be totally wrong, but also arrogant and hubristic, to demand that the old generation should excise its personal, emotive, and subjective reactions and just 'tell it how it was'?

And, of course, all that would be true and correct—on some level—and one does not need to be a postmodernist to recognise that. But it would also be somewhat beside the point. Because none of us actually disagrees with any of these arguments either as a matter of theory or as a matter of politics, but the reason why we nevertheless keep coming back over and over to the same vulgar request for 'facts and evidence' has, in fact, nothing to do with any of this beautiful theorising. Most intergenerational conflicts have a fundamentally economic logic and the one we are findings ourselves in here is not any different in this regard. This may sound vulgar and perhaps even too simplistic, but the dull economic reality on our end—the lived everyday reality of our structural position in the discipline's broader economy of power/production—is that, quite simply, many of us still have no jobs, let alone tenures; and we are not that fresh-out-of-college anymore; and we feel we are probably working as hard as most of our peers 'in the mainstream', and yet our career trajectories seem to be entirely dissimilar to theirs. And it is not like there appears to be any kind of obvious witch-hunt going on against the NAIL crowd that would explain this state of affairs as a function of some crude political struggle. And, of course, each of us knows it was never going to be easy to swim against the main stream—and, just for the record, we are not complaining about that, we really do like it here, in the NAIL house, even if you insist that it does not exist anymore. And it is not that we are asking for any kinds of paternalistic interventions on our part—we all have seen how this sort of quasifeudal dynamic plays out with our peers 'in the mainstream' and we are not sure we would like to be part of something like that. But it certainly would not hurt if those who came here before us would start telling us a bit more about 'what actually happened' to the house of NAIL before we arrived in it.

For let us face it: the job situation is not getting any better and the terms of trade between the 'new stream' and the mainstream are not really improving either. Given how many of us still find ourselves on *this* side of the tenure line, given how much more of a challenge it seems to be even to get one's foot through the door these days, how could anyone be surprised that the 'vulgar question of facts' keeps coming back again and again? Would it not help someone in that sort of position before they take on the job market to know already more or less clearly how, why, and in what way their being associated with the NAIL tradition can affect their employability? Would it not help them to know what sort of disciplinary wars and quarrels the movement may have had in the past that might still linger on beneath the surface so that they could at least figure out in which direction the minefields are and who their inherited adversaries may be? Would it not help them to learn also what sort of things other NAIL people had tried in the past that ultimately backfired, so that they would not repeat the same mistakes, and what sort of things they tried which ultimately succeeded, so that they could recycle that know-how in their own professional lives?

And maybe this sort of economism does not reflect that well on anyone, the young or the old, the mentors or the mentees. It certainly does not seem to be that easy to reconcile this kind of discussion with the traditional notion of what radical, progressive, and critical people are meant to talk about. But, surely, it would be a very strange definition of radicalism if it implied that one should somehow refuse to learn before one joins a struggle about what its actual parameters are.

And so, exasperated and disappointed with what we have been able to receive from our elders, we gradually take up the task of getting it for ourselves. In between conferences and over coffee breaks, in libraries and during plenary panels we set out on our own 'fact-establishing missions'. We talk to one another and exchange 'findings'. We read, we listen, and we watch our elders ever more attentively than before, but now much more with an eye to uncovering their hidden symptomatologies than following their immediate arguments. We draw our own inferences and project our own hypotheses about what their past successes and failures must have been and what sort of political inheritance they will be leaving behind them.

Inevitably, all this leads to a whole set of its own mythopoetic moments with all the attending mystifications, reifications and generalisations. But since the jobs question does not go away, ending the exercise does not appear to be an option. The results it yields may be no less confusing than the stories we get from our elders, but we stick with it nonetheless, gradually refining our 'guiding questions' and adjusting our investigative optics as we go along, in the hope that perhaps even if there can be no 'outside mythology', not all mythologies must be alike.

What comes out of this, in the end, often seems possible to organise in a way that would allow the NAIL movement to 'say something about itself' without actually 'saying it'. Sometimes the general picture this allows one to reconstruct comes out looking even more contradictory than anything one finds in the movement's oral tradition. And sometimes it comes out looking more or less like what you can see in Table 6.2 (p. 187–188 infra).

Like with all such instruments, there is not just one correct angle from which you can approach Table 6.2. One way in which it can be understood would be by conceiving it as a depiction of the NAIL tradition considered *as an ideology* as that ideology is experienced from the vantage point of today's young generation—provided, of course, that one would understand the word ideology to mean here something like 'vision', 'episteme', or 'mental map'. Another way to interpret it would be to regard it as a representation of what it seems the general structure of pathways taken by the NAIL enterprise in its *formal discursive dimension* has become over the last 20 years. Whichever interpretation is more convincing, the basic aim here is to try to explore how it seems from today's point of view the NAIL movement, despite its self-mythologising efforts, has actually evolved in terms of its discursive practices.

There are a number of different insights that one can take away from this exercise.

First, note how the idea of the steady progression from the age of organic unity to the age of a disintegrating confederacy that was so central to the internal logic of Table 6.1 appears to be completely undermined by the general pattern implied in Table 6.2. To be sure, from a purely 'quantitative' point of view, the intellectual scope of the NAIL tradition seems to have expanded very impressively over the last 20 years: the sheer diversity of conversations that people lead now within the movement appears to be a lot greater than it has been at any point in the past. And yet all the rifts and disjunctions that are visible within the tradition today, if you look at them closely, have all already been there in the early 1990s. The confederacy, to put it differently, had never actually been that united in the first place.

Second, consider also how much more difficult it would be, on the basis of what Table 6.2 indicates, to support the thesis that as it progressed beyond its golden age the NAIL tradition somehow increasingly distanced itself from its early CLS roots. Even if we only limit ourselves to the most talked about texts entry, the constant recurrence of Duncan Kennedy's article on the semiotics of legal consciousness and the enduring relevance of Martti Koskenniemi's *from apology to Utopia*—by far the most CLS-ish of all early NAIL texts—rather unequivocally seem to suggest that NAIL's connection to the CLS tradition continues to remain as central to its discursive operation today as it was 20 years ago.

Naturally, none of this disproves in any way the fact that the average NAIL scholar of 2012 will on the whole tend to have a much weaker grounding in the classical CLS canon than their predecessor did in 1990, but perhaps what this pattern represents should not be interpreted so much as a sign of some sort of intellectual distancing between the NAIL and the CLS traditions but only as an indication that a sufficiently extensive 'indigenous' referential archive has been built up within the NAIL tradition itself. There just seems to be a lot more literature within the NAIL's own library these days—one does not need anymore to pack one's reading lists and teaching curricula with early CLS texts about contract law or the politics of judicial reason.

Thirdly, consider furthermore, in the same vein, that even as the 'semiotic turn' does indeed appear to have given way to the 'political-economic turn' at some point between the early 1990s and today, the particular manner in which the latter has unfolded indicates that this process may not, in fact, have been quite as simple and straightforward as it might look. Note, more specifically, which particular strands of the broader political-economic tradition (Wallerstein's heavily structuralist world systems theory, Polanyi's proto-speech-actist institutionalism) and in combination with which other related enterprises (Kennedy's 'three globalizations' theory, biopoliticist interpellatory analysis) seem to be enjoying the greatest degree of reception within the NAIL intellectual space today. Could it be that what we are witnessing here is some sort of intradisciplinary epistemic transmigration? If so, what might be the animating dynamics behind it? Is it just a matter of the natural evolution of the structuralist *problematique* or did it have something to do with the latent institutional struggle for resources?

Fourthly, changing the levels slightly, note also how much 'stickier' the textual focalization patterns seem to have become in 2012 as compared to the early 1990s. The 'Three Globalizations' essay,[16] though formally published in 2006, had been making rounds at least within the movement itself, since the turn of the century.[17] Most of the chapters in Antony Anghie's *Imperialism* book[18] similarly had been published in article form quite a few years before they were rearranged into a book. The same goes for David Kennedy's *The Dark Sides of Virtue*.[19] What is more, in terms of their overall critical temperament both *Imperialism* and *The Dark Sides of Virtue*, just like Koskenniemi's *Gentle Civilizer of Nations*,[20] read a lot more like the product of the mid-1990s than the mid-2000s.

Clearly, it would be quite implausible to suggest that no interesting or intellectually rewarding NAIL scholarship has been produced after the year 2006. And yet the dominant points of reference in the movement's internal discursive space today seem to be articulated in a pattern which implies precisely that: the average 'age' of the most talked about texts in 2012 is considerably greater than it was in 1992. What should one make of this phenomenon? Could it be somehow indicative of some broader cultural transformation taking place within the movement's social field? Or is it the case rather that it is simply becoming ever more difficult to draw up a reading list that will appeal to everyone—either because the tradition itself has become too 'big' or because there are just far too many people inhabiting its social field today, spread across a network of institutional sites that connect with one another only sporadically? None of these options can be ruled out; each of them, however, points towards a completely different ideological dynamic (and thus a completely different regime of intradisciplinary power/production relations).

Last but not least, consider too what the general pattern in the right-hand column of Table 6.2 seems to imply about the internal evolution of the TWAIL project. No strand of the original NAIL tradition in the last 20 years, it seems safe to say, has had an intellectual career quite as successful as TWAIL. And yet to what extent can the TWAIL tradition today be considered a direct continuation of what had first been attempted under that label in the 1990s? If the whole idea of there being such a thing as a 'TWAIL' project is meant to reflect the general degree of penetration of the postcolonial studies tradition into the broader field of critical international legal studies, how much attention should one give then to the fact in the basic conceptual architecture of the new TWAIL discourse a great deal

---

16 See Kennedy 2006.

17 Cf. Kennedy 2003.

18 See Anghie 2004.

19 See Kennedy 2004.

20 See Koskenniemi 2002.

of space seems to have been reserved for the intellectual legacies of Edward Said and Karl Marx—and even Wallerstein and Andre Gunnar Frank too—but not that much for Frantz Fanon, Gayatri Spivak, or critical race theory? And what should one think then also, in the same context, of the fact that even as there seems to be so much interest among the new TWAIL scholars in taking up the general problematic of 'international law and its others' and talking and thinking about 'history as a counter-narrative', there does not seem to be any interest left in pursuing the former exercise via the lens of any form of psychoanalytic tradition or supplementing the latter exercise with talking and thinking about history also as a 'meta-narrative'? And why, furthermore, is it also the case that this new TWAIL tradition seems to have such a strong predilection for closely reading and deconstructing various landmark judicial decisions but not treaty regimes; exploring the legacy of Robert Hale and the distributive impact analysis but not that of Eugen Ehrlich and the 'living law' theory; investigating the reactionary effects of liberal legalism and the supranational proliferation of neoliberal economic institutions but not the law of finance and the transnational proliferation of tax havens?

Could it be that what stands behind all this is some 'natural' shift in intellectual fads? Or is it more that, as one senior colleague suggested, the new TWAIL 'simply latched' on to those parts of postcolonial studies which it found easier to read, without adding anything substantive to its borrowings, so that, pretty much like with legal semiotics before it, there now seems to be nothing specifically *legal* about the general theoretical architecture of legal postcolonialism?

## 6.5 The Challenge of Structuralism: Koselleck's Lesson

One of the most important theoretical implications raised by the Hobsbawmian distinction between the order of history and the order of memory from the epistemological point of view, undoubtedly, has been the formulation of the so-called problem of *diachronic structures*, that is to say, those configurations of causational factors which produce such transformational patterns that, as Reinhart Koselleck puts it, tend to 'prevail, whether encouraged or opposed'—historical processes that sweep across the full range of the participant historical forces, progressing relentlessly and irreversibly, according to their own immanent logic, seemingly regardless of which political camps and dramatis personae may hold the heights of power.[21]

Often, the essential facticity of such structures, notes Koselleck, can be perceived relatively directly, in the empirically observable flow of everyday experience. In most cases, however, the transformational patterns they produce will tend to unfold so slowly and on such a grandiose scale that their reality will entirely

[21] Koselleck 2004, 108.

escape the limits of their contemporaries' perceptive capacity—they will slip into the hole of the empirically unknowable.

The temporality of such structures, even if it is still 'comprehensible [only] in the medium of the events within which [it is] articulated', becomes thus impossible to reduce to any 'strict sequence of *experienced events*'. As a result, none of its constituent elements can lend themselves to registration within the order of memory, which is to say that it will be only by resorting to some form of 'social science or [the idea of] *history as a science*' that we will be able to detect the basic contours of its immanent logic.[22] 'Both levels, event and structure, [thus reveal themselves to be] related to each other without merging'.[23] Each, consequently, necessitates the development of its own epistemology and its own methodological apparatus, and the 'priority of the eyewitness accounts' that will be typically considered an unquestionable given in one case will have to be rejected as a matter of principle in the other.[24]

What follows from all this at the level of general historiography, observes Koselleck, is the unavoidable recognition of a certain untranscendable gap between the two levels of the historical inquiry, 'a methodological aporia' occasioned by the fact that the 'temporal extension [of events and structures] cannot be forced into congruence, neither in experience nor in scientific reflection'.[25] In practical terms, the most obvious consequence of this realisation, as Koselleck sees it, becomes the following two-pronged methodological postulate: (1) 'It would be wrong to attribute a greater reality to "events" than to … structures merely on the grounds that the concrete course of the event is bound up with an empirically demonstrable before and after in a naturalistic chronology'[26]; and (2) 'Historical semantology shows that every concept entering into a narrative of representation … renders relations discernible [only] by a refusal to take on their uniqueness'[27]—or, in other words, the only way in which any historical experience can become analytically representable is through the systematic deployment of conceptual categories the principal effect of which is always to bring forward their essentially nonsingular, i.e. structurally conditioned, character.

A slightly different way of putting all this would be to say that, however wide the ontological hiatus between the order of events and the order of structures may appear, the logical conflict between the two philosophies of investigative praxis that correspond to the study of events and the study of structures—and thus, by extension, the methodological opposition between the enterprise of history-as-biographies-and-memoirs and history-as-social-science—because of the very nature of historical representation as a form of knowledge-production will always-already be resolved in favour of the latter. The notion of telling history 'as

[22] Id. 107–109.
[23] Id. 108.
[24] Id. 105-8.
[25] Id. 110.
[26] Id. 111.
[27] Id. 112.

concrete events', put bluntly, is a logical impossibility. The idea that one can separate the exercise of recording any set of personal subjective experiences from the depersonalised investigation of their structural determination is a complete fiction. Even when you think you 'don't do structures', structures still 'do you'.

The practical relevance of these last few remarks should not be too difficult to figure out. If structuralism should indeed be an epistemic inevitability, the only question that we ought to ask at this point is how exactly we can 'structuralize' our inquiry more effectively. What sort of configurations of causational factors, in other words, will it make more sense for us to focus on in order to obtain a more insightful understanding of the NAIL history?

## 6.6 Third Image: Material Bases

There also exists another tradition of thinking about ideology, one that does not put such a great premium on the reconstruction of narrative patterns and conceptual frameworks but rather places its main emphasis on the study of institutional loci and forms of collective organisation. Whatever it is that one might imagine the word 'ideology' to stand for, on this view of things can only come into being and acquire practical effectivity through the combination of a certain institutional apparatus and the related pattern of social practices.[28] Seen from this angle, thus, the basic theoretical challenge of identifying the historical meaning of something like NAIL *taken as an ideological phenomenon* cannot, in the final analysis, be resolved in terms of any exercise centred around the identification of 'guiding ideas', 'standard reading lists', 'dominant problematics', etc., but only in terms of an inquiry whose principal focus lies with the investigation of those material apparatuses and forms of collective interaction which the various groups of people associated with this phenomenon typically work with.

Virtually every given set of ideas can in principle give rise to a 'tradition'. And yet only very few of them do in practice. The reason for that lies partly in what one might call the dampening effects of the 'ambient background noise': the 'natural static' that is always present in every discursive field, created as the result of the myriads of interactions between all its constituent traditions.[29] But above and beyond all such entropic factors stands the fact every tradition, first and foremost, is a product of strategy.

Legacies, as Regis Debray put it, are never created by pure chance: the transmission of any given set of ideas, epistemic conventions, or aesthetic sensibilities from one point in time to another can only be achieved through a great expenditure of effort and strategic planning.[30] Just 'as in the Darwinian biosphere',

[28] Althusser 2001, 112.

[29] Debray 2000, 5.

[30] Ibid.

in the field of knowledge-production 'place is not available to all'.[31] To be sure, on some fundamental level, every tradition in the final analysis depends for its survival on its capacity to sustain a relatively stable system of communication so that the respective social space can be integrated into an internally unified community—in that sense the question of narratives and epistemic predispositions certainly carries a great deal of importance. And yet what really determines, in the greater scheme of things, how well any given tradition is going to be able to transmit itself through time, ultimately, has far less to do with its standard narrative protocols than with its capacity for the creation of sufficiently steady social networks, the conquest of institutional sites of power, investment and accumulation of the necessary stocks of organisational capital, the putting into place of appropriately configured hierarchies of actors, 'bureaucracies', and 'chains of decision-making', as well as the installation of suitably calibrated internal geographies and territorial regimes.[32]

Above all, it seems, the task of tradition-building always requires the deployment of considerable strategic resources, and every strategy, in the last instance, inscribes itself in the basic material givens which condition the collective life of the respective communities: their personnel structures, logistical bases, exchange and distribution systems, and the corresponding 'property holdings' through which all these conditions are secured. No tradition, let alone a movement, can survive in the long run without creating a corresponding system of enabling bureaucracy, not least because every act of 'cultural transmission' necessarily entails a careful distribution of tasks and a relatively functional chain of decision making.[33] 'If you wish to understand a theology, examine its corresponding ecclesiology'.[34] No tradition likewise will be able to survive also without setting into place an appropriate system of institutional apparatuses: research institutes, publishing outlets, educational curricula committees, grant and scholarship foundations, conference centres, academic appointments committees, chair endowments, editorial board positions, etc.[35]

Also no tradition can come into existence without the effectuation of a suitably organised territorial framework, that is to say, a suitably calibrated system of intracommunal geographic circulation.[36] The ecclesiology of the mediaeval church was established not least through the institution of extensive pilgrimage routes (with all the accompanying interpellatory dynamics of seasonal timetables, collective rituals, and standard routines that this enabled) as well as the elaborate territorialisation of the formal hierarchy of ecclesiastical appointments, that is to say, the institution of a clearly articulated core-periphery

31 Ibid.

32 Ibid. 9–16.

33 Ibid. 13–15.

34 Ibid. 20.

35 'What would Plato have amounted to had he not had the brainstorm of purchasing a plot of land near the Athenian suburb of Colonus where he established a sanctuary of the Muses?' (Ibid.).

36 Ibid. 4.

structure within the underlying economy of internal power/production relations.[37]

How has the ecclesiological organisation of NAIL manifested itself over the course of the last 20 years? What is the essential structure of its core-periphery dynamics? What is its geography and what is its structure of enabling institutional apparatuses? What do its personnel structures and its chains of decision making look like? What institutional sites has it conquered and in what sequence? For how long has it retained control over them? What sort of patterns of socialisation did it express itself through, more generally? How did it inscribe these patterns in its economy of power relation? The further away we move from the image of NAIL as a collection of oral histories and common epistemic predispositions, the more difficult it becomes to grasp the exact contours of its ontological basis. The higher also become, however, the practical stakes of resolving that challenge.

How has the NAIL movement manifested itself in material terms over the last 20 years? The core institutional locus of the NAIL enterprise—what one might call its patriarchal see (to continue with Debray's metaphor)—should not be that difficult to discern. From the late 1980s until about 2007, it was the European Law Research Center at Harvard Law School. From 2007 to about 2009, there was a temporary shift from Harvard to the Brown International Advanced Research Institute at Brown University. After 2009, the centre of gravity once more shifted to Harvard. This time, however, the principal focus became the newly established Institute for Global Law and Policy.

Nor should it be difficult to identify the principal 'semi-peripheral powers' of the NAIL movement. As of today, this category seems to include the combination of three relatively long-established largersize 'archdioceses'—the University of Helsinki/Erik Castren Institute in Finland, the SOAS-LSE 'corridor' in London, and the University of Toronto/Osgoode Hall tandem in Canada—and a host of somewhat lesser scaled 'dioceses'—Cornell, Bogota, Melbourne-Sydney, the American University in Cairo, as well as potentially the new English-speaking law school at the Sciences-Po in Paris—connecting to one another primarily via the Harvard link or through the three archdiocesan centres (but not, as a rule, directly).

Crucially, at each of these institutions, that is to say, both in its core and on the semi-periphery, the movement realises itself through the same basic arrangement of social practices: (i) conferencing (predominantly within the movement's own social space); (ii) academic publishing (almost exclusively in reputable scholarly publications); and (iii) graduate-level teaching and PhD supervision.[38] Put differently, inasmuch as the NAIL enterprise has any existence as a material

---

[37] Ibid. 16.

[38] The ideological effects of this arrangement should not be difficult to hypothesise. Cf. Bourdieu 1993, 115: 'The field of restricted production can only become a system objectively producing for producers by breaking with the public of non-producers, that is, with the non-intellectual factions of the non-dominant class. … By an effect of circular causality, separation and isolation engender further separation and isolation, and cultural production develops a dynamic autonomy. Freed from the censorship and auto-censorship consequent on direct confrontation with a public foreign to the profession, and encountering within the corps of the producers itself a public at once of

phenomenon, it exists almost exclusively *through* and *on the basis of* an overwhelmingly *academic ideological apparatus* and stereotypically academic social practices and rituals. Mainstream-style 'reaching over into the world practice', whether in the form of 'consultancy' or 'activism', does not on the whole seem to be a regular feature, nor for that matter does there seem to be any enthusiasm for any kind of 'advocacy masquerading as scholarship'.[39]

A different way of interpreting all this would be to say, for example, that what the practices of the NAIL movement seem to indicate is the spread of a relatively mild form of solipsism or a certain kind of political conservatism in self-denial. A more interesting reading, however, would be to say that the consistent eschewal of the politico-ethical turn in NAIL's practical self-realisation in favour of a more 'aesthetic' mode of scholarly work could be regarded as a functional replication of what in Thorstein Veblen's language one would describe as the conspicuous leisure model of economic activity.[40] The similarities seem all the more striking if one adds to the consideration the fact that the levels of the implied educational capital expected of the typical producer/model reader[41] of a NAIL text from the point of view of the general patterns of international legal discourse appear often not just abnormally high but virtually prohibitive.

On the other hand, the switch into the aesthetic mode could also be relatively legitimately interpreted, after Andre Gorz, as an indication of the beginning of the systematic transcendence of the traditional bourgeois model of 'work as wage labour' premised as it is on the direct insertion of the labouring process into the broader system for the circulation of exchange value.[42] The less the NAIL discourse tends to lend itself to direct exchangeability with, say, the discourse of the European Court of Human Rights, the more effectively the NAIL tradition can be said to challenge the entrenchment of capitalistic labour practices within the social space of the international legal discipline.

Or one could read it as a symptom of international law's ever-accelerating slippage into a culture of half-hearted narcissism or even perhaps draw a parallel with Debord's 'society of the spectacle'. Hearing about some of the projects pursued by some of my postmodernistically inclined peers, it certainly would not be difficult to come up with a fairly compelling argument in favour of that interpretation.

Then again, putting the matter in such terms may very well obscure more than it will help to reveal. To cite just one example: however, superficially one might define the idea of the aesthetic turn, it would be difficult not to acknowledge that

(Footnote 38 continued)
critics and accomplices, it tends to obey its own logic, that of the continual outbidding inherent to the dialectic of cultural distinction.'.

39 The phrase comes from Kalman 2002, 359.

40 See Veblen Veblen 1994.

41 On the 'production of model readers' and the construction of 'author' and 'reader' as textual strategies, see, generally, Eco 1979, 7-11.

42 See Gorz 1982, 2.

that particular expression which it received, for instance, in the early works of Nathaniel Berman,[43] in fact, seems to have very little in common in terms of its implied knowledge-production model with the expression it was given, say, in *from apology to Utopia*.[44] Detailing the structural grammar of the international legal argument and tracing Hegelian-style continuities between the phenomenologies of Robert Redslob, Wasily Kandinsky, and Bela Bartok may both be expressions of some form of disciplinary rebellion, but in terms of their implied operative logics they very obviously belong in entirely different genres.

Putting aside for a moment the question of NAIL's typical labour practices, the broader question that begins to emerge at this point, as one starts to consider the relevance of the various differences between Koskenniemi and Berman's socioeconomic contexts when they set out to work on those two texts, is to what degree the NAIL movement's general material bases may have evolved over the last two decades.

Admittedly, looking at things from this angle does not point towards any self-evident conclusions patterns. But it does indicate a number of interesting possibilities.

First, seeing how far and wide the institutional territoriality of NAIL events has spread in recent years, one might say the material bases of the movement have expanded pretty remarkably since the early 1990s. One seems as likely today to attend a NAIL-themed conference, partake in a NAIL-inspired reading group, or read a NAIL-style article at Cairo or Melbourne as at Harvard or Helsinki.

On the other hand, even the briefest look would be enough to note that nearly three decades after its inception the NAIL movement still has not developed any proprietary publishing line: there exist no NAIL-specific journals or a NAIL-aligned publishing house. Nor do there exist any endowed NAIL chairs or a NAIL professional society. To be sure, one can find now a whole range of NAIL-related institutes and research centres that did not exist some 15 or 20 years ago, and with a certain degree of imagination between all them one can also make out now the faint outlines of a modest structure of NAIL-related doctoral scholarships, postdoc fellowships, and travel grants. But one will still find no structures of systematic excellence recognition behind all of this—there exists no NAIL equivalent of the Deak or the Guggenheim prizes—and the general numbers of the dedicated support staff that the movement is meant to rely on seem at best rather negligible.

At the same time, those 'chains of decision-making', even if they may not be so easy to identify at first glance, are all definitely there. Their underlying logic of operability may still appear to be premised on a certain kind of contradiction, but they have certainly already taken form.[45] The nature of that contradiction,

---

[43] See Berman 1992.

[44] See Koskenniemi 1989.

[45] Some observers have cited this sense of ambiguity as evidence of the fact that NAIL must somehow be a 'cult'. Others took from it the notion that 'what NAIL really needs now is a 1968 moment'. Both deductions seem to be driven more by some form of fantasy-play than reasoned argument. But they are certainly 'there' and this fact, too, contributes an important element to the determination of the economy of power/production relations within the movement's social space.

furthermore, seems to be as revealing as it is intriguing. Historically, having inherited the early CLS tradition's New Leftist culture of theoretical pluralism, the movement, rather decidedly it seems, chose to develop its formal discursive identity in a relatively decentralised rhizomatic manner. Over time, however, when it came to constructing the structure of its day-to-day institutional operation, the basic organisational logic which it selected broke with the New Left's spirit of anti-hierarchism in favour of a more centralised, vertically integrated model of operative management. How much of this came by accident and how much by design is difficult to say. But in the long run it seems very likely this fundamental disjunction between its order of formal discursive practices and the dynamics of its institutional organisation is going to produce a much greater impact on how the NAIL tradition will be able to transmit itself through time than virtually any other related factor.[46]

One way to start uncovering the historical materiality of the NAIL enterprise would be to map out the basic evolutionary trajectory of its principal institutional sites. The logic of the exercise may not be particularly complicated, but it seems it would be quite useful to start by distinguishing between those sites in which NAIL historically established its principal academic bases and those that served primarily as the nodal points in the territorialization of its common social space, for, indeed, the two trajectories as one can see from Table 6.3 have not for the most part converged or fed into one another.

## 6.7 The Enigma of Helsinki: The Core-Periphery Logic and the Challenge of Disciplinary Survival

Note an interesting pattern that seems to emerge in Table 6.3: one of the two most long-established institutional centres of the NAIL movement both in what concerns its academic and its social materialisation, at least since the mid-1990s, has been the University of Helsinki (more specifically, the Erik Castren Institute). What could explain this pattern?

As one might expect, traditionally, one of the most commonly cited reasons for the enduring relevance of the Helsinki cluster both within and outside the NAIL context has been its long-term close association with Martti Koskenniemi. Surely, though, not even the presence of leaders as charismatic and as well connected as him, even if one makes allowance for whatever extensive stocks of institutional capital he must have been able to accumulate in the broader context of Finnish legal academy, could sustain a whole economic enterprise over such a protracted period of time. As Marxists would say, a man might make his own history, but he

---

[46] Note also the possible parallels with the so-called post-hierarchical model of management. See Boltansky and Chiapello 2005, 75–76.

certainly cannot make a whole economy. The 'little Sartrian God',[47] so beloved of in the liberal humanist tradition of disciplinary historiography,[48] is an empty illusion that typically helps to disorient the historical analysis far more than it helps to illuminate it. The thesis that the keys to understanding the historical evolution of the international legal discipline should be sought in the deeds and works of individual scholars might be considered a very effective critical platform if one were struggling, say, against a conception of international legal historiography premised on the assumption that the evolution of international law is a projection of the inexorable march of Reason or the ends of Providence. But that is not, thankfully, the context in which we find ourselves today. And so the question inevitably arises: why has the Helsinki cluster remained so prominent over such an extended period of time?

The logic behind seeing this issue as a potential historiographic conundrum may not be immediately obvious, but the following excerpt from Boris Kagarlitsky should help set up the discussion. First, however, recall something Pierre Bourdieu once observed: like every domain of cultural production, modern academia effectively operates as an economic system.[49] Secondly, consider against this background that inasmuch as the field of international legal academia because of the essentially global character of the international legal discipline is probably set to replicate the same dynamics of circulation which is typically characteristic of the contemporary global economic system, bearing in mind that that system today is unquestionably dominated by the capitalist mode of production, any attempt to answer the question posed above must necessarily begin with the consideration of what sort of 'foreign investment attraction' and 'income repatriation' regimes underpin the material bases of the Helsinki cluster.

As Kagarlitsky points out:

> The tendency for the accumulation, concentration, and centralization of capital … is [an economic] constant [under the capitalist mode of production. And] it is precisely the logic of accumulation and concentration of capital that leads to its systematic redistribution in favour of global 'leaders'. Even a sharp increase in the rates of economic growth on the periphery cannot result in a radical change of the existing state of affairs. Indeed, under certain circumstances, quick growth can actually weaken the national economies of these countries. The better the country's economy works, the more of 'free' or 'excess' capital it generates, which then is redistributed towards the principal centres of accumulation.[50]

Looking at the two institutional trajectories sketched out in Table 6.3, it seems difficult to avoid the conclusion that the law of the accumulation and centralisation of capital, at least to some extent, must govern the evolution of the NAIL movement.[51]

---

[47] The phrase comes from Althusser 1976, 44.

[48] For a typical sense of which, see, for example, the so-called 'European tradition in international law' series run by the European Journal of International Law since the early 1990s.

[49] See Bourdieu 1988.

[50] Кагарлицкий 2009, 30-31.

[51] Or, as Bourdieu puts it, it is always those who are most endowed in scientific capital that end up leading the scientific revolution, not those who are deprived of it. (See Bourdieu 1990, 184.).

Consider, after all, which particular NAIL clusters, outside Helsinki, seem to have developed the strongest base and endured the longest: Harvard, LSE/SOAS, Toronto, possibly also Melbourne. Consider also which clusters had peaked for a brief spell in the past before quickly fading away: Utah, Northeastern, Birkbeck. What the first group all seem to have in common is that each of these institutions appears to constitute what in the context of international legal academia could be regarded as the functional equivalent of a 'principal centre of accumulation'. What marks the second group, on the other hand, is the fact that each of these institutions appears to have replicated the fate of those peripheral economies which, having achieved rapid unexpected growth, become ultimately victims of their own success.

Harvard, Toronto, LSE/SOAS, Melbourne—it is not even so much the question of how much prestige each of these institutions can command within their respective academic environments as their capacity to position themselves at the top of the respective global extraction/attraction chains. Top law schools in leading academic markets, each of them is commonly believed to attract first-rate faculty of international standing and to offer highly rewarding intellectual experiences for each of their students which allows them to implement highly selective admission policies. The possibilities implied by such sort of setup inevitably capture the attention of the most ambitious and academically capable strata of potential graduate students. The possibility of working with the most attractive graduate student material strengthens the interest and commitment on the part of the academic heavy-hitters and faculty leaders. The guaranteed presence of internationally recognised faculty ensures the steady inflow of generous external funding. Higher levels of institutional affluence make it easier to retain top student talent through various grants, stipends, and bursaries as well as top faculty talent through higher wages, more efficient institutional structures, and more extensive research and teaching support. The combination of greater financial and organisational resources, in turn, allows the pursuit of higher profile academic projects commanding a greater degree of intradisciplinary clout which, in turn, helps reinforce the interest both of the faculty and the graduate student community and to raise the institution's profile among the 'donor community'. The brighter the lustre, the stronger the corps, the greater the money inflows—and thus *ad infinitum*.

All of which raises the question: given that none of these conditions should in principle be achievable in the context of a small-scale academic economy, how can one explain then the Helsinki phenomenon? Harvard, Toronto, LSE/SOAS, Melbourne—however, different the particular situations of each of these institutions may be, all of them actively position themselves, and are commonly perceived, as *global players*. All of them also come from, and are commonly associated with, an English-speaking educational culture, which in an international academic market in which English remains the dominant language of exchange confers an obvious economic advantage. All of them carry globally recognisable brand names that enable them, among many other things, to diversify their sources of financing beyond the immediate context of their respective territorial states. To what extent could the same thing be said about Helsinki?

To put the matter in a somewhat different way, is Helsinki's enduring relevance as a NAIL powerhouse one of those exceptional situations that only serve to highlight the general rule or is it a reflection of some other, as yet unidentified structural pattern?

After all, as Kagarlitsky notes, the law of the 'inevitability of the redistribution of capital towards the centre' is closely connected to the imposition of the 'open economy' principle on the respective peripheral regions: '[t]hat is why only Japan, Stalin's Russia, and the states of South East Asia, which in different times and in different ways managed to "secede" from the global capital markets, were able to radically change their position in the global hierarchy.'[52] Could the Helsinki Erik Castren institute be NAIL's equivalent of the 1960s Japan or the 1980s Four Asian Tigers? The answer is not easy to work out, but the question still deserves to be raised.

Putting aside the enigma of Helsinki, another core-peripheral question that merits attention in this context is the question of the causal importance of the internal evolution of the NAIL enterprise within the Harvard cluster. To what extent has the general trajectory of the NAIL tradition been determined by the trajectory of its development within Harvard?

Note the apparent continuities between the first and the third rows and the 'organic' stability of the third column in Table 6.4 (p. 189 infra). From the greater diversity of personnel and the adoption of an organisational model presupposing the use of a shorter time-span for the execution of basic social interaction follow the emergence of a broader sense of disciplinary identity and a progressive dissipation of emphasis on the specifically *legal* tradition of critical academic thought.

Note also the additional twist which the logic of the third column in Table 6.4 gives to the general narrative suggested in Table 6.3 (p. 189 infra): did the sudden mushrooming of the new clusters in recent years reflect the turn to the research institutes model at Harvard? If so, what does this say about those discursive configurations which were detected earlier in the right-hand column in Table 6.2?

## 6.8 Fourth Image: The Spirit of *Avante Garde*

There is an interesting passage that appears towards the end of one of Terry Eagleton's books. Its immediate subject is the determination of the inherent ideological dynamics of a certain aesthetic attitude that took shape in West European culture at the beginning of the last century. In Eagleton's taxonomy, this attitude can be best described as *avante garde*, and here is what he proposed were its most characteristic features:

[52] See Кагарлицкий 2009, 31.

> Like the left-aesthetic lineage, the *avante garde* has two moments, one negative and one positive. The negative aspect is perhaps the best known: shock, outrage, moustaches on Mona Lisa. It is difficult to base politics on it, and [it is] difficult to do it twice. This current of the *avante garde* takes up the negative aesthetic of modernism and destroys meaning. What is it, in the end that the bourgeoisie cannot take? Meaninglessness. Don't strike at this or that bit of ideological meaning, for if you do you stay within the orbit of orthodoxy; strike instead at the very structure and matrix of meaning, and confound ideology in this scandalous way. There is also the positive moment of the *avante garde*, that of Brecht rather than Dada. This proclaims: there is indeed a way of resisting incorporation by the ruling order, whatever the fashionable jeremiads about how they will simply hang Picassos on the walls of their banks. That, claims this *avante garde* trend, is not the point. If they can place your revolutionary artefacts in their banks then that means only one thing: not that you were not iconoclastic or experimental enough, but that either your art was not deeply enough rooted in a revolutionary political movement or it was, but that this mass movement failed. How idealist to imagine that art, all by itself, could resist incorporation! The question of appropriation has to do with politics, not with culture; it is a question of who is winning at any particular time. If they win, continue to govern, then it is no doubt true that there is nothing which they cannot in principle defuse and contain. If you win, they will not be able to appropriate a thing because will have appropriated them. The one thing which the bourgeoisie cannot incorporate is its own political defeat. Let them try hanging that on the walls of their banks. The negative *avante garde* tries to avoid such absorption by not producing an object. No artefacts: just gestures, happenings, manifestations, disruptions. You cannot integrate that which consumes itself in the moment of production. The positive *avante garde* understands that the question of integration stands or falls with the destiny of a mass political movement.[53]

There seems to be a rather striking parallel between Eagleton's 'negative moment' and the way one normally tends to perceive today the common disciplinary legacy of the NAIL tradition.

The 'negative aesthetic of modernism [that] destroys meaning': what was Nathaniel Berman's attempt to draw on Bartok and Kandinsky *while proposing to construct a practically operable legal-historical analytic* if not an all-out attack on the traditional protocols of disciplinary knowledge that sought to extinguish every possibility of their continuous employment as heuristic instruments?[54]

'Drawing moustaches on the Mona Lisa': how else could the orthodox international law scholarship understand Ed Morgan's attempt to interpret the meaning of the Badinter Commission's pronouncements on the law of statehood by reading them through the prism of a Borges tale about firing squads and delayed executions?[55]

To use Picasso's *Les Demoiselles d'Avignon* to unlock the meaning of the League of Nations minority protection system, to explain the appeal decision in the *Tadic* case with a metaphor drawn from a tale about a 'dreaming magician'—what better examples could there be of a Dada aesthetic within the medium of international legal scholarship?

---

[53] See Eagleton 1990, 371-2.

[54] See Berman 1992.

[55] See Morgan 2001.

To homologise a hallucinatory dream of a writer sentenced to execution to an advisory opinion about the meaning of self-determination, to file Redslob and Sarah Wambaugh together with Alban Berg and Federico Garcia Lorca—how about turning *that* into a method on which one could build a politics *for* the discipline or at least apply it again?

Things do not seem to be as simple with the 'positive moment'. On the one hand, there does clearly exist a great deal of consensus, traceable both within and outside the NAIL field, that the measure of NAIL's successes must ultimately be sought in something like the persisting purity of its rebellious attitude. In its more sophisticated form the argument goes along the lines of: 'how can what you do be regarded as an emanation of a disciplinary rebellion when a Whewell professor writes an endorsement blurb for your book[56] or a mainstream primer on positivist dogma recognises your contributions alongside those of Tunkin and Anzilotti?'[57] In its more vulgar form the argument tends to turn back to the age-old tactic of 'arm-chairing the radicals': 'you aren't allowed to be employed by a rich, prestigious Western university and still call yourself critical.'

One can imagine a whole spectrum of possible responses to each of these arguments, but the most common reaction would usually be to go with Eagleton's 'yes, but how idealistic would it be to demand that art, all by itself, could resist incorporation.' How infantile and how disingenuous would it be to berate a scholarly tradition for managing to survive in the aftermath of its apparent failure to reach an objective it never set for itself? What, would it be more fitting if, once the universal elimination of oppression/legal fetishism/the ruses of imperial reason proved itself to be unachievable, the NAIL scholars stopped writing and publishing entirely? Would that make their social position more authentic? Would its members' radical credentials become more impressive if no one ever cited their works or gave them jobs?

Then again, as Eagleton's reasoning seems to imply, this sort of strategy will remain successful only so long as one can identify, even if only in the abstract, the possibility of those 'revolutionary masses' whose political engagement has so far failed to back up the *avante-gardist* momentum coming to its support in the future. What sort of a mass political movement could be said to have *failed to support* the NAIL 'vision'? More importantly, if NAIL in this formula should be equivalent to Eagleton's order of art, at what level of international legal disciplinary reality would one have to search for its missing counterpart in the order of revolutionary political action?

The argument may seem a little abstract but what it is working towards is, of course, the question of the movement's sense of strategic self-perception. One of the most common anxieties shared by the young critically minded international law scholars today has its roots in precisely that type of dilemma: to what extent is the NAIL enterprise *really* meant to be different from all other disciplinary

[56] See, e.g., Koskenniemi 2002.

[57] See Corten 2009.

movements and traditions? What if that point about 'selling out' and 'getting co-opted' is somehow correct? Better still, what if it is *not* correct, but not because 'they have go their facts wrong', but because this way of thinking about this issue is completely beside the point? What if the real question that one should ask—but no one has yet—is not whether we should feel anxious or threatened whenever the legacy of our purportedly critical tradition comes to be recognised in the citadels of disciplinary orthodoxy, but *what kinds of recognition* and *in what contexts* merit such sort of reaction?

The consciousness against which the NAIL movement raised its banners, historically, has never been a perfectly monolithic phenomenon. Some segments of the disciplinary orthodoxy undoubtedly still persist in characterising the NAIL enterprise as a despicable scandal. Others, however, quite clearly do not. Many areas of the disciplinary doxa in the last 20 years opened themselves to NAIL's influence, enabling the NAIL tradition to start remoulding the corresponding institutional politics and discursive habits and in return becoming gradually remoulded itself. Side by side with large tracts of mutual newstream-mainstream unreceptiveness, thus, there extend now sizeable tracts of a more or less actively functioning disciplinary symbiosis.[58] Why can that not be seen as something to feel optimistic about? After all, in a world where critique can no longer claim to have any kind of privileged relationship with 'science', and the very idea of having a 'science of good life' can no longer be taken seriously, to insist that there should be an automatic virtue for the critical project in retaining a principled state of isolation seems, at best, rather irresponsible.

That said, all these arguments represent, of course, only one side of the story. The other side of it is that 'if they are not coming for us with guns, it must be because we have already surrendered'. However, elegantly one may manoeuvre around it, the possibility that recognition indicates co-optation is never really going to go away. Nor will the idea of the liberal kiss of death, the concept incorporation through defangification, or the threat of a mutual cross-sterilisation.

Put in such terms, the prospects certainly seem rather bleak, if not exactly dispiriting. The real kicker in all of this, however, is that we will never be able to know in advance which of these scenarios we are living in 'until it is too late'. This does not mean, of course, that we should not therefore have any conversations about such matters. But perhaps, before we begin, it would be a good idea to work out what form they should have and in how public a setting they should take place (Table 6.5 at p. 190 infra).

[58] In Britain alone in recent years there have been several NAIL-related appointments at institutions that no one previously would have associated with any form of anti-establishment disciplinary sensibility: LSE, Durham, St. Andrews, Kings College London. Even Cambridge—partly through the expansion of its publishing business, but mainly through Allott's and Koskenniemi's personal influence—has opened its doors to some form of NAIL-inspired work.

## 6.9 In Lieu of a Conclusion

The investigative sequence sketched out above—from oral histories to discourse patterns, material bases, and aesthetic models—is not, of course, meant to suggest that this must be the only way in which one can meaningfully discuss the historical meaning of the NAIL enterprise from the vantage-point of the new generation of critical international law scholars. There exist many other angles from which one could explore the ideological effectivity of the NAIL movement, its intradisciplinary legacy, and politico-institutional lessons.

Notably, however, almost all of the existing discussions of NAIL appear to ignore these possibilities. Whether one takes China Miéville's brief chapter on the subject in *Between Equal Rights*,[59] Deborah Cass's iconic essay,[60] Nigel Purvis's early classic,[61] or pretty much anything attempted by Jason Beckett,[62] the general concept of the NAIL enterprise one typically tends to find in the literature today allows no space for the consideration of its material infrastructure. The challenge of trying to explain how NAIL came to be and 'what it is all about' is answered instead through a series of relatively protracted discussions of various abstract concepts, tropes, and slogans that in the popular perception have come to be associated with some of the movement's better known earlier texts. (The general inclination in this context appears to be almost always to focus on the first few chapters of *from apology to Utopia*.) The underlying suggestion, in other words, seems to be that it should be possible to discover something inherently special behind these slogans, concepts, and tropes, some sort of hidden intrinsic essence that can explain everything one really needs to know about NAIL: why its arguments came to develop the way that they did, what kind of logic moves its intellectual evolution and determines its intradisciplinary politics, etc. One does not need to be a diehard Marxist to see the fundamental problematicity of this approach.

To be sure, it must make perfect sense, to borrow the point from G. E. White, for 'persons whose principal business is the production of scholarship in which they seek to persuade others of the soundness and validity of their ideas'[63] to proceed on the presumption that ideas make history or that, at the very least, the logic according to which ideas develop through time must be fundamentally internal, that is to say, one can perfectly understand it 'on its own merits', independently from the messy realities of politics, power struggles, and economic exploitation by which it is conditioned. But virtually everything modern historiography has taught us belies that assumption, and one could cite any number of

[59] See Miéville 2005, 45–60.

[60] See Cass 1996.

[61] See Purvis 1991. In a similar vein, see also Carty 1991.

[62] See, typically, Beckett 2005.

[63] White White G 2003, xi.

occasions on which NAIL scholars themselves have made precisely the same argument.

Note that my point here is not to dispute the fact that it may be a worthwhile enterprise in general to ruminate on the theoretical implications of relative indeterminacy or the idea of 'the culture of formalism', or to deny the possibility that the use of some tropes and slogans in practice can carry a considerable symptomatic value. It seems to me rather self-evident that one would not be able to gain a full understanding of any collective project, especially one so complex as NAIL, without looking very closely at its internal landscape of ideas and narrative patterns that help to shape the project's 'official ideology' and filter its members' lived experience—and not just in what comes to their apprehension of whatever real-world phenomena are meant to serve as their objects of discourse but also in what concerns their understanding of the internal politics of that broader social space vis-à-vis which this project seeks to distinguish itself. But the notion that an abstract logical analysis of any given set of concepts or slogans, however comprehensively mapped out and referenced, can supply a meaningful insight into what that particular collective project is 'all about' or even how the logic behind its discourse 'really works' seems to me, at best, fundamentally untenable.

Surely, if there is one thing we can take away from NAIL's own 'turn to history', it ought to be that one must always question the explanatory value of any historiographic analytic that purports to be constructed around a decontextualized (and, therefore, inevitably formalist and also inevitably essentialist) exegesis of abstract concepts. One does not need to subscribe to any kind of vulgar economistic theory to see the validity of this point. If there is anything the study of history should have taught us about 'ideas', it is certainly that every time one observes the rise of a certain group of heretofore not very popular concepts or tropes, be it 'relative indeterminacy' or 'foregrounding the background', one is always going to be able to find behind this development a clearly identifiable pattern of some prior accumulation of institutional and ideological resources whose investment enabled the resulting spike in ideational interest to occur.[64] And it is that pattern—and the sense of strategic self-posturing vis-à-vis the rest of the discipline that informs it and is enabled by it in return—that we should try to comprehend and theorise.

## 6.10 Postscript: An Alternative View

It seems to be a common trend in much of NAIL scholarship to describe various intradisciplinary movements and traditions as projects and enterprises. Throughout this essay I, too, have drawn on this vocabulary rather liberally. But what exactly are the implications of calling something an 'enterprise' as opposed to, say, a

[64] Cf. Kennedy 2000, 498–500.

'school'? How should one understand the ontology of a 'project' as distinct from, say, a 'method'?

The most helpful definition of 'project' in recent critical legal literature to my mind comes from Duncan Kennedy's *Critique of Adjudication*:

> A project is a continuous goal-oriented practical activity based on an analysis of some kind (with a textual and oral tradition), but the goals and the analysis are not necessarily internally coherent or consistent over time. It is a collective effort, but all the players can change over time, and people at any given moment can be part of it without subscribing to or even being interested in anything like all its precepts and practical activities. ... It isn't a project unless people see it as such, but the way they see it doesn't exhaust what outsiders can say about it.[65]

Looking from this angle, it seems possible to attempt yet another imaging exercise for NAIL. The details of the argument can be changed, but the basic structure would be something like this:

1. In its socio-political dimension, NAIL first and foremost constitutes an academic project. It exists within—and is completely unthinkable outside—the material-institutional conditions of late-twentieth century Western academia. Its practices are richly saturated in conspicuous academicism (highly theory-intensive, sophisticated knowledge protocols) and it poses relatively prohibitive academic-capital entry tariffs to all potential entrants. Being an essentially Western (and decidedly Anglophone) phenomenon, NAIL, nevertheless, exhibits a rather sophisticated territorial-institutional logic. At the core of this logic lies a core-periphery-style dynamic of capital accumulation which on some basic level triggers a similarly structured pattern of personnel migration (jobs, education, social reunions, pilgrimage).
2. In socio-ontological terms, what NAIL essentially stands for is just a group of people brought together in the context of a common set of academic practices. The composition of the group has evolved over time, so have the common points of reference around which their collective practice was organised. The main organisational components of this practice, however, have remained unchanged: teaching (graduate-level law students), publishing (almost exclusively in professional scholarly contexts), conferencing and workshopping (both for networking and ideas-dissemination purposes), and securing of necessary socio-institutional capital to enable all of the above. A large part of NAIL's specific approach to workshopping derives from the organisational experience accumulated through the so-called 'Dighton weekends' exercises.
3. In ideational-thematic terms, what brought the NAIL project together does not, on the whole, lend itself to articulation in terms of any kind of common programmatic vision or even a common method or approach. Inasmuch as there has ever been any 'continuous goal-orientation' behind NAIL, it was most probably limited to nothing more than a vaguely shared sense of rejection

[65] Kennedy 1997, 6.

directed against the traditionally accepted disciplinary dogma, in particular, the traditional protocols of knowledge.

4. In socio-psychological terms, what gives the NAIL project its sense of collective identity was a New-Left-style culture of protest. To be a NAIL person has always been much more about *being-against* something called the 'mainstream' than *being-for* any specific research agenda, theory, ideology, or analytical method. Sharing in this culture is what ultimately explains point (3) above and point (7) below.
5. In material terms, what secures the continuation of the NAIL project beyond the point where the dynamics of (3) and (4) may expire is the retention of the collective academic practices and institutional loci described in point (2) above and point (6) below. It is this combination of logistical elements which supports the primary forms and modes of NAIL's practical self-realisation (conferences, symposia, summer institutes), and temporal reproduction (graduate student training).
6. Institutionally, the practical reality of NAIL has always remains inseparable from the Harvard Law School's graduate programme and, in chronological order, the institutional and financial support provided through the Harvard European Law Research Centre, the Brown International Advanced Research Institute, and the Harvard Institute for Global Law and Policy. Other centres, institutes, and common initiatives—most notably the Erik Castren Institute at the University of Helsinki—have also played an important but limited role in the maintenance and development of the NAIL project at various stages during its evolution.
7. Ideologically and disciplinarily, the collective identity of the NAIL project seems to remain much more incoherent, contradictory, and fragmented in the eyes of its participants than in the eyes of those who view it 'from outside'. This brings a great deal of anxiety and frustration to the former. The latter do not seem to care as much.
8. Many of those who have been part of the NAIL project over the years would have probably continued to write and teach 'against the grain' even if NAIL had never come into existence. But many more would not. For a volume with this kind of title, this seems a comforting enough thought on which to finish this essay.

## Appendix

**Table 6.1** The NAIL quest

| Timeframe | Organisational forms and institutional dynamics | Geography |
|---|---|---|
| Pre-history: early to mid-1980s | • Separate efforts and disparate projects of the founding figures coalesce into a common awareness of disenchantment and dissatisfaction with the disciplinary orthodoxy<br>• No movement yet, only a diffuse critical impulse rooted as much in 'theory' as in 'practice'<br>• No clearly identifiable institutional locus | Strong European orientation |
| 'Overture': Mid- to late-1980s | • Movement inception at Harvard: the formation of the first NAIL generation<br>• The foundations of the 'canon' laid down: *FATU*, *Decay of International Law*, *Eunomia*, and *Spring Break*—'high theory'<br>• The semiotic turn in NAIL<br>• The linkup with CLS and the Harvard JD programme | US institutional base and European 'cultural' orientation |
| First crisis: late 1980s | • Slaughter of all things CLS<br>• Movement-building freezes<br>• Scholarly work continues, but the NAIL project itself goes into hibernation | Residual dynamics in US institutions |
| Take-off and rise to the summit: early to mid-1990s | • The NAIL enterprise is reinvented through a strategic distancing from both CLS and the Harvard JD programme<br>• Primary institutional locus shifts to Harvard graduate programme<br>• Movement grows rapidly and organically: the second generation of the NAIL community enters the stage<br>• 'Dighton weekends'<br>• The NAIL tradition takes off: canon at zenith—NAIL as a theoretical confederacy<br>• The cultural turn in NAIL<br>• Sustained attacks from the disciplinary orthodoxy: accusations of obscurantism, faddishness, parasitism, nihilism, and irrelevance | Strong North American focus with a steady infusion of 'third-world elements' |

(continued)

**Table 6.1** (continued)

| Timeframe | Organisational forms and institutional dynamics | Geography |
|---|---|---|
| Dispersion and fragmentation: mid- to late 1990s | • The NAIL movement increasingly turns into a confederacy not only in theoretical but also in institutional terms: the 'long march through institutions' that began in the previous period leads to the emergence of various rifts and 'secessionary' dynamics<br>• Internal struggles within the community over the meaning of 'critique' and 'strategy'<br>• Break from CLS is completed both at the ideological and at the theoretical levels<br>• Rise of TWAIL | Increasingly global reach as NAIL is re-exported into Europe (Helsinki, London, etc.) |
| Second crisis and 'rebirth': turn of the millennium to early-2000 s | • Counter-revolution within the Harvard graduate programme<br>• 'Fin de NAIL' : the movement is dead, though the tradition survives<br>• Canon closed<br>• Some strands of the NAIL tradition go mainstream<br>• Disintegration of confederacy through fragmentation and successful secessions<br>• 'Young Turks' take off: FNRIL in Europe, TWAIL in the US<br>• The 'turn to history'—*Gentle Civilizer*<br>• Disciplinary orthodoxy loses interest in NAIL | 'Global' in image, North American, UK, and continental European in practice |
| 'Now': late 2000 s onwards | • 'Exodus' to Brown and return to Harvard: research institutes as new form of institutional linkage—the Dighton formula recycled<br>• No sign of a movement—'many scenes', 'autonomous scenes', 'ephemeral scenes'—but the tradition is partially brought back together<br>• The turn to political economy<br>• Even more 'history'<br>• CLS is a foreign land<br>• The third generation of NAIL—conspicuous academicism as a given<br>• Reinvention of TWAIL | Global in image and practice: North America, UK, Australia, with some outposts in between |

**Table 6.2** The patterns of discourse

| | 1988–1992 | 2008–2012 |
|---|---|---|
| Most talked about texts | *From apology to Utopia*[66]<br>*A new stream of International Law Scholarship*[67]<br>*Modernism, nationalism, and the rhetoric of reconstruction*[68]<br>*Spring break*[69]<br>*Decay of International Law*[70] | *Imperialism, sovereignty and International Law*[71]<br>*From apology to Utopia*<br>*Gentle civilizer of nations*[72]<br>*Dark sides of virtue*[73]<br>*Three globalizations of law*[74] |
| Most read authors | Martti Koskenniemi, David Kennedy, Anthony Carty, Nathaniel Berman | Antony Anghie, Martti Koskenniemi, David Kennedy, China Mieville, Susan Marks, Anne Orford |
| Main projects | Foucauldian archaeology<br>Legal semiotics<br>'Invented traditions' criticism | TWAIL (and law-and-imperialism studies more generally)<br>International law and political economy<br>'Global governance' studies (including governmentality studies)<br>Microhistory and biographization of international law<br>New Law-and-Development |
| Secondary projects | FemCrit, law and culture studies | Neo-Marxist ideology critique, non-Foucauldian genealogy and history of 'big' ideas, comparative international law studies |
| Notable absences | Marxism, eco-criticism, law and development, indigenous peoples' rights | FemCrit, eco-criticism, legal semiotics, sociology of international law, macrohistory, indigenous peoples' rights |

(continued)

66 Koskenniemi 1989.

67 Kennedy 1988.

68 Berman 1992.

69 Kennedy 1985.

70 Carty 1986.

71 Anghie 2004.

72 Koskenniemi 2002.

73 Kennedy 2004

74 Kennedy 2006.

**Table 6.2** (continued)

| | 1988–1992 | 2008–2012 |
|---|---|---|
| Theoretical inspirations and primary interdisciplinary debts | First generation US CLS<br>'French' (literary) theory and semiotics<br>Frankfurt School<br>Psychoanalysis | Foucault and the biopolitics tradition (Agamben, Hardt and Negri, etc.)<br>Non-liberal traditions of political-economic thought (Polanyi, Wallerstein, Marx, Hale, etc.)<br>Postcolonial studies (Said)<br>(American) Legal realism<br>Carl Schmitt<br>Slavoj Zizek |
| Key themes (*topoi*) | Legal indeterminacy and relative autonomy of the law; scepticism towards reconstructive projects; 'death of reason'; 'it's all semiotics'; international law as an 'invented tradition'; private as political; international law as a field of desire; international law and identity construction; international law as culture; intersectionality | 'Empire'; good governance as ideology; 'state of exception'; Schmittian critique of liberalism; 'blind spots'; role of experts; lawfare; 'law as constitutive'; 'international law and its subalterns'; international law as a system of core/periphery relations; economics is about institutions; economy is politics; 'dark sides of virtue(s)'; internationalism as ideology; 'false contingency'; foregrounding the background; critique of rights-lite |
| Main reaction against | Liberalism<br>Liberal legalism and juridificationism<br>Representational theory of the IL discourse<br>Normativist (prescriptivist) model of legal scholarship | Managerialism<br>Formalism and anti-formalism<br>Legal fetishism and legal nihilism<br>Progress narratives on the macro level<br>Depoliticization of economy and development/internationalism<br>Human rights fetishism (and human rights heroism too) |

**Table 6.3** General timeline of NAIL in its institutional dimension

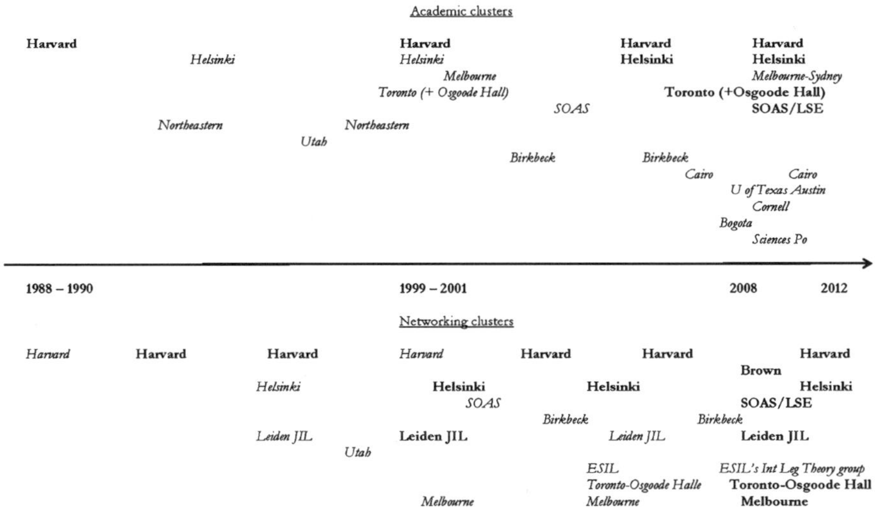


**Table 6.4** Evolution of NAIL at Harvard

| | Late 1980s | Mid-1990s | Late 2000s |
|---|---|---|---|
| Primary site and apparatuses of educational reproduction | • Harvard JD programme<br>• International law curriculum<br>• Seminars and reading groups | • Harvard LLM and SJD programmes<br>• International law curriculum broadly so conceived<br>• Large-scale conferences, graduate student workshops<br>• Dighton workshops | • Summer research institutes at Harvard (and Brown)<br>• Law and development and history of legal thought curriculum<br>• 'Dighton-lite': writing workshops as part of the summer research institutes |
| Profile of a typical NAIL newcomer at Harvard | Harvard-based, US American in origin, predominantly white, gender-balanced, almost exclusively legal-trained | Harvard-based, predominantly non-US American in origin, much weaker gender balance, racially mixed, predominantly legal-trained | Predominantly non-Harvard based, predominantly non-European and non-US American in origin, gender-balanced, racially mixed, disciplinarily diversified but primarily legal-trained |
| Typical posture of an average NAIL newcomer vis-à-vis US CLS | NAIL is an organic continuation of CLS. | CLS has run its course. | 'CLS? Yes, I heard of it before.' |

**Table 6.5** General timeline of NAIL

NAIL tradition

**International law semiotics** **FemCrit** *TWAIL* **TWAIL** **New TWAIL**

*FemCrit* *Sociology of international law* *Sociology/History* **History** **History**

*'Invented traditions' criticism* *Comparative international law* *Comparative international law*

*World systems tradition* **Political economy**

*Law and culture studies* *Neo-Marxism* *Neo-Marxism*

**1988 – 1990** **1999 – 2001** **2008** **2012**

International Politics: Principal Themes

'End of History' Yugoslavia and Rwanda Kosovo 9/11 Iraq 2003 Arab Spring
International community Tribunalization and peacekeeping ICC 'War on terror' Global financial crisis
Markets! 'Second generation reforms' at BWI 'Augmented' Washington Consensus Repudiation of neoliberalism Sovereign debt
EU created OSCE 'Fortress Europe' Great wave of EU expansion Merkozy
End of Comecon WTO created Asian crisis End of 'new economy' 'Death' of the Doha round

International Legal Discipline: Mainstream Trends

*Manhattan School* *Transnational Legal Process* *European neo-formalism* *'Governance theory'*
*Global administrative law*
*Human rights legalism* *'Empire and Law'* *Human rights constitutionalism*
*'New World Order'* *Liberal internationalism* *Constitutionalism and international law*

# References


Althusser L (1976) Essays in self-criticism. NLB, London

Althusser L (2001) Lenin and philosophy and other essays. Monthly Review Press, New York

Anghie A (2004) Imperialism, sovereignty and the making of international law. Cambridge University Press, Cambridge

Beckett J (2005) Countering uncertainty and ending up/down arguments: prolegomena to a response to NAIL, EJIL 16:213–238

Berman N (1992) Modernism, nationalism, and the rhetoric of reconstruction. Yale J Law Hum 4:351–380

Boltansky L, Chiapello E (2005) The new spirit of capitalism. Verso, London

Booker C (2004) The seven basic plots. Continuum Publishers, London

Bourdieu P (1988) Homo academicus. Polity Press, Cambridge

Bourdieu P (1990) In other words: essays towards a reflexive sociology. Stanford University Press, Stanford

Bourdieu P (1993) The field of cultural production. Columbia University Press, New York

Carty A (1986) The decay of international law? Manchester University Press, Manchester

Carty A (1991) Critical International Law: recent trends in the theory of International Law. EJIL 2:66–96

Cass D (1996) Navigating the newstream: recent critical scholarship in International Law. Nord J Int Law 65:341–383

Corten O (2009) Methodologie du droit international public. Editions de l'Université de Bruxelles, Brussels

De Toledo C (2008) Coming of age at the end of history. Soft Skull Press, Berkeley

Debray R (2000) Transmitting culture. Columbia University Press, New York

Eagleton T (1990) The ideology of the aesthetic. Blackwell Publishing, Oxford

Eco U (1979) The role of the reader: explorations in the semiotics of texts. Indiana University Press, Bloomington
Gorz A (1982) Farewell to the working class: an essay on post-industrial socialism. Pluto Press, London
Hobsbawm E (1989) The age of empire. Vintage Books, New York
Кагарлицкий Б (2009) Периферийная империя: циклы русской истории, Алгоритм-Эксмо, Москва
Kalman L (2002) Professing law: Elite law school professors in the twentieth century. In Sarat A et al (eds.) Looking back at law's century. pp 337–385
Kennedy D (1980) Theses about international law discourse. Germ Yb Int Law 23:353–391
Kennedy D (1985) Spring break. Tex L Rev 63:1377–1423
Kennedy D (1988) A new stream of international law scholarship. Wisc Int Law J 7:1–49
Kennedy D (2000) When renewal repeats: thinking against the box. NY Univ J Int Law Policy 32:335–500
Kennedy D (2004) The dark sides of virtue: reassessing international humanitarianism. Princeton University Press, Princeton
Kennedy D, Tennant C (1994) New approaches to international law: a bibliography. Harv Int Law J 35:417–460
Kennedy D (1997) A critique of adjudication (fin de siècle). Harvard University Press, Cambridge
Kennedy D (2003) Two globalizations of law and legal thought: 1850–1968. Suffolk Univ Law Rev 36:631–679
Kennedy D (2006) Three globalizations of law and legal thought: 1850–2000. In: Trubek D, Santos A (eds.) The new law and economic development: a critical appraisal. pp 19–73
Koh H (2003) The law under stress after September 11. Int J Legal Info 31:317–322
Koselleck R (2004) Futures past: on the semantics of historical time. Columbia University Press, New York
Koskenniemi M (1989) From apology to Utopia: the structure of international legal argument. Lakimiesliiton Kustannus, Helsinki
Koskenniemi M (2002) The gentle civilizer of nations: the rise and fall of international law 1870–1960. Cambridge University Press, Cambridge
Miéville C (2005) Between equal rights: a marxist theory of international law. Brill Publishers, Leiden
Morgan E (2001) The other death of international law. Lei J Int Law 14:3–24
Poulantzas N (1978) Classes in contemporary capitalism. NLB, London
Pratchett T (2011) I shall wear midnight. Corgi Books, London
Purvis N (1991) Critical legal studies in public international law. Harv Int Law J 32:81–127
Skouteris T (1997) Fin de NAIL: new approaches to international law and its impact on contemporary international legal scholarship. Lei J Int Law 10:415–20
Teles S (2008) The rise of the conservative legal movement: the battle for control of the law. Princeton University Press, Princeton
Tushnet M (2005) Critical legal theory (without modifiers) in the United States. J Political Phil 13:99–112
Veblen T (1994) The theory of the leisure class. Dover Publications, New York
White G E (2003) Tort law in America: an intellectual history (rev. edn.). Oxford University Press, New York
Wright E (1998) Rethinking, once again, the concept of class structure. In: Wright E (ed.) The debate on classes pp 269–348

# Chapter 7
# Innovative International Law Approaches and the European Condition

**Outi Korhonen**

**Abstract** This chapter explains the European reception of new approaches to international legal theory through three locations of debate: 'Europe', 'international law', and 'theoretical innovation'. Exploring the intersection of these new approaches to each debate in turn, the chapter explores how its influence transcends mere re-formulations or rhetorical changes in the field of international law and remains resistant to conventional doctrinal vocabularies or mainstream conceptions. Moreover, the chapter considers how the debate being situated in the context of Europe has in turn shaped the concerns and argumentation of new approaches outside of the United States. In the spirit of the critical tradition, the author reserves her doubts on each claim, and focuses on examining the conditions of their validity, motivation, and interaction.

## Contents



O. Korhonen (✉)
American University in Cairo, Cairo, Egypt
e-mail: korhonen@aucegypt.edu

J. M. Beneyto and D. Kennedy (eds.), *New Approaches to International Law*,
DOI: 10.1007/978-90-6704-879-8_7,

## 7.1 Introduction

The Madrid workshop (2010), which celebrated David Kennedy's scholarship and its global influence and, in particular, the book-length version of the innovative Spring Break/Rights of Spring, commissioned a number of accounts on international legal writing including a panel on new international legal theory in Europe. To take up the claim of newness, while celebrating a person as well and as deeply versed in the archives and achievements of international law as Kennedy, poses problems. Among other lessons, Kennedy has been the one to press on us that only a few things, if any, are new under the international legal sun and there is always a politics attached to a claim of renewal. He has touched on this issue in his epochal writings e.g. Primitive Legal Scholarship, The Turn to Interpretation, The Move to Institutions, When Renewal Repeats and others.[1] Let us consider, for instance, what he writes in the introduction to the latter in 2000:

> The discipline of international law today is cheek by jowl with people calling for new thinking and renewal, even as they offer up the most shopworn ideas and initiatives (…) (And, he continues that) (f)or international lawyers, the performances of renewal, criticism, and reform are central for professional identity and competence."[2] Kennedy says this about the past 100 years of international law.

Further, Kennedy maintains that placing the disciplinary renewalism in a context of the turns and moves that have taken place since the late nineteenth century still fails to explain 'how one or another argument common in the discipline for more than a century will in a given moment be experienced as novel and another as passe.'[3] Thus, Kennedy reminds us that what we experience as or choose to call new is an effect or a performance, behind which many more and less intentional motives work, rather than being new in any strict/genuine/pure or objective sense. When speaking of new—even if only new theory—one should bear in mind its complications and see the concept of the new as performative, motivated, effect willing, projective instrument rather than an objective scientific appraisal.

Thus, it is with apparent reservations if not unease that I have taken up this topic—new international law theory in Europe—inside which at least three arguments nest. They are:

(1) That there is theoretical innovation rather than just faddish re-formulations, performances, or rhetorical changes in the field of international law;
(2) That there are different approaches to international law, which cannot be reduced to doctrinal debates and could be characterized as theory (in a robust sense of 'theory'), and

[1] Kennedy 1986; Kennedy 1987b; Kennedy 1991; Kennedy 2000b.
[2] Ibid., 337.
[3] Ibid., 338.

(3) That Europe or Europeanness influences or conditions some of these approaches and the innovativeness in them in some way.

The topic could be treated in short by referring to Kennedy's discussion about the politics of renewalism and by concluding that the task here is to trace the politics of the European international lawyers at given eras—even if not often openly proclaimed. In that case, the conclusion would be that a political challenge to the mainstream ideology is really what any claims of there being new theory are all about, and this article would become one about academic ideology debates in our field. Such discussions, however, are many and I intend to pursue another path. There are other dimensions to entertaining the idea of what new is (or new is what), which one may call e.g., an ethics of encouragement, a pedagogy of passion, or a strategy of responsibility, as Kennedy also infers.[4] These merit a deeper look into the phenomenon of the new.

In the spirit of critical tradition, I reserve my doubts on each and all of the three claims above i.e., the existence of theory, innovation, and Europeanness. My aim is not to discredit but to examine the conditions of their validity, motivation, and/or interaction. The claims embed many further dimensions and debates that are quite important and, by no means, concluded as of to date. I shall first touch on those underlying debates and issues before moving on to my conclusions about whether and how the European condition influences—and, indeed, conditions—innovation in international law today.

## 7.2 Is There Theory Innovation?

In a traditional sense, theoretical innovation can be defined as a discovery of a new way of excavating, organizing, interpreting, and/or critiquing knowledge in an academic discipline. A theoretical innovation may be a general way of formulating something that practice seems to demand. It may also be a new discovery that springs from abstracted problem solving. It can be many things as long as it reaches beyond the systematization, recitation, and repetition of existing findings or the normal scientific paradigm to use Kuhnian terminology. While this paper is based on the multidimensional dialogues honoring Kennedy's work, it cannot but acknowledge the presence of theoretical innovation in international legal academia today and do so fully aware of the disciplinary politics involved. Yet these aside, Kennedy's two exceptional and early writings, the original Spring Break and Autumn Weekends,[5] merit a special mention when renewal is discussed. They were different enough to teeter on the outer brink of the discipline while they introduced an innovative melange of stances from existential phenomenology to

[4] Ibid., 337; this dimension of renewal is also treated, more or less explicitly, in Charlesworth and Kennedy's joint epilogue to a recent project on international law directed by Anne Orford. See, Charlesworth and Kennedy 2006.

[5] Kennedy 1985; Kennedy 1993.

historiography, journalism, American CLS, and beyond to an international lawyer's practice merged with academic analysis. In addition, they interconnected levels of substance that law more often seeks to avoid, to cover or to defer to other disciplines. In Spring Break (1985), Kennedy wrote in the first person unraveling the narrative logic at the same time as spinning it kaleidoscopically. It was authorship that had not been seen before. In Guenter Frankenberg's analysis, Kennedy...

> (...) aim(ed) to present an ever-densifying, multilayered report on the mutual constitution and reciprocal exclusion of determinacy and indeterminacy in everyday social life and thought. Kennedy offer(ed) a theory of motion that orients itself on shifting situative contexts (...) The reader is not to be supplied with aprioristic knowledge, totalizing concepts, or doctrinal truths, but rather should learn to adjust to surprises, the interplay of indeterminacy and determinacy, and a never ending critique.[6]

Kennedy's approach was so strikingly new that he was invited to write a methodological appendix[7] to the piece by the editors of the Texas Law Review. The following is what Kennedy says in the main text about why a new approach needed to be forged:

> For all (the) potential narrative variety (...) it seems that no matter which story I tell, our moment with Ana (the torture subject) is bound to be rendered too lucid, its own ambiguity lost to history. The difficulty is that both the analysis and the activism respond to narrative demands. Both enterprises struggle against the confusion of moments like ours with Ana, continuously creating new ambiguities and confusions. Although one point of a story like this one is to remember what was put aside in our moment with Ana, the telling reinforces a deeper social practice of conflict management: we defer coming to terms with the confusion of the moment by embroidering it into the fabric of numerous comforting stories.[8]

Such statements were, however, not sufficient from the point of view of the editors and a whole theory/method appendix was added. Since the time, many of the issues that Kennedy says in the quote above have been revisited by renewalist writers in the field e.g., the narrativism, the logic of history, the social practice of deference, to name but a few themes.

Kennedy's claims may not have been new in any absolute sense but the way they informed international legal discussion was new at the time and they have retained their renewalist power even today. It is indeed a very happy occasion as well as, perhaps, an improbable journey that has brought the book The Rights of Spring, containing Spring Break and Autumn Weekends,[9] onto the center stage of our celebration again, nearly a quarter century after the disciplinary break-through that they entailed. Kennedy hardly predicted this when he wrote the explanatory

---

6 Frankenberg 1989, pp 395–396.

7 Kennedy 1985, p 1417.

8 Ibid., 1380; I have discussed this condition in terms of situationality e.g. in Korhonen 2000.

9 Kennedy 2009.

appendix at the behest of the editors. He explained the innovative style in the following terms:

> I wanted to see whether it might be possible to think about and experience a legal situation while refusing to locate its determinate and indeterminate aspects in any specific locale, historical or ahistorical (...) This is, of course, a dangerous goal, for any attempt at ruthless dislocation will be its own victim.[10]

Thanks to Kennedy, we have been guided in thinking about, articulating, discussing, and experiencing this situation—and alerted to its risks but also potentials.

## 7.3 What is Innovation?

Innovation, in any case, is far from a self-evident proposal nor can it be a compelled renaissance move. When everyone calls for it, it easily becomes a lame act or a trickster's performance devoid of inspirational power, policy significance, or ethics. Authors, who have been charting the chronology of theoretical renewal e.g., the New Approaches to International Law (NAIL) movement, the new stream, critical theory, or 'deconstruction' in international law, that often ended up describing a cage out of which the birds had flown or something that was vague, lucid, and/or fragmented to the extent that it was not useful.[11]

Many renewalists would probably not have recognized themselves e.g., in Nigel Purvis's analysis in 1991 stating that ''the New Stream of international legal writing has sought to renew the coherence of the discipline' nor accepted his claim that the new stream itself is European although the international legal theory element American.[12] They may not have agreed with Dencho Georgiev that their critical moves were broadly speaking inherited from legal realism.[13]

More recently in 2000, when Gerry Simpson's excellent article stated that '(t)he rejuvenation of international law in the last decade has its source in two developments. On the one hand,'critical legal scholarship' (...) On the other hand (...) International Relations scholarship (...)'[14] many of the participants to the concurrent conference "International Law in Ferment: A New Vision for Theory and Practice" by the American Society of International Law (ASIL) would not easily have subscribed to any of these two sources—at least, not without a host of caveats and disclaimers.[15]

---

[10] Kennedy 1985, p 1420 and note 20.

[11] A random selection of the early analyses of 'new' writing in international law include, e.g., Georgiev 1993; Boyle 1985; Carty 1991; Onuf 1985; Purvis 1991; Scobbie 1990; Wrange 1990–1991; Wrange 1994.

[12] Purvis 1991, pp 88–89.

[13] Georgiev 1993, p 1.

[14] Simpson 2000, p 439.

[15] ASIL 94th Annual Meeting April 5–8 (2000).

Hilary Charlesworth, one of the foremost international legal innovators, discussed the internal contradictions and the practical frustrations of disciplinary renewal in the above-mentioned ASIL conference and said:

> (T)he critiques may have quite different agendas and may often end up in tension with one another (…) (furthermore,) these (new) approaches have had very little impact on actual practice of international law (although) (w)e may be able to point to some salutary developments in terminology and structure.[16]

She did, however, conclude with optimism that guerilla warfare type interventions here and there in the discipline, including practice, offered a hope in destabilizing oppressive narratives and exposing blind spots even if the process remained contradictory, fragmented, partial, and "in ferment".[17]

Be the source of renewal what it may, and be it an eternal repetitive trope or not without any guarantee of effectiveness, there is no question about the significance of the innovative-minded Movements Era in the discipline that started in the late 1970s. Assuming that this timing is about right, it is not very informative to claim that the international law renewalism were a subset of the Critical Legal Studies (CLS) since their beginning and development practically coincided and an order of primacy between the sites and authors would be non-sensical. First Kennedy, then Martti Koskenniemi, in their early work, departed from the tradition of international law literature. The two published their doctoral dissertations International Legal Structures (1987) and from apology to Utopia (1989).[18] Kennedy's early 'Theses' had already signalled that a paradigm shift was under way in 1980.[19] In discussing his point of departure from preceding legal argumentation styles, he said:

> The key to developing a style of legal analysis which could aid in elaborating the connections between practice and theory (…) is concentration upon discourse and upon the hidden ideologies, attitudes and structures which lie behind discourse, rather than upon the subject matter of legal talk.[20]

Below, it will be argued that the way in which the practice–theory nexus was worked in renewalist writing may be one site of difference between European and other innovators.

Elsewhere in the world at this time, Bhupinder Chimni and others were working on redesigns of the world according to international law in what later spurred the Third World Approaches to International Law (TWAIL). Chimni wrote about international commodity arrangements and criticized the acts of the transnational ruling elite.[21] The publications were followed by talks, seminars, conferences,

[16] Charlesworth 2000, p 74.

[17] Ibid., 74–75.

[18] Kennedy 1987a; Koskenniemi 1989.

[19] Kennedy 1980.

[20] Ibid. 355 (footnote contained in original excluded).

[21] Chimni 1987.

lectures, students, disciples, and networks started forming. At the 94th Annual Meeting of the ASIL in 2000, the same year as Charlesworth and Chinkin's award-winning book The Boundaries of International Law[22] was published, Kennedy redefined the subject itself—international law, not as the law governing state behavior, but as:

> a group of people sharing professional tools and expertise, as well as a sensibility, viewpoint, and mission (and) (t)heir disciplinary consciousness or lexicon (as) composed of typical problems, a stock of understood solutions, a vocabulary for evaluating new ideas, a sense about their own history and a way of looking at the world.[23]

Anthony Carty had described Kennedy's view of international law as one of an aesthetic achievement that absents the referent.[24] Kennedy had perplexed many with his ideas but what was sure is that he emphasized the disciplinary commitment to anti-complacent self-reflexion and renewal; he highlighted that international lawyers as a professional group were continuously launching internal criticism and reform projects as a part and parcel of the 'sensibility', 'viewpoint', 'mission', even 'the professional identity and competence', and demanded more attention to them than to the consolidation of canons and doctrines.[25] Yet, it was not that the definition of international law as the law governing state behavior was to be abandoned. The stage had merely been turned on it and it was being revisited from various perspectives with a strong heuristic strategy, of which the general trend was to center on the blind spots, the theoretical and political underpinnings of the missions, vocabularies, rhetorics and other moves, and the human agency and the power dimensions involved in everything that made international law a phenomenon of the world, a "this-worldly law"[26]—beyond a mere term in a lexicon.

Many things attested to Kennedy's success in turning the tables on international law and its sophisticated yet 'shopworn' discipline. In the 1990s, the NAIL conference series took place profiting from an internationally representative crowd; feminist, post-colonial, critique-race, post-structural, and other progressive approaches took hold in the discipline; the Australian and Third World Approaches to International Law (TWAIL) authors gained fame and influence. Makau Mutua defined TWAIL as a 'broad dialectic of opposition to international law', which it sees as a part of an illegitimate governance system that is...

> (...) premised on Europe as the center, Christianity as the basis of civilization, capitalism as innate in humans, and imperialism as a necessity also citing Kennedy's Primitive Legal Scholarship on international law's colonial origins.[27]

---

[22] Charlesworth and Chinkin 2000; it earned the ASIL's Gloer T. Butcher Prize in 2005.

[23] Kennedy 2000a, 104.

[24] Carty 1991, pp 70–72.

[25] Kennedy 2000a.

[26] See Frankenberg 1989, 360–361.

[27] Mutua 2000, 31, 33.

Charlesworth drew the audiences straight into the dialogue at the launch of feminist analyses of international law after the path-breaking conference at the Australian National University (ANU, 1990) in her manifesto that foregrounded the audience: 'Alienating Oscar? Feminist Analysis of International Law'.[28] In response to criticisms towards feminists' incoherence, she defined the feminist project in international law in the following way:

> We remain unrepentant. The feminist project in law is less a series of discrete interpretations than (...)'a sort of archeological dig'. Different techniques are appropriate at different levels of the excavation (...).[29] She concluded that alienation of the reactionary establishment was an inevitable incidence in the course of the work.[30]

At the turn of the millenia the ASIL devoted the above-cited 94th Annual Meeting to the arrival of movers in the field. The discipline embraced renewalist performances or, at least, tastes, confirming Kennedy's definition emphasizing in-built reformism. Still, only a few of the participants to any of these conferences could be or would even like to be defined as 'theoretically innovative'. For good reason: There are many other significant ways to shake a discipline beyond focusing on its theory or becoming inventors—e.g., politically, morally, ecologically, globalistically motivated stances. Also, there are many of the 'mpm' people and practitioners, who are simply not into theory, at least in the traditional sense, which they see as an item of politically reactionary or otherwise unnecessary intellectual paraphernalia. Although innovative-minded international lawyers come in many varieties, the ones influenced by Kennedy mostly share a consciousness of the 'mpm' i.e., the modern/post-modern era. Mpm is used here as an acronym coined by Duncan Kennedy and denoting the modernist/postmodernist situation or double bind, in which one cannot really escape one or the other despite their epistemic and cultural crossfire.[31] The origins for the dislike towards theory among a number of people experiencing the mpm-bind are evident in Duncan Kennedy's explanation:

> "Modernism/postmodernism (mpm, in orig.) (...) is a project with the goal of achieving transcendent (...) experiences (...) in the interstices of a disrupted rational grid. (...) The analytics, which in modernism are always ex post, are incorporated into performance by postmodernists and emphasize the omnipresence of (...) (e.g.) the plasticity of the formal media that presuppose that they are not plastic."[32] This, he says, with the understanding that the said "postmodernists" can never escape the vestiges of modernism ingrained in their pm-performances.

There were, however, other reasons not to innovate theoretically or to make such claims. For some, to be 'theoretical' was anything but a merit and risked to

---

[28] Charlesworth 1993, 1.

[29] Ibid. 3.

[30] Ibid 13; note that Charlesworth has explained that the Oscar Schachter ("Oscar") himself was not at all 'alienated' when approached by this suggestion directly by HC.

[31] Kennedy 1997, p 7.

[32] Ibid. 7–8.

reduce real-life relevance and effectiveness, the very virtues that e.g., Charlesworth had called for (above). These included e.g., a number of academics and consultants who imagine that their practical assignments involve, above all, time-efficient, i.e., supposedly theory-free, resoluteness. And, naturally, a number of those whose projects evaluated their achievements frequently in terms of the life-world changes for their target groups e.g., women, the aboriginals, subsistence farmers, refugees or others, who were more directly impacted by policy changes than 'theory'. This is because effective decision making is more often than not associated with minimal theory, although no necessary link exists. To identify with 'theory' is not without political and strategic risks.

Thus, to speak of a rush of 'new theory' and to assume that it means something beyond normal science, the status of which Kennedy defined as one of innate and repetitious renewal projects, is a paradoxical call. Also, when there are claims of newness, the innovations are not necessarily politically or theoretically new even if they fulfil the criterion of a disciplinary performance that becomes significantly more common at a given moment than previously. As noted above, newness or innovativeness have much broader scopes than theoretical. There is also the fact that many new approachers have seemed inclined to do away with reifications such as (grand) theory and methodology since, at least, the 1990s. If we take all of the above as given, renewal of theory or method becomes obsolete while the subject matter to renew can hardly be recognized—and as such it is not 'solid' enough to demonstrate change and transformation. The same urging applies as with the discipline itself—it is not the subject matter of new theory itself but what lies behind it where we should center our attention.[33]

## 7.4 New and Old Scenes?

Despite its paradoxes, ebbs, and flows, the Movements Era (late 1970s to present) took hold. For the movements to form, the 'new continent' and, later, the 'new world' were undeniably the main set-up. The European-origin international lawyers, who were riding the new waves, did not do so in isolation from America and the emerging world at large—quite the contrary. Kennedy spent time in Europe, cultivated European ties, Europeans sought him out at Harvard Law School, attended the ASIL and NAIL conferences, published in the American and Australian edited collections, embraced critiques of neo-capitalism/colonialism, and sympathized eagerly with the TWAIL although the latter tended to shut down apologetic passes. Many Europeans had grown weary and even quite sick of their old institutionalized ways of looking at their discipline and tapped into the new continent and the new world energy fields that offered hope in so many different ways against the stagnating weight of the European establishment.

[33] See above quote from Kennedy (with fn. 20 *supra*). Cf. Kennedy David 1980, p 355.

Thus, on the one hand, the European engagement with the new stream took place thanks to the work of Transatlantic personalities, such as Kennedy, who may be more European through their European ties and in a constructive sense than many who tread knee deep in European soil. On the other hand, there were innovative-minded European lawyers, who affiliated with the ranking chart topping academic institutions, the Ivy League, and forged co-funding initiatives with them. They were needed as intellectual incubators as much as protective shells against that part of the European establishment and disciplinary culture that appeared reactionary or defensive in the face of the movements. The innovatively minded appealed to the authors and disciplinary positions on the new continents (America, Australia) and the new world (developing world) exploiting the gentleness of liberal internationalism. They also drew on a good measure of post/neo-colonial guilt. The liberal European circles could not but acknowledge the calls of inclusiveness, multiculturalism, pluralism, developmentalism, the subalterns, and the others, not to appear conservative and defensive of the neo-colonially infested Fortress Europe. Thus, even in Europe, some conference series took place although mostly in the margins leaning on the new continent for acknowledgement and support. While at home, a typical European new streamer would learn to think of herself as the token critique in good days and, in bad days, someone trying desperately to pass through never-ending legitimization exercises and apologetic justifications for her 'sensibility of renewal', which Kennedy identified as a non-threatening and commonplace professional posture on the other side of the Atlantic. It was more as with the response to feminists that Charlesworth described, namely that if new and subversive enough, a novel approach would be construed as downright 'mad' from the perspective of the normal science canonists and be sidelined if tolerated at all. Although it seems but logical that to bring new is to bring challenges to the old and, thus,

> (f)eminist methodologies challenge many accepted scholarly traditions. (…) (Still) (f)or this reason, feminist methodologies are regularly seen as unscholarly, disruptive, or mad. They are techniques of outsiders and strangers.[34] Having collaborated widely also in Europe, Charlesworth's views applied equally to European experiences and to any approach that was new enough.

The European new streaming and its innovation potential was, thus, more of a constricted resource than its American and emerging world counterparts. Throughout the Movements Era, European renewalism seemed to have clustered into small pockets, sticking to their countries of origin without large-scale, or in-depth cross-exchange between academic institutions. Often notable innovative authors worked completely alone. The networks were small and depended, mainly, on the British scholars, because of the dominant language set its own conditions that were not at all always appreciated in the lesser linguistic Empires. The renewalist circles that functioned in Europe did not have strong interconnections or an umbrella organization even given the inauguration of the European Society of

[34] Charlesworth 2004, p 160.

International Law (ESIL) in 2004—not, at least, in comparison to other academic fields. Nevertheless, one cannot de-emphasize the renewalist impact on the European scene of a set of notable, yet extremely diverse initiatives by individuals and institutions such as the ones calling forth and sponsoring the present collection.

The Movements Era has thus been a different one in Europe than in other places. Geography does matter although not in simplistic terms. The embrace and co-optation of the movements in the discipline at large e.g., in the America, seemed much less of a high-stakes debate. There was less hyperbole, hyperventilation, hassle, and self-torment about post-modern discourse pervading the discipline in the new world than on the very continent where post-modern theory had reined supreme in other disciplines for several decades already. In Europe, one seemed to remain as wrought as ever about the self-irony, tragedy, paradoxality, and the rest of the mpm symptoms to which renewalists had (allegedly and irresponsibly) plunged the discipline—as if closing one's eyes and ears would have made the whole mpm condition disappear. Beckett implied to the general unease about the associations that had emerged while he has the following to say about 20 years of Koskenniemi's influence in European international law academia:

> (I)t is technicalization itself (...) which forms the true enemy, and Koskenniemi joins forces, perhaps unpalatably, with Carl Schmitt, but also with Isaiah Berlin and Michel Foucault. Their aim being to re-center contingency and decision-making (...) (r)ejecting the bland, technicalising, discourse of the correct answer (...) (Yet it is) this naive belief, in progress, in justice, in universality, in the technically/objectively correct answer (that) is the Iron Cage of juridical modernity: the poisoned chalice bequeathed to us by the discipline's founders (...) It is, tragically, that irony which will preserve the value and relevance of Martti's (Koskenniemi) work.[35]

If we compare the picture of the disciplinary tradition described by Kennedy above—as a group of people with a set of professional tools and a propensity for renewal—and the other by Beckett—a group of people drinking out of a poisonous chalice handed down by the founders—we can see that the scene set-up for scholarship is very different. Kennedy speaking and writing to an international audience at the ASIL and Beckett discussing Koskenniemi's significance at a debate organized by the European Journal of International Law (EJIL) described a very different mood and climate in which the discipline and innovation was supposed to thrive. To put it crudely, in Europe, renewalists seemed to ravel in uneasy irony often feeling caged in an eternal search for legitimisation; in America they tapped onto the discipline's innate strengths with much less apologetic voices. It must be noted, of course, that both of the venues above (ASIL, EJIL) are inclusive of the other continents and, thus, do not represent an American versus. European dichotomy in any definite terms. Notwithstanding such allowances there was a remarkably different emphasis, mood, and climate. To better understand the European side, it may be instructive to consider what Guenter Frankenberg,

[35] Beckett 2009.

another Transatlantic yet European based thinker, said about law, irony, and seriousness:

> Since the time of the Mosaic Law and Solomon's, supposedly, wise judgements, law and judicial decisions have been enveloped in an aura of solemn, austere seriousness. This seriousness is reflected in the specialized language of jurists, in their esoteric logic, in legal rituals and ceremonies far removed from everyday life (...) Form, formality and formalism are all taken seriously. They are said to stand for matters of substance demanding seriousness (...) (Yet) (c)ritique and irony have long accompanied this mulish seriousness on its quest for transcendental fixed points in a stubbornly fickle and this-worldly law.[36]

This duality applied also to (international) legal theory and discussions. It was, perhaps, more openly and readily accepted in sites where European-style establishment culture carried less credence i.e., outside the European mainstream scenes. Perhaps, the litmus test was, paraphrasing Frankenberg, whether one could imagine the blindfolded justice laughing or even smiling on one's theory–or 'non-theory' as will be discussed below.[37]

Having said this, one must not forget that Kennedy's early Theses[38] appeared in a European publication, the German Yearbook of International Law, and were described thus by one reviewer:

> (...) 1980 is the date of Kennedy's Theses on International Legal Discourse, the very title of which signals Kennedy's arrival on the international legal scene with a manifesto in his hand and revolution in his heart.[39]

It was a defined and serious way of opening a renewal debate. Would this choice of posture have been influenced by the European experiences and audiences of the author? Certainly different from the tone in 2000 and even reminiscent of Luther's solemn hammerwork at Wittenberg four centuries earlier, the nailing of theses was received, on the one hand, with a liberated cheering but also, on the other, a reserved and defensive response. Since then, a fair measure of self-effacement replaced'revolution-at-heart'. The voice was toned down and ironized. Ironically, as much as the manifesto-stance caused a stir in both positive and negative senses, the increase of irony seemed to balm the European mpm ailment and the initial defensiveness against renewal calls. For instance, Beckett claimed that even the most sceptical early opponents to renewalist writing had since come around and mentioned specifically Ian Scobbie, who wrote a review (in 1990) the title of which already said much: 'Towards the Elimination of International Law: Some Radical Scepticism about Sceptical Radicalism'.[40] It was in response to Koskenniemi's from apology to Utopia and other 'new theory'. Then, Scobbie found that...

---

36 Frankenberg 1989, pp 360–361.

37 Ibid., 360.

38 Kennedy 1980.

39 Onuf 1988, p 638.

40 Scobbie 1990.

> Mr Koskenniemi's deconstruction might simply prove to be a pitfall gift-wrapped for the intellectually pretentious in that it seems to be a new and powerful method of analysis (...) (D)econstruction, in so far as law is concerned, is only a rehashing of established analytical methods, dressed up in modern linguistics, and predicated on a naive truth-theory, which ultimately would appear to be self-defeating.[41]

In the course of the two decades, according to Beckett and Scobbie himself, there has been a clear rapprochement. For one, it was thanks to the change of tone on the renewal-side that shifted from hearty revolution and/or strict theory emphasis to irony and mpm resignation. Today, we find that there is much agreement between the 'sceptical radicalism' and 'radical scepticism', i.e., between a token renewalist critique and a token mainstream defender in Europe. Kennedy explained why this would occur by his redefinition of international law in 2000 (quoted above) in which he pointed out that repeated reform performances lie at heart, tides change, and arguments get eternally recycled in the discipline. If we believe Kennedy, the rapprochement was but an inevitable step in the game inside the disciplinary frame. One may indeed wonder what the function of the newness claim is in this context today. Should it be abandoned or does it serve a valuable politics, pedagogy or even an ethics? It seems that the most celebrated authors identified with the renewalist-spirit are cautious in the use of the 'new'. Thus, it may appear that it is a chimera to juxtapose the old and the new except for specific purposes at specific times, places, and strategic situations.

Yet, many cannot escape a sense of a veritable loss of faith if we were to abandon 'renewal', 'innovation', and 'newness' as phenomena and resign to their dispassionate, discursive recycling according to the disciplinary logic as described by Kennedy. Would it matter? Let us consider what the general theorist Peter Sloterdijk said about the situation of caged newness and how it was experienced by the younger generations. In his main oeuvre Critique of Cynical Reason in 1983,[42] Sloterdijk explained how the critique and the mainstream could not ultimately differ and were pervaded by the same disillusionment and (self-)irony. He said:

> Critique, in any sense of the word, is experiencing gloomy days. Once again, a period of pseudocritique has begun, in which critical stances are subordinated to professional roles (...) (T)he hollowness of the critique that (tries) to drown out its own disillusionment (can) be felt. Such a critique realizes that having success is a long way from having an effect. It writes brilliantly but in vain, and that can be heard through everything.[43]

This reflects the same worry that was expressed by Charlesworth about the disciplinary renewal and its practical effectiveness as quoted above. So is there anything to be done in order to avoid the tragic irony, disillusionment, resignation, hollowness and practical ineffectiveness if we acknowledge that renewal may often be a chimera? As suggested e.g., by TWAIL, the feminists or as alluded by Kennedy, a politics and/or ethics must be uncovered; but how to do so without

[41] Ibid. 346.
[42] Sloterdijk 1983.
[43] Ibid. xxxvi (preface).

shipwrecking in politics as so many European thinkers have done from Machiavelli to Hobbes, Heidegger, or Schmitt and beyond? How to cross-over to ethics or to situate our renewal efforts in a multidisciplinary push that stimulates embodied and, preferably, transcending disciplinary experience that does not suffer from an incurable mpm anxiety?

## 7.5 What is Theory Anyway?

In a modern sense, theory is a way to organize ideas and to assess their validity. If we were operating in the pre/modern modes, it would be easy to identify theories of international law: positivism and naturalism, post/realism, and idealism, their derivatives, and the ones that can be based on Kennedy's redefinition of international law above. However, conscious of the mpm situation, the two influential dissertations by Kennedy and Koskenniemi seemed to take us out of such modes beyond a point of no return. The discipline used to be so deeply embedded in its reigning theory that the illusion of theorylessness prevailed.[44] At the launch of the Movements Era, the cover was lifted and it was faced off with semiotics, structural linguistics, deconstruction, post-structuralism, and all of what Scobbie chose to call 'scorched-earth radicalism of modern French philosophy.'[45]

Kennedy had, however, made his theory-scepticism and methodological disclaimers explicit already before the publication of International Legal Structures (1987) despite writing e.g., the methodological appendix to the original Spring Break (above) and other occasional overtures on theoretical problematics. Koskenniemi later joined the move away from theory and method statements. There was a clear abandonment of what were taken as disciplinary fixtures and academic reifications. Before long, many renewalists landed in the paradoxical mpm stance on theory. If it was important, as Charlesworth said, to expose the way we organized disciplinary ideas and assessed validity through getting away from the illusion of theorylessness, then how could we do it if we did not believe in theory any longer?[46] If theory dissolved into non-theory, so did the baseline of comparison between old and new theory.

The substitutes for the concepts of 'theory' and 'method' started appearing in international legal writing at the turn of the 1990s, and they still abound ranging from sensibility, intuition, voice, style, credo, rhetoric to performance. Somewhat more firm concepts, such as discourse, strategy, approach, and stance have also become commonplace. For sure, these did their work to maintain distance to theory-building, and there is little doubt that a grand theory became a self-defeating quest after the mpm struggle colonized our thinking.

---

[44] Charlesworth 2000, p 75.

[45] Scobbie 1990, p 339.

[46] See Kennedy 1986, p 13.

There were, however, clear differences in how one opposes being fixed in and locked down by theory. One difference in the approaches influenced by Kennedy and Koskenniemi remained, at least, until the mid-1990s. While Kennedy had disclaimed against theory and method from early on, in Europe, as Koskenniemi's dissertation (from apology to Utopia) demonstrates, at the very least in academic degree work, some sort of theory and method was not let go even among the renewalists.

Whether the theory and method that the renewalist-minded Europeans tolerated could be described as small-theory/small-method or theory-like temporary scaffoldings for academic degree purposes, concepts such as phenomenology, deconstruction, linguistics, and (neo)formalism stuck although the trend was to adopt ever more disclaimers. Koskenniemi moved away from the theories and methods that the 1989 from apology to Utopia embraced between the former and his second major oeuvre. George Rodrigo Bandeira Galindo in reviewing Koskenniemi's the gentle civilizer[47] paid attention to the author's dislike of terms such 'ideas'or 'history'and their replacement with 'sensibility', 'intuition', and 'narrative'.[48] Moreover, Galindo discussed the fact that little by way of definition or the significance of these preferences was articulated beyond what we were supposed to understand on the basis of our mpm consciousness ourselves.

Interestingly, the reviewer's tone had also changed: Whereas Scobbie dissected and reconstructed Koskenniemi's theoretical and international legal claims spinning them into unintended contradictions in 1990, Galindo was merely expressing a resigned worry that central operating terminology of the 'sensibility', 'intuition', and 'narrative' did not receive any explanation in such a leading piece of disciplinary writing.[49] In 2005, Galindo felt only baffled, not 'sceptical' like Scobbie, about the loose terminologies of major work in theoretical renewal. However, there was one exception to the abandonment of theory in Koskenniemi's work and this was what Galindo said about Koskenniemi's attraction to formalism:

> Koskenniemi sets out his own theoretical (or non-theoretical, as he would prefer, in orig.) approaches to international law (…) (I)nternational law should allow itself to be guided by formalism (…) (while) it is not possible to ignore the fact that formalism feeds off a culture of resistance to power, a social practice that involves responsibility, openness and equality (…) (And,) (t)he universalism preached by formalism is based on the idea of 'lack'; that is, the universality that such a culture purports to have is negative rather than positive.[50]

Thus, based on Koskenniemi, Galindo found that the theory substitute that would not be rendered useless by the mpm consciousness was a non-theory that emphasised the lack of, the void, and the escape from substance i.e., also the political/ethical action—a negation at work. Here emerged hence a contradiction to the call of substance without which renewal seemed rather non-sensical or obsolete as was argued in the discussion of the above section.

---

[47] Koskenniemi 2002.

[48] Galindo 2005.

[49] Ibid. 546.

[50] Ibid.

On the other hand, if we take renewal as a disciplinary performance with a contingent effect, Koskenniemi's performance as a renewal figure regardless of the criteria of renewal was undoubtedly and always a top performance. Even his paradoxical renaissance moves toward such an old school theory as formalism did not reduce the effect of newness and this was true regardless of how such formalism would fare e.g., in light of a critique of the plasticity of forms as, e.g., Duncan Kennedy's argument or in regard of Frankenberg's suggestion of the misguided seriousness about formalism (above) that were also discussed in the Movements. There was, however, the tragic side of paradoxality of the mpm situation that became more articulated when in the mode of negation. Going back to Sloterdijk again, who discussed the struggles and paradoxes in general terms in 1983, the escape from substance tended to bear the undoing of critical theory, which finds little shelter if its crux rests merely on guiding sensibilities and a denial of substance. Sloterdijk said that

> In this sensitive critique (sensibility-tradition indebted to Adorno), there is a paralyzing resentment (…) (T)his sensitive theory is based on a reproachful attitude, composed of suffering, contempt, and rage against everything that has power. It makes itself into a mirror of the evil in the world, of bourgeois coldness, of the principle of domination, of dirty business and its profit motive (…) It is inspired by an archaic No to the world of the fathers, legislators, and profiteers. Its basic prejudice is that only evil power against the living can come from this world. That is the reason for the stagnation of Critical Theory." As an antidote Sloterdijk recommended that "(t)he impulse of Critical Theory is becoming mature enough to burst open the strictures of negativism.[51]

Thus, the abandonment, denial, and lack of theory as well as renewal faced the same challenge: to harness elitist sensibility only worked so far, to formulate a politics risked shipwreck, to avoid them may mean ineffectiveness, frustration, and the undoing of critique itself.

How these challenges were mediated differs among the renewalists. The differences were clear between e.g., Koskenniemi's formalism as the non-theory of the 'lack', Charlesworth's demand of effectiveness and critique of the illusion of theorylessness, and Kennedy's critical voice that sometimes jumped between stances to the extent of appearing 'unsure'.[52] Yet another path has been taken. A number of renewalist authors embarked on avenues that were characterized as 'high theory' with an implied (self-) criticism of the intellectual chauvinism involved.[53] The health benefit of these approaches was that they steered beyond the mpm theory–anxiety and employed anything and everything from modern art to neo-conceptualizing philosophy in their attempts to achieve accuracy and to bring

---

[51] Sloterdijk 1983, xxxv.

[52] Onuf 1988, p 631.

[53] While at Harvard Law School Jean Thomas was conducting a workshop on high-theory discussions (HLS Graduate Programme 1997–1998); several authors in Anne Orford's project and book International Law and its Others might be characterised, at least to some extent, as high-theory writers including e.g. Douzinas, Duncanson, Parsley, Orford, Grbich, Hoffmann and others. See Orford 2006.

issues into discussion that had remained outside the disciplinary syntax, grammar, and idiom. An example can be drawn from Karen Knop, who, in discussing the creation of meaning in international law and the role of domestic courts, likened it to David Henry Hwang's play M. Butterfly's critical relationship to its inspiration Puccini's opera Madame Butterfly. Comparing domestic courts' work on international law to local art productions, Knop said:

> (I)nstead of thinking of the local production as second-rate, we might think of it as embedding the play in that time and place, and forging a bond with other productions in other times and places. Beyond this, each and every local production might be seen to change the meaning of the play.[54]

The multi-dimensionality of the local meaning-giving was discussed by Knop in reference to a post-colonial opera critique and international law in a revealing manner emphasizing the situationality of legal performance and its this-worldly significance.[55] Explicit and uninhibited about creating new languages and idioms for discussions about international law such authors benefit from not being (entirely) fixed and bogged down by the limitations of the frame within which the discipline operated. The challenge for these approaches was, however, one with audience-interest/alienation through what may have seemed private languages and a perceived hi-brow multidisciplinary stance. There are a number of readers, be they academics or practitioners, who do not have the time for, the patience with or the respect for newly conceived, metaphor-rich, discipline-crossing , or art-combining lingos, the concepts and references of which may seem utterly foreign or ones never to be heard of again. There were, however, always also those hungry for the foreign terrains and the'hi-theory' pieces attracted a number of afecionados in the same way as heavy poetry or ultra-modern conceptual art may do. Thus, mind-exercising, fulfilling, adventurous, and/or admirable in their accuracy and transcendence-seeking as they may be, the practical effectiveness issue remained, as did the mpm issues that critics would quickly be able to spin in the way Scobbie did in the early days of Koskenniemi, Kratochwil, and others.

Whichever of the above stances one chose in regard of the theory-problematique, a universal solution to defeat frustration, paradoxality, vacuity, and tragic denial seemed difficult to conceive. The Movements Era inspired many alternatives that tackled the challenges in very different ways. They did, analogously to Knop's local courts, also sometimes produce situated and shifting meanings and innovative steps. Difficulties and challenges did not mean that there were no successes and no possible stances to be taken in theoretical terms. For instance, the TWAIL and the feminist stances achieved guerilla-style success and firmness against hegemony-producing elements, and emancipation for both practical and theory purposes, and so did

[54] Knop 2000, 533.

[55] Similar approaches have been discussed above e.g. in Kennedy's original Spring Break (Kennedy 1985), in Orford's collection (Orford 2006), and in Korhonen, International Law Situated (Korhonen 2000).

Kennedy's Spring Break.[56] Some produced a local effect, some exercised a lasting influence on the discipline and, above all, one that was dynamic and anti-stagnating in terms of law as well as our self-awareness whatever our stance to theory may be. Whether local and momentary or global and lasting had nothing to do with situated significance, as Knop's article showed, and this applied also to theory—including its negatives.

## 7.6 What is Europe?

To accept to discuss something assuming a fixable European identity is, of course, an aporia par excellence for anyone experiencing the constraints of post-modernity and the mpm situation. The caveats abound: What is 'Europe' as a geographic, political, communal, economic, ethno-religious, essentialist, semantic, philosophical, and cetera project? What are the various dimensions of consequences that emanate from even a momentary fix of an imagined European community, its membership, and a European identity? What are the politics of such a fix? Should one opt for the Kennedy–Koskenniemian language of a European sensibility, style, or, indeed, a Europeanness of non-Europeanness—to escape or, at least, vaccinate against the tragic paradoxes involved in assuming an mpm-conditioned Europeanness?

It may indeed seem that the only option is to ask what the European is not e.g., in comparison to the New World. Or, one may consider Europe as a mere symbol. A mere symbol 'Europe' is different from Europe as economic might, polished metropoles, self-conscious institutions, or deep secret archives, and its is different from the Europe-as-project e.g., of the European Union, the Council of Europe, or the Organization for Security and Co-operation in Europe, while, despite all of the logical indeterminacy, 'Europe' as a universal signifier floats in the global intellectual discourse invoking associations of over-saturation, stagnatedness, class-consciousness, and an overkill of a governance grip unseen ever before.

However, for various reasons not unrelated to a personal situation, all of these solutions for identifying the European condition may seem dissatisfactory. Descriptions of European sensibilities, styles, the various identity projects of Europe, or the symbol/signifier Europe hit the nail a bit angularly at best. Although it may seem a linguistic trick to some, I find it more accurate to tease out the European condition and its implications to new theory through 'traces', as the concept is made famous by the European thinkers from Heidegger to Derrida. If and when a trace of the Europeanness can be found, it should be remembered that a trace points to that which is absent—i.e. that which was or will be; at most, a sign, a footprint suggesting a dusted-over path. E.g., one could ask whether Koskenniemi's longing for the 'lack' theory of formalism is of this nature and simultaneously tell of the European condition? Is it the European condition that made Kennedy nail his theses on the pages of the German Yearbook of International Law in both a protestant and a

[56] See references to Charlesworth, Chinkin, Chimni, and Kennedy above.

self-ironical yet serious performative gesture? Is it the European condition that made Scobbie so sceptical of radicalism in 1990? And, is it the same Europeanness that made Pål Wrange and the successive generations embrace from apology to Utopia and the main work influenced by it as star-quality "jam-sessions" so overdue and welcome?[57]

If, hypothetically, there are European traces in the former, it seems that the outcome of this article is very different from the proposals by Thomas Skouteris in this volume and others claiming that history/historiography is the key to or the core of European new theory in the field of international law.[58] It is not about history —not about the subject matter as Kennedy said—it is about traces hidden in history-related and any number of other moves and performances. In other words, there can very well be a trace of 'Europe' (however defined) e.g. in Kennedy's Theses in 1980, his history critique (Primitive Legal Scholarship 1986) and, in his subsequent historical, religion-related, structural/post-structural, cultural, managerial, and humanitarian quests of international law[59]—one or all of them. However, there is nothing exclusively European in all the de/re-constructive and sensibility seeking history writing that has taken place since 1980s. For one, in Kennedy's case, the European influence could be traced to the performances, their time and place, rather than to the subject matter of these performances if his redefinition of the discipline above is taken to weigh on how we should read renewalist writing.

Undoubtedly, the ignoble role of Europe in world history weighs heavily on any innovative theorising; the progress narratives, and their mirrors—i.e., the narratives of decay of European efforts at international justice. These demonstrate as much as anything our take of 'international law as therapy', although Koskenniemi coined the phrase specifically in reference to Allott's revolution of the mind—in a conservative idealist sense.[60] From conservative to vanguard, there seems to be no end in sight for the need of therapeutizing and counter-therapeutizing for our frustration with justice, fragmentation of our world and our law, the dark sides of our humanitarian sentiments—aspects that class discussions also reveal without exception. Thus, one might also suggest that the Europeanness (if any) in the newer discourse surfaces most plainly as the struggle with the symbolical package of Europe—or the package of the symbol 'Europe' as described by Sloterdijk and many others. The European condition forces one into a particularly gloomy mpm struggle accentuated by the utter saturatedness of all fields from legal policy to theoretical innovation; a struggle with the homage to founding fathers and history; the struggles with the aversion to pragmatics and embodiment; and with the resort to non-personal discipline as personal and collective therapy. No wonder that many simply want to react with the archaic 'No' to everything that 'Europe' in these many senses represents.

---

57 See, Wrange 1994.

58 See e.g. Galindo's taken on Koskenniemi discussed above.

59 See note to Kennedy's history discussions above.

60 Koskenniemi 2005.

In these struggles, however, as in Simone Weil's analysis of the European mind, there is the possibility of both grace and gravitation, the latter ranging from despair to paralysis.[61] The gravitation, at worst, may produce an imprisonment with a mode of analysis, e.g., the historicization, if it becomes dominant of the renewalist or any other paradigm and freezes change, versatility, and the importance of the 'here and there' of meaning-creation that Knop showed in the discussion above. The grace is the obvious self-therapeutical effect that emancipates us not only from the historical but the broader range of the pre-conscious (Vorverständniss-level) fixations e.g., the cultural, communal, moral, political, ethical situational limitations without voiding, emptying, or vacating them. The emancipation may be limited in terms of empowerment if the personal and political can only be imagined and projected through others elsewhere at another time (only 'there'). For those laboring under the European condition (in one way or another), to align with the dead, the Americans, the feminists, the aboriginals, or the third or fourth world may seem strategically commendable cooperations but they do not resolve the limitations inherent in the European condition. It could be suggested that the European disciplinary innovativeness tends to insist too much on keeping our options open, on remaining vacant, and riding on the wings of others rather than adding to substantive local, timely innovation, that is accused of "second-ratedness", and to theory-flexing dialogue in the sense discussed in reference to Knop above.

There are exceptions, however, including e.g., the anthropology and culture conscious studies of international law that many authors have applied. Feminist scholarship has paved the way to inject an interdisciplinary, embodied, timely, personal-political methodology into the study of international law not excluding Europe. Authors from Emmanuelle Jouannet, Christine Chinkin to Susan Marks, and many Finnish colleagues working with anthropological or cultural critique and international law have transcended into new horizons when looking into issues such as democracy, community, and human rights leaving behind the old-hat debates between universalism and cultural relativism. They have proposed to connect the law (be it international law, human rights, law) with the embodied person, culture, and politics in ways that do not seek divorce from particularized substantive struggles nor reductions and deferences of foreign-seeming merits. Surely, one cannot claim that feminist innovations in international law could be homed to Europe any more than the latest historicist or conservative approaches. Quite the contrary. The difference, however, is that through embracing openly and explicitly the embodied personal–political (plus), they bring their Europeanness, if any, consciously into the action. In a deeper sense, none of the approaches can escape it. A therapeutical reading applied e.g., to the historicist scholarship cannot escape its personal–political either but—through backgrounding—its ever-so-important tracks and traces remain under cover and de-emphasized. With the feminist-influenced authorship the reverse is true, and, thus, their Europeanness is truer to color. It is possible and probably important to be extremely critical of any general

[61] Weil 1952.

proposition to the effect that the European condition would be best seen in European feminist authorship. The Europeanness is in the eye of the beholder or, at the very least, in the relationship between the observer and the observed—author and audience. Earlier we saw how Charlesworth foregrounded this relationship as the starting point of the effort.[62]

An obvious alternative—that has come up in the discussions above on theory and innovation—is that we toss the Europeanness altogether. We may arrive at such a conclusion through reading Kennedy again but on a recent subject i.e., humanitarianism which bears a trace of something that most international lawyers would undoubtedly share in Europe as elsewhere. One of Kennedy's observant urgings for those, who are ready for re-assessment of their business is to '(a)sk not for whom the humanitarian toils.' He says:

> Humanitarian advocates and policy makers routinely think of themselves not only speaking truth to power—but speaking to power as representative of someone else (...) Too often we have enchanted our fantasies about these unrepresented, transforming them into truth. We have acted as if speaking for them immunized us from challenges to the truth of our positions or removed us entirely from responsibility for both truth and power.[63]

Could we say: Ask not for whom the Europeans toil? This and Kennedy's other questions unapologetically, even rudely, reduce the conditions emanating from our subjects, under which we think we are laboring, into trivia. It is not that we are media for some other deserving things and people, even the law—even Europe. Turning the tables on ourselves this way helps us refocus on what we ourselves make of law's/Europe's/our discipline's powers and truths despite their limitations here and today. Kennedy has again alerted us to the danger of being imprisoned and shortsighted by the pre-project and its imagined pre-conditions. For different reasons, older and newer strands of theorizing about international law often exhaust themselves with their historicizing and their mpm struggle. Equally, the innovators be they critiques, neo-communitarians, interdisplinaries, conservative idealists, historicists, or other, are not necessarily significantly better than canonists or doctrinalists in getting beyond re-narrating our condition. They—or we—are so pre-occupied and fascinated about our mpm-selves, the paradoxes or their denial, our enlightened false consciousness[64] whether about history, culture, power, community, or the state of international law today that we exhaust ourselves in revisiting and recycling these idioms. This way—staring at one's feet and looking over one's shoulder—the Europe-bearing international lawyer never gets to the here, the present, and the forward orientation. Knop's argument above implied that a local court may be more meaning-creative and innovative of international law in this respect than any first-rate, brilliantly written renewalist piece that remains hollow. It happens if Kennedy's urging for the self-re-assessing humanitarians to foreground the

---

[62] Charlesworth 1993; Charlesworth 1996.

[63] Kennedy 2004, p 351.

[64] Sloterdijk 1983, p 5.

background[65] is lost and as long as one remains 'mulishly serious' about one's discipline, the law, and oneself as their medium in the fore.[66] Still, one could call it 'international law as therapy' and one must not forget that it applies across the board with differences in the awareness achieved and the hollows filled with reality effects.

One alternative would be to engage with the actors from a less-fixed perspective that would enable one to reflect on and even reshuffle fore- and backgrounds without forcing a divorce and a hierarchy. Similarly as above, the value and insight generated by the innovative theorizing on the controversial fixtures of the international legal system, its traditions, structures, and dynamics with the particular emphasis on the role of Europe, the British Empire and/or Nazi Germany cannot be undervalued. No doubt, the foregrounding of the disciplinary idiom, its grammar and discourse, or structure and history has offered ever new highly stimulating research questions that new European international lawyers have approached applying the insights from a host of famed theorists from Derrida to Lacan, Irigaray to Saussure, Foucault, Sartre, and Levi-Strauss to Habermas and beyond. As Charlesworth and Kennedy say, however, the most important revelation here is that "there remains so much we do not know" still.[67]

## 7.7 Tracing the European Condition

Next, let us consider briefly an evergreen of theoretical debate namely pragmatism. New theorizing has many times clustered around common denominators in a neo-pragmatist vein. The pragmatic move seems certainly one of the renewals that constantly repeat. It seems, indeed, that getting minds out of the box has often been helped by a skilled dialectic or closer convergence of practice and theory in the newer world, while in the renewalist circles in Europe there is a certain reservation to the concept.

Pragmatist moves have been taken for granted in America at the very least since Oliver Wendell Holmes and many would claim that this is a common law benefit.[68] On the other side of the Atlantic many feel that Europeanness must be precisely something that will not allow the practice/theory distinction to collapse. It is not uncommon, e.g., that the goal is defined as 'getting the students away from the practice'[69] rather than seeking a deconstruction of the distinction. In this scenario, the pragmatic approach is seen as a compromise to a practice that breeds false consciousness. Thus, theory is sought as a cure. Is there a trace of something distinctly European in this scepticism towards practice and pragmatism? Is there

---

65 Kennedy 2004, p 349.

66 See also Frankenberg's discussion on seriousness in Frankenberg 1989, 360–362 and passim.

67 Charlesworth and Kennedy 2006, 401.

68 Hantzis 1987–1988.

69 This was a written note to me by a young chair in a progressively-minded international law department (Fall 2010). Note on file with author.

another tragic subjectivity that regrets contamination by reality? This is one aspect of what Koskenniemi's 'concretivism' as the other pole of the pendulum denoted in from apology to Utopia.[70]

The concretia appears as a diversion that comes back to haunt the discipline feeding frustration. Simultaneously, the concrete may appear immune to fundamental reform. This is the mirror anxiety of the theory-paranoia that was discussed above. Such a view is also embedded, e.g., in theories according to which Europe's coloniality supported by practical evidence precludes any kind of transcendence for everyone in any way associated with it. Interestingly, e.g., Koskenniemi's work has rarely entertained pragmatism although, on the one hand, the frustrating concretivism plays a significant role in the argument structure (above) and, on the other hand, a hope and an optimism is derived mainly from the ways of the practitioners. Consider e.g., the following conclusion by Koskenniemi in a collection titled Theory and International Law (1991):

> The tension that exists between international law and sovereign statehood is quite similar to the tension between constraint and freedom, or determinism and indeterminism. In each case we are dealing with a structuring or defining principle of the human condition itself and not with a problem which could be somehow 'solved' in favor of one or the other by fixing the relation between the two in some permanent way. It is what we do—how we act—as practising lawyers, and not how we theorise about what we do, that establishes—for the moment—that relation and determines who we are.[71]

However, the savoir-faire of the practicing lawyers did not quite amount to a pragmatist pose in Koskenniemi's account. Pragmatism as a practice-derived theory was bracketed to maintain the non-theory posture. Another move would be an explicitly pragmatic theory such as e.g., Florian Hoffmann's recent proposition, who derives it precisely from the human rights professionals in action and activism.[72] In comparing his pragmatism to Koskenniemi's endorsement of the practitioners' ways but only in support of the formalist pose, Hoffmann describes, in other words, the problem with plasticity of the form that Duncan Kennedy discussed above:

> (N)ot all those (practioners) within the formalist 'dialect group' are aware that it is but a placeholder for an unattainable unity (...) Indeed, a good part of the (formalist) legal profession (...) manifests a hegemonic gatekeeperism that does not quite square with the—albeit 'gentle'—transgressive capacities of the uses of formalism (...), Hoffmann continues by distinguishing his own action-based stance: (I)f the entirely contingent character of such decisionism (by practitioners) is always recognized, it becomes no more than an imposing gesture, a cautious 'jump in the dark' (...) which cannot control its

[70] Koskenniemi 1989, p 46.

[71] Koskenniemi 1991, p 45.

[72] See e.g. Hoffmann 1980.

> consequences. It seeks to establish a temporary hegemony (...) subject to revision at any moment (...) It engages an 'other' in its (or her/his) otherness, and it is, thus, intrinsically political (...).[73]

In its political stance it departs most clearly from the also praxis-derived formalist culture. Hoffmann concludes by likening such an open-ended and precautious pragmatism to an algorithm that keeps reapplying itself—which seems very much like the micro-level theoretical offspring of the repetitious disciplinary renewal of the macro-scale (by Kennedy) both conscious of their political package. Is it that the palate for pragmatism turns on the ability to tolerate a substance package, however, transgressive and temporary it may be as in Hoffmann's? Is it that the compromising connotation of pragmatism that implies the incubation of one politics or power-exercise after another is an un-European disciplinary posture? Is this a Weimar trauma? Is it that even with action, decisionism, and praxis the European condition forces one off the pragmatic road? It is intriguing to mirror Hoffmann's pragmatism to Koskenniemi's culture of formalism in order to tease out European traces while both straddle and embrace their several identities and origins so beautifully through their work—bearing their European packages too.

If the key to tracing the European out of the pragmatism/formalism approaches that derive from international law in action has to do with the Weimar trauma, it should be better defined. The Weimar era has been extensively analyzed also in the international law discipline by e.g., Nathaniel Berman in various pieces. In a discussion of Schindler and Kelsen's interwar work, he said:

> We seesaw uncritically between a faith in new legal orders and a panic at the spread of violent irrationalism; we dream of an enlightened, supranational world and, yet, remain alternately fascinated and repelled by mythic images of national identity. The interwar effort to deal with these same questions and shifting moods is daunting both in its intellectual sophistication and absolutely catastrophic conclusion.[74]

It is the "perilous ambivalence" of the professionals, the panic, and the interlocking of fascination, and repulse at a renewal, and any revitalizing political or ethical stances that mix into the Weimar trauma also in the European international law discipline. An European cannot simply be as pragmatic and easy-going about substance and pragmatism as an American without invoking the ghosts of the holocausts. Sloterdijk speaks of Weimar as the era of double decisions and matter-of-factness unto death.[75] In his discussion the pragmatic compromises, intentional ambivalences and, indeed, a 'positivistic grand-tactical spirit' of the anti-fascists are shown in a way that is sure to traumatize many a future generation of anti-totalitarians. As Sloterdijk said, the anti-fascist forces together with Moscow's supertacticians accepted Hitler's coming as inevitable but did not notice how their own resignation to and strategizing around it escalated into the diabolical as they...

---

[73] Hoffmann (2005).

[74] Berman 1992, p 356.

[75] Sloterdijk 1983, p 521.

> (…) bet on Hitler just like someone bets on a catastrophe. Thus, one could fight against him and nonetheless still find something good in his probable victory: that, as it was thought, he was specifically suitable to bring about the total bankruptcy of the system.[76]

The appeal to the tactical, strategic or pragmatic spirit seem eternally tainted by this trauma that, in some ways, seems to hit harder on those geographically close to the location of the former concentration camps. The elevation of praxis without a pragmatic pose is one form of therapy for it. For praxis has been late-modernity's recourse from irrationality and from the fall of theory since it has "always (been) held to be the most legitimate child of reason."[77] However useful as a therapeutic program, Sloterdijk warned against the mythologization of praxis and activism by noting that…

> (e)very active deed is etched in the matrix of passivity; every act of disposing over something remains dependent on the stable massiveness of what is not at our disposal; every change is borne also by the reliable perseverance of what is unchanged, and everything that is calculated rests on the indispensable base of what is unpredictably spontaneous.[78]

Most people would probably disagree with, choose to ignore or defer Sloterdijk's warning. Many audiences also found it preposterous when Jacques Derrida claimed that the act of feeding his cat in Paris presented ethical aporia in the face of all the famine in the world.[79] The therapy of small practical acts by the good guys and bracketing the big picture is still in strong demand after the Weimar trauma, the holocaust, the bomb, and the general demise of grounding in our mpm 'monde concentrationnaire'—we cannot simply be accountable for the 'stable massiveness of what is not at our disposal' too, can we?[80]

The biographical trend in European international law writing is linked to this problematique too for often we write about the practice in which our forebears engaged. Sometimes, the biographizing turn in the scholarship is equated with a historiographical turn. Koskenniemi's The Rise and Fall of International Law[81] is, perhaps, a most famous example of alternating between the two. In addition to it, European academia is particularly rich with Festschrifte—i.e., celebratory publications for the grand old figures. Projects, conferences, name-bearing institutes, and anniversary publications for notable persons provide a sense of active remembering and reassuring continuance in the face of historical discontinuity, recycled renewal, doctrinal fragmentation, and the general disruption of the rational grid. The biographical scholarly style is well known and respected. It brings a human touch to the technical expertise and enlivens the matter-of-fact-dryness leading to (metaphorical/disciplinary) death, as criticized by Sloterdijk

76 Ibid. 525–526.

77 Ibid. 539.

78 Ibid. 540.

79 Derrida 1996, p 71.

80 Sloterdijk 1983, xiv (foreword by A. Huyssen).

81 Koskenniemi 2002.

above. It has demonstrated potential for overcoming the gloomy days of critical theory, as discussed above. It bears a momentum of professional affiliation and networking. A critique of disciplinary history through biographies is a sort of inductio ad personam. What is slightly surprising is that the biographizing or small narratives-style historiographies in our field, despite their radical critique, experientalist, emancipatory, and/or embodying sympathies, have not pierced the veil into microhistory. One may wonder why the Montaillou[82] of international law still remains to be written after quarter of a century past Spring Break.

Be it as it may with the relevance of microhistory to international law, the innovativeness of the biography-style lies in spinning the small narratives together with the doctrinal grand narrative(s) and thereby making the latter richer—and more real. Quite conscious of not escaping yet another production of a reality effect[83]—however more persuasive through the personalization—the authors and their audiences know that the great men and thoughts cannot be cut loose from the establishment or the Empire. The question is what the Montaillou-style critique of the history of international law would look like? Would it be likely to be written in Europe or somewhere else? Why? International law's no-name-practitioners have certainly left a paper trail for centuries and the depths of the uncovered European archives are well known. Would we read the history of international law as it has passed down from the no-name cadre to the next as eagerly as we follow the grand projects e.g., of Europe?

Another point is that through biographizing scholarship we can mirror our autobiographical as much as the discipline's sensibilities and, hence, also self-therapeutize from a distance. While the best scholars would know to escape accusations of subjectivism, there is a very subjective subtext present in the unveiling of another life's intrigues, tragedies, and intimacies even if in the professional interest field. It is also through this biographical projection that one can model otherwise unpalatable stances e.g., the pragmatisms of others. The benefit of biographizing is that the pragmatisms, strategies, tactics, and the politics of the discipline, however, intimately moulded into a portrait remain those of someone else, while the biographist can retain a vacant distance. However, one cannot forget to check them against Kennedy's urgings to the humanitarians—i.e. the illusions of self-effacement and representation.[84]

---

82 Le Roy Ladurie 1975. Montaillou—the book sold in millions and was translated to tens of languages—it is a multilayered study of peasant life in the light of an Inquisition court case in a small mediaeval village. It represents an anti-grandnarrative effort that was called forth by the developments by the Annales school of historiography. It is one of the foremost examples of microhistory as a 'theoretical' choice - the antithesis to field's macrohistorians, such as e.g. Niall Ferguson, who is a vociferous critic of it. The point is to reimagine and renarrate historical events, even eras, through the record left by the silent 99,9 %—the persons who do not become the grand figures of establishment History.

83 I am refering to Roland Barthes' term *l'effet de reelle*. See, e.g., Korhonen, International Law Situated, Chap. 4 (History) (supra).

84 Kennedy 2004, p 351; see discussion above.

One may again suggest that the desire of a distance would probably appeal to many a European as discussed above. It is, however, not the case that e.g., American international law scholars would not biographize. The question is thus if they biographize less or if they biographize with the politics of such performances more openly in view? If one compares e.g., Kennedy's discussion of John Jackson or Liliana Obregon's discussion of the creole consciousness and international law[85] to my own discussion of the Finnish international lawyers of the early twentieth century, one may make such a claim. In the first paragraph of the International Style in Post-War Law and Policy focusing on Jackson's contribution, Kennedy foregrounds the precepts of his project as follows:

> (M)odern internationalists (...) share a pragmatic sensibility or style, at once down to earth or case by case and technocratically sophisticated. I come to international economic law (and to Jackson's work) to explore this sensibility, its attitudes towards internationalization, its thoughts about politics and the role of international law.[86]

Kennedy's portrait starts with the I-author well articulated and with an explicit project. A similar statement is difficult to find among the European examples. It is also not a coincidence that the Jackson discussion focuses on the development of different pragmatic voices, polemics, and even a pragmatic conscience.[87] The politization of the authorship and the readership projects do not delegitimize or embarrass—but constitute the relevance of—the biographizing when Kennedy does it. This sort of openness about their projects is not often celebrated in the European publications. The seriousness and matter-of-factness ("unto death") comes back to haunt the Europeans—both authors and audiences—who struggle to maintain the illusion that it is possible to erase the gravitating mpm condition out of the discipline and forget that it means erasing the human embodiment and the potential of the grace as well.

## 7.8 Conclusion

The claim in the title of this paper is that there is a three-dimensional intersection of 'Europe', 'international law' and 'theoretical innovation'. From the many issues touched above, we can deduce that the interplay of this trinity is complex. We would have to consider a range of non-theories in a situation of repeated performances of renewal and the question of their politics in a Europe permeated by a European identity that authors and audiences regard very differently if they recognize it at all. Nevertheless, as Kennedy reminded us, any attempt at ruthless dislocation would not work since it risks many a false pretense of neutrality and ends up a description of a statistical'das man' from a no man's land. This has been the problem with public international law—the discipline—through many decades.

---

[85] Obregon 2006; see Korhonen 2000, passim.

[86] Kennedy 1995, p 671.

[87] Ibid. 682.

If we relax our attitude, we could perhaps summarize that a range of innovative disciplinary writing from Kennedy to Marks and Chinkin, from Koskenniemi to Hoffmann, from Simpson and Simma to Allott, and others is more or less'European'. If we dissect the texts, idioms and subtexts, we find traces of the European, which we cannot, however, in any way determine or fix without inserting the personal–political of the specific authors and their audiences into the 'algorithms'—the cultural geography of origin being one lesser figure among them.

In my earlier work, I have spoken about the encounter—in other words, the need to have the law, the lawyer and the world meet whenever discussing justice or international law. I have emphasized taking account of the situations and conditions of each three in every decision making i.e., determining situation. Above, I have shown that co-ordinates, determinants, and conditions—e.g. innovation, theory, Europe—appear hollowed-out and negative if not situated. I agree with Sloterdijk that even a brilliant (pseudo)critique fails to rise above the gloominess, and deadly matter-of-factness of the system, the establishment, and the logic of the Empire without the situational questions—what is the 'here' and the 'now'—posed, as I have argued in this article.

With all the reservations still valid, I claimed that there was a double-anxiety that conditioned innovation in Europe: an anxiety of pragmatism as well as of theoretical posture. Becoming immobilized by such a double anxiety would lead to what Weil called gravitation or what Sloterdijk called the critique's inability to burst out of its negativism. I found that with colonial history and the Weimar legacy hanging over Europe, it was particularly difficult to free oneself and one's approach to international law from the ironical escalation, from the resignation as in gulping down Beckett's "poisoned chalice", from Frankenberg's "mulish seriousness" or, at least, from a trace of Sloterdijk's "matter-of-factness unto death". It was not that European authors did not recognize or struggle against these pitfalls and malaises. There were different kinds of "international law as therapy" as well as robust feminist stances that unrepentantly attacked diabolical resignation or the bounds of what is tolerated or else "mad". It seemed, however, that responses often may stop short of taking a final step and, thus also, the transcending step while they remained in the negative descriptive mode. The end of history, i.e., what needed to be said, was not only acknowledged but recognized and admitted. Even if Europeans went into the personal or the micro-level, thus, seeking an embodied discipline, it was often in the name of something at a distance, something grander e.g., humanitarian politics, conservative idealism, or grand ideas. It seemed troubling to bear with the massive, spontaneous, and unpredictable world that is not at our discipline's immediate disposal, in which, however, our acts rest embedded. The inclination was to leave it to the practitioners and decline theorizing about the 'great unknown', which, however, would be the 'forward' mode.[88]

[88] Charlesworth and Kennedy 2006.

Thus, although European authors often do write modern and/or hi-theory, the non-theory stance has won more prominence in the renewalist movements. Similarly, although Europeans rely very much on practice, any articulated pragmatisms tend to be shallow, reserved, and/or rare. The European condition demands therapeutic efforts to settle with the colonial and the World War sins. We may ask whether the therapeutic stances are innovative or repetitive renewal moves? On the one hand, we saw that to claim renewal is to make a (disciplinary) policy claim. On the other hand, we found that European renewalist authors often took distance to politics and policies. European renewalism may often seem imprisoned by this paradox—of wanting a change but refusing to direct it. Depending on how one defines "politics" this might be the end of the discussion: without politics, there can only be recycled renewal performances. In the narrow sense of partisan politics, it would, however, not be true. Only if politics is taken to encompass care about the world, the pedagogic aim of unveiling this-worldly law, and stimulating a desire to seek solutions to its problems in the future generations, and an ethical demand of embodied justice, would it serve as a good criterion for innovation. Yet, the question rises whether such a broad criterion can be applied usefully. I conclude quoting Kennedy's description that matches also innovatively minded international lawyers laboring under the European condition:

> (W)e find a distinct group of (international lawyers) struggling with the relationships between their work and the realms of thought and political practice. They are anxious about both politics and thought. And they have no theory or practice or client or party which can resolve their anxiety. As their work has developed, they have simply altered their accommodation to their situation (...).[89]

The caveat is that Kennedy's description is not meant to be about European international lawyers; he wrote it in 1989 to describe American legal academics to a German audience. The fact that we can apply it to European innovators of international legal theory today does not testify to everything being the same but to a complexity of issues that this article has hoped to show: from the repetitive renewal to the mpm struggle with theory, to the plurality, mobility, and fragmentation of identities, but, also to the possibility of transcending differences and bounds in our discipline, and the push to burst out of the anxiety.

## References

Beckett (2009) The politics of international law—twenty years later: a reply. In: EJIL: Debate! (May 19, 2009) at 3, available at http://www.ejiltalk.org/the-politics-of-international-law-twenty-years-later-a-reply . Accessed 10 August 2010

Berman N (1992) A perilous ambivalence: nationalist desire, legal autonomy, and the limits of the interwar framework. Harv Int'l L J 33:353–379

[89] Kennedy 1989, p 393.

Boyle J (1985) Ideals and things: international legal scholarship and the prison-house of language. Harv Int'l L J 26(2):327–365
Carty A (1991) Critical international law: recent trends in the theory of international law. Eur J Int'l L 2(1):66–96
Charlesworth H, Chinkin C (2000) The boundaries of international law: a feminist analysis, Manchester U.P
Charlesworth H (1993) Alienating oscar? feminist analysis of international law. In: Dallmeyer DG (ed.) Reconceiving reality: women and international law, ASIL, pp 1–18
Charlesworth H (1996) Cries and whispers: responses to feminist scholarship in international law, Nord. J. Int'l L. Nos 65(3–4):557–568
Charlesworth H (2000) Remarks by Hilary Charlesworth. ASIL Proc 94:74–75
Charlesworth H (2004) Feminist methods in international law. Stud Transnat'l Legal Pol'y 36:159–184
Charlesworth H, Kennedy D (2006) Afterword: and forward—there remains so much we do not know. In: Orford A international law and its others, Cambridge U.P. pp 401–408
Chimni BS (1987) International commodity agreements: a legal study, Routledge Kegan & Paul
Derrida J (1996) The gift of death (David Wills transl. orig. in French, Donner la mort, 1992), University of Chicago Press
Frankenberg G (1989) Down by law: irony, seriousness, and reason. Northw U L Rev 83(1 and 2):360–397
Galindo GRB (2005) Martti Koskenniemi and the historiographical turn in international law. J Int'l L 16(3):539–559
Georgiev D (1993) Politics or rule of law: deconstruction and legitimacy in international law. Eur J Int'l L 4(1):1–14
Hantzis CW (1987–1988) Legal innovation within the wider intellectual tradition: the pragmatism of oliver wendell holmes, Jr. Northw U.L Rev 82(3):541–595
Hoffmann F (1980) Human rights, the self and the other: reflections on a pragmatic theory of human rights. In: Orford A, International law and its others. Cambridge U.P. pp 221–246
Hoffmann (2005) Shooting into the Dark': towards a pragmatic theory of human rights (activism), paper in B. & A. Rapoport Centre for Human Rights and Justice & Texas International Law Journal, Symposium'Representing Culture, Translating Human Rights' (Nov. 3–4, 2005), 24 available at http://repositories.lib.utexas.edu/bitstream/handle/2152/4082/hoffman.pdf?sequence=2. Accessed 10 August 2011
Kennedy D (1980) Theses about international law discourse. Germ Yb Int'l L 23:353–391
Kennedy D (1985) Spring break (including methodological appendix). Texas L Rev 63(8):1377–1423
Kennedy D (1986) Primitive legal scholarship Harv Int'l L J 27(1):1–98
Kennedy D (1987a) International legal structures, Nomos
Kennedy D (1987b) The move to institutions. Cardozo L Rev 8:979–988
Kennedy D (1989) A rotation in contemporary legal scholarship. In: Joerges C, Trubek DM (eds.) Critical legal thought: an American-German debate, Nomos, pp 353–395
Kennedy D (1991) Images of religion in international legal history. In: Janis M (ed) The influence of religion on the development of international law. Martinus Nijhoff, Dordrecht, pp 137–146
Kennedy D (1993) Autumn weekends: an essay on law and everyday life. In: Austin S, Kearns TR, Law and everyday life, University of Michigan Press, pp 191–235
Kennedy D (1995) The international style in postwar law and policy: Jackson J and the field of international economic law. Am U J Int'l L Pol'y 10(2):671–716
Kennedy D (2000a) My talk at the ASIL: what is new thinking in international law. ASIL Proc 94:104–125
Kennedy D (2000b) When renewal repeats: thinking against the box. N.Y.U. J. Int'l L Pol'y 32(2):335–500
Kennedy D (2004) The dark sides of virtue, reassessing international humanitarianism, Princeton U.P
Kennedy D (2009) The rights of spring: a memoir of innocence abroad, Princeton U.P

Kennedy D (1997) A critique of adjudication: fin de siecle. Harvard U.P

Knop K (2000) Here and there, international law in domestic courts. NYU J Int'l L Pol 32(2):501–536

Korhonen O (2000) International law situated. The Lawyer's Stance to Culture, History and Community, Kluwer

Koskenniemi M (1989) From apology to Utopia: the structure of international legal argument, Finnish Lawyers Publishing

Koskenniemi M (1991) Theory: implications for the practitioner. In: Philip A (ed.) Theory and international law, Brit Inst Int'l & Comp L pp 1–46

Koskenniemi M (2002) The gentle civilizer of nations. The rise and fall of international law. Cambridge University Press, Cambridge, pp 1870–1960

Koskenniemi M (2005) International law as therapy: reading the health of nations (by Philip Allott), Eur. J Intl L 16(2):329–341

Le Roy Ladurie E (1975) Montaillou: village occitan de 1294 à 1324, Gallimard

Mutua M (2000) What is TWAIL? ASIL Proc 94:31–38

Obregon L (2006) Completing civilization: creole consciousness and international law in nineteenth-century Latin America. In Orford A International law and its others, Cambridge University Press, Cambridge, pp 247–264

Onuf N (1985) Do rules say what they do? from ordinary language to international law. Harv J Int'l L 2:385–410

Onuf N (1988) International legal structures (By David Kennedy). Am J Int'l L 83(3):630–640

Orford A (2006) (ed.) International law and its others, Cambridge University Press, Cambridge

Purvis N (1991) Critical legal studies in public international law. Harv Int'l L J 32(1):81–128

Scobbie I (1990) Towards the elimination of international law: some radical scepticism about sceptical radicalism. LXI Brit Yb Int'l L 61:339–362

Simpson G (2000) The situation on the international legal theory front: the power of rules and the rule of power. Eur J Int'l L 11(2):439–464

Sloterdijk P (1983) Critique of cynical reason, Michael Eldred transl. (originally published in German), University of Minnesota

Weil S (1952) Gravity and grace (French orig. Pesanteur et la Grace, originally published in 1947), Routledge

Wrange P (1990–1991) En diskussion utan innehåll? Critical legal studies och folkrätten. Juridisk Tidskrift 2:256–270

Wrange P (1994) Från domstolsession till jamsession eller Martti Koskenniemi och juridikens slut. Retfaerd 17(64):3–23

# Chapter 8
# Notes for the History of New Approaches to International Legal Studies: Not a Map but Perhaps a Compass

**Ignacio de la Rasilla del Moral**

**Abstract** This work offers the first introductory chrono-bibliographical approach to David Kennedy's highly diversified, greatly heterogeneous, and provocatively engaging scholarly work, since his pioneering application of structuralism to international law to his latest inquiries on the nature of expertise in the age of global law and governance. This survey of three decades of Kennedy's work is contextualized within the intellectual scaffolding of New Approaches to International Legal Studies (NAILS) since the early-mid 1980s.

*Lasciate ogni speranza voi che entrate*
Dante, Inferno.

## Contents



---

LL.B. (Complutense) MPhil & Ph.D. cand. (UPO, Seville) M.A. & Ph.D. (The Graduate Institute, Geneva) LL.M (Harvard)

---

I. de la Rasilla del Moral (✉)
Post-Doctoral Max Weber Fellow in Law, European University Institute, Florence, Italy
e-mail: ignaciodelarasilla@post.harvard.edu

J. M. Beneyto and D. Kennedy (eds.), *New Approaches to International Law*,
DOI: 10.1007/978-90-6704-879-8_8, 

## 8.1 Introduction

What Ernesto Sabato once wrote about his relationship with literature being "the same that a *guerrillero* may have with the regular army" applies to David Kennedy's relationship with international law. Kennedy's work is an endeavor of faith in the humanistically emancipatory, the politically empowering, and the socially transforming potential of one's scholarly engagement with the retrieval and dissemination of critical knowledge at the global level. This premise illuminates the assortment of ethical preoccupations, deconstructed analytical positions, and discursive strategies that have accompanied his 30-year-long creative (re)thinking of the field of international legal studies. Although Kennedy has invested his intellectual career in international law as an academic field,[1] his work extends far beyond this intra-disciplinary compartment to penetrate inter (and even counter) disciplinarily into other branches of legal thought. Indeed, throughout the years, Kennedy's explorative interventions have included the fields of comparative law, international economic policy, American legal thought and, as of late, the areas of law and development, global law and governance, and the nature of international expertise.[2] Kennedy's contributions to international legal studies have been a key factor for the ongoing evolution of a corpus of international legal scholarship that stands for a broad, heterogeneous, and multifaceted global critical legal movement since the mid-1980s. Such a mass of legal scholarship has received a number of generically descriptive doctrinal labels; among them, *Newstream*[3] or New Approaches to International Law (NAIL)[4] have gained significant doctrinal reception.[5] Yet, it is equally possible to find other liminal denominations to interchangeably refer to the body of scholarship produced by this critical generation of international law scholars; these include the anti-foundational critique,[6] the post-modernist turn, the international legal branch of Critical Legal Studies (CLS),[7] the

[1] The expression is by Kennedy, see Kennedy 2006a, 983, 984.

[2] In the area of his contribution to the study of global governance and the politics of expertise, see among others: Kennedy 2008, 2009, 2011a Kennedy 2005, 5 and Kennedy 2001b, 117.

[3] See for the seminal work, Kennedy 1988a, 1.

[4] See Tennant and Kennedy 1994. See, e.g. also, Skouteris 1997; Skouteris and Korhonen 1998.

[5] See MacDonald 2011.

[6] See Paulus 2001.

[7] See Cot 2006, 587–589. See also Koskenniemi 1997, 391.

non-instrumental theories of international law",[8] the critical approaches to international law[9] or, merely, the *"crits"* work. Such a little-understood on-going academically activist effort has resulted in that international critical legal doctrine had already deeply planted the seeds of its own tradition in the contemporary international legal consciousness in the late twentieth and early twenty-first centuries.

Among the traits that characterize the new approaches to international legal studies are, first, a profound distrust for grand narratives and the proclamation of abstract and universalizing principles that characterize modernist thinking; second, a leaning for deconstruction and a tendency to dwell on the paradoxes and ambivalences that emerge from the unstitching of the creases of legal thought; third, a devoted attention to efforts for unveiling the justifications embedded in the rhetorical repetition of patterns of discourse; fourth, a commitment to highlight the often unassumed complicit character of individual scholarly work in oppressive and conservative structures of international legal thought; fifth, a related ethical-oriented awakening call inspired by the abhorrence of "legal managerialism" which is addressed to those shaping the expert field for them to assume the political character of their legal expertise instead of hiding behind the lego-technical and technocratic forms of legal thinking; sixth, a connected invitation to experts to engage in self-reflection as social intellectual actors and to foster socio-resistance with their work; seventh, a turn back to theory and history against doctrine and technocratic practice oriented to combat the depersonalization of legal thinking; eight, a focus on place, gender, and origin in approaching relations of domination; ninth, a keen awareness of the legacy of colonial, racist, and patriarchal heritage inserted in international law with the consonant challenge to regimes of "truth" that are bound up with "systems of power"; tenth, a regeneration of history and (of the stories) of the discipline as open fields of reflective contestation; eleventh, an insistence on the examination of international law's indeterminacy and structural biases combined with an attempt to deflate, in the critical theory's vein, the pretensions of dominant approaches so as to recast enquiry in a new key; twelfth, a scholarly commitment that "relates theorizing to life" or, if preferred, one that insists that professional writing should remain intrinsically linked to a non-transferable personal existential call; thirteenth, a compromise with the ever self-regenerating creative perplexity that informs the critical legal scholars' emancipatory approach to knowledge when they examine that form of social practice that we know as international law in the early stages of the twenty-first century.

[8] See Scobbie 2006, 83, 102. See analyzing the notion of "intrumentalism" in international law Koskenniemi 2003, 89.

[9] See Korhonen 1996, 1.

## 8.2 The 1980s: Or Between Post-Structuralism and History

Kennedy's international legal work in the 1980s pioneered the transposition of critical theory (with a special emphasis on the Frankfurt School) and of a series of post-modern trends (post-structuralism, deconstructionism) to the study of international law.[10] From an intra-disciplinary perspective, David Kennedy's book length work, *International Legal Structures*[11] and a number of his articles starting as early as 1980[12] pioneered the application of the structuralist method to international law. Kennedy's acknowledged aim was to "reformulate the relationship between law and politics in rhetorical terms".[13] By looking at "public international law from the inside",[14] he sought to focus upon "the relationships among doctrines and arguments and upon their recurring rhetorical structure".[15] In seeking "to unify the historical, theoretical, doctrinal and institutional projects of the discipline" through "a methodological reformulation,"[16] Kennedy's efforts were aimed, in his own words, at dislodging, the "discipline of international law from its stagnation"[17] in "the tragic voice of post-war public law liberalism".[18] Kennedy's attention to the critical mapping of the specificities of the U.S academy of international law has accompanied him ever since. By the 1980s, the echoes of a post-Vietnam challenging generational tone are patent in his description of the international legal U.S. academy in the late 1970s as "one in which no one seemed to think international legal theory could offer more than an easy patois of lazy justification and arrogance for a discipline that has lost its way and kept his jobs".[19] Kennedy insufflates his spirit to an American counter-tradition that was criticizing the U.S.' mainstream approach, both internally and externally. Internally, "for failing to complete its own anti-formalist project, for continuing ambivalence about the state, about legal sovereignty, and so forth"[20] so as to

[10] For Kennedy's contribution to critical theory in international law in the 1980s, see, among others: Kennedy 1980, 353—this work is regarded as the first application of structuralism to international law. See also Kennedy 1987a, 1988a. Kennedy's work had a great influence in Koskenniemi 1989.

[11] See Kennedy 1987a.

[12] See Kennedy 1980, 353.

[13] Kennedy 1988a, 7.

[14] Ibid. 11.

[15] Ibid. 10.

[16] Ibid. 11.

[17] Ibid. 6.

[18] Ibid. 2.

[19] Ibid. This phrase constitutes a clear homage echo to a classic phrase of the CLS' manifesto by Roberto Unger, otherwise, the well-known "When we came, they [the law professors] were like a priesthood that had lost their faith and kept their jobs. They stood in tedious embarrassment before cold altars. But we turned away from those altars and found the mind's opportunity in the heart's revenge". Unger 1986, 116.

[20] Kennedy 1999, 34.

unearth the blinds spots, overstatements, or elisions which are part of the discipline's normal doctrinal and/or institutional practices.[21] Externally, by seeking "to link the mainstream to an ideological bias", and to come up with a "situated historical and strategic" project that could investigate "how one or another mainstream blend of rule and policy may function as a cover or polemic for particular interests".[22]

Kennedy shares with the first generation of the CLS' movement an intra-American regenerative will to pursue the anti-formalist lineage of "the frenzied locust eaters"[23] of American legal realism from the 1930, against post-legal realist pragmatic oriented efforts of legitimization that could be found in international law under the cloak of a "strong anti-formalism with an insistence on realism about sovereign autonomy as the basis for a world community"[24] (as in the Yale School) or as the combination (in the Columbia School) of "a weak anti-formalism with a commitment to neutral norms and humanist institutions as law for the modern international community".[25] Indeed, CLS[26] retook a number of features of the radical strand of American legal realism[27] including (so as to name but a few) its objection to the formalism of previous legal and social thought; its emphasis on the interplay of external factors, or biases in the development of legal doctrine and the fear of reification of legal concepts. One of the founders of the CLS movement justified this very "resurrecting (of) the critical strands in pre-World War I legal progressive thought and legal realism, so that we could claim a tradition for our highly controversial positions in the domestic legal debate while at the same time finding a place in the larger development".[28] Indeed, CLS' kinship to American legal realism[29] has been, commonly, located in their "adoption of the Realist's twin orientations toward an iconoclastic historiography and a rigorous analytic jurisprudence".[30] Echoes of this linkage are apparent behind a critical approach that favors an understanding of "the identity of internationalism as a whole, not as that of a system with a fixed ideology, but as a work-in-progress, subject to constant revision through situational engagement". This call for situationality in international law as well as other legal realist insights were developed, on a more radical transformative political basis, under the influx of a general epochal mood

[21] Ibid. 35.

[22] Ibid. 35.

[23] Llewellyn 1931, 1922, 1938.

[24] Kennedy 2000a,117.

[25] Ibid. 118.

[26] For a book entirely consecrated to offer a thematically ordered perspective to the scholarly literature associated to critical legal studies, see Bauman 1996.

[27] For an introduction to CLS see Anon. 1982, 1669.

[28] Kennedy 1997, 366.

[29] Portrayed as "a reaction against American classical thought which in turn was a reaction against pre-classical legal thought" see Singer 1988 465, 476.

[30] See Anon. 1982, 1677.

of "expanding eclecticism"[31] by a new generation of critical oriented academics when their re-appraising of the methods of legal (and, by extension, lego-international) scholarship in the late 1970s and 1980s.

The latter methodological turn benefitted from the influence of the Frankfurt School, and its "critical theory", as well as from the new structuralist lenses provided by anthropological and psychoanalytical cognitive insights. Although diverse in their location of the core of a binary "deeper level" (whether ideology/false consciousness or *langue*) that "reproduces or structures both doctrines and theory"[32] at the surface level or *parole,* the common orientation of these two supplementary critical traditions at displacing the "relationship between theory and practice with which legal scholars are familiar"[33] was key for CLS to come to grips with the "fundamental contradiction" between -self and -other, -individuality and -community. This duality that was, originally, examined in the legal field by Duncan Kennedy[34] was one of the key background influences in the analysis of the structure of the international legal argument developed by M. Koskenniemi in *from apology to Utopia*. From this perspective, the critical approach constitutes a doctrinal reaction to the inherent contradictions of political liberal theory, in respect of which international law appears as a subsystem that led to its characterization as "ethically incoherent, intellectually constraint, logically indeterminate, and self-validated in terms of its own authority".[35] Both Kennedy(s) foregrounded Koskenniemi's thesis, in what is "perhaps, the last modern treatment of the field"[36] according to which "international law should be seen, first and foremost, as a rhetorical movement "from emphasizing concreteness to emphasizing normativity and vice versa".[37]

Although this structuralist insight was oriented to demonstrate how legal doctrines, as a manifestation of the ideology of liberalism, contribute to an unjust social structure, it will, nonetheless, be the implicit underlying "foundationalism" (understood as the pretension[38] of having found the "true, essential" structure of legal doctrine) what deconstruction, as a post-structuralist technique of analysis *pace* what is perceived as "Derrida's most enduring philosophical legacy today" (otherwise "the theory that all binary oppositions are essentially unstable"[39]—or différance) will make the distinguishing mark of the post-structuralist challenge in

---

31 See Kennedy 1985–1986, 209, 210.

32 Ibid. 271.

33 Ibid.

34 Kennedy 1976, 695.

35 Purvis 1991, 81.

36 Kennedy 1990, 385, 386. See also Kennedy 2006a, 983 (noting that FATU "could well turn out to have been the last great original treatise in the international law field").

37 Ibid. 347.

38 Otherwise, "The more sophisticated a person's legal thinking, regardless of her political stance, the more likely she is to believe that all issues within a doctrinal field reduce to a single dilemma of the degree of collective as opposed to individual self-determination", Kennedy Duncan 1979, 213.

39 Rasulov 2005, 799, 800.

legal thought. It is this trans-disciplinary post-structuralist challenge—that affected international law too—understood as a "response to the difficulties encountered by the synchronic of the structuralist tradition and the dialectics of critical theory"[40] what determines the, otherwise, admittedly, blurred divide-line between the first and second evolutionary-oriented generations of CLS' scholarship.[41] This post-structuralist challenge also affected, by ricochet, the defining features of the internal (or epistemological) and external (or normative) branches of the critical movement in international legal scholarship. In this sense, the radical methodological eclecticism and the inter-disciplinary ambition of the critical movement found in the use of post-structuralism a methodological justification for its ambition to confront the sempiternal distinction between theory and practice that, in accordance with the writings of David Kennedy in the mid-1980s neither the school of Frankfurt in its application to the science of international law nor structuralism have been able to transcend.

The contours of the internal (or epistemological) and external (or normative) branches of the critical movement in international legal scholarship shall be fleshed out by a new generation of critical scholars in international law. Indeed, although David Kennedy's initial critical interventions in international law were pursued under the influence of the Critical Legal Studies movement (CLS) understood as a political intervention in the legal theory and history of the United States of the 1970s and 1980s, Kennedy also intervened in the CLS' internal "American" debates in the 1980s in his search for a post-structuralist turn of the screw.[42] In doing so, he traced a map of the legal trends of this time built on the axis of the quasi-chirurgical exam of the confuse relationship between academic work and intellectual work or politics.[43] As already noted, in his analytical deconstruction of the individual lawyer's conscience as academic actor in the complex scenario of post-legal realism, Kennedy insisted on how, somewhat, critical and theory and structuralism were merely reiterating the problem between theory/practice against which the legal scholar was looking for relief.[44]

The 1980s also saw Kennedy engaging, in parallel, with a series of studies on the configuration and generational geography of international law from a historical intra-doctrinal perspective. Indeed, David Kennedy's generic platform for renovation and critique is supported by the broad background offered by his extensive studies on the history of international law that cover its evolution from the times

[40] Kennedy 1985–1986, 276.

[41] Kennedy offers in his work as a clear sample of this post-structuralist challenge in stressing that "neither structuralism nor critical theory has provided a method which lawyers can deploy against their theoretical and doctrinal malaise" one which he identifies as "transcending the theory/practice distinction", Ibid.

[42] For Kennedy's contribution to the exam and shaping of critical theory in American Law in the 1980s, see, among others, Kennedy 1986, 1989.

[43] Ibid. 364.

[44] Ibid. 372.

(and even before of) the Peace of Westphalia.[45] Kennedy, who was certainly aware that the "discipline of public international law has a keenly developed sense of history (and that) indeed much of the field's theoretical and doctrinal debate is conducted as a debate about history",[46] also engaged in the perennial debate on whether Vitoria was or not (contra James Brown Scott)[47] the founding father of international law as discipline or, instead, a "primitive" scholarly precursor who did not distinguish between law and morality.[48] In arguing that it was not possible to see Vitoria as "father" of international law, but that he should, instead, be seen as a representative of "primitive legal scholarship" (together with Suarez, Gentili and Grotius) because of his failing to normatively differentiate between different kinds of norms: moral, scriptural, or strictly legal, Kennedy also contributed to *"toute la question des origines de droit international (qui) est entourée d'une épaisse couche d'interprétations partisantes et déformantes qui se succèdent depuis plus de deux siècles et qui conditionnent inévitablement toute considération à son sujet"*.[49] Moreover, Kennedy's suggestion of the "tendentiousness of an historiography which termed these men (pre-1648 scholarship) precursors"[50] was influential in Koskenniemi's assessment that the distinction between "ascending" and "descending" approaches to international law did not arise until 1700[51] that is, in the pre-classical period. This re-conceptualization of historical origins of the discipline also began to set the ground for a gradually emerging new conceptualization of the late nineteenth century of international law[52] as well as for what, many years later, would emerge as today's intra-disciplinarily influential and scholarly "hip" critique of the colonial origins of international law.[53] It will be, however, in the 1990s and the twenty-first century when the strengthening of the historical turn in international law was to take place.

Other than pioneering the use of structuralism in international law and pushing for post-structuralism in the U.S. legal academy debates, as well as to consecrating a considerable attention to the history of international law, from the early/mid-1980s one sees Kennedy's engagement with critical activism in the field of human rights. *Spring Break*[54] a provocative essay that had, later on, been revisited and extended with reflections on the evolution of the field for two decades,[55] soon

[45] In the area of Kennedy's contribution to the history of international law in the 1980s, see among others: Kennedy 1986, 1987b, 841.

[46] Kennedy 1998, 1, 12.

[47] See Brown Scott 1934.

[48] See Kennedy 1986. See, De la Rasilla 2012.

[49] Haggenmacher 1983, 27, 80.

[50] Kennedy 1988a, 1, 16.

[51] See Koskenniemi 1989, and Kennedy 1990, 390.

[52] See Koskenniemi 2002.

[53] See e.g. Anghie 2004.

[54] Kennedy 1985b, 1377.

[55] See Kennedy 2009.

became the flagship of this approach. One accompanies the *avant-gardiste* telling of the vicissitudes and reflections of a young (untenured) Harvard professor in humanitarian visit to political prisoners in Uruguayan prisons during the latest stage of the military dictatorship and the repression led against the *Tupamaro* movement. The essay was originally provided with an appendix that abounds with references to critical legal thought and post-structuralism so as to place strategically the narrative within the debates over legal indeterminacy that, thanks to the CLS, were very much in vogue in the 1980s. Kennedy's talent for focalization on the argumentative core of a line of thought and his ability to peel it off and to regurgitate in a finely laminated form can be seen in the ironically methodological justification he presented of the purpose of *Spring Break* in this appendix that he co-wrote with Nathaniel Berman. Here, the author defines his methodological approach as an "argumentation against the enterprise of asserting a dogmatic indeterminacy as an attack against the normative discourse of liberalism".[56] He justifies this deconstructionist challenge by "demonstrating the ways in which any such assertion of indeterminacy undermines itself by reliance upon a shifting, yet nevertheless inescapable image of determinacy".[57] In twisting to the break-point of yet another turn of the screw the most sophisticated arguments, Kennedy notes that with Spring Break he wanted to open "the legal experience to the understanding" that "the acknowledgement that reading and writing a piece of legal scholarship is as much a matter of mood, its critical bite a product of its tone, as it is of a deployed methodology or a revealed truth about the reality of legal situations"[58] This ex post-facto wrapping up of the narrative in the intellectual seam of American-*French Theory* seems to square the introspective and iconoclast style of *Spring Break* within the parallel evolution of *Cultural Studies* in the U.S. academy in the 1980s as well as with certain radicalization of the trend *Law and Society*––and within the latter of the sub-trend *Law and Everyday Life*.[59] The latter can be seen as an experimental variety of legal anthropology that places the conscience of the lawyer at the forefront of his narrative. Such style found a sequel in Kennedy's work in the 1990s where the author gave free rein to his causticity in writing in first person about law, the human rights' movement and the limits of professional activism in his *Autumn Weekends*.[60] This line of introspective and mischievously demystifying approach to the work of the international lawyer definitively transcended the previous confines of the discipline. Since then, this line of international legal scholarship has been nurtured by other authors who have written on international law with a considerable ironical freshness.[61] Kennedy's work in the area of human rights is heavily influenced by its linkage with the critique of the

56 Kennedy 1985b, 1420.

57 Ibid. 1417–1423.

58 Ibid. 1423.

59 See e.g., Sarat and Kearns 1995.

60 See Kennedy 1995, 191.

61 See especially Talgren 1999.

discourse of human rights in CLS.[62] This is a line of thought to which he continued contributing provocatively asking whether human rights were "part of the problem"[63] in the following decades. The critical success of these rights' critiques of Marxian underpinnings should not be seen in isolation from the background of liberal triumphalism that characterized international law since the fall of the Berlin Wall and the gradual entry into the globalization age. Kennedy's own work, and through his mentorship of third world approaches to international law, has served as counterpoint to the duo neo-liberal Washington consensus/empire of the rule of law on the international plane until the very present.

The 1980s also witnessed the beginning of Kennedy's reflections on a thematic that has accompanied him ever since: the nature of international legal education. Adopting a retrospective perspective on his, by then, very recent experience as student, he describes international legal studies as being condemned to endure an "uncomfortable oscillation between cynicism and enthusiasm".[64] In these reflections, that constitute a valuable and rare testimony of the study of international law in the *per excellentiam* U.S.' elite legal institution, are some of the sharpest and most activistically optimistic pages for the reform of the study of the discipline of international law. Writing in first person, in his lucid exam of the evolution of the academic discipline in EE.UU., as well as in his analysis of the alienation and promise that the various professional path-careers offered to him, Kennedy vindicates a new intellective existential space grounded on the "resurrection of the doctrine and history of public international law".

The development of his early reformist critical work, anchored on the axes of post-structuralism, history, and the study of the intra-disciplinary evolution of international law, together with Kennedy's interest for legal education, were bound to prefigure—but, only in part—the evolution of his writing in the following two decades in which, as a corollary, he also served as fundamental agglutinative for the development of new and alternative approaches to international legal studies—or New Stream.[65]

## 8.3 The 1990s: Between the New Approaches to International Law and the Counter-End of History

After the fall of the Berlin Wall, Kennedy, who founded the European Law Research Center at *Harvard Law School* in 1991, has been developing a very critical and influent parallel work in the framework of the process of European integration

---

62 Kennedy 1997.

63 Kennedy 2001a, 101. Kennedy 2004.

64 Specially, Kennedy 1985b, 361, 362.

65 See in the 1980s, Kennedy 1988a, 1.

which he observed was encapsulated in historical frames of international renovation(ism), and reiteration(ism), or continuism. With these early 1990s' works, Kennedy inaugurated his very minutious and detailed inter-disciplinary exam of the strategies of economic development and policy. Indeed, if, by the very early 1990s, Kennedy's interest on this topic was focused on the Eastward extension of Western economic and legal regimes in Europe, the fields of law and development and political economy have accompanied his polyhedrical and all-encompassing work up to the present.[66] By the early 1990s, he also stressed, in parallel, the exam of what was, by then, the dawn of a New World Order and the role of international institutions in shaping it. International institutions are one of the great axis—almost magnetic in his scholarship until this very day. This area of studies renews, however, itself in his work, through new and bifurcated waves of generational enthusiasm[67] that are punctuated by his engaged contribution to the development of critical alternatives to the prevailing modes of international legal thought that have been accompanying these institutional developments.

However, it is his role as agglutinative and primus motor of the development of New Approaches to International Law, one of the more defining features of the 1990s. This is, indeed, a decade marked by his reflections and scholarly activism in favor of constituting a critical school in international law.[68] His very direct contribution to the renewal, and emergence of critical contemporary schools of international law, extended the doctrinal challenge embodied by CLS to the sphere of international law. The fruit of these efforts is a heterogeneous galaxy, intellectually identified under the label of New Approaches to International Law (NAIL),[69] which is a term that was originally (but see Falk)[70] used by Kennedy in 1988 by reference to his own work that he described as one that "borrows from recent linguistic and literary theory and from the work of contemporary critical legal scholarship—which has itself drawn on the European legal traditions of structuralism and post-structuralism—in order to reformulate the relationship between law and politics in rhetorical terms".[71] This project became gradually constituted around a series of conferences and academic events and overlapped with a number of other academic projects including in Kennedy's own words "'Third World Approaches to International Law", "International Legal Feminism", the "Feminism, Law Sexuality and Culture project" (FLASC), "the New

[66] Kennedy 1991a, 373. See also Webb and Kennedy 1990, 633.

[67] Kennedy 1994a, 330.

[68] In the area of Kennedy's contribution to the study of critical trends of international legal thought in the 1990s. See Tennant and Kennedy 1994 and Kennedy 2000a, 104. For an introduction in Spanish Contreras and De la Rasilla 2007.

[69] See Cass 1996. See also Purvis 1991.

[70] See Falk 1967, 477.

[71] Kennedy 1988a, 7.

Approaches to Comparative Law Project", the "Poscolonialism and Sexuality Project".[72] To those mentioned by Kennedy, one can also add a number of strands of research and thought such as international legal history, international economic law, and regulatory policy, critical race theory, critical approaches to human rights, new social movements, a resurgent interest on Marxian perspectives on international law as well as law and development, post-colonial studies, Lacanian studies etc.[73] Defined by Koskenniemi as a "new critical sensitivity consciously self-reflective",[74] these strands can be, broadly, included within what Duncan Kennedy has identified as "*mpm/left*"—otherwise "modernism/postmodernism and leftism"[75]—a generic trend of legal thought that combines or follows a critical left-wing orientation in methodology, and approach and/or applies or it is influenced by the post-modernist turn in its approach to international legal studies.

Despite its heterogeneity, and the rejection of compartmentalization that defines the, otherwise, very diverse and extensive work that is, generally, identified under the label of new and critical approaches to international law, the critical trend may be characterized as a movement loosely united by its will to, as Kennedy has remarked, "escaping (…) the neo-liberal triumphalism of the post-Cold War discipline".[76] Merely descriptive in orientation, this feature coincides with the fact that it is during the post-Cold War era when the critical movement in international law gained a broader scholarly influence. To attempt to order, in methodological terms, a general retrospective perspective and to situate Kennedy's role in it, one can have recourse to the superficial yet, introductorily useful,[77] division of two strands in the post-modernist critique of international law understood by Anthony Carty as "the assertion that the discipline is governed by a particular historically conditioned discourse which is, in fact, quite simply, the translation onto the international domain of some basic tenets of liberal political theory."[78] This methodological division is used for basic explanatory purposes to account for what is an extremely complex scholarly relationship—including one of intestine opposition—among critical scholars themselves who regularly dismiss any attempt at being conceptually pigeonholed in their scholarly pursuits.

The first trend or branch of the critical project in international law has been identified as one of internal or epistemological character, while the second is characterized by its external or normative academic features. The second strand possesses its own scholarly roots, though in its international legal dimension, it has, to a great extent, evolved or has, otherwise, both methodologically and historically benefitted from the background work of the first trend. While loosely

---

[72] Kennedy 1999, 15.

[73] For a chart Ibid., 36.

[74] Koskenniemi 1996, 337.

[75] See Kennedy 1997.

[76] Kennedy 2000b, 491.

[77] Paulus 2009, 69.

[78] Carty 1991, 66.

distinctive, both strands influence each other. In its attempt to reconceptualize the idea of international law through a 3-fold conceptual, methodological, and strategic challenge,[79] the internal or epistemological critical trend has been exploring the apologetic-utopian complementary double nature of the international legal argument—which, as explained by Koskenniemi, is able to "provide a criticism of any substantive position, but unable to justify any".[80] Although the internal critique has evolved throughout the 1990s, and the first decade of the twenty-first century, it was *ab origine* oriented to challenge the "narrative of continuation with the past" identified with the classical liberal approach to international law. The "indeterminacy thesis" set the ground for ulterior critical approaches to international law that are radically subjectivist as it corresponds to the internalization of post-modernist's insights, and their definition of international law as both an intellectual discipline and a professional culture. Among the goals of these approaches is that of informing the task of a new generation of critical-oriented international lawyers who, in becoming more attentive to the dark sides and limitations of its own disciplinary vernacular, become elevated to the rank of social engineers in their approach to the international *ars boni et aequi.*

Integrating perspectives borrowed from sociology, political theory, the theory of language, or anthropology, this project of scientific reconceptualization opened the Pandora's Box of critical studies in a discipline that was earlier been firmly rooted in an orthodoxy that had, traditionally, conceptualized its own history in terms of progress in the accomplishment of liberal values, and that was trained to present the art of its officium in terms of professional objectivity and lego-technical neutrality. The critical preoccupation with revealing the relations of power undergirding international law is premised in the previous demonstration of the legal indeterminacy *ab origine* of any pretension of dominance of any legal position *vis-à-vis* other. Such a stressing on the indeterminate nature of the duality of concretion and normativity on which the expansive ideal of the rule of law is inspired in the internationalist imaginary determines a return to a renovated political combat that is more acutely sensitive to the injustices behind contemporaneous reality and to the role of law in relation to them.

Against the scientific background-setting for the politicization of the discipline, the second and parallel critical project possesses a complementary external character. This second project makes the core of its scholarly criticism, the reflections of international law's historical as well as methodological complicity with, among others, the structures of *macho* and patriarchal dominance (feminism), racist (critical race theory), euro-centric, and imperialist (third world approaches to international law), or (among others) economic inequality. Although rooted in the internal critique, this so-called external trend also benefits from the "turn to history". In fact, for Koskenniemi, such an intra-disciplinary turn is "an effort to set aside the conditionings of the structural method in order to infuse a sense of

[79] Cass 1996, 341.

[80] Koskenniemi 2003, 4, 8.

historical dynamism and political struggle—even on the personal level—to the study of international law".[81] One of the innovative lines of research explored by the historic turn as a generational disciplinary challenge[82] is, precisely, grounded on the effort, as noted by Kennedy, of "mapping international law's disciplinary lexicon"[83] through the examination of successive generational shifts of repetition and renewal in the field. Critical historians of international law such as Nathaniel Berman have, consequently, argued that the genealogical approach to international law is the examination of "the appropriation and re-appropriation of law by the heterogeneous forms of power as well as the constitution and reconstitution of power by the heterogeneous forms of law".[84]

According to the genealogical perspective, the importance of "discontinuity" as a working concept for the historian and the stress on a form of writing which is rooted in the analysis of history as discourse sets itself in the way of any doctrinal attempt at using "continuous history" as a "reassurance to "subjectivity" for international law. This feature alone may suffice to evince an immediate fault-line between a genealogical historical approach, and other alternative visions of the relationship between international law, and its history that were previously exemplified in connection to the feeling of "increased political possibility" brought about by the end of the Cold War. Such methodological gap becomes even more patent if the structuralist faith in the analysis of history as discourse is replaced by a post-structuralist stress on relations of power over relations of meaning.[85] Indeed, doing so, allows an interpretation, extrapolated to the field of the history of international law, according to which, as noted by Foucault, "the purpose of history, guided by genealogy, is not to discover the roots of our identity, but to commit itself to its dissipation".[86] This historical turn has been greatly cultivated by Third World Approaches to International Law (or TWAIL). Instead of following the footprints of "early scholarship (that) tended to treat the colonial encounter as marginal to the story of international law", thus attempting to "recast colonial international law as universal international law", TWAIL offered a "foundational critique of the history of international law" by situating the "colonial project at the very heart of international law".[87]

The 1990s saw a series of Kennedy's works devoted to retrace the lines of discursive evolution of the discipline of international law from the aftermath of the

---

81 Koskenniemi 2002.

82 See an interesting approach by Kemmerer 2008, 71.

83 Kennedy 1988a, 122.

84 Berman, 2008, 88.

85 See among the extensive bibliography, Beaulieu and Gabbard 2006.

86 Foucault 1977, 162.

87 See Anghie 2004.

II World War onwards.[88] His contemporary historical studies were complemented by his attention to the history of international law in other epochs[89] that becomes a fundamental object of inquiry to subvert categories of international legal thought as well as a strategy to counteract "liberal de-politization and neutralization of political options"[90] by exposing the historical social relations of domination on which they are built. To these works one should sum new inquiries on the interpenetration between the politics of international relations and international legal order[91] as well as studies on the role of culture, and the influence of religion in the shaping of international law.[92] The external critical project in which Kennedy participates and fosters in the 1990s, benefits, in generational academic terms, from the extended critical *Zeitgeist* that was brought about by the scholarly repolitization of the field channeled by the internal critique in the 1980s'. Alongside the evolution of the internal project, the scholarly tropes of the external project have been gaining momentum through the 1990s, and the first decade of the twenty-first century. Together, these two branches mirror the parallel modernist-postmodernist/left distinction that, as noted by Duncan Kennedy, is "one that is helpful in understanding many of the debates that occurred in CLS when it was a live movement and that still arise about CLS as a school and theory of law".[93] Although loosely indicative, this distinction helps to account for the doctrinal map of the different trends that make up for the heterogeneous scholarly work of emancipatory spirit, and anti-continuist, and critically de-legitimating of the internationalist traditional *status quo* that was earlier captured as the New Approaches to International Legal Studies.

## 8.4 The Twenty-First Century or Between the Continuity of a Multi-Thematic Exploration and the Way Ahead

Kennedy helped inaugurating the internal critical branch of international law in the 1980s, and he continued to flesh out its external branch by enlarging the traditional boundaries of the discipline of international law in the 1990s. Driven by a powerful intellectual curiosity, by his active challenge against being pigeon-holed and by his commitment to the practical enshrining of an intellectual program, the

---

88 In the area of Kennedy's contribution, through the 1990s and early twenty-first century to the study of the discipline of international law in the U.S., Kennedy 1994b, 7. Kennedy 1999, 9. Kennedy 2000a, 335, 386 and Kennedy 2003b, 397.

89 See Kennedy 1996, 385.

90 Koskenniemi 2002, 15.

91 In the area of Kennedy's contribution to the study of the interpenetration between international law and international relations see, among others, Kennedy 1995 330. Kennedy 1992, 237.

92 In the area of Kennedy's contribution to the analysis of the influence of religion on international law, see among others Kennedy 1988b, 1991a. 1998.

93 Kennedy 1997.

twenty-first century has seen Kennedy continuing his earlier work through magisterial approaches to the history of American legal thought[94] and to the area of comparative law.[95] He has done so without abandoning traditional domains of international law, such as critical approaches to international law of human rights[96] and the socio–corporative evolution of the international human rights movement,[97] while also devoting a considerable attention to the study of both humanitarian international law and war.[98] In his writing in the twenty-first century, there is an even greater push for inter-disciplinarity—with references to materials from sociology and social theory, economics or history—that breaks further away with the molds of established international legal thought. Kennedy has also explored the domains of global law and governance and related debates on global constitutionalism[99] in the age of institutional proliferation and fragmentation. He has, furthermore, found new channels of scholarly expression in the fields of law and development,[100] economic policy,[101] and political economy. Kennedy has approached these fields through the lenses provided by his on-going exploration of the nature of professional expert knowledge at the international level in respect to whom (as well as in respect to the rest of multiple semi-autonomous regimes of decision and influence—both social and private—that shape the real international policy) he defends the necessity of an "aperture to the human experience of the responsible discretionality and freedom".[102]

Indeed, if Kennedy's project of critical cognitive renewal has, since its inception, been a cry against disciplinary intellectual stagnation, his scholarly rebellious perspective is, as of late, ultimately grounded on the epistemological importance he concedes to the "work of experts and the significance of expert knowledge in governing our world".[103] As the author himself notes "over the last several years, I have studied the work of various experts—international lawyers, human rights activists, military professionals, experts in economic development—to understand the nature of their expertise, the knowledge they bring to bear, their background consciousness about what is and is not part of their domain, the terms through which they argue for one or another position, and the channels through

---

94 See Fisher III & Kennedy 2006a.

95 In the area of Kennedy's contribution to the study of comparative law see Kennedy 1997, 2. See also Kennedy 2003a, 131.

96 Kennedy 2004.

97 Kennedy 2009.

98 In his area of contribution to the study of war and humanitarian international law, see among others, Kennedy 2006a. Kennedy 2007, 173.

99 In the area of his contribution to the study of global governance and the politics of expertise, see among others Kennedy 2011a, 2008, 2009; Kennedy 2005, 5 & Kennedy 2001b 117.

100 In the area of Kennedy's contribution to the study of the inter-relation between law and economic development see, among others, Kennedy, 2012. Kennedy 2006a, c.

101 Kennedy 2011b, 1.

102 Kennedy 2006–2007, 395, 398.

103 Kennedy 2008, 827, 846.

which they make what they know real".[104] In the pages that follow, I shall devote some attention to Kennedy's recent engagement with the nature of expertise in the field of Global Governance[105] which is a corollary of Kennedy's drive to problematize the epistemological given framework of current perspectives on international legal studies.

In his recent work "The Mystery of Global Governance",[106] Kennedy, who is former chair of the World Economic Forum's Global Advisory Council on Global Governance, has presented his own architectural approach to the field of global governance. This is built around a three-layered literature review of the available international legal approaches—traditional and new. At the first level of the literature review that Kennedy engages in critical dialogue, one finds the category of "conventional disciplines". Identified with the tradition of international law and its background architecture (norms, entities, powers, and history), this is the very epistemological framework against which Kennedy had originally projected his now more than 30 years long project to "write new stories of our conventional fields".[107] Pursuant to his longstanding project, Kennedy's writing on global governance pertains to the critical tradition (as opposed to problem-solving theory) and it is, ultimately, oriented at problematizing the cognitive framework of international law and the study of global governance. Kennedy's dialectical strategy proceeds through carefully orchestrated argumentative steps. Before examining Kennedy's engagement, however, with the second and third layer of approaches to global law and governance and his critical stance on global constitutionalism, I will review—in a critical exegetic fashion—the first three of those argumentative moves present in "The Mystery of Global Governance".[108] This exegesis of a couple of pages of distilled pure critical theory in action shall help to evince the extent to which David Kennedy's complex writing requires attentive engagement on the part of his reader. Let's call these three argumentative steps, I shall show by reference to Kennedy's own writing, the critical techniques of, first, generation of an epistemological expectation; second, engagement through interrogation; and, third, intra-disciplinary reassurance after methodological disorientation.

Kennedy begins his writing by generating an epistemological expectation through the stressing of the disciplinary as well as trans-disciplinary scholarly momentum gained by the object of its inquiry, and the innovative characteristics of the methodologies employed to approach it. It is against this background that Kennedy interprets that the growing scholarly interest in the area of global governance reveals the existence of an "unknown unknown". This both explains the emergence, and calls for new modes of thinking to unravel it. Contrary to what one may tend to think, Kennedy's initial assumption is not fatally weakened by the

---

104 Ibid.

105 Kennedy 2011a.

106 Kennedy 2008, 827.

107 Ibid. 835.

108 Ibid. 827.

realization that the very mechanics of the production of forms of social inquiry are structurally conditioned by a professional academic market. Moreover, the fact that the very production of knowledge constitutes an industry that creates its own necessities in the form of interrogations and cognitive queries does neither detract from the empirically observable growth of the scholarly literature in this area nor from the assumption that such a growth can be interpreted as an adaptative response of the field to ongoing external transformation. However, the recurring preoccupation showed by Kennedy with the double descriptive and constitutive character of academic knowledge throughout this work, and the social effects he ascribes to the existence of disciplinary blind spots in different modes of thinking, may still have profited from a previous measuring of the weight of professional industrialization over the levers of production of academic knowledge on the topic at hand.

Having effectively generated an epistemological expectation in his reader, the second technique employed by Kennedy is what one can term engagement through interrogation. The answer to the ensuing question of who are the customers of both the descriptive and constitutive knowledge to whom Kennedy attempts to appeal through his so-portrayed "mystery of global governance" makes, logically, for step number two of his dialectical strategy. Those customers of knowledge are invoked through an array of engaging interrogations. Because, who is not to "care deeply about how much poverty can be sustained in a world of such plenty"?[109] The powerful grasp of Kennedy's interrogations' technique closes its dialectical grasp over his audience through an humanist almost irresistible appeal: if we unveil the mystery that I am (not unlike the sorcerers of primitive ages) conveying to exist, we shall "begin to know how to make the world a better place".[110] Step three of Kennedy's dialectical strategy begins by showing the monumental magnitude of the intellectual endeavor that lies ahead. Kennedy employs a double technique to further problematize this epistemological task: an intervention in the discipline of international law and the casting aside of alter-disciplinary vocabularies. The exclusion of the latter is done through an argument of expert authority "As an avid consumer of their work, I must say I would not want to navigate by their maps of world power"[111] The author completes this technique by invoking a reservoir of background knowledge about every field from political science and sociology and anthropology and economics ("everywhere there is important knowledge, promising new initiatives, intriguing insights").[112] This reservoir of knowledge is one to which the author will be made claim of expertise, at different reprises, throughout his work. A related technique is employed by Kennedy to dispel any sense of disciplinary certainty in the international lawyers' mindset. The idea is conveyed through the projection of an ever-inclusive new area of

[109] Ibid. 828.

[110] Ibid.

[111] Ibid.

[112] Ibid.

knowledge: Global governance. This finds itself, consequently, portrayed as the result of the breaking down of all legal disciplinary boundaries by which the field was earlier defined. Thus, global governance is not anymore "the sum of private law and public law, national and international law", "each served by its own disciplinary experts",[113] but has, instead, gained an identity of its own which cannot be but holistically apprehended. And, the reason why the contemporary international lawyer is not prepared to do so is intra-legal disciplinary specialization. At this point, any background methodological preoccupation with Kennedy's legalist approach to the definition of global governance has, moreover, been superseded by the intra-disciplinary relief on the part of its legal audience. Indeed, the author is implicitly arguing that the mystery of global governance can be apprehended by recourse to law if only one leaves aside one's compartmentalized knowledge. Moreover, by now, Kennedy has convinced his audience that the maps provided by other disciplines, although useful, are as elusive as the promise offered by the old legal schemes to penetrate this new and ever-inclusive domain. The projection of such a new background intellectual frame is, furthermore, strategically instrumented to convey a sense of imperfection of all maps available to describe the answer to the question "how are we governed at the global level?". This is the elusive mystery that Kennedy presents as the mechanical running-hare for his project of epistemological renewal. It is also an ever inclusive framework for critical approaches to international law through the use—as this exegesis has attempted to briefly show—of a technique of intra-disciplinary reassurance after methodological disorientation.

A series of highly interesting and innovative further dialectical techniques used by Kennedy follow in his writing—but the limited scope of this work does not allow me to describe them in detail. It may suffice to note that they are, nonetheless, all oriented to prepare the ground for Kennedy's engagement with the second level of his literature review that he describes as the three "mothers-of-all-reinventions in the field of global governance."[114] Kennedy engages these trends of thought as methodological forerunners of his own project. This is because they share the traits of rejection of conventional disciplinary boundaries, of the blurring of public and private, of the national and international, find their inspiration in the social sciences, and are all united by the rejection of traditional approaches. Kennedy engages with the insights offered by the policy-oriented jurisprudence of the New Haven School, the works of the Manhattan School, and those of Transnational Legal Process and Liberal International representatives as well as with some of their precursors (like e.g. Jessup) whether in their own right as influential methodological lenses (like in the case H. Koh) or as objects of critical study by authors pertaining to the new approaches to international law (NAIL). The latter one is, as already seen, a multifaceted critical trend of thought that has evolved as a dialectical counterpoint to these perspectives since the early 1990s onwards. Kennedy's assessment that "even

---

[113] Ibid.

[114] Ibid. 836.

at their best, these more recent traditions remain rudimentary and partial answers to the question how are we governed at the global level"[115] complements his more than 30 years-old project of problematization of what he earlier examined as the first layer of "conventional disciplines" of international legal thought that this very second layer of literature is portrayed (according to Kennedy) to have cognitively overthrown.

The third level of engagement of literature in the field of global governance opens the way to Kennedy's analysis of what he terms the "contemporary frameworks for thinking about global governance".[116] These new ways of explaining global order rank from projects of legal sociology (such that of Braithwaite) to global administrative law frameworks (as in Kingsbury) or systems-theory (*à la* Teubner) as well as others that flag the constitutional metaphor to normatively describe the current global legal order. Kennedy's critical take on this "group of large proposals to interpret the world of law surged in the last few years"[117] is evinced by the "check list against which I would judge the constitutionalist, or any other, project to rethink global governance".[118] This check list includes from the insufficient attention paid to the "sheer density of rules and institutions in the global space", to the "disorderliness, the pluralism, the uncertainty, the chaos, of all those rules and principles and institutions" as well as the "series of issues we might think of as the inverse side of law", and the worry that "our projects to rethink global governance fail to grasp the depth of the injustice of the world today and the urgency of change",[119] Kennedy's critical vein, as a way of illuminating the polemics, insights, assumption, blind spots, and biases of these new approaches to the global legal order ends by devoting a special attention to the most conventional of these emerging vernaculars. His complex attack-front against the constitutionalist literature is based, among others, on the assumption by this trend that the world is constituted as well as due to its own proceduralist and settlement biases. Kennedy's rejection of constitutionalist lenses is, further, undergirded by his suspicion of universal ethics, and his leaning for legal pluralism as a site of creative legal contestation.

Kennedy's "The Mystery of Global Governance" is one among many interesting examples of the author's general attempt at epistemological subversion of the discipline. This subversive approach is undergirded by a preoccupation with the constitutive role of knowledge in reproducing hierarchies and inequalities and with the role of law as superstructure in examining how the world is legally constituted. Ultimately, in coming up with his focus on general modes of expertise and the work of experts in global law and governance, Kennedy is interested in scrutinizing the knowledge accessible to "the man behind the throne" as well as in

---

115 Ibid. 840.

116 Ibid. 845.

117 Ibid. 840.

118 Ibid. 848.

119 Ibid. 848–849.

encouraging the emergence of a parallel multiplicity of cognitive sites where people are encouraged into the human experience of exercising responsible freedom. Animated by a self-regenerating scholarly impulse this approach is characterized by an ethos of rebellion and anti-stagnation. Kennedy's attention during the twenty-first century to the role experts play as the producers and conveyor belts of specialized critical knowledge with a transformative potential is, therefore, less a recipe than a call for resistance and imagination in the task of remaking global politics in the twenty-first century.

## 8.5 Conclusion

This introductory study has surveyed three decades of an intellectual trajectory that benefits from an American university system in which there is a considerable inter-lego departmental teaching mobility among law professors as well as an extraordinary curricular richness. This intellectually diversified career appears as, somewhat, still structurally unthinkable in the European academy where a more clearly defined professional pigeon-holing tends to prevail among its members. This feature of thematic inter-disciplinary (and even counter-disciplinary)[120] diversification situates Kennedy in the antipodes of a general trend toward the pragmatic compartmentalization of one's legal expertise. Preaching emancipation and becoming the personification of emancipation in one's intellectual work sum up two lacerations in a creative intellectual plot that the majority of the *invisible college* only aspires to baste in the given framework of an imposed legal formalism. This constitutes a super-structure that, when it is interiorized, conditions the self-examination of the scientific viability of one's own work through the underlying operation of a complex system of professional carrots and sticks. Against this background, Kennedy's success as the man behind the throne of the "other" international law are a salute to diversification, experimentation as well as intra, inter (and even counter) disciplinary dissonance understood as the most profound embodiments of such intellectual emancipation. It is not that Kennedy has gone beyond the confines of international law as a field, rather it is the field of international law that has grown thanks, partly, to his salutary influence in the last decades being now, as a result, considerably more diverse and, therefore, more democratic than when this extremely gifted scholar came to it. Kennedy's extensive work appears, in retrospect, as almost polihedrically impermeable to any holistic appraisal; the latter makes it welcoming, in a beehive-like manner, of many diverse explorations; but, in essence, it epitomizes the freedom of an intellectual program that ultimately consist in finding something as basic and essential as "our place in the world"[121]—a vital attitude that evinces itself in the

[120] See Kennedy 1985b, 361, 380.

[121] Ibid. 381.

existential, evolutionary, and creative exploration of one's full potential as an international legal scholar. David Kennedy, who remains up to this day, a catalyzer of creativity, innovation, and intellectual rebelliousness among new generations of academics in international legal studies (and elsewhere) can often be found today answering e-mail messages from his Wireless Blackberry® around the world.

## References

Anghie A (2004) Imperialism, sovereignty and the making of international law. Cambridge University Press, Cambridge
Anon. (1982) Round and round the Bramble Bush: from legal realism to critical legal scholarship. Harv Law Rev 95:1669
Bauman B (1996) Critical legal studies. A guide to the literature. Westview Press, Boulder
Beaulieu A, Gabbard D (eds) (2006) Michel Foucault and power today. International multidisciplinary studies in the history of the present. Lexington Books, Lanham
Berman N (2008) Dans le sillage de l'empire. In: Berman N (ed) Passions et Ambivalences: le colonialisme, le nationalisme et le droit international. Pédone, Paris
Brown Scott J (1934) The Spanish origins of international law. The Clarendon Press, London
Carty A (1991) Critical international law, recent trends in the theory of international law. Eur J Int Law 2:66–96
Cass D (1996) Navigating the Newstream: recent critical scholarship in international law. Nordic J Int Law 65:341–383
Contreras FJ, De la Rasilla I (2007) Humanitarismo crítico y crítica del humanitarismo. In: Kennedy D (ed) Los lados oscuros de la virtud. Editorial Almuzara, Córdoba, pp 9–40
Cot JP (2006) Tableau de la pensée juridique américaine. Révue Générale de Droit Int Public 3:109
De la Rasilla I (2012) The Zero Years of Spanish International Law. In: Jouannet E and Motoc I (eds) Les doctrines internationalistes durant les années du communisme réel en Europe. Société de législation comparée, Paris, pp 95–135
Falk (1967) New approaches to the study of international law. Am J Int Law 61:477–495
Fisher III W and Kennedy D (eds) (2006) The Canon of American legal thought. Princeton University Press, Princeton
Foucault M (1977) Nietzsche, Genealogy, history. In: Bouchard DF (ed) Language, counter-memory, practice: selected essays and interviews. Cornell University Press, Ithaca
Haggenmacher P (1983) La place de Francisco de Vitoria parmi les fondateurs du droit international. In: Truyol Serra A et al. (ed) Actualité de la pensée juridique de Francisco de Vitoria. Bruylant, Bruxelles, p 27
Kemmerer A (2008) The turning aside: on international law and its history. In: Bratspies RM, Miller RA (eds) Progress in international law. Martinus Nijhoff Publishers, The Hague, pp 71–93
Kennedy D (1980) Theses about international law discourse. Ger Yearb Int Law 23:353
Kennedy D (1985c) Spring break. Tex Law Rev 63:1377–1423
Kennedy D (1985–1986) Critical theory, structuralism and contemporary legal scholarship theory. N Engl Law Rev 21:209–289
Kennedy D (1986) Primitive legal scholarship. Harv Int Law J 27:1–97
Kennedy D (1987a) International legal structures. Nomos, Baden–Baden
Kennedy D (1987b) The move to institutions. Cardozo Law Rev 8:841–988
Kennedy D (1988a) A new stream of international law scholarship. Wis Int Law J 7:1
Kennedy D (1988b) Religion and international law. Proc Am Soc Int Law, 82:1–49

Kennedy D (1989) A rotation in contemporary legal scholarship. In: Joerges C, Trubek D (eds) Critical legal thought: an American-German debate. Nomos Verlagsgesellschaft, Baden–Baden, pp 353–396
Kennedy D (1990) Book review. Harv Int Law J 31:385
Kennedy D (1991a) Turning to market democracy: a tale of two architectures. Harv Int Law 32:373
Kennedy D (1994a) A new world order: yesterday, today and tomorrow. Transnatl Law Contemp Probl 4:330–376
Kennedy D (1994b) The international style in postwar law and policy. Utah Law Rev 1:7
Kennedy D (1995) Autumn weekends. An essay in law and everyday life. In; Sarat A and Kearns TR (eds) Law in everyday life. The University of Michigan Press, Ann Arbor, pp 191–235
Kennedy D (1996) International law in the nineteenth century: history of an illusion. Nordic J Int Law 65:385–420
Kennedy D (1997) New approaches to comparative law: comparativism and international governance. Utah Law Rev 2:545
Kennedy D (1998) Losing faith in the secular: law, religion and international governance. In Weiner A and Kaplan L (eds) Graven images, vol 4: transgression, punishment, responsibility and forgiveness. University of Wisconsin Press, Madison, p 115
Kennedy D (1999) The disciplines of international law and policy. Leiden J Int Law 12:9
Kennedy D (2000a) My talk at the ASIL: what is new thinking in international law. In Proceedings of the 94th annual meeting of the American society of international law, pp 104–125
Kennedy D (2000b) When renewal repeats: thinking against the box. N Y J Int Law Polit 32:335–500
Kennedy D (2001a) The international human rights movement: part of the problem. Harv Hum Rights J 15:101–125
Kennedy D (2001b) The forgotten politics of international governance. Eur Hum Rights Law Rev 2:117–125
Kennedy D (2003a) The politics and methods of comparative law. In: Bussani M and Mattei U (eds) The common core of European private law: essays on the project. Kluwer Law International, The Hague, pp 131–207
Kennedy D (2003b) Tom Franck and the Manhattan school. N Y Univ J Int Law Polit 35:397–435
Kennedy D (2004) The dark sides of virtue. Reassessing international humanitarism. Princeton University Press, Princeton
Kennedy D (2005) Challenging expert rule: the politics of global governance. Syd J Int Law 27:5–28
Kennedy D (2006a) Of war and law. Princeton University Press, Princeton
Kennedy D (2006–2007) Speech: assessing the proposal for a global parliament: a skeptics view. Widener Law Rev, 13:395–399
Kennedy D (2006b) The last treatise: project and person. (Reflections on Martti Koskenniemi's from apology to Utopia). Ger Law J 7:983
Kennedy D (2008) The mystery of global governance. Ohio North Law Rev 34:827–860
Kennedy D (2009) The rights of spring. A memoir of innocence abroad. Princeton University Press, Princeton
Kennedy D (2011a) Global governance? New thinking about law and policy. Princeton University Press, Princeton
Kennedy D (2011b) Some caution about property rights as a recipe for economic development. Account, Econ Law: A Convivium 1:1–64.
Kennedy D (2012) Economic development: an intellectual history. Princeton University Press, Princeton
Kennedy D (1976) Form and substance in private law adjudication. Harv Law Rev 88:1685
Kennedy D (1979) The structure of Blackstone's commentaries. Buffalo Law Rev 28:205, 213
Kennedy D (1997) The Paradox of American legal realism. Eur Law J, 3:366
Korhonen O (1996) New international law: silence, defence of deliverance? Eur J Int Law 7:1–28

Koskenniemi M (1989) From apology to Utopia. the structure of the international legal argument. Finnish Lawyers', Helsinki

Koskenniemi M (2003) What is international law for? In: Evans M (ed) International law. Oxford University Press, Oxford, 89–116

Koskenniemi M (1996) Editor's preface. Nordic J f Int Law 65:337–340

Koskenniemi M (1997) Le style comme méthode: lettre aux organisateurs du symposium. In: Koskenniemi M (ed) La politique du droit international. Pédone, Paris

Koskenniemi M (2002) The gentle civilizer of nations. The rise and fall of international law, 1870–1960. Cambridge University Press, Cambridge

Llewellyn K (1931) Some realism about realism—responding to Dean Pound. Harv Law Rev 44:1222–1238

MacDonald E (2011) International law and ethics after the critical challenge: framing the legal within the post-foundational. Martinus Nijhoff, The Netherlands

Paulus A (2001) International law after postmodernism: towards renewal or decline of international law. Leiden J Int Law 14:727–755

Paulus A (2009) The international legal system as a constitution. In: Dunoff JL and Trachtman JP (eds) Ruling the world? Constitutionalism, international law, and global governance. Cambridge University Press, Cambridge, pp 69–112

Rasulov A (2005) International law and the poststructuralist challenge. Leiden J Int Law 19:799–823

Sarat A, Kearns TR (eds) (1995) Law in everyday life. The University of Michigan Press, Ann Harbour

Scobbie I (2006) Wicked heresies or legitimate perspectives? Theory and international law. In: Evans M (ed) International law, 2nd edn. Oxford University Press, Oxford, pp 83–112

Singer J (1988) Legal realism now. Calif Law Rev 76:503

Skouteris T and Korhonen O (1998) Under Rhodes's eyes: the 'old' and the 'new' international law at looking distance. Leiden J Int Law 11:429

Skouteris T (1997) FIN de NAIL: new approaches to international law and its impact on contemporary international legal scholarship. Leiden J Int Law 10:415

Talgren I (1999) We did it? The Vertigo of law and everyday life at the diplomatic conference on the establishment of an international criminal court. Leiden J Int Law 12:683–707

Tennant C and Kennedy D (1994) New approaches to international law: a bibliography. Harv Int Law J 35:417

Unger R (1986) The critical legal studies movement. Harvard University Press, Cambridge

Webb D, Kennedy D (1990) Integration: eastern Europe and the European economic communities. Columbia J Transnatl Law 28:633–675

# Part III
# Reassessing the Use of Force in International Law?

# Chapter 9
# Formalization and Deformalization as Narratives of the Law of War

**Olivier Corten**

**Abstract** In his seminal of war and law, David Kennedy demonstrates how the shift from formalism to realism can be observed in the evolution of the law of war. This shift, which can be characterized as a "deformalization" narrative of the law of war, is the main object of this chapter. More precisely, I argue that, especially in regard to the codification of relevant rules in *jus contra bellum* and in *jus in bello*, formalism must not be underestimated. On the one hand, the formalization narrative appears far more convincing than the deformalization one to understand the evolution of the law of war from the nineteenth century. Every time a war is waged, it leaves no doubt that a large range of actors will debate about its formal legality. On the other hand, formalism must not be overestimated. It provides only a strategy which can—or not, depending on the circumstances of the case at hand—be used to support or combat a war. And, of course, the efficiency of the argument will depend both on the audience concerned and on the political context in which the debate takes place.

## Contents



---

O. Corten (✉)
Center of International Law, Université Libre de Bruxelles, Brussels, Belgium
e-mail: ocorten@ulb.ac.be

J. M. Beneyto and D. Kennedy (eds.), *New Approaches to International Law*,
DOI: 10.1007/978-90-6704-879-8_9, 

## 9.1 Introduction:

In his seminal *of war and law*, David Kennedy argues that the "Cold War", and later the "War on terror", are formulae which tends to blur the classical distinction between war and peace.[1] This rhetorical strategy enables political leaders to obtain extraordinary powers to combat "the enemy", inside and outside national borders. Against this backdrop, law is not—or at least not only—a humanist force external to war. It is rather a tool, similar to a "commercial asset",[2] used by the authorities to proclaim a 'state of war", to launch and lead wars, or to justify wars in the (national or world) public opinion. Law as such is neutral: it can be used either to make or to combat war. It is as a common language used by political and military leaders as well as by humanitarians.[3] But this "culture of rules" has also led to an erosion of the experience of personal decision making and responsibility. It is, thus, crucial to take into account the limits of law in order to revitalize our responsibility for war,[4] which foregrounds more troubling questions: when is warfare necessary? What is the hierarchy of the aims to pursue? Should such warfare be carried out through economical or military means? Addressing the sole question of the legality of war can obviously not provide an answer to these crucial issues. In brief, "Kennedy's book appears as an attempt to show how the shift from formalism to realism" can be observed in the evolution of the law of war.[5] This shift, which can be characterized as a "deformalization" narrative of the law of war, is the main object of this chapter.

In the first page of his book, David Kennedy observes that "people write about the wars of their own time and their own country".[6] *Of war and law* is written by an US international lawyer, who had many discussions on the ground with humanitarians as well as military personnel, about the role and the limits of law.[7] In contrast, by way of example, I think and write as a European citizen of a small country with limited powers, particularly in the military domain. My practical experience with humanitarians and military institutions is rather limited. I wrote a book called *The Law against War* from my desk, conceiving law as a (at least) theoretical roadblock to war, drawing primarily upon classical sources of international law (e.g. official positions of States in and outside the United Nations, case-law of the ICJ, work of the ILC, …).[8] My position is, thus, culturally and politically oriented,[9] namely holding that the deformalization, presented as a

[1] Kennedy 2005.

[2] Kennedy 2005, 36.

[3] See also Kennedy 2004.

[4] See Haskell 2007.

[5] Contreras and de la Rasilla 2008, 776

[6] Kennedy 2005, 1.

[7] See e.g. Kennedy 2005, 32–33.

[8] Corten 2010.

[9] For more details, see Corten 2008; and Corten 2009a, b, c, d.

self-evident characteristic of the evolution of international law since the nineteenth century, is only one way to describe the history of the "law of force".[10] Another possibility—far more convincing and desirable, as far as I am concerned—is to promote a "formalization" narrative. One can indeed choose to emphasize that formalism still remains a method and a language shared by the different actors of a war when they decide to use law. In fact, "formalization" and "deformalization" constitute two narratives which can possibly be equally used to navigate the history of the law of war. This core question will be exposed by commenting on four ideas which are built upon in David Kennedy's book: (1) law as an argument, (2) the erosion of sharp legal distinctions, (3) the deformalization of the law of war and (4) the choice between formalist and antiformalist narratives every jurist needs to make. Given my privileged sphere of competence, I will mainly focus on *jus contra bellum* to support my reflexions on the "law of war", with *jus in bello* being evoked in a more incidental way.

## 9.2 Law as an Argument

*Of war and law* is obviously grounded on a "critical approach" of (international) law.[11] According to the author, law is not a static set of rules, nor the product of ethics, nor is it established by a decision of the sovereign. The rule of law cannot, therefore, be proved to be "valid" *in abstracto*. It is rather a process, an instrument of reason used to support a claim or to justify an action in a political context. Accordingly, the meaning of law cannot be determined in general. The question is not "what does law mean?" but "whose interpretation of the law will, in fact, prevail, and before what audience?"[12] In this context, David Kennedy points to the growing importance of experts networks, which share common legal vernaculars for debating the necessity of warfare and the manner it will be waged. Law has become an "alternative way of thinking [...] which emphasizes the persuasiveness, rather than the validity of norms."[13]

I feel personally comfortable with this general conception of law, which can be characterized as a classical "critical approach". Yet, I would like to formulate two remarks in relation to the role and limits of legal formalism.

First, this aspect of the book does sound rather familiar, even to a "European formalist". Of course, it is grounded in classical American writings.[14] David Kennedy expressly quotes the well-known "Holmes" theory of law (a prophecy of what a judge

[10] For more details, see Corten 2009b.

[11] We could also use other expressions, like the well-known "New Approaches to International Law" (see Kennedy 2009).

[12] Kennedy 2005, 35.

[13] Kennedy 2005, 92.

[14] See Haskell 2007.

will decide),[15] as well as Oscar Schachter's concept of the "college of international lawyers".[16] But this part of the reasoning could be founded on classical European legal writings as well. "Law as an argument", if it can be summarized as such, is an idea that can obviously be rooted in the Marxist theory of law.[17] In the Marxist tradition, law is denounced as a tool used by those in power to impose their domination, either by force (which is justified and organized by law) or by ideology (law must be presented as good and fair).[18] Law is not the (even imperfect) realization of justice; it is an instrument of power.[19]

But, beyond this "law of power", there is also a more general "power of law". Law can actually be used by all actors, including those who combat the power, to support their view.[20] This way of thinking was applied to international law in the 1970 and 1980s by the well-known "Ecole de Reims".[21] Charles Chaumont, a former legal adviser to the French Ministry of Foreign Affairs, defended in his Hague course an openly Maoist conception of international law.[22] There is no fixed or rigid meaning of the rule of law. The rule is the result of a political contradiction, and expresses this contradiction without resolving it.[23] The contradiction, characterized as "primitive" as it is linked to the creation of the rule, will simply be transformed into another contradiction, characterized as "consecutive", which will focus on the interpretation of the rule.[24] This template can be easily applied to the rules prohibiting the use of force. Article 51 of the UN Charter, for example, does not put an end to the contradictions among the different

---

15 Kennedy 2005, 95–96.

16 Kennedy 2005, 81.

17 See Contreras and de la Rasilla 2008, 773.

18 See generally Hunt 2010.

19 See e.g. Marx and Engels 1947.

20 Pashukanis 2002.

21 See *Annales de la faculté de droit et des sciences économiques de Reims* (Université de Reims, 1974); *Réalités du droit international contemporain. Force obligatoire et sujets de droit*, Actes des seconde et troisième rencontres de Reims (Université de Reims, 1976); *Réalités du droit international contemporain. La relation du droit international avec la structure économique et sociale*, Actes de la quatrième rencontre de Reims (Université de Reims, 1978); *Réalités du droit international contemporain. Discours juridique et pouvoir dans les relations* internationales, Actes de la cinquième rencontre de Reims (Université de Reims, 1981); *Réalités du droit international contemporain. Discours juridique sur l''agression et réalité internationale*, Actes de la sixième rencontre de Reims (Université de Reims, 1982); *Réalités du droit international contemporain. Le discours juridique sur la non-intervention et la pratique internationale*, Actes de la septième rencontre de Reims (Université de Reims, 1986); *Réalités du droit international contemporain. Les rapports entre l''objet et la méthode en droit international* (Université de Reims, 1990).

22 Chaumont 1970.

23 See Jouannet 2004.

24 See Chemillier Gendreau 2004.

conceptions of self-defence.[25] It only offers a formula which will be interpreted differently by States and other actors of the international society in each particular context. Against this background, it would, of course, be convenient to invoke an "experts" "consensus" to support their position. One could mention[26] Pierre Bourdieu's theory of the *champ juridique*, i.e. a network of legal actors who share the same intellectual framework and which, even if it remains autonomous, will be mobilized by other actors to justify their position.[27] Alternatively, Jean Salmon's works[28] on the topic might be evoked, this latter author relying both on contemporary Marxist theories and authors like Chaïm Pereleman,[29] to insist on the importance of the audience as a criteria of persuasiveness of an (legal) argument.[30]

What about formalism, at this stage? On the one hand, (neo) and (post) marxist approaches cannot be considered as "formalists" since, according to these authors, law could not be understood without connecting it to economical, sociological, and political factors.[31] On the other hand, however, one cannot conclude that any kind of formalism is excluded from this theory. As part of the 'superstructure", law is supposed to be distinguished from the "infrastructure". A distinction is therefore possible, not on substance, but formally. As an instrument of power, law is simply a formalization of the will of the ruling class through the State. And, as an ideology, law has to be formally separated from morals and politics.[32] The formalization of law indeed favors the fiction of an objective and neutral law, rationally applied by experts and professionals.[33] In this perspective, the persuasiveness of the legal argument relies on its formal validity,[34] which leads me to another observation.

In some parts of the book, David Kennedy notes that "the point about a norm is not its pedigree, but its persuasiveness"[35]; or "the point is no longer the validity of the distinctions, but the persuasiveness of arguments".[36] At the same time, he observes that "if the rules can be shown to be invalid, their persuasiveness may crumble".[37] This latter remark is perfectly in line with the critical neo-Marxist

---

[25] See *Réalités du droit international contemporain. Discours juridique sur l'agression et réalité internationale*, Actes de la sixième rencontre de Reims (Université de Reims, 1982).

[26] Banchand 2009, 16.

[27] Bourdieu 1986.

[28] See Salmon 1982, 2002.

[29] Perelman and Olbrecht-Tyteca 1991.

[30] Other European authors, like Derrida or Foucault, could also be evoked as relevant to interpret David Kennedy's position; Contreras and de la Rasilla 2008, 780–781.

[31] See Salmon 2001, "critique" and 290 and Corten 2009a, 59–68.

[32] Corten 2002; see also Althusser 1969.

[33] Bourdieu 1991, 99.

[34] See Weber 1978.

[35] Kennedy 2005, 93.

[36] Kennedy 2005, 96.

[37] Kennedy 2005, 97.

theories. Of course, there is no validity as such, no "objective validity". Validity is part of the dispute; it will be contended, contested, perhaps formally upheld by an international body and, if it is the case, certainly interpreted by the actors concerned. In fact, and this seems especially true in the realm of the "law of war", there is no persuasiveness without argument on validity.[38] When a State resorts to force, it will use several ranges of arguments, political (e.g. to defend democracy, to maintain peace), moral (e.g. to stop slaughters, to protect the victims) but also legal, even in a defensive way (the war was not prohibited by the UN Charter).[39] This is what Guy de la Charrière, a former legal-adviser to the French Ministry of Foreign Affairs and Judge at the International Court of Justice, called the *politique juridique extérieure*.[40] When the US, the UK, and its allies decided in 2002 to attack Iraq, they asked their legal department to establish a legal argument, founded on the interpretation of the existing (the formal) rules of positive international law.[41] And, as we know, the argument was perhaps the most formalist one can imagine: the March 2003 war would have been based on a Security Council resolution adopted in November 1990 (Security Council Resolution 678), which would have been temporarily suspended by another resolution adopted after the April 1991 cease fire (Security Council Resolution 687).[42] Of course, the US and its allies also contended that they would promote democracy in the Middle East and stop Saddam Hussein's regime's atrocities.[43] But these political and moral arguments were invoked separately, the formalist legal argument still being advanced in a parallel way.[44]

As far as international law is concerned, persuasiveness cannot operate without arguments based on formal validity. This is true when the debate is brought to an International Court, like in the DRC-Uganda case where the two parties using a

---

38 See also Beetham 1991, 67.

39 Corten 2009c.

40 De la Charrière 1983.

41 Kennedy mentions this episode; Kennedy 2005, 40–41.

42 *Letter dated 2003/03/20 from the Permanent Representative of the United States of America to the United Nations addressed to the President of the Security Council*, S/2003/351, 20 March 2003 (and "Contemporary Practice of the United States" (2003) 97 *AJIL* 419–432; (2005) 99 *AJIL* 269–270); *Letter dated 2003/03/20 from the Permanent Representative of the United Kingdom of Great Britain and Northern Ireland to the United Nations addressed to the President of the Security Council*, S/2003/350, 20 March 2003 (and Attorney General, Lord Goldsmith, *Legal basis for use of force against Iraq*, Attorney General Lord Goldsmith, 17 March 2003, http://www.number10.gov.uk and "United Kingdom Materials on International Law" (2003) 74 *BYBIL* 779–812; (2004) 75 *BYBIL* 829–845; (2005) 76 *BYBIL* 907–913 and 919–920; (2003) 52 *ICLQ* 811–814; (2005) 54 *ICLQ* 767–778 (Attorney General, Lord Goldsmith, "Iraq: Resolution 1441"); Letter dated 2003/03/20 from the Permanent Representative of Australia to the United Nations addressed to the President of the Security Council, S/2003/352, 20 March 2003.

43 See e.g. Sharp 2006.

44 See Spiliopoulou Akermark 2005, 222–223.

classical positivist reasoning to convince judges.[45] But this can also be the case when the debate takes place in an international political forum, like the Security Council (see the debates about the legality of the Iraqi war from september 2002 to April 2003)[46] or even in a national forum, as it was evidenced in the 2004 Spanish elections, (former) Prime Minister Aznar being criticized for having supported an "illegal" war (i.e. in formal violation of the UN Charter).[47] In sum, formalism and persuasiveness are not to be opposed, but rather to be linked. A rule, or a legal position, cannot be said to be valid *in abstracto*; it must be "proved"/argued to be valid; and the persuasiveness of a legal argument will be most likely based primarily on a formalist reasoning.

## 9.3 Erosion of "Sharp Legal Distinctions"?

*Of war and law* strongly insists on the erosion of the sharp legal distinctions that characterized the nineteenth century, when two clear bodies of law—law of peace on the one hand, and law of war on the other—were alternatively applicable. David Kennedy denounces "the increasing continuity between war and peace",[48] stating: "In short, the boundary between war and peace has become something we argue about, as much or more than something we cross [...] War today is both a fact and an argument".[49] Here again, these observations seem undeniable. One can add to the illustrations given in the book the widening definition of the "threat to peace" within Chapter VII of the UN Charter.[50] Since the beginning of the 1990s, the notion has extended not only to a threat by a State against another State in violation of Article 2.4, but also to various situations such as civil strifes, humanitarian disasters, collapsing State structures, unconstitutional changes of regime, acts of "terrorism". In the 2000s, the dilution of the notion was theorized and linked with the concept of "human security",[51] the threat being progressively extended to environmental dangers, social problems, grave diseases (AIDS), and

---

[45] ICJ, Armed Activities on the Territory of the Congo (Democratic Republic of the Congo *v.* Uganda); see the Written and Oral Proceedings on the website of the Court; http://www.icj-cij.org/docket/index.php?p1=3&p2=3&code=co&case=116&k=51.

[46] See e.g. S/PV.4625 (Resumption 1), 16 October 2002; S/PV.4625 (Resumption 2), 17 October 2002; S/PV.4644, 8 November 2002; S/PV.4709 (Resumption 1), 19 February 2003; S/PV.4726, 26 March 2003; S/PV.4726 (Resumption 1), 26 March 2003.

[47] See e.g. Martinez 2009.

[48] Kennedy 2005, 5.

[49] Kennedy 2005, 4–5.

[50] See e.g. de Wet 2004.

[51] See e.g. http://www.hsrgroup.org/human-security-reports/2005/overview.aspx, and *2005 World Summit Outcome*, A/RES/60/1, 24 October 2005, para 143.

so on.[52] The result is that today, it seems that we are in a permanent state of "threat to peace", i.e. in a situation which cannot be reduced either to peace or to war.

This does not mean, however, that all kinds of legal distinctions have disappeared. If one compares the current situation with that prevailing in the nineteenth century, it can rather be said that the terms of the distinction have changed, especially as far as the "law of war" is concerned.

This can first be shown by assessing the evolution of *jus contra bellum*. We know that, prior to the UN Charter, international law contained limited restrictions on the right to resort to war.[53] By contrast, "measures short of war", like limited and targeted military actions on the territory of another State, were not necessarily prohibited.[54] In 1945, the word "war" disappeared from the legal vocabulary, the Charter adopting a broader prohibition, the use or the threat of "force".[55] This marked the end of the distinction between a 'state of peace" and a 'state of war", as all kinds of attacks by a State against another State could be covered under the umbrella of "force".[56] However, the threshold conditioning the applicability of the *jus contra bellum* did not disappear; it was only displaced, at a lower level. In the nineteenth century, just as today, one is faced with an alternative: the applicability or inapplicability of *jus contra bellum*. In the system of the Charter, an action is characterized as a use of "force" according to Article 2.4 (and it is only permitted within the limited and restrictive framework of the Charter), or it may be defined outside of force and thereby governed by another set of rules (e.g. legality of entry into a foreign territory by the agents of a State, legality of the interception of a foreign aircraft according to the Chicago Convention, legality of a seizure in the high seas according to the Montego Bay Convention).[57]

The problems related to the determination of this threshold can be illustrated by various precedents. In the *Fisheries case (Spain v. Canada)* for example,[58] Spain contended that the seizure of one of its vessels (the *Estai*) by the Canadian coastal guards was an actual "use of force" which rendered the rules of the UN Charter applicable.[59] Canada replied that this seizure was rather a simple conservation and management measure under national regulations, not being equivalent to a "use of

---

[52] *In larger freedom: towards development, security and human rights for all. Report of the Secretary-General*, A/59/2005, 21 March 2005, at 29, para 78 and *A more secure world: Our shared responsibility*, U.N., 2004, at 21 *ff* and at 65, para 200; *2005 World Summit Outcome*, A/RES/60/1, 24 October 2005, at paras 9 and 71.

[53] See generally Neff 2005.

[54] Waldock 1952, 467–468, 471–472 and 475–476; Brownlie 1963, 59–60.

[55] Rumpf 1984.

[56] Randelzhofer 1982.

[57] Corten 2010, Chap. 2.

[58] ICJ Rep (1998) 443 *ff*, para 19 *ff*.

[59] Application instituting proceedings, 28 March 1995, at para 2(h); Sanchez Rodriguez, 9 June 1998, CR 98/9, at para 20; Pastor Ridruejo, 15 June 1998, CR 98/13, at para 8; Dupuy, 15 June 1998, CR 98/13, at para 22.

force" according to the Charter.[60] If Spain was right, the Canadian measure could only be justified by a Charter exception to the prohibition on the use of force; if Canada was right, this measure should rather be justified by other legal arguments (like "necessity" as a circumstance precluding wrongfulness, for example), but the Court could not pronounce on it, such issues being excluded from the Court's jurisdiction by Canada's declaration under Article 36 of the Statute.[61] The Court implicitly upheld Canada's position and refused to pronounce on the merits of the claims based on the alleged violation of the rules prohibiting the use of force.[62] This example clearly confirms that the principle of a sharp legal distinction, conditioning the applicability of *jus contra bellum*, did not disappear. In the nineteenth century, the distinction was between "war" and "peace". Today, the distinction is among a use of "force" and a simple "enforcement" or "police" measure. But the principle still remains.

Let's turn now to *jus in bello*. Here again, "war" is no longer the relevant legal criterion. The contemporary vocabulary refers to the more general expression of "armed conflict".[63] This notion is clearly broader, as it covers any use of force between States, or even any armed "hostilities" between "organized groups" in a civil strife.[64] This seems perfectly logic, *jus in bello* being adapted to the evolution of *jus contra bellum* that has just been described. And here again, one must note that the principle of a sharp legal distinction remains: either there is an "armed conflict" according to the Geneva Conventions, and the "Law of Armed Conflicts" applies; or there is not, and this set of rules does not apply. It is true that it is generally agreed nowadays that human rights law is applicable whatever the situation is, armed conflict or not.[65] But here again, a principle of distinction remains relevant. Either there is a "time of public emergency which threatens the life of the nation"[66] and the State concerned can invoke derogations, and therefore temporarily declare not to be bound by certain human rights obligations; or there is no such situation, and all human rights are applicable.

---

[60] Counter-Memorial of Canada, 29 February 1996, at para 31; Kirsch, 11 June 1998, CR 98/11, at para 45; see also Weil, 12 June 1998, CR 98/12, at para 31 and 32; Hankey, 17 June 1998, CR 98/14, at paras 14, 15 and 56.

[61] Counter-Memorial of Canada, 29 February 1996, para 4.

[62] ICJ Rep (1998) 466, para 84.

[63] See Article 2 common to the Geneva Conventions: « the present Convention shall apply to all cases of declared war or of any other armed conflict which may arise between two or more of the High Contracting Parties, even if the state of war is not recognized by one of them » (http://www.icrc.org).

[64] Article 1.1. of the Protocol Additional to the Geneva Conventions of 12 August 1949, and relating to the Protection of Victims of Non-International Armed Conflicts (Protocol II), 8 June 1977 (http://www.icrc.org).

[65] See e.g. ECHR *Issaïeva, Youssoupova et Bazaïeva v. Russia*, 24 February 2005, n°57947/00, 57948/00 and 57949/00.

[66] Article 4 of the UN Covenant on Civil and Political rights.

Of course, each qualification will depend on a process of interpretation which cannot be reduced to a rational or mechanical reasoning, i.e. to a "formalist", restrictive approach. The questions, whether one is faced with a "use of force" according to the UN Charter or whether there is an "armed conflict" according to the Geneva Conventions, are to be resolved in each particular context. And the answer will largely depend on the situation, notably on the audience concerned. "Law as an argument" is an idea that must be kept in mind in assessing the interpretation of these sharp distinctions. But once again it can be shown in relation to practice that these distinctions will be used as a formal argument to argue in favor of the applicability of a certain set of rules. To that extent, formalism—broadly defined as the possibility to use forms to distinguish between law and politics or moral, or to distinguish between different sets of rules—is far from having disappeared.

## 9.4 Deformalization of the Law of Force?

The thesis of the "deformalization" of international law seems shared by many scholars.[67] For his part, David Kennedy states that:"For a century, law—and particularly international law—has been in revolt against formalism [...] The revolt has been successful".[68] He, then, distinguishes three historical periods: the classical period (from sixteenth/seventeenth century to 1815), characterized by the "just war" theories, the positivist period (from 1815 to the mid-twentieth century), characterized by the formalization of the law of force and the current period, which would be marked by a movement of deformalization. More specifically, Kennedy notes that "the nineteenth century rules and sharp distinctions were joined in the twentieth century by broader standards and looser criteria for judgement".[69] But he also emphasizes that "at the same time, we should not exaggerate the move from rules to standards".[70]

In my view, the movement of deformalization—here defined as a move from rules to broader standards or "principles"[71]—is extremely difficult to establish, at least on an empirical basis. If one looks at legal texts as applied in practice, such conclusion seems rather debatable, regarding both *jus contra bellum* and *jus in bello*.

Did *jus contra bellum* in the nineteenth century (considered to be the golden age of the positivist period) include precise rules and distinctions rather than general principles? It is far from obvious. Actually, according to a large part of the

---

67 See e.g. Jayasuriya 2005, 52 ff; Krisch 2005.

68 Kennedy 2005, 45.

69 Kennedy 2005, 87.

70 Kennedy 2005, 88.

71 Contreras and de la Rasilla 2008, 777–778.

contemporary legal scholarship, there was, at that time, no *jus contra bellum* at all.[72] It was a period of *jus ad bellum*, and this *jus* was not really framed in a positive international legal system. Following this interpretation, the use of force was not really a right, but rather a sovereign's prerogative.[73] Accordingly, when they resorted to force, States used moral or political arguments, without ever referring to (positive) law.[74] Legally, war was, therefore, limited neither by rules nor even by standards. Other authors advocate another position. According to them, regarding the law of war in the nineteenth century, either one considers that the right to go to war was unlimited. However, if this is the case, it seems difficult to conceive the existence of any international legal order at all.[75] "Law", whatever the definition one gives to this concept, implies commitments to be bound by obligations and to respect the right of other subjects of the legal system. This would obviously not be the case if subjects were totally free to attack one another.[76] In this hypothesis, the obligation to recognize existing boundaries (*uti possidetis*), the respect of existing treaties, the duty of non-intervention, or more generally the classical rule *pacta sunt servanda* become simply meaningless. This would still be a state of nature, not yet an *état de droit*. Or, and this is the second term of the alternative, one must consider that the right to go to war was, even in the nineteenth century, legally framed.

At that time, States were able to use force if they could invoke "legitimate grounds" largely defined: self-preservation, autoprotection, redress of torts or outrages, and so forth.[77] This can be illustrated by the doctrinal debate about the right of "humanitarian intervention" (or *intervention d"humanité*) in the late nineteenth century. Some authors argued that this right was in conformity with international law if certain conditions were met: it was, in a certain way, an exceptional right.[78] Of course, this presupposes that there were certain kinds of limitations to use force in principle. If one follows this line of reasoning, the nineteenth century *jus ad bellum* did exist as a legal regime. Yet, legal limitations were still so broad that it would clearly be excessive to contend that these were equivalent to precise rules. These limitations—like 'self-preservation", for instance—must rather be characterized as broad standards. And, if one looks at the justifications given at that time, these standards can be characterized as a sort of blend between legal and moral/political considerations.[79] No 'sharp distinction" between law and moral thus prevailed. Finally, whatever interpretation of the

---

72 Wehberg 1928.

73 Verzijl 1968, 215; McMahan 2010, 495–496.

74 Verzijl 1968, 215; see also Draper 1990, 201.

75 Kelsen 1946, 332 ff, 1953, 28.

76 Lauterpacht 1933.

77 Martens 1858, 203; Nys 1894, 173; Redslob 1923, 242 and 470; Verdross 1929, 497–498.

78 See Rolin-Jacquemyns 1876; Rougier 1910.

79 See e.g. the official justification given by France during its 1866 intervention in Mexico; A.Ch. Kiss, Répertoire de la pratique française de droit international, vol. II, at 106, para 198.

nineteenth century legal regime is chosen, it seems patent that only very broad general principles, if any, limited the use of force. International law was, therefore, not "formalist" at all.

The situation changed radically with the adoption of the UN Charter in 1945. At that moment, formalism undoubtedly characterized the new *jus contra bellum*. States were officially no longer capable to invoke broad (legal/) moral principles to make war, such as self-preservation, autoprotection, redress of torts, and humanitarian grounds.[80] The use of force is henceforth framed in legal terms. States have established rules conditioning the legality of war. Self-defence, according to Article 51 of the UN Charter, is not defined anymore as a general right to protect a State's "rights" or "interests". It has become a technical institution the States seek to define as precisely as possible. The riposte is admissible in the case of an "armed attack", i.e. an actual use of force by a State against another State, regardless of the legitimacy of this resort to force.[81] And this riposte must be "necessary", as a condition which, according to the International Court of Justice, is not "purely a question for the subjective judgement of the party",[82] but rather 'strict and objective, leaving no room for any "measure of discretion"'.[83] This would not be the case, as expressly specified in Article 51, if the Security Council has taken appropriate measures according to Chapter VII of the Charter.[84] More generally, collective security measures can be decided by the Council if certain substantial (the existence of a threat to peace) and procedural (mainly the conditions of vote enshrined in Article 27.3) conditions are met.[85] In my opinion, this formalist conception still prevails: a use of force is in conformity with the Charter if, and only if, it is justified by self-defense (narrowly defined in Article 51) or a decision by the Security Council, and this remains true even if the military intervention is presented as morally or politically justified. The legal consecration of the "Responsibility to protect" concept in 2005 did not entail any evolution in that respect.[86] The text accepted in the World Summit Outcome document does not refer to broad and legal-moral principles, but to the existing rules.[87] Paragraphs 138 and 139 indeed require, if the sovereign is unable/unwilling to stop genocides,

---

80 Corten 2001.

81 Corten 2010, Chap. 7.

82 ICJ Rep (1986) at 141, para 282.

83 ICJ Rep (2003) at 196, para 73.

84 Institut de droit international Resolution on Self-defence, 27 October 2007, Santiago Session (http://www.idi-iil.org/idiE/navig_chon2003.html), para 9. See also Greig 1991.

85 Corten 2010, Chap. 6.

86 Comp International Commission on Intervention and State Sovereignty, *The responsibility to protect* (December 2001), http://www.iciss.ca/report-en.asp and A/RES/60/1 of 24 October 2005; see also *A more secure world: Our shared responsibility*, Report of the Secretary-General's High-level Panel on Threats, Challenges and Change, (U.N. 2004) 65–66, para 199–203) and *Report of the Secretary General, In larger freedom: towards development, security and human rights for all,* A/59/2005, 24 March 2005, A/59/2005, 24 March 2005, at 39, para 125.

87 See e.g. Boisson de Chazournes and Condorelli 2006; see also Delcourt 2008.

crimes against humanity or ethnic cleansing, a decision from the UN Security Council adopted in conformity with the Charter.[88]

Regarding this historical evolution, it seems, to my mind, that the "formalization" is more relevant that the "deformalization" to characterize the evolution of *jus ad/contra bellum*. A brief assessment of the evolution of *jus in bello* could lead to similar conclusions. The nineteenth century gave rise to a late and incomplete codification, so that one could consider that it remained largely composed of general and broad principles. The well-known "Martens clause", introduced in the Hague Conventions of 1899/1907, is significant in this regard:

> Until a more complete code of the laws of war is issued, the High Contracting Parties think it right to declare that in cases not included in the Regulations adopted by them, populations and belligerents remain under the protection and empire of the principles of international law, *as they result from the usages established between civilized nations, from the laws of humanity and the requirements of the public conscience*.[89]

This obviously illustrates a merger of law, moral and politics, but certainly not formal law. By contrast, the twentieth century is a period of "codification", i.e. a work of rationalization of the law of armed conflicts. The rules were increasingly clarified and organized in conventional or non-conventional texts, not only the Geneva Conventions and Protocols, but also in many instruments specifying the prohibited weapons and means of combat.[90] One of the latest achievements of this codification movement was the ICRC work on the customary rules of the law of armed conflicts.[91] Against this background, it can be stated that *jus in bello* was "formalized" rather than "deformalized" over the last decades.

Of course, and to conclude this part of the reasoning, things are not that simple. Another reading or interpretation of the history of the law of war is certainly possible, emphasizing the limits, or even some kind of decline of the formalization process. I am perfectly aware that the narrative proposed above is profoundly subjective, as it depends upon an interpretation of the facts and of the rules of law. This narrative could perhaps be denounced as "European formalism", given the

---

[88] See Gray 2008, 51–55.

[89] Emphasis added.

[90] See e.g. Convention on the Prohibition of the Development, Production and Stockpiling of Bacteriological (Biological) and Toxic Weapons and on their Destruction, 10 April 1972; Convention on Prohibitions or Restrictions on the Use of Certain Conventional Weapons Which May be Deemed to be Excessively Injurious or to Have Indiscriminate Effects, 10 October 1980; Protocol on Non-Detectable Fragments (Protocol I), 10 October 1980; Protocol on Prohibitions or Restrictions on the Use of Mines, Booby-Traps and Other Devices (Protocol II), 10 October 1980; Protocol on Prohibitions or Restrictions on the Use of Incendiary Weapons (Protocol III), 10 October 1980; Convention on the prohibition of the development, production, stockpiling and use of chemical weapons and on their destruction, 13 January 1993; Protocol on Blinding Laser Weapons (Protocol IV to the 1980 Convention), 13 October 1995, Convention on the Prohibition of the Use, Stockpiling, Production and Transfer of Anti-Personnel Mines and on their Destruction, 18 September 1997… (all texts and State parties available on: http://www.icrc.org/ihl.nsf/TOPICS?OpenView). Accessed April 2012.

[91] Henckaert and Doswald Beck 2006.

emphasis put on legal forms as separated from—even if these forms remain interlinked with—moral and political factors. In any case, it is clear that the narrative contained in Kennedy's *of war and law* is in many aspects different. If one admits the relativity of perceptions, representations, and interpretations, one must admit that none of these two narratives can be claimed to be the only possible one. Of course, the "European formalist" approach could be more persuasive to some audiences, whereas the "American critic" approach could be more persuasive to others. But to claim that there exists only one 'scientific" assessment of this evolution would only be possible in an orthodox—and, to say the truth, old-fashioned—positivist way of thinking. If, by contrast, one considers law, but also the representations of law (including of its history), as an argument, the terms of the debate become different. The question is not (only): which version is the more persuasive? It is also, and perhaps mainly: why should I argue in favor of this or that version?

## 9.5 "Deformalization" and "Formalization" Narratives: Which to Choose From?

To argue in favor of a "deformalization" or a "formalization" narrative is thus a matter of choice. And this choice cannot be decided *in abstracto*; it will be made by each of us depending on the situation at hand, and in relation to our beliefs, representations and faiths. I was struck by the use of "we" in David Kennedy's *of war and law*: "we think of international law as a broadly humanist and civilizing force"[92]; "we make war in the shadow of law, and law in the shadow of force"[93]; "we have bureaucratized and professionalized warfare".[94] It seems that this "we" is aimed at characterizing, or at promoting the existence of, a community. But at the same time, it is not always easy to identify which community this could be. In any case, it is far from obvious that any community of international lawyers exists, especially if one takes a look at the various and contradictory opinions expressed on current "law of war" issues. Looking more specifically to controversies surrounding *jus contra bellum*, the situation could be summarized as follows: in general, "antiformalists" support new justifications to make war; by contrast, "formalists" seem to be more restrictive, and therefore much more reluctant to accept such justifications.[95]

On the one side, and particularly in the US scholarship, several authors defend a broad conception of the possibilities to use force. Those authors argue in favor of the existence of a right of anticipatory self-defence, of a right to pursue "terrorists" on

[92] Kennedy 2005, 6.

[93] Kennedy 2005, 165.

[94] Ibid.

[95] Corten 2005.

the territory of another State anywhere in the world, of a right of humanitarian intervention or "pro-democratic" invasion, to give only some examples.[96] Those legal possibilities should be recognized given the evolutions of international relations today: increasing threats posed by terrorists and rogue States, emergence of values of democracy, rule of law, human rights, "moralization" of international law.[97] What is striking about this literature is the firm rejection of a narrow interpretation of the UN Charter as too restrictive, rigid, inaccurate to address the current challenges of the contemporary world—in a nutshell, as too "formalist",[98] "legalist"[99] or "positivist".[100] These authors allow the interpreter to take account of non-legal considerations,[101] including the resort to "just war" theories.[102] In this perspective, it is necessary to evaluate the legality of military action "[n]ot simply in terms of certain rules, that are supposed to form part of a black-letter code of international law, but in terms of the acceptability of those responses in different contexts, to the contemporary international decision process".[103]

One the other side, many authors focus on the construction of a "textually-oriented, hierarchical series of rules set out in Articles 31 and 32 of the Vienna Conventions".[104] They indeed remain attached to the rules of *jus contra bellum* as enshrined in the Charter, in the subsequent instruments defining these rules (GA resolutions 2625 (XXV), 3314 (XXIX), 42.22, 60/1, ...) and as interpreted by judges, especially by the International Court of Justice (*Nicaragua*, *Oil Platforms*, *DRC/Uganda* cases, among others).[105] According to those authors, admitting arguments of opportunity or morality would represent a reversal to pre-Charter *jus ad bellum*, and not a "progress" of international law in any way.[106] On the contrary, any revival of just war theories would open the door to "arbitrariness and subjectivity".[107] Formalism appears as a tool used to counter the imposition of a subjective interpretation of what is "legitimate" by the great powers.[108] As far as legitimacy of wars is concerned, there is no univocal view shared by States or groups, no "international community", no "we". Every State, group, person, has its own opinion about what is a "just" war. Until the adoption of the Charter, the

---

96 Schmitt 2002; Franck 2002; Buchanan 2003, 134.

97 Sofaer 2003; Taft and Buchwald 2003; Biggio 2002.

98 See Koskenniemi 2002; Gardner 2003; Schieder 2000.

99 Falk 1999.

100 Ibid, 854.

101 Wedgwood 2000, 2003, 578; Franck 2002, 94; Falk 2003; Garcia 2003.

102 Garcia 1999, 68; Sofaer 2003, 225; Stromseth 2003, 268; Biggio 2002, 20–22.

103 Reisman 1999; Reisman and Schachter 1984; see also Schmitt 2002, 56.

104 Byers 2002, 25; see also Bothe 2003.

105 See e.g. Simma 1999; Constantinou 2000, 22; Hofmann 2002; Sicilianos 2002; Randelzhofer 2002, 803; Byers and Chesterman 2003; Christakis 2004, 2005, 209–211; Laghmani 2004, 16–17.

106 Corten 2001.

107 Bothe 2003, 239; see also Verhoeven 2002, 61–62.

108 See Gowlland-Debbas 2000.

most powerful political actors could use a blend of moral/political/legal arguments to justify the use of force, with very limited—if any—forms of constraint and control. By contrast, contemporary international law formalized what it is a "just"—now said to be "legal"—war. War is legal if decided as such by the Security Council following a particular procedure. Legality is thus procedural (not substantial) and relative (not absolute): "It is traditional wisdom of legal theory that where substantive law cannot bring about a sufficient degree of legal certainty, procedural rules must be used to obtain results which are socially or politically acceptable".[109] Law has, of course, not become objective, as it depends on the balance of powers prevailing in each situation concerned; but it has surely become less subjective, as no particular State or group of States (even "civilized" or "democratic") can decide in the name of the "international community".[110] Actually, the legality of a war may better be characterized as "inter-subjective", as the decision to go to war must have been accepted by States with very different cultural backgrounds and political views. In sum, in this perspective, formalism is both a shield against raw power and a sword of a new form of (procedural) justice.

This is, of course, only a general overview, which openly overlooks subtleties and particularities. Antiformalists are not necessarily hawks, supporting the war against terror in all its manifestations; formalists are not necessarily doves, tirelessly fighting for peace. As previously stated, formalism can also be used to justify a war,[111] and anti-formalism could also be used to combat it. As David Kennedy rightly points out, even if it had been approved by the Security Council, it is probable that the 2003 Iraqi war would have been criticized (as the 1991 war was, although duly authorized).[112] The fact remains, however, that a general overview of the literature favors, in my opinion, the description given above. Likewise, my personal experience makes me believe that formalism is a more efficient tool to combat war than antiformalism, as it appears more neutral and more objective, even if, ultimately, it is not.[113] "Formalism" can, thus, generally be considered as a more efficient argument against war, "antiformalism" being associated with an intent to revive or to rekindle "just war" theories, and therefore to enhance great powers to justify their acts.[114]

On the other hand, it must be kept in mind that this "formalist" choice is a strategic, pragmatic, and therefore relative one. It does not bear any "faith" or "belief" in formalism as such. At this stage, several limits of this approach must be emphasized.

---

109 Bothe 2003, 239.

110 Gowlland-Debbas 2000, 383.

111 It is possible to interpret in this sense some writings of Pellet 2000; Eisemann 2002, 239; O'Connel 2002a, b; or Murphy 2002.

112 Kennedy 2005, 162.

113 See Corten 2009a, b, c, d, 37–44.

114 See Anghie 2005.

- Firstly, it must be recalled that the possible success of a formalist argument presupposes that the audience concerned shares this mode of reasoning.[115] To focus on the formal illegality of war will be efficient in certain fora, like the international Court of Justice, and most of the time the UN General Assembly or the Security Council. The persuasiveness would be more doubtful in other contexts, in which international law does not appear legitimate or credible as a normative system. In any event, to contend that a war would be illegal does not mean that this war would be unjust, or even lesser that the war will not be waged because of its illegality. The "illegality" of war appears rather as a technical information which could take an ethical dimension only if the participants of the debate think that legality is a necessary (even if not sufficient) condition of the legitimacy of a war.
- Secondly, formalism is here presented like a strategic choice in the realm of the law of war, not in all the fields of international law. To invoke the formal validity of the rules of the UN Charter implies a certain adherence to the content of those rules. Mainly, we have seen that the legality/justness of war according to this system lies in a procedural criteria, i.e., a multilateral decision of the Security Council, as opposed to a unilateral decision by a State or a group of States. By contrast, this does not mean that a (strategically) "formalist" scholar would support the content of rules in international economic law which, for example, require all States to pay their international debts, even if it implies keeping millions of people in a situation of extreme poverty. This is why, personally, I prefer to focus on certain particular fields of international law, notably the law of war.
- Thirdly, even in this latter domain, the formalist choice, being only strategic, is always dependent on the case at hand. It appears, therefore, crucial to think about the legitimacy of every war before making any pronouncement on its legality. To pick up just one example, when NATO States triggered their campaign of bombardments against Yugoslavia on March 23, 1999, I personally did not focus first on the legality problem (indeed, it appeared self-evident that this was not a real "problem", the illegality of the war not being doubtful at all).[116] My concern was rather to know if this war was really legitimate in a broad meaning. At that time, the main justification raised by NATO States was the rejection of the "Rambouillet plan" by the Yugoslavian authorities.[117] But, in my view, after reading this plan,[118] the Yugoslavian counter-proposals[119] and

[115] See the developments and references above.

[116] See e.g. Spinedi 1998, 27–28; Kohen 1999; Valticos 2000, 8–9; Dubuisson 2001, 154–158; Brownlie and Apperley 2000, 895.

[117] NATO 2001, 304.

[118] Text available on http://www.diplomatie.gouv.fr/fr/pays-zones-geo_833/kosovo_650/colonne-droite_2743/textes-reference_2741/accord-rambouillet-27.05.99_5375.html or, in English, in Weller 1999, 453 ff.

[119] *Ibid*, 480ff.

the relevant OSCE and Secretary general of the UN Reports,[120] this did not justify the war, as all the peaceful means had not yet been exhausted.[121] In sum, my main concern was the "necessity" (but in a broad and non-formal meaning) of the war. And, because I truly thought that this war was unnecessary and therefore illegitimate, I choosed to denounce its formal illegality.[122] If, by contrast, I had thought that the war was legitimate, I would simply have avoided asserting anything about its legality. This example shows that the formalist approach choice is only a strategic one, which implies the possibility not to use it if it appears inappropriate in a particular case.[123]

All this leads me to another problem. What if formalism would be inappropriate, either because it would enforce a rule considered as unjust (like in the example of international economic law) or because it would be an obstacle against what would be considered as a "just" or "necessary" war? In my view, two options are possible in those cases. The first would be to interpret existing legal forms in order to adapt them to my personal values. This could mean, for example, to raise a formal argument justifying not paying a debt (like "necessity" as a circumstance precluding wrongfulness), or to contend that a (just) war would be legally justified (because it would implicitly be authorized by a Security Council resolution, for example). But, to be sustainable, this mode of reasoning should be grounded on strong formal arguments. Otherwise, my credibility as a (formalist) lawyer would be undermined. Perhaps, in this case, should I prefer the second option, which could be simply to remain silent on the matter. This 'silent option" seems perfectly appropriate and sensible if, as a lawyer, I think that the "just" solution cannot be supported "legally" (i.e. formally) with some credibility.

In sum, formalism must not be underestimated. The formalization narrative appears far more convincing than the deformalization one to understand the evolution of the law of war. And every time a war is waged, it leaves no doubt that a large range of actors will debate about its formal legality. On the other hand, formalism must not be overestimated. It only provides a strategy which can—or not, depending on the circumstances of the case at hand—be used to support or combat a war. And, of course, the efficiency of the argument will depend both on the audience concerned and on the political context in which the debate takes place. Finally, we can return to the Marxist approach, conceiving law, and more generally legal discourse, both as an argument and as a narrative generating

120 Those reports (see S/1998/1068, November 12, 1998, at para 48; S/1998/1221, at para 13; S/1999/99, 30 January 1999) show that the UCK bears the main responsibility for breaking the cease-fire which was concluded on 15–16 October 1998 under the supervision of NATO and OSCE (S/1998/978; S/1998/1991).

121 See Corten 1999.

122 Actually, I pleaded as a member of the Yugoslavian legal team appearing in May 1999 before the ICJ to complain against the armed attack launched by NATO States; CR 1999/15, 12 May 1999, 17–23.

123 See also Corten and Delcourt 1999.

particular representations and ideologies. The tension between formalism and antiformalism in the legal sphere, as well as the use of the formalist or antiformalist narratives, can usefully be assessed by resorting to this critical approach. In this perspective, one must always keep in mind David Kennedy's core interrogation: "whose interpretation of the law will, in fact, prevail, and before what audience?".[124]

## References

Althusser L (1969) For Marx. Penguin Press, London

Anghie A (2005) The war on terror and Iraq in historical perspective. Osgoode Hall Law J 43:45–66

Banchand R (2009) Présentation. In: Kennedy D (ed) Nouvelles approches du droit international. Pedone, Paris

Beetham D (1991) The legitimation of power. Macmillan, London

Biggio FA (2002) Neutralizing the threat: reconsidering existing doctrines in the emerging war on terrorism. Case West Reserv JIL 34:1

Boisson de Chazournes L, Condorelli L (2006) De la "responsabilité de protéger", ou d'une nouvelle parure pour une notion déjà bien établie. RGDIP 110:11

Bothe M (2003) Terrorism and the legality of pre-emptive force. EJIL 14: 229

Bourdieu P (1986) La force du droit. Eléments pour une sociologie du champ juridique. Actes de la recherche en sciences sociales 64:3–19

Bourdieu P (1991) Les juristes, gardiens de l'hypocrisie collective. In: Chazel F, Commaile J (eds) Normes juridiques et régulation sociale. L.G.D.J., Paris

Brownlie I (1963) International law and the use of force by states. Oxford University Press, Oxford

Brownlie I, Apperley CJ (2000) Kosovo crisis inquiry: memorandum on the international law aspects. ICLQ 49:879

Buchanan A (2003) Reforming the international law of humanitarian intervention. In: Holzgrefe JL, Keohane RO (eds) Humanitarian intervention: ethical, legal and political dilemmas. Cambridge University Press, Cambridge

Byers M (2002) The shifting foundations of international law. A decade of forceful measures against Iraq. EJIL 13:21

Byers M, Chesterman S (2003) Changing the rules about rules? Unilateral intervention and the future of international law. In: Holzgrefe JL, Keohane RO (eds) Humanitarian intervention: ethical, legal and political dilemmas. Cambridge University Press, Cambridge

Chaumont C (1970) Cours général de droit international public. RCADI 129:333–528

Chemillier Gendreau M (2004) Actualité de la pensée de Charles Chaumont et perspectives du droit international. Revue belge de droit international 37:290–308

Christakis T (2004) Vers une reconnaissance de la notion de guerre préventive? In: Bannelier K et al (eds) L'intervention en Irak et le droit international. Pedone, Paris, pp 9–45

Christakis T (2005) Existe-t-il un droit de légitime défense en cas de simple "menace"? Une réponse au "Groupe de personnalités de haut niveau" de l'ONU. S.F.D.I., Les métamorphoses de la sécurité collective. Droit, pratique et enjeux stratégiques, Pedone, Paris, pp 198–221

Constantinou A (2000) Right of self-defense under customary international law and article 51 of the United Nations charter. Bruylant, Brussels

[124] Kennedy 2005, 35.

Contreras FJ, de la Rasilla I (2008) On war as law and law as war. LJIL 21:776
Corten O (1999) Se habian agotado realmente todos los medios diplomaticos? El fracaso del "plan de Rambouillet". Informe sobre el conflicto y la guerra de Kosovo, ediciones del oriento y del mediterraneo, Madrid, pp 295–306
Corten O (2001) La référence au droit international comme justification du recours à la force: vers une nouvelle doctrine de la guerre juste? In: Dillens AM (ed) L'Europe et la guerre. F.U.S.L, Brussels, pp 69–94
Corten O (2002) La persistance de l'argument légaliste. Eléments pour une typologie contemporaine des registres de légitimité dans une société libérale. Droit et société. Revue internationale de théorie du droit et de sociologie juridique, 50:185–203
Corten O (2005) The controversies over the customary prohibition on the use of force: a methodological debate. Eur J Int Law 16:803–822
Corten O (2008) Le droit international comme sport de combat. In: Jouannet E, Ruiz Fabri H, Sorel JM (eds) Regards d'une génération sur le droit international. Pedone, Paris, pp 169–175
Corten O (2009a) Le droit international comme sport de combat. In: Corten O (d) Le discours du droit international. Pour un positivisme critique. Pedone, Paris, pp 37–44
Corten O (2009b) Méthodologie du droit international public, ed. Université de Bruxelles, Brussels
Corten O (2009c) Droit, force et légitimité dans une société internationale en mutation. In: Corten O (ed) Le discours du droit international. Pour un positivisme critique. Pedone, Paris, pp 71–112
Corten O (2009d) Les ambiguïtés de la référence au droit international comme facteur de légitimation. Portée et signification d'une déformalisation du discours légaliste". In: Corten O (ed) Le discours du droit international. Pour un positivisme critique. Pedone, Paris, pp 105–138
Corten O (2010) The law against war. Hart Publishers, Oxford
Corten O, Delcourt B (1999) Portée et limites du discours légaliste dans le débat sur la guerre du Kosovo. La revue nouvelle, Brussels November
De la Charrière G (1983) La politique juridique extérieure. Economica, Paris
De Wet E (2004) The chapter VII powers of the United Nations Security Council, Hart Publishers, Oxford & Portland Oregon
Delcourt B (2008) La responsabilité de protéger et l'interdiction du recours à la force: entre normativité et opportunité. SFDI, La responsabilité de protéger, Pedone, Paris, pp 305–312
Draper GIAP (1990) "Grotius" place in the development of legal ideas about war. In: Bull H, Kingsbury B, Roberts A (eds) Hugo Grotius and international relations. Clarendon Press, Oxford
Dubuisson F (2001) La problématique de la légalité de l'opération "Force alliée" contre la Yougoslavie: enjeux et questionnements. In: Corten O, Delcourt B (eds) Droit, légitimation et politique extérieure. L'Europe et la guerre of Kosovo, Bruylant, Brussels
Eisemann PM (2002) Attaques du 11 septembre et exercice d'un droit naturel de légitime défense. In: Bannelier K et al (eds) Le droit international face au terrorisme. Pedone, Paris
Falk R (1999) Kosovo, world order, and the future of international law. AJIL 93:847–857
Falk R (2003) What future for the United Nations charter system of war prevention? AJIL 97:596
Franck TM (2002) Recourse to force. State actions against threats and armed attacks. Cambridge University Press, Cambridge
Garcia RB (1999) Cuestiones actuales referentes al uso de la fuerza en el Derecho Internacional. Annuario de derecho internacional 15:3–70
Garcia RB (2003) El Debate sobre la legalidad internacional tras la crisis de Iraq y las Naciones Unidas. Annuario de derecho internacional 19:56
Gardner RN (2003) Neither bush nor the "Jurisprudes". AJIL 97: 585
Gowlland-Debbas V (2000) The limits of unilateral enforcement of community objectives in the framework of United Nations peace maintenance. EJIL 11: 381
Gray C (2008) International law and the use of force, 3rd edn. Oxford University Press, Oxford

Greig DW (1991) Self-defence and the Security Council: what does article 51 require? ICLQ 40:366–402
Haskell J (2007) David Kennedy, of war and law. Nord J Int Law 76(2):323–326
Henckaert JM, Doswald Beck L (eds) (2006) Customary international humanitarian law. ICRC, Cambridge
Hofmann R (2002) International law and the use of military force against Iraq. GYIL 45:30
Hunt A (2010) Marxist theory of law. In: Patterson D (ed) A companion to philosophy and theory of law. Blackwell Publishing, Oxford
Jayasuriya K (2005) Reconstituting the global liberal order: legitimacy and regulation. Routledge, London
Jouannet E (2004) The legal theory of Charles Chaumont. Revue belge de droit international 37:259–289
Kelsen H (1946) General theory of law and state. Harvard University Press, Cambridge
Kelsen H (1953) Théorie du droit international public. RCADI 84:28
Kennedy D (2004) International humanitarianism: the dark sides. Int J Not-For-Profit Law 6. Available on www.icnl.org/knowledge/ijnl/vol6iss3/special_2.htm. Accessed Dec 2010
Kennedy D (2005) Of war and law. Princeton University Press, Princeton
Kennedy D (2009) Nouvelles approches de droit international. Pedone, Paris
Kohen M (1999) L'emploi de la force et la crise du Kosovo: vers un nouveau désordre juridique international. RBDI 32:133
Koskenniemi M (2002) Iraq and the "Bush Doctrine" of pre-emptive self-defense. Expert analysis. Crimes of war project, Aug 20. Available on http://www.crimesofwar.org/expert/bush-koskenniemi.html. Accessed Dec 2010
Krisch N (2005) International law in times of hegemony: unequal power and the shaping of the international legal order. Eur J Int Law 16:392
Laghmani S (2004) La doctrine américaine de la "preemptive self-defense": de la guerre par "mesure de prévention" à la guerre par "mesure de précaution". In: Ben Achour R, Laghmani S (eds) Le droit international à la croisée des chemins. Pedone, Paris
Lauterpacht H (1933) The function of law in the international community. Clarendon, Oxford
Martens F (1858) Précis du droit des gens moderne de l'Europe, vol II, éd. Guillaumin, 641 Paris
Martinez G (2009) Aznar's war: understanding Spain's decision to participate in the 2003 US-led invasion of Iraq. Aust NZ J Eur Stud 1:36
Marx K, Engels F (1947) The German ideology. International Publishers, New York
McMahan J (2010) Laws of war. In: Besson S, Tasioulas J (eds) The philosophy of international law. Oxford University Press, Oxford
Murphy SD (2002) Terrorism and the concept of "Armed Attack" in article 51 of the United Nations. Harv ILJ 43:41–51
NATO (2001) Statement by the secretary general. Press release (1999)040, 23 March 1999. In: Krieger H (ed) The Kosovo conflict and international law. an analytical documentation 1974–1999. Cambridge University Press, Cambridge
Neff SC (2005) War and the law of nations. A general history. Cambridge University Press, Cambridge
Nys E (1894) Les origines du droit international, ed. Castaigne, Bruxelles; ed. Fontemoing, Paris
O'Connel ME (2002), Lawful Self-Defense to Terrorism. Univ Pittsbg LR 63:889
O'Connel ME (2002A) The Myth of preemptive self-defense, ASIL August 2002. Available on http://www.asil.org/taskforce/oconnel.pdf. Accessed Dec 2010
Pashukanis EB (2002) General theory of law and marxism. Transactions Publishers, New Brunswick
Pellet A (2000), Brief remarks on the unilateral use of force. EJIL 11: 385
Perelman C, Olbrecht-Tyteca L (1991) The new rhetoric. A treatise on argumentation. University of Notre Dame Press, Notre Dame
Randelzhofer A (1982) Use of force. In: Bernhardt R (ed) EPIL, vol 4. North-Holland Publishers, Amsterdam, p 267

Randelzhofer A (2002) Article 51. In: Simma B (ed) The charter of the United Nations. A commentary, 2nd edn. Oxford University Press, Oxford
Redslob R (1923) Histoire des grands principes du droit des gens de l'Antiquité jusqu'à la veille de la Grande Guerre. Rousseau éd, Paris
Reisman M (1999) International legal responses to terrorism. Houst JIL 22:5–6
Reisman M, Schachter O (1984) Coercion and self-determination: construing charter Article 2(4). AJIL 78:642–645
Rolin-Jacquemyns G (1876) Note sur la théorie du droit d'intervention. RDILC 8:673–682
Rougier A (1910) La théorie de l'intervention d'humanité. RGDIP 14:468–526
Rumpf H (1984) The concept of peace and war in international law. GYIL 27:429–443
Salmon J (1982) Le fait dans l'application du droit international. RCADI 175:261–414
Salmon J (ed) (2001) Dictionnaire de droit international public. Bruylant, AUF, Brussels
Salmon J (2002) Le droit international à l'aube du XXIe siècle. VI Cours Euro-méditerranéens Bancaja de droit international. Tirant lo blanch, Valencia, pp 35–363
Schieder S (2000), Pragmatism as a path towards a discursive and open theory of international law. EJIL 11:691
Schmitt MN (2002) Counter-terrorism and the use of force in international law. George C. Marshall European Center for Security Studies, Garmisch-Partenkirchen
Sharp JM (2006) U.S. democracy promotion policy in the middle east: the Islamist dilemma. CRS Report for Congress, The Library of Congress
Sicilianos LA (2002) L'autorisation par le Conseil de sécurité de recourir à la force: une tentative d'évaluation. RGDIP 106:47
Simma B (1999) NATO, the UN and the use of force: legal aspects. EJIL 10:1–22
Sofaer AD (2003) On the necessity of pre-emption. EJIL 14:212
Spiliopoulou Akermark S (2005) Storms, foxes and nebulous legal arguments: twelve years of force against Iraq, 1991–2003. ICLQ 54:222–223
Spinedi M (1998) Uso della forza da parte della NATO in Jugoslavia e diritto internazionale, Quaderni Forum, vol XII
Stromseth JE (2003) Rethinking humanitarian intervention: the case for incremental change. In: Holzgrefe JL, Keohane RO (eds) Humanitarian intervention: ethical, legal and political dilemmas. Cambridge University Press, Cambridge
Taft W, Buchwald T (2003) Pre-emption, Iraq and international law. AJIL 97:557
Valticos N (2000) Les droits de l'homme, le droit international et l'intervention militaire en Yougoslavie. RGDIP 104:5–18
Verdross A (1929) Règles générales du droit international de la paix. RCADI 30:471
Verhoeven J (2002) Les "étirements" de la légitime défensem. AFDI 54:49–80
Verzijl JHW (1968) International law in historical perspective, vol I. Sijthoff, Leyden
Waldock CHM (1952) The regulation of the use of force by individual states in international law. RCADI 81:455
Weber M (1978) Economy and society: an outline of interpretive sociology. University of California Press, Berkeley
Wedgwood R (2000) Unilateral action in the United Nations system. EJIL 11:352
Wedgwood R (2003) The fall of Saddam Hussein: security council mandates and pre-emptive self-defense. AJIL 97:576
Wehberg H (1928) Le problème de la mise de la guerre hors la loi. RCADI 24:306
Weller M (1999) The Crisis in Kosovo 1989–1999. International documents and analysis. Cambridge University Press, Cambridge

# Index



J. M. Beneyto and D. Kennedy (eds.), *New Approaches to International Law*,
DOI: 10.1007/978-90-6704-879-8,

Printed by Printforce, the Netherlands